Eastern Europe

A Geography of the Comecon Countries

Eastern Europe
A Geography of the Comecon Countries

Roy E. H. Mellor

COLUMBIA UNIVERSITY PRESS
New York   1975

Roy E. H. Mellor is Professor of Geography
at the University of Aberdeen.

© Roy E. H. Mellor 1975
Published in Great Britain in 1975 by The Macmillan Press Ltd
Printed in Great Britain at
THE PITMAN PRESS
Bath

Library of Congress Cataloging in Publication Data

Mellor, Roy E H
Eastern Europe.

   1.   Europe, Eastern.   2.   Soviet ekonomicheskoĭ
vzaimopomoshchi.   I.   Title.
DR16.M44   1975   914.7   74–12198
ISBN 0–231–03940–9
ISBN 0–231–03945–X(ptk)

Contents

List of Illustrations

List of Tables

Preface

The copious geographical literature on the Soviet Union in the English language is unmatched by material for the Socialist states of Eastern Europe, which remain relatively little known to English-speaking students. At the present pace of change in Europe, it would be a pity to concentrate our interest on Western Europe and omit to examine the remarkable developments taking place in the other half of Europe. The language problem has certainly been a barrier for most interested people and few of us are fortunate enough to have access to Magyar, Rumanian and the several Slav languages, let alone to Albanian and German. This is unfortunate, because several of the countries have a long, respectable if little known tradition of geographical study and have produced a valuable literature in their own vernaculars. This book has sought in particular to draw on this excellent if relatively inaccessible source material.

For reasons of length it has been decided not to expand on the physical background other than to set a backcloth for the study, and the work is primarily concerned with the complex and diverse human geography. Particular attention has been paid to the historical background, especially in the past two hundred years, since it is felt that the great changes arising from the acceptance of a Marxist–Leninist order of society and economy in the last twenty-five years can only be fully appreciated if seen in their historical setting. Stemming from this approach, the reader may sense the emphasis on the political–geographical pattern, but he will well appreciate that in this part of Europe, with the upheavals of centuries, political geography is a spectre that has to be lived with. Indeed the contemporary scene cannot be adequately interpreted without an understanding of what has gone before. Even a quarter of a century of the rigorous impress of Marxist–Leninism and the more recent changes that have begun to emerge from Comecon cannot conceal the imprint, remarkably fresh inspite of events, left by the great empires that confronted each other in a relentless power struggle over this part of Europe. Attention has also been given to the way in which Sovietisation and the interpretation of Marxist–Leninist dogmas have been remoulding the visible landscape, an aspect of political geography too long given little consideration.

The study of an area so diverse and complex as Eastern Europe presents numerous methodological and interpretive challenges. An initial challenge is to find a thread of identity for the study to make it, some would claim, regionally respectable. This thread seems to be presented by the apparent unity created by the acceptance of Soviet-style Marxist–Leninism and its imposition on divergent ethnic and economic backcloths. In a sense, a new region—Eastern Europe of the eight Socialist states—has emerged from what were previously a part of Central Europe (in itself an elusive concept), and the Balkans, sometimes more generously defined spatially as South-eastern Europe, besides the true eastern marchlands of Europe that lap into the Soviet Union. With eight countries at different levels of social and economic development and possessing sub-

stantial organisational divergences, the treatment must naturally be a little uneven, but every attempt has been made to give a reasonably equal coverage of
each country in relation to its size and diversity and its role in the area's affairs.
The deficiencies are most apparent in the statistical material, both on a comparative scale between countries and over time, especially for those countries
that have undergone violent territorial change.

The work owes much to many helpful people in Eastern Europe, too
numerous to name. I might, however, mention especially Professor Dušan Brkić
of Sarajevo whose wide conceptual view of the problems of Europe's Socialist
states has been a long-standing inspiration. Dorota and Manfred Alexander of
the University of Cologne have combed Eastern Europe's bookshops for me. For
my own travels I owe a grateful acknowledgement of help received from the
Carnegie Trust for Scotland. Much laborious compilation was done by my assis-
tant, Miss Sheila Bain, while the maps were produced by Laurie McLean and Bert
Bremner, the quality of whose work will be readily appreciated. The manuscript
was typed by Mrs I. J. Greig, who mastered with incredible success the eccen-
tricities to the British eye of Slav and Magyar spelling. Whenever my spirit has
flagged I have been grateful for the encouragement received from colleagues,
particularly Kenneth Walton and Alistair Smith. The latter along with Chalmers
Clapperton gave noble help in reading a remarkably illegible series of drafts.
Much of the original encouragement came from my wife, whose intimate
knowledge of the Slav lands, their peoples and languages, has been invaluable.
She has also done so much of the drearier tasks of reading manuscripts and
checking text, besides using her culinary skills without which no energy-
consuming author can survive. For errors, slips and deficiencies, I alone am
responsible.

Roy E. H. Mellor

Part One
Physical Environment and
Political Geography

1 The Physical Environment

1.1 Definitions of Eastern Europe

The eight states, which since 1945 have been organised on Marxist–Leninist principles, are commonly referred to collectively as Eastern Europe, but it would be more appropriate to speak of them as comprising 'East Central and South-eastern Europe'. Although there has always been much disagreement over the extent and definition of the major regional divisions of Europe, the term 'Eastern Europe' has commonly included the so-called European Russia, while much of the study area was before 1945 included in the vaguely defined but conceptually live Central Europe. Likewise, South-eastern Europe has come to have a wider connotation than its predecessor, the Balkans. In common usage, Eastern Europe has come to mean in the last quarter of a century the eight states associated with the Soviet Union through their political ties in the immediate post-war years, so that the German Democratic Republic has been included under a label which was unthinkable before 1945. In nineteenth-century and early twentieth-century Europe, central Europe was a real image, but the division of Europe between conflicting ideologies in the years of the Cold War split it asunder, leaving only a vacuum, so that it is now a term seldom heard. Whatever arguments may be made to the contrary, we must accept that common usage has made a bodily shift in the concept of Eastern Europe, from which the Soviet Union is now generally excluded.

Defining Eastern Europe to include the eight Socialist states of the study area certainly should not suggest a sense of unity among them in their physical environment, for relief, climate, hydrology and soils are extremely diverse and bear no relation to the political divisions. There is similar diversity in the human patterns, the sole unifying factor being the acceptance of Marxist–Leninist principles in the organisation of their economic and social life. Even here, however, an increasing polycentrism has reduced the unity of interpretation of classical dogmata. Within the physical environment, a comparison of the countries might be made on a relief basis (figure 1.1), for there is a contrasting juxtaposition of mountain and lowland: the characteristically plain-like German Democratic Republic, Poland and Hungary stand in contrast to the chiefly mountainous and hilly Czechoslovakia, Jugoslavia, Albania and Bulgaria, while Rumania falls into an intermediate category, with much plain as well as mountain. A division on a climatic basis is less evident—the German Democratic Republic and Poland along with Czechoslovakia, by reason of their cooler summers, can be distinguished from the other countries, while in easternmost Poland and Rumania the influence of the continentality of the Russian plains is felt.

1.2 The six major landscapes

Within the study area, six major landscapes can be distinguished, three of them essentially plains and three preeminently mountainous and hilly. The open vistas of the North European plains where glacial features predominate in the detail of relief, imparting a subtle contrast in landscape between north and south, typify the German Democratic Republic and Poland. The Hercynian landscapes of gentle rolling forested uplands of remarkable concordant elevation, separated by broad basins or deeply incised valleys, are characteristic of the south and south-west of the German Democratic Republic and of Bohemia. The central relief feature of Eastern Europe is the majestic bow of the Carpathians, curling through Slovakia and Rumania, comprising both rolling, forested ranges and strikingly rugged mountains, rising to impressive altitudes in the High Tatra and higher parts of the Eastern Carpathians. Here they stand as a great bastion

Figure 1.1. The major intra-regional contrasts in relief are readily apparent in the contrast between the great northern plain, the splendid bow of the Carpathians and the true 'Balkan' mountain country in the south-east.

facing the open plains of southern Russia and sheltering behind them is the rich hill country of Transylvania, to which access from the west is guarded by isolated massifs. In northern Jugoslavia, the Julian Alps and Karawanken form a formidable wall, dying away eastwards in low hills on the edge of the Pannonian Plains. From them, extending south-eastwards, separating the Mediterranean lands and the Pannonian Plains lie the Dinaric mountains, whose landscape is made particularly distinctive by the calcareous rocks that impart an impression of aridity and display well-developed underground drainage. With many deeply incised, canyon-like valleys and steep-sided depressions, this is hard country to cross, and a sheer and forbidding white face rises from the island-studded blue waters of the Adriatic. The northern flanks, where karstic phenomena are absent, are more congenial, with well-watered and forested country.

The structurally mixed Balkan mountains lie east of the broad Morava–Vardar corridor. The northern ranges are similar to the Carpathians, with the long narrow Stara Planina on whose northern flanks a wide belt of rolling hilly and mountainous country dips away to the Danube platform, while on the south a wide trench-like depression separates the Sredna Gora and the great Maritsa Trough from the Stara Planina. The southern mountains are huge, inaccessible shattered pieces of an ancient massif, with wide erosion surfaces and many basins.

One of the most striking landscapes comprises the great open plains of Pannonia, sometimes called the mid-Danube or Hungarian basin. East of the Danube is an almost steppe-like landscape, but to the west and north, pieces of the ancient basement pierce the plains to form scenically attractive hill country. There are also remnants of volcanic hills not dissimilar to those around the inner flanks of the Carpathian bow. Less striking on a small scale map but thoroughly impressive on the ground are the plains of Wallachia and Moldavia. The Wallachian Plains spread from the marshy course of the Danube into the rolling foothill belt of the Carpathians, while the Moldavian Plains become rolling country towards the north and merge with the Prut and Dnestr valleys on the east. A hidden massif, the Dobrogea/Dobrudscha, deflects the Danube north to its wet and swampy delta with the Black Sea.

In the mountains, elevations are not great: in the High Tatra, the maximum height is the Gerlachovský Štít, 2655 m, a modest peak compared to the eight peaks in the Western Alps each over 4000 m. In the Transylvanian Alps (the southern Carpathians) Mt Moldoveanu, 2543 m, is the highest summit; in the Stara Planina, Botev reaches 2376 m and in the Rila Massif, Musala attains 2925 m, while in the Dinaric mountains, in the Prokletije, Jezerce reaches 2694 m. The Julian Alps rise to 2863 m in Triglav. At the other end of the scale, parts of the Pannonian Plains are as low as 90 m and large areas of Wallachia are no more than 50–60 m above sea level. Characteristic elevations in the Hercynian uplands are 150–70 m in the Bohemian Polabi, 250–390 m in southern Bohemia; the Krušné Hory rise to 1244 m in Klinovec and the Šumava to over 1400 m; while the Sudeten mountains reach 1602 m in Sněžka (Schneekoppe).

Although mountain barriers appear to bar the way from one lowland to another, there are several important corridors. Most significant has been the great Morava–Vardar routeway from the Aegean to the mid-Danube basin; access from the Danube basin to the northern plains can be made easily through lowland Moravia. The low passes across the Forest Carpathians have been historically important routeways from the wooded steppe into the Pannonian Plain. The geomorphological evolution of the Eastern and Southern Carpathians has left numerous inter-montane basins and river gorges that provide easy ways through—none more striking than the defile of the Olt and the Red Tower Pass, the gorge of the Jiu and the Bicaz Pass. Important passes cross the

Balkan mountains. Of these the Isker gorge gives access from the Danube to the Sofia basin and the Dragoman Pass allows movement from this basin to the Morava–Vardar corridor. In the south the Struma valley and the Maritsa valley (the 'road to sorrow') provide ways to the Aegean and to the Bosporus.

1.3 Structure

East of a line from Koszalin south-west towards Lvov, the North European Plain overlies an ancient basement structure associated with the East European Platform, now deeply covered by sedimentaries laid down by later shallow marine transgressions. In a few places in north-east Poland, this basement is masked by only a thin veneer of Quaternary deposits. West of the Koszalin–Lvov line, the basement complex is even more deeply buried and Hercynian structures underlie much of the German sector. They come to the surface in Upper Silesia and in the uplands of Little Poland. Under Mecklenburg, the structures may be Caledonian, but in the Elbe basin salt domes associated with petroleum and natural gas rise from great depths.

Hercynian (sometimes termed Variscan) structures, composed of Palaeozoic sediments deposited in a contemporaneous geosyncline and later folded and uplifted, form an important element in the Central European landscape. The remains of these mountains show structural trends; but in later times they were eroded and levelled by seas in which Permian, Triassic and other sediments were laid down, only to be uplifted, warped and dislocated when the Tertiary alpine orogeny created the broader features of the existing relief. The younger sediments have been denuded over large areas to reveal the older rocks, but in places between the uplands young rocks remain as broad lowlands, while movements have cast them into striking ridges and hogbacks. After such violent disruption, the old structural trends of the original folds have little significance in contemporary relief, which now displays rounded uplands with remarkably concordant summit levels, broad basins or deeply incised valleys, with classical *horst* formation (for example the Harz, from which the name is derived), and fault scarp features (for example in the Bohemian face of the Krušné Hory and the parallel scarps of the Sudeten mountains). Tilting and breaking of old erosion surfaces have strongly influenced the drainage pattern, and Tertiary transgressions left abrasion platforms and deserted coastlines. The dislocation gave rise to striking volcanic landscapes (České Středohoři, Doupov Hills) or to mineral springs that mark the sites of many spas. From the swamps of the Carboniferous period have come the line of bituminous coalfields along the northern flanks—in Saxony, in Bohemia and in Silesia—and such coals are buried under the northern plains. The Tertiary transgressions left an immense wealth of brown coal in Bohemia and in the northern plains, while rich mineral salt deposits cluster round the Harz flanks and there is a wide selection of metallic ores.

The mountains are the product of the Tertiary alpine orogeny, of which the most imposing monument is the great north-facing bow of young, soft, folded sediments, volcanic materials and shattered spikes of older and more resistant country, of the Carpathians. A product of the gigantic impact of earth movements in the Oligocene-Miocene, the mountains have a total length of over 1300 km and yet through their curvature, their two ends, on the west near

Bratislava and on the east near Turnu Severin, are only 500 km apart. Extending south-eastwards from the Julian Alps to the Black Sea, the mountains of the Dinaric and Balkan system form another part of the Tertiary orogenic belt, though incorporated within the structures are remains of older massifs in the south-west. These mountains differ from the Alps in their lower elevations and the lesser influence of glaciation, though structurally there are many similarities, particularly in the Carpathians. Structural links between the outliers of the Eastern Alps and the westernmost Carpathians are clearly evident, even though the link is deeply buried beneath the Danube valley and the Marchfeld, but the continuity is marked in the Leiser Berge and Pavlovské Vrchy that break the surface of the Vienna basin.

The movements that built the Carpathians appear to have come from within the bow, so that in places thrusts and overfolds have over-ridden the Hercynian basement on the northern flanks, while pieces of older crystalline Hercynian materials are found among the Tatra structures. Characteristically, the Carpathians have a broad foreland or piedmont depression filled with material eroded from the mountains. The main mountain belt is flysch country eroded into roughly dissected hill country, revealing thrusting and overfolding, while where softer clays have been removed there are generous basins and vales. On the south-west, this belt terminates in Jurassic limestones known for their steep isolated hills. The most impressive scenery of the High and Low Tatra belongs to a double row of isolated crystalline massifs, while there is also an inner belt of prominent hills in young volcanic rocks. In the Eastern and Southern Carpathians, erosion has left many basins, in some instances tectonically controlled, and extensive remnants of old erosion surfaces exist. The drainage pattern suggests its existence before uplift of the mountains.

The Dinaric–Balkan Tertiary mountains tend to rise in altitude as they extend south-eastwards from the Julian Alps. Predominant are calcareous rocks that suggest origin as deep water deposits in Tethys. Pressure seems to have come from the north-east, with folds overthrusted towards the Dalmatian coast, while depressions excavated in soft flysch deposits in the Adriatic coast have been flooded by a late glacial rise in sea level. Terraces marked at several elevations along the coast were reputedly cut by a Pliocene sea. Inland the ranges have been excavated into long depressions by differential erosion and cut into isolated *horsts* by canyon-like transverse valleys of allogenous rivers. There are almost plateau-like summits, with surfaces of early Tertiary date pockmarked by solution phenomena on the calcareous rocks. East of the calcareous belt lies the Dinaric schistose belt, where Palaeozoic crystalline schists have penetrated the sedimentary cover, a generally rolling landscape, but wherever gabbro or hornfels occur, a more rugged effect has been imparted, and there are also young volcanic phenomena and steep-sided karstic plateaus. This belt drops in altitude to merge into the Pannonian Plains.

East of the Vardar, the Balkan ranges—the Stara Planina—form a continuation of the Carpathian structures south of the Danube, separated from the Transylvanian Alps and the Banat mountains by the Danube break through. The ranges have a strongly crystalline character on the west, but eastwards the core is increasingly dominated by a mass of folded Mesozoic sediments and demonstrate uplift after planation, with broad open surfaces and antecedent drainage. The ranges drop southwards in a number of long depressions to the Sredna Gora. The south-eastern part of the system, in Macedonia and southern Bulgaria, comprises the large 'median mass' of the Hercynian Pelagonian–Thracian massif, composed of gneiss, granite and crystalline schists as well as some old Palaeozoic calcareous rocks. On the west the block has been much dissected by rivers of the Morava and Vardar system, with much down-cutting on the south to adjust to a lowered level of the Aegean Sea. The subsidence and instability are still marked by earthquakes, often of destructive force. Since Jurassic times there has been deposition of young sediments by marine transgressions and lake formation. The high crystalline blocks of the centre and the east have been cut by numerous small basins, while the higher mountains stood above the Pleistocene snowline and reveal evidence of glaciation. In these blocks, much of the relief originates from a Pliocene dislocation and disturbance, with associated vulcanism marked by thermal mineral springs. Upper Miocene erosion surfaces occur at different altitudes in the Pirin and Rhodopi, which suggest the massif underwent prolonged continuous uplift and arching as the Morava–Vardar depression sank, reflected by numerous features of antecedent and epigenetic drainage. The structures on the south reveal the influence of the Aegean subsidence, which may have occurred as late as the Quaternary. Eastern Bulgaria is marked by a long trough of subsidence in the Maritsa valley and in the Tundzha depression, possibly all related to the Pleistocene. The Strandzha Planina forms a belt of young uplift blocking the through passage of the Maritsa trough to the Black Sea.

The mountain systems are partly orientated by the resistant blocks of ancient (Hercynian or pre-Hercynian) massifs against which the soft sediments were forced in the process of folding. One such massif, the Getic–Moesian, lies deeply buried under an infill of young sediments on the lower Danube, conditioning the orientation of the Transylvanian Alps and the Stara Planina. Its surface forms the broad, low plateaus and river terraces of the Wallachian Plains and the calcareous Bulgarian Platform south of the river, where sinking long continued. The lowermost reaches of the Danube are deflected northwards to their delta by the smaller buried massif of the Dobrogea. The southern Dobrogea part of the Getic–Moesian massif is separated from the northern part by the Karasu depression, an ancient channel of the Danube (apparently blocked by gentle uplift in Würm times). The Eastern Carpathians derive their orientation from abutting on to the Podolian–Azov arch of the Russian Platform.

A most imposing macrorelief feature is the mountain-ringed Pannonian Plain, which overlies a down-warped median mass. The ancient crystalline base, dislocated in numerous fragments, sank along with its Mesozoic sediments, becoming a large sea in early Tertiary times, slowly filled by a great depth of sediment. Later rivers deposited sheets of sands and gravels and *loess* was blown in. The deposits are thickest in the Tisza basin and in the continued area of subsidence of the Rába basin. In the Mecsek and the Bakony Forest, the old basement protrudes through the younger sediments. The dislocation of the basement is reflected in mineral springs and volcanic phenomena (for example Tapolca, Tihany), with outliers of the Dinaric system and uplifted parts of the basement on the southern edge in the Sava–Drava mesopotamia. The Tertiary hill country of Transylvania is regarded by many students as part of the Pannonian massif which did not founder so deeply, but was covered by deposits from Tertiary seas and later dissected by rivers in a complex way. The massifs that block access to it, notably the Bihor mountains, may be Carpathian structures affected by sinking and gross disturbance that has left volcanic phenomena.

The emergence of new concepts of 'plate-tectonics' in geological studies may help in the future to explain how the various structural elements of Europe came to be pieced together and by what mechanisms the main tectonic features were developed.

1.3.1 The North European Plain

Across Germany and Poland, the North European Plain, widening eastwards, bears the imprint of the great Quaternary ice sheets which at their maximum extent reached from Scandinavia to nudge against the southern uplands. Glacial landforms have been much modified by later meltwaters and by strong winds around the ice cap flanks, so that in the south are large areas of fine yellow dust—*loess*—which these winds carried from the periglacial deserts. Farther north, resorted fluvio-glacial sands form undulating heath country with fossil dunes. The northernmost plain has the youngest and freshest evidence of the ice sheets, with well-developed moraines and lakes in glacial hollows. The central part is seamed by broad, shallow valleys of streams that carried immense quantities of sediment-laden water from the decaying ice sheets, still used in part by modern drainage, though at several places the rivers have broken through the low interfluves to flow north towards the Baltic Sea.

The rough outline of the drowned Baltic coast has been smoothed by long spits protecting water-filled or silted lagoons, though the coastline is commonly irregular in shape and the veneer of ground and end moraine fretted by the sea into low cliffs. Where the underlying hard rocks emerge at the surface, there are impressive cliffs (for example Kap Arkona). Old drowned meltwater valleys form shallow straits behind low offshore islands such as Rügen, formed of fifteen patches of moraine joined by sand spits. Of the lagoons, the most striking lie along the East Prussian coast, in the Frisches Haff and Kurisches Haff. The rivers have narrow, shallow, drowned estuaries making modest harbours.

A broad lowland of rolling ground moraine behind the coast rises gently to the lake-studded morainic plateaus of Mecklenburg, Pomerania and Masuria, where the two major Baltic end moraines lie 15–40 km apart, with low, steep-sided hills, remnants of the moraines, mostly forest covered, separated by marshy or lake-filled hollows, with complex and imperfect drainage systems. The lakes vary greatly in size and shape (including the subglacial *Rinnenseen*—ribbon lakes—of Masuria) but are mostly shallow. Pasture typifies moister hollows, while potatoes flourish on the extensive light sandy soils, but heavy ill-drained clays are unattractive to farming. The forest is both sombre coniferous woodland and more open beech stands.

The central belt of meltwater valleys (*Urstromtäler* or *Pradoliny*) is a featureless countryside. On low interfluves lie older ground moraine and much modified moraines of the earlier glaciations. Towards the south, sandy outwash, moraine and fossil dunes are marked by heaths broken by major valleys, in the Lüneburg Heath, the Fläming, the Lusatian Heaths and north of Wrocław. Much heath has been reclaimed for farming or its poorer parts planted with conifers. The meltwater valleys have considerable areas of blown sand in dunes, as well as swampy or lake-filled hollows, like the complex system of interlinking channels from which Berlin derives much of its character. The meltwater valleys are comparatively poorly developed east of the Vistula, but there are large areas of indeterminate drainage in the famous Pripyat marshes. Forest and pasture are characteristic land uses in the *Urstromtal* belt.

Spread across the older drift, the plains of Central Poland are particularly featureless and the moraines marked on maps are hardly visible in reality, though in a few places they give rise to low hills, again less marked east of the Vistula. Moist, peat-filled hollows are common and the river valleys are broad, almost imperceptible and usually swampy. Sand resorted by wind and water from the great *pradoliny* and from the glacial clays, makes infertile country like the 500 km^2 of the Puszcza Kampinoska, though sands are often marked by pine stands and some forest covers the low hills. Central Poland has a dense rural population that farms a high proportion of its modest soils.

The evidence of the extension south of the ice sheets is hard to decipher and in places almost obliterated. More impressive are the large areas of *loess* on which soils of remarkable fertility have developed, most clearly seen in the great embayments of the northern Plain into the southern uplands. Here, a largely treeless landscape of open fields and nucleated villages forms the grain and beet districts of the *Börde* in Saxony and Thuringia, often broken by forested ridges of the underlying solid rock. Similar *loessic* country occurs in Lower Silesia south of the Oder and around Kraków, Kielce and Lublin, where a very high proportion of the land is farmed and where there has been acute rural overpopulation supported by the maintenance of soil fertility despite simple farming methods.

1.3.2 The Hercynian Lands

The 'middle-aged' Hercynian–Variscan uplands form a scenically attractive element in the landscapes of Central Europe, generally represented by massive tilted blocks of country or steep-sided but relatively flat-topped plateaus on which ancient erosion surfaces at different levels may be traced. Triassic, Jurassic and Cretaceous materials, now warped and distorted, form striking ridges and cuestas, particularly on the northern edge of the Hercynian lands, standing above the rich farming country of the *loess*-covered foreland. The great dissected, forested *horst* of the Harz on the northern edge has given its name to these structures. Seen from the surrounding lowlands, it looks like a range of rounded hills incised by valleys, but from the air its massive and classical *horst* form is visible. It was one of the great metal mining areas of late mediaeval Central Europe. The Thüringer Wald, forming a barrier to communications between central Germany and Bavaria, is a north-westwards pointing ridge, some 80 km long and 16–20 km wide. It is extensively forested and bounded by steep, fault-defined flanks eaten into by deeply incised valleys. On the east, it merges into a wide, dissected slaty plateau (elevation 500–750 m) broken by rounded residual hills. With poor podzolic soils, farming is unattractive and much ground remains under spruce or beech forest, while the valleys draining to the Elbe have been used for reservoirs to store water for the industries of the plains.

East of the Thüringen Plateau, the Erzgebirge (Ore Mountains, Krušné Hory) extend for 160 km as a high dissected plateau rising to over 1200 m. The north-west face is gentle, weakly terraced by reputedly marine abrasion surfaces, but the south-east face is an immense faultline scarp, dropping precipitously from weakly rounded summits. This configuration made colonisation by Saxons from the north relatively easy and an important mediaeval and later incentive was wealth of lead, zinc, silver, nickel and cobalt associated with granitic intrusions. Uranium has been important since the Second World War. The hills still remain forested, though farming is practised at surprisingly high altitudes and some of the highest settlements in the Hercynian lands are found here.

Between the Erzgebirge and the Lusatian Hills, where a 25 km wide block of Hercynian country sank between faults, there are soft sedimentary materials through which the Elbe has incised its valley. Its tributaries have cut the soft but massive sandstone into *buttes* (Tafelberge), whose steeper slopes are forested with mixed and coniferous woodland while their tops are heathy and between them lies well-cultivated farmland, though their grotesque form has made them a popular tourist area. The Lusatian Hills (500–600 m), a rounded granitic northern upland border of Bohemia, have a relief gentler than the Erzgebirge and the soils, with an admixture of *loess* in places, are agriculturally attractive. The hills merge into the highly complex Sudeten Mountains, mostly large faulted and tilted blocks of metamorphic and crystalline rocks broken into segments. On the south a series of ridges drop towards the Bohemian basin, their scarped faces towards the mountains. The western Sudeten Mountains are dominated by the Eulengebirge (Krkonoše, Karkonosze) and the Jizerské Hory which reach 1605 m in the Schneekoppe/Sněžka/Śnieżka. The middle part of the mountains lies mostly in Polish territory, where the Kłodżko (Glatz) Basin is a fertile countryside flanked by forested mountains of gneiss and schists (Orlické Hory). The eastern Sudeten ranges, broad, rounded upland rising to well over 1000 m, sink gently eastwards to the Moravian Gate and steeply to the south and south-west. These mountains are still extensively forested, though they rise above the tree line in their higher parts, but well-farmed vales with small industrial towns lie between the ranges, and around Wałbrzych (Waldenburg) coal is mined.

The south-west flank of Bohemia is formed by imposing upland covered by almost virgin forest, particularly in the Šumava, the most massive part of Bohemia's mountain rim. Throughout much of its length, summits over 1200 m are not unusual, rising above a flattish uplifted Tertiary peneplain. The open moors on some of the highest parts form one of Bohemia's major 'reservoirs'. This mass of granite and metamorphic rocks, lacking in easy crossing points, forms a sparsely settled no-man's-land with Germany; but on its northern edge, a depression cut by the Berounka and the Regen forms a major routeway into Bohemia and separates the Šumava from the crystalline but lower and narrower dissected upland of the Český Les, whose highest point (over 1000 m) overlooks on the northern edge another significant routeway into Bohemia through Cheb and the Ohře valley.

Three principal landscapes comprise the interior of Bohemia, with the north largely formed by the broad plain of the upper Elbe (Polabi), a crudely triangular basin eroded early into the Bohemian massif and subsequently filled by Cretaceous and Tertiary sediments, now forming an undulating lowland, mantled by sand, silt and veneer of *loess*. Drained by the Labe (Elbe) and the Vltava (Moldau), the good 'black earth' type soils are intensively cultivated and this is the granary of Bohemia. On its northern side, a fantastic landscape of forest-clad volcanic hills forming outliers of the Středohoři breaks the intensely farmed countryside. Southwards the plain rises to the plateau that forms most of southern Bohemia, a rolling and in places quite hilly area composed of ancient rocks intensely folded and reduced to a peneplain in Tertiary times. The poor acidic podzols are unrewarding for farming and large forests remain. The rivers flow across the plateau that tilts gently downwards towards the north, but there appears to have been warping of the surface, for the middle and lower reaches of the rivers towards the north have incised themselves in meandering, trough-like valleys, demonstrated by the gorge of the Vltava at Prague. The massif has been broken and faulted and long narrow schistose ridges break the surface. The Brdy with its mineral resources has encouraged settlement, while near Plzeň a synclinal trough contains small but locally important coal deposits.

The fracturing of the Bohemian massif is reflected in volcanic rocks and landforms, notably on the west along the trough of the Ohře river and in the Doupovské Hory, where the better soils have been well settled. The most rewarding soils of the Bohemian Plateau are associated with shallow Tertiary lakes that left sands and clays, as well as extensive peat deposits.

The Bohemian–Moravian Uplands (Českomoravská Vrchovina) form most of eastern Bohemia, a great, gently sloping crystalline mass between Bohemia and the Moravian Plains. Late movements or warping are suggested by the broad, open upper valleys of the rivers and their deeply entrenched lower courses. The summits are usually forested domes (600–700 m) above the modestly dissected hill country. The soils are poorer and the higher tops wetter and cooler, with snow lying longer, than in central Bohemia, so that much rough pasture and forest remains, while potatoes and hardy cereals are important in local farming. It is a generally sparsely settled country with employment in small industrial towns.

The broad depression of the Moravian Plain, the structural junction between Hercynian and Carpathian structures, is a major route way from the North European Plain to Danubia. The northern part of the plain around Ostrava, covered by materials carried by meltwater from the Quaternary ice sheets, forms a rich agricultural area renowned for its sugar beet, while on its south is a constriction known as the Moravian Gate (Moravská Bráma), a passageway probably enlarged by Quaternary meltwater. The western side of the Moravian Plain is formed by hilly country, lower but more roughly dissected than the Bohemian–Moravian Uplands. Unfortunately, though the Moravian Plains have good soils and much sunshine suited to cereal cultivation, so that a large proportion of their area is farmed, they suffer from a tendency to drought.

The Hercynian structures under the North European Plain are concealed by younger sediments in the German sector, but in southern Poland hills and low plateaus break through the drift cover to reveal some of the oldest rocks known in Poland. They account for the important coal-bearing rocks of the Upper Silesia coalfield, while in the impressive limestone scarps of the Jura Krakowska there is well-developed karst, notably near Ojców, and settlements show a springline distribution. These limestones contain lead, zinc and iron ore. The eastern anticline forms the most striking relief in Poland north of the Carpathians, in the forested Góry Świetokrzyskie that rise to 611 m in the Łysogóry and are associated with the Little Polish Upland (Wyżyna Małopolska), an area of ancient settlement where a high proportion of the ground is intensively cultivated.

1.3.3 The Tertiary Mountain Structures

The Carpathians

The great east–west Tertiary orogenic belt extends across much of the southern part of Eastern Europe. The Carpathians form a majestic mountain landscape extensively forested, with deeply entrenched valleys and broad well-cultivated basins. Compared to the Alps, elevations are moderate and only in the High Tatra is a truly rugged mountain landscape found, though impressive mountainous country is seen in the Ceahlău and Făgăraş Massifs. Many parts of the Carpathians remain remote and backward, though intensive tourist development like the Alps is beginning to emerge.

The western Carpthians are low forested hills, prominent in the landscape inspite of modest height. The south-westernmost part ends at the Danube near Bratislava, whose castle stands on a commanding prominence above the river. Towards the north-east, the Malé Karpaty expand to 60 km wide, comprising forested ridges, but about 80 km north of the Danube, they merge with the Bilé Karpaty and the Javornik, whose harder rocks appear as summits up to 1000 m, and a northern plateau has been dissected into a series of forest-clad ridges, dropping relatively gently to the Moravian Plain, but with a sharp drop to the trench-like valley of the Váh. Inspite of road building, this country remains an effective barrier between Bohemia–Moravia and Slovakia.

The more dissected country of the western Beskids has summit levels well over 1000 m. As a result of the dissection, the headwaters of the Oder and Váh have cut an easy crossing of the Moravian–Silesian Beskids in the Jablunkov Pass (553 m), route of the main east–west arterial railway in Czechoslovakia. The ranges continue across Poland, straddling the Polish Podhale territory that extends to the crestline of the High Tatra. The Polish Carpathians comprise largely the outer zone of younger rocks (mostly Cretaceous and Tertiary) that display intense alpine-type folding. The landscape is not dissimilar to the Sudeten mountains, though of quite different geological character, with broad forested ridges, rounded summits and a concordant skyline characteristic of mountains produced under a warm humid climate. The valleys are wide and open, forming good farming country, though narrow gorge-like defiles occur where the rivers cut across the ridges. One of the most impressive landscapes is along the Dunajec river, where the southern Beskid ranges form the Pieniny mountains, while it has also cut formidable valleys in the Beskydy Wysprowy and the Pogórze foothills that seldom rise above 500 m.

In the Babia Góra, the Beskids rise to 1725 m but become markedly lower and more dissected east of the Biała river, where important passes—the Tylicka, Dukielska and Łupowska—cross the mountains. East of the Poprad valley, the

Low Beskids, whose summits seldom exceed 400 m, have the appearance of a rolling but highly dissected peneplain. The headwaters of the Dnestr mark the western end of the Bieszczady, a sparsely populated, rolling forested country, the principal part of the so-called Carpatho-Ukraine, while on the east, towards the Rumanian frontier, the Gorgany and Cherniye Gory rise to more rugged heights of 2058 m (Goverla/Howerla). In these Eastern Beskids, there are wide tracts of rolling and gently rounded hills, with large forests and much good pasture. Sometimes known as the Low Forest Carpathians, this sector is crossed by important passes (Uzhotskiy, Tatars' Pass).

South of this outer zone of predominantly younger rocks lies an inner Carpathian zone, best developed in the mountains that form the heart of Slovakia, which shows a much higher proportion of harder crystalline rocks, with widespread igneous rocks and granite. In many parts Mesozoic rocks cover the older materials, but the Tertiary sediments so marked in the outer zone are largely absent. Nevertheless, a similar trend in orientation from west to east in a slightly curved face concave to the south is found. Three main lines of ranges appear amid the seething complexity, with broad intervening basins floored by young sediments. On the west and south, the ranges tend to fan out and die away into the Pannonian Plain, so that the main rivers rise in the higher parts of the Tatra and flow in curving courses between the ranges towards the Danube.

The western part of the Central Carpathians is the granite massif of the Malá Fatra, cut by the Váh in a magnificent gorge common to superimposed rivers. The Malá Fatra dies away south into undulating country of the lower Nitra valley. The core of the Central Carpathians is formed by the Tatra (Tatry), with the northern High Tatra as the most rugged landscape resulting from intense glaciation. This small area extends east–west for only about 60 km between the Poprad on the east and the Orava on the west and yet within a distance of 40 km there are several peaks over 2000 m, with typical corrie lakes on the northern slopes, while on the south the range drops to the Liptov Basin in a steep and formidable face. Bare rock faces rise well above the treeline and the mountain pastures, most impressive when seen from Zakopane in Poland. The eastern end is an abrupt drop from the Vysoké Tatry (High Tatra) overlooking Poprad, but the west, the Západné Tatry (Western Tatra), drops in steps towards the Váh. This is poor agricultural country, but forms the tourist focus on both the Czech and Polish flanks.

South of the Liptov Basin and the upper Váh lies the Low Tatra (Nizké Tatry), about 80 km in east–west extent, which rises to a smooth and levelled upper surface (2043 m, Ďumbier). The core is mostly granite and gneiss, but calcareous rocks impart a rugged landscape with karstic phenomena and there is evidence of the work of ice. Only the highest surfaces are alpine meadow and much is forested by good stands of timber. To the south and south-east lie the Slovak Ore Mountains (Slovenské Rudohorie), a tangled mass of low rounded hills, dropping from west to east, with large forests but more farmland in the broader valleys than in the Tatra. The highest point (Stolica) reaches only 1477 m on the west, while elevations in the east do not exceed 1200 m. A conformity of rounded summits over considerable distances suggests a series of erosion surfaces. Erosion and lithology give the mountains their character, with numerous caves and canyons in the Slovak karst, where there is little forest and much open pasture. The Slovak

Ore Mountains have long been known for their mineral wealth—gold, silver, copper and lead were mined in mediaeval times in the west, but iron in the east was of later interest, with some lignite from Tertiary basins.

East of the Central Carpathians lies the lower, rolling but forested and farmed hilly country of the Spišská Magura, Levočské Pohorie and other groups that extend beyond the broad valley of the Hornád. Though cool and moist, the lower elevations are well farmed and carry a relatively thick population. The landscape is a complex but pleasing mixture of hill masses, basins and valleys with rolling hills, though it is poor and backward in appearance. Some of the hills drop eastwards and southwards into the gentle outwash fans of the Tisza drainage (Potiská Nižina, Tiszahát), on whose northern edge stand the splendid forested cupola-shaped hills of the volcanic Vihorlat. The outwash fans with good alluvial soils are well cultivated.

East of the uppermost Tisza, the ranges begin again to widen out into the Rumanian Carpathians, of which three major systems are distinguished—the Eastern, the Southern and the less commonly known Bihor. The Eastern and Southern Carpathians form a massive eastward-facing bow, while the Bihor Carpathians comprise several separate massifs. In the north the Eastern Carpathians resemble the landscape of Slovakia, with parallel ranges of Secondary and Tertiary rocks around a crystalline core, separated by upland basins of varying size and importance in the human geography of the country. On the inner side there are also igneous rocks. The Eastern Carpathians extend south-south-eastwards for 240 km before a sharp turn in the ranges west-south-west forms the Southern Carpathians—the Transylvanian Alps—to run for 200 km until they merge with the southern part of the Bihor Carpathians in a gentle curve towards the Danube gorges. Similarities in structural history produce landscapes in these three components with many features in common, so that the marked *Boresco* erosion surface, a remnant of an ancient peneplain, may be found at widely different points around an elevation of 2000 m, while a lower but similarly prominent *Riu Ses* surface can be found in the Southern and Bihor Carpathians. An exceptionally extensive surface is also found at around 1000 m in the Eastern Carpathians, though less definitively elswhere. From these surfaces it is obvious that much of the Eastern and Southern Carpathians are a highly dissected plateau cut by deeply entrenched valleys and broken by wart-like residual hills.

The Eastern Carpathians, cut into separate segments by a rectilinear drainage pattern, display three distinct landscapes. On the northern half, there is a rugged crystalline core of well forested mountains that rise into broad grassy erosion surfaces over 1300 m. On the outermost side of the bow is a zone of intensely folded Secondary rocks covered on the outer side by less disturbed flysch deposits, whose width increases southwards. Although the relief is more gentle and valleys broader, elevations are considerable. Eastwards the zone turns into rolling hills and melts away as a footslope belt into the undulating Moldavian Plateau and piedmont country. To the west of the central core is a line of volcanic mountains, structurally related to the Vihorlat in the north, that still bear evidence of cones and craters and reach 2100 m in the Călimani Mountains, though elevations are much less towards the south.

The Eastern Carpathians are generally marked by broad upland surfaces and deep, steep-sided valleys unattractive to settlement, which is clustered in the intermontane basins and wider valleys. Most of the eight main basins lie between the volcanic mountains and the crystalline core. The largest and most impressive are the Giurgeu–Ciu Depression and the Bîrsa–Tirgu Depression, floored by *loess* and aluvium, so that they are well settled and much cultivated. Other basins like that of Muramureş, Dornei and Cimpulung have a rougher relief and lie at greater altitudes, making them agriculturally less attractive. These basins and the transverse valleys provide routes through the otherwise formidable-looking mountains. Apart from these basins and valleys this is a sparsely settled country of endless forest or mountain grassland in which old ways of life persist.

The Southern Carpathians, not so markedly broken into isolated segments, are generally higher and more continuous, largely the result of more widespread exposure of the crystalline core. The prominent erosion surfaces are broken by extensively glaciated hard residual masses, with well-developed corries (particularly on north faces over 2000 m) and striking *aretes*, and terminal moraines occur in some higher valleys. The northern flanks of the mountains are usually straight and steep, while the southern faces are more gentle and dissected by rivers flowing to the Danube, gradually merging into the broad footslope belt. The Făgăras Massif has a distinctly alpine character, rising to over 2000 m in its length of 45 km. Its western end is marked by the deep gorge of the Olt, a river that rises in the Eastern Carpathians and flows through several mountain basins and then runs along the northern edge of the Făgăraş Massif before cutting across the mountains, through the Lovistea Depression, to join the Danube. The more complex mountains west of the Olt, on whose upper surface the broad erosion platforms are well developed, comprise rough terrain without adequate roads and rise to over 2500 m. The western end is marked by the deep entrenchment of the Jiu that drains the Petroşeni Depression, a down-faulted part of the massif floored by Tertiary materials that have attracted a dense settlement. West of the Jiu, an extremely complex area is dominated by the rough and rugged Retezat Massif, rising to over 2500 m, where the occurrence of soft rocks between belts of harder materials gives a lithological control in the pattern of relief. On the higher parts of the Retezat, Godeanu and Vîlcan massifs the remains of the *Boresco* surface are common, while there is much evidence of glaciation, but this is less inaccessible country than the Făgăraş Massif. The western end of this belt is the Timiş–Cerna Depression that leads from the Iron Gate of Transylvania to the Iron Gate of the Danube.

'Western Carpathians' is a term used by Rumanian geographers for the mountain masses along the west side of the great Transylvanian Depression, likened to a chord across the arc of the Eastern and Southern Carpathians. These are highly complex mountains comprising three separate massifs and belts of low foothills. They are separated from the Southern Carpathians by the Timiş–Cerna Depression and Hateg Basin. The Bihor or 'Western' Carpathians extend over some 34 000 km², an area of irregular depressions and stranded massifs, though in general relief lower than other parts of the Carpathians. In the Banat Mountains and the Poiana Ruscă Massif elevations are not more than 1400 m, while in the Apuseni or Bihor Massif, a few peaks rise to over 1800 m. The pattern of the mountains has a radial character that throws knots of mountains into sharp focus. On the western side are great gulfs of lowland, with clustered villages and cultivated land penetrating far into the mountains. The relief is generally smoother than elsewhere because they were not hosts to Quaternary glaciers, but they do show well-developed erosion surfaces that are settled up to 1200–1300 m. Limestone is very common, giving well-developed and extensive karst, with imposing 'klippen' places, while in the Muntii Metalici Teriary eruptive forms impart a 'haystack' appearance.

Two main ridges form the Banat Mountains, each over 1000 m on the east but not more than 500–700 m on the west. Wherever crystalline schists appear, these mountains are miniatures of the Southern Carpathians. Though unimpressive these mountains are rich in minerals. Their southern limit is the transverse valley of the Danube, the longest in Europe, from Bazias to Turnu Severin, comprising four gorges interspersed by wider basins. North of the Bistra Depression lies the powerful Poiana Ruscă Massif, typical of the older crystalline schists, radially intersected like the spokes of a wheel by many valleys, between which broad ridge-like interfluves are well settled and farmed. The broad valley of the Mures, a main access into Transylvania, separates the Poiana Ruscă and the Apuseni/Bihor Massif. Whereas the former rises to only 1380 m, the latter nearly reaches 1800 m, though a few peaks are higher and dominate the massif like castles. Within the massif are extensive erosion surfaces, 'suspended plains' that carry settlements and cropland well above the levels elsewhere in the Rumanian Carpathians. In parts of the west-centre and south limestone has produced a karstic landscape with gorges, ice caves and similar features while in the south, volcanic activity has left a rich mineral wealth—gold, silver, mercury and other metals have been mined for nearly 2000 years. The Bihor itself forms the highest part of the Apuseni Massifs, with a broad open top broken by more resistant knobs that rise to 1848 m.

Almost entirely surrounded by the Carpathians, the Transylvanian Basin is really a massive representative of the many small intermontane basins and extends 150 km east–west and 200 km north–south, clearly differentiated from the surrounding mountains, except in the Somes Plateau in the north-west. The relief is gently undulating Tertiary hill country between 300–600 m. As a vast late Tertiary lake, it was slowly filled by sediments washed from the surrounding mountains that were later slightly warped. Erosion of these beds and deposition of *loess* and alluvia are the keys to the contemporary landscape. Some rougher relief occurs where there was volcanic activity or where more marked foldings nearer the massifs, and there are also marked salt domes. Nevertheless, some parts are a strikingly flat plain. Apart from the Olt drainage to the south, most rivers flow to the Pannonian Plains. With gentle relief and fertile soils, Transylvania has been extensively taken into cultivation, with endless fields and small patches of woodland, mostly on the higher ridges.

The Dinaric Mountains

Northernmost Jugoslavia lies within the outliers of the Eastern Alps in the Karawanken and Julian Alps and the hilly and mountainous country of Slovenia, but to the south these merge into true Dinaric structures stretching away to the south-east. Rising to over 2000 m, the Karawanken form an impressive northern frontier range with Austria, while to the south lies a series of short broken ranges, with well-settled basins and valleys between them. A limestone plateau between the Sava and Drava basins reflects some Dinaric characteristics. These northern landscapes of forests, fields and clustered villages with imposing churches are reminiscent of Austria, while the Julian Alps, with forest and mountain meadow, are similar, where Triglav (2863 m) is one of the highest peaks in Eastern Europe.

The dissected plateau seamed by steep ridges south of the Julian Alps rises to 1000 m and is distinguished by its limestone and its structural trends as Dinaric. A lower lying saddle of country, it has had a long history as a routeway from north-west to south-east. To the south lies the glacis of the high *Dinarids*, whose structural zones widen towards the south-east. The country comprises a series of nearly parallel ridges following the general structural trend between which lie depressions and plateaus, but the essential landscape contrast is between the karstic and non-karstic areas. Erosion has commonly reduced the ranges to flattish ridges and rounded protuberances, but their sides are steep, and they are dissected by steep-sided valleys. Much of the Dinaric belt rises above 600 m, but there are also considerable areas over 1500 m and in the south, summits may exceed 2000 m, with evidence of glaciation. A markedly trellised pattern is seen in the drainage flowing to the Adriatic or to the Pannonian Plain, with the longitudinal valleys often much wider than the gorge-like transverse sections cutting across the ranges.

One of the most distinctive landscapes occurs in the broad limestone uplands of the Karst, extending some 550 km along the Dalmatian coast and varying in width from 60–100 km, rising in general elevation towards the south. With occasional patches of sandstone and shale, the limestones are generally massive but vary in age and character, so that in places—like the sinuous Gulf of Kotor—differing lithological characteristics have influenced relief. The uplands are bleak and bare, and chemical action of rainwater in the remarkably pure limestone has produced typical surface forms and an elaborate underground drainage. A common feature is the solution hollow—either small *doline* and *uvale* or the large flat-floored, steep-sided basins (*polja*) up to 70 km long. These hollows show distinct alignment along structural trends. The *polja* are often the only farmed areas, floored with silt or red soils, though some are flooded in winter when the water table rises. Lake Skader is a *polje* permanently flooded because its bottom is below modern sea level. Springs (*vrela*), swallow holes (*ponori*) and caverns (*jame*) are everywhere common and there are impressive waterfalls and dry valleys derived from the underground drainage. Above the depressions are the open surfaces of the *planine*. The landscape is arid with sparse vegetation.

The Dalmatian coast is backed by steep, white faces of the mountains, scaled in many places by remarkable roads (Lovćen road), while the promontories and offshore islands reflect a classic drowned landscape. Drowned valleys provide fiord-like entries inland. Only in the south, in Montenegro, are modest beaches developed; further south in Albania, there is a broad marshy and one-time malarial coastal plain, while low coastal platforms distinguish the Istrian Peninsula and the Ravni Kotari between Zadar and Šibenik.

The southern karst, south of the Neretva and Bosna, changes to a high continuous plateau rather than parallel ranges. The plateau over wide areas is almost devoid of surface water, with so much bare limestone that there is hardly room for poor xerophytic plants.The *polja* are sunk deep into the surface and suffer acute cold air drainage in winter. Montenegro, a truly mountainous country, is geologically more varied and there is abundant surface drainage. It is exceptionally rugged between the Zelengora and the Prokletije on the Albanian frontier, with many summits well over 2000 m (Durmitor, 2522 m). With more water and modest soils, it has been more attractive to man inspite of its ruggedness.

Between the karst and the valleys that form the southern outliers of the Pannonian Plains lies a belt of mountains and hills that drops to the plains and extends from north-west to south-east for over 500 km though seldom wider than 80–100 km, except in the south. The landscape of forested slopes and cultivated valleys, with patches of mountain pasture, besides the abundant surface water and the much denser settlement, form substantial contrasts to the karst. A Palaeozoic and igneous core is covered by younger sediments, with sandstones, shales and not much limestone. Between Sarajevo and Zenica, the soft Tertiary materials have been excavated into a wide and shallow basin, but elsewhere the landscape comprises short sections of hills and mountains running with the Dinaric trend and separated by broad vales but cut by transverse gorges. Elevations are generally greater towards the south. The country is scattered with villages and small market towns.

Most of Serbia and Montenegro comprise an ancient massif of early rocks with igneous intrusions and much broken and faulted. Triassic and Cretaceous seas left a coating of younger deposits, notably limestones. The Secondary rocks are, however, extensive only in the north, in the Šumadija, and in the basins of Kosovo and Metohija. Some relief features were cut by water draining from late Tertiary lakes, but the impervious schists have greatly accelerated erosion by quick run-off. In the older rocks there is considerable mineral wealth. The Šumadija has been extensively cleared of forest, though pigs once kept in large numbers depended on acorns for forage. In the Kapaonik, much beech and oak forest remains, though some parts rise above the treeline. Throughout the area, as in many Balkan mountains, *šibljak*, deciduous brushwoods, reflect overgrazing in the forests. The flora contains Balkan, Mediterranean and Central European elements as well as relics of the Tertiary vegetation.

East of the Morava–Vardar corridor, the southern mountains belong to the ancient Rhodope–Pelagonian Massif and in the north, to a southern extension of Carpathian structures. The Balkan Mountains, including the Stara Planina and the Sredna Gora, are a narrow and continuous range over 600 km long. The northern flank is a foothill zone that merges into the platform south of the Danube, while the Stara Planina is a complex of mountains and upland basins. The foothill belt comprises younger sedimentaries resting against the core of the Stara Planina, so that harder strata stand out as sharp ridges across which transverse valleys have been cut, with intervening broad and well-cultivated clay vales. Some of the ridges exceed 1000 m. There is much forest, but also large clearings for grazing, while small towns lie at the entrance to passes across the mountains. East of the Jantra river, the ridges become a broad plateau. The Stara Planina comprises true folded mountains cut by transverse valleys and numerous low passes (about fifteen roads cross the range, the most famous being the Shipka Pass). It slopes relatively gently to the north, but the south is steep and partly fault-controlled. The range is well forested, though it rises to rough alpine grazings and the summits are usually gently rounded (maximum elevation, Botev, 2376 m). The lower eastern part is divided into the easily-crossed ranges.

Narrow, elongated tectonic basins lie along the southern flank of the Stara Planina. The largest, the Sofia Basin (1165 km²) has its surface broken by isolated hills, but floored by good soils and with resources of lignite, inspite of cold air drainage and temperature inversion, it carries a substantial population. However, farming requires irrigation to supplement precipitation. To the east, the basins merge into a trench-like depression that forms an attractive farming area amid the mountains, widening into the Tundzha Basin, the lowest and economically most important part. South of the depressions, the Sredna Gora forms structurally a part of the Rhodope Massif, but unlike it, with a covering of Secondary rocks and flysch. Large areas remain in forest, but the warm south-facing slopes are well cultivated as they drop to the broad plain-like basin of the Maritsa, whose Tertiary and recent deposits cover the old massif to a great depth and give good soils that are intensely farmed.

The plain-like valleys of the Maritsa and Tundzha are the economic core of Bulgaria, extending over 20 000 km², broken by occasional hills, where older rocks are found. The landscape is like a vast market garden, but the steep slopes of the hills and mountains are usually forest clad. It is here that some of the strongest Turkish influences remain. The low hills of the Strandzha (up to 600 m) separate this lowland from a coastal plain around Burgas, whose poor soils and low rainfall result in a less prosperous agriculture, with much rough grazing and stunted thicket of an almost Mediterranean character.

The Rhodope Massif of ancient rocks and igneous materials is a dominant feature of Balkan relief. As a result of Tertiary uplift its steep flanks have been scarred by deep and narrow valleys to give difficult access to the interior, though small basins, the foci of settlement, occur where there are less resistant rocks, with farming on the alluvium of their floors. Many valleys, like the Arda, Mesta and Struma, lead out of Bulgaria into Greece. The inaccessibility of the interior of the massif long made it a refuge from the Turks, with high level planation surfaces that offered grazing. The highest parts are the Rila and Pirin massifs, both rising to over 2900m, with evidence of past glaciation and cool summers even in present times. Snow may lie all the year on high north-facing surfaces, though an 'alpine' relief is developed only in the Pirin. Hardwood forests of the lower slopes change to conifers with altitude and transhumance from valleys to high summer pastures remains. One of the most northerly outliers, Vitosa (2290 m), a great igneous mass with steep and forested slopes, overlooks the Sofia Basin.

1.3.4 The Pannonian Plains

The mountains of Central and South-eastern Europe surround an immense plain, broken sporadically by lines of hills and drained by the Danube, which enters through the gap between the Eastern Alps and the Carpathians and leaves through a narrow gorge between the Carpathians and the Balkan mountains.

The oval-shaped Pannonian Plains are split into segments by the hill masses. The north-west, framed by hills, is the Little Plain (Kisalföld) which rises south-eastwards into the hills and extends westwards to the Neusiedler See (Fertö) and the outliers of the Eastern Alps. On the north is the Danube and the plains of southern Slovakia that extend up the major valleys between the long southward pointing fingers of the Carpathian structures. An area of subsidence in recent geological time, it is marked by the broken and braided Danube course. The country is well farmed, with forest and meadow by the river and large areas of reeds. Weathering of limestone has left important bauxite deposits and there is also lignite and, in the hillier country towards the Jugoslav border, some petroleum.

Between Lake Balaton and the Danube, the Magyar Trans-Danubia (Dunántül) suggests the view of a people infiltrating from the east. This is a triangular plain, sometimes rolling, sometimes flat, broken by the Mecsek and Hegyhát hills, though south-westwards it merges into the Drava basin. With a cover of sand and *loess*, some good soils are much cultivated for arable crops. The southwest has remarkable low ridges and shallow valleys in a peculiar corrugated drainage system, possibly a structural control. The hillier parts are often forested. The Mecsek, part of the ancient basin, has steep sides and rounded tops rising to over 600 m, perhaps belonging to the same planation as the Bakony Hills. This is a forested landscape with farming wherever there are patches of *loess* and here are also Hungary's main bituminous coal resources.

The Kisalföld and the Dunántül are separated by the central Bakony Hills and related masses (Dunántúli–Középhegység), extending from the Danube at Visegrád south-westwards and divided by shallow rift-like transverse valleys into three segments. The hills are characteristically flat-topped ridges in calcareous rocks, and there are also well-farmed longitudinal depressions. In the south basalt creates striking monadnocks. The higher parts are well forested, with much oak and beech, but the slopes are extensively farmed, though the Vértes Hills are scarred by large bauxite mines. The highest and steepest part is the volcanic Pilis, rising to over 700 m. Along the southern flank of the Bakony Forest lies the remarkably shallow Lake Balaton, a major recreational area, and a remnant (like the Fertö) of a former more extensive water body.

The Hungarian Northern Mountains—Északi–Középhegység—in many respects comparable to the Slovak Ore Mountains, though separated by the valleys of the Ipel (Ipoly) and Sajó, consist of five main massifs. The greatest elevations are the Mátra (1015 m) and the Bükk (959 m), the roughest and scenically most impressive. These hills have the main Hungarian resources of timber, mostly oak and beech, while their *loess*-covered lower slopes are well farmed and the sunny southern slopes of the Tokaj Hills have famous vineyards. The karst of the Borsod contains considerable mineral wealth.

East of the Danube, comprising about half the area of the Pannonian Basin, is the vast plain of the Alföld. Everywhere relief is slight, but the north-western, northern and eastern flanks really comprise gently merging outwash fans of rivers from the surrounding mountains and provide good, warm, dry soils. Dunes of blown river sands form the most striking relief within the plain, while subtle differences in the landscape arise from surface materials—sand, *loess* or alluvium—and from the level of the water table. Much of the sand derives from the Quaternary Danube and Tisza, with a broad influvial area of coarse sand partly overlying *loess* between the two rivers (Kiskunság). Parts are a natural wilderness (Bugac steppe) though modern methods can make it suitable for fruit and vine growing. The marshes of the Tisza valley trapped easterly moving sand, so that little is found east of the river, except in the Nyírség in the north-east. Many old meanders along the rivers have been straightened and drained marsh provides moist meadowland, while the higher alluvium has been cultivated since removal of the flood danger in the nineteenth century. Once a great grazing country, then a cereal growing area, the Alföld now has a varied farming economy.

The steep upper course of the Tisza and its sudden change in gradient when it reaches the plain renders it liable to sudden floods, so that even reclamation has not eliminated the danger. The flood plain still has many abandoned meanders and the river changes course abruptly. In the windblown river sands of the Nyírgség in the great upper bend of the Tisza there is much birch forest (*nyír*) and rough grazing. Further south the Hajdúság is a sandy, *loess*-covered area intensively cultivated, while completion of the Eastern Main Canal has provided valuable irrigation water, though on the west lies the grassy treeless Puszta of Hortobágy, where pastoral traditions have survived longest. Unfortunately, much ground water in the Alföld is saline, little use for irrigation, and where it comes near the surface, saline soils occur or even shallow pans that dry out to salt encrustations in summer. Several factors combine to make this a grassland, though there is dispute about its origin. South of the Hortobágy, the Nagykunság has good black soils—acacia and poplar-ringed farms with their well sweeps dot an extensively cultivated landscape.

The south-eastern part of the Pannonian Plains is the focus of the drainage system, with the confluence of the Tisza, Sava and Drava in the Danube. The landscape is a broad plain, covered with *loess* and alluvium and a water table high enough to attract farming. This polyglot country of the Banat, Bačka and the southern Baranya, was resettled after long depredations by the Turks. Much improvement took place in the nineteenth century by the construction of drainage canals and flood prevention measures. To the west the southern part of the Pannonian Plains has forested ridges and broad cultivated valleys along the Drava (Podravina) and the Sava (Posavina), with extensive *loessic* but also patches of infertile sands. The Slavonian Hills and the Bilo Gora are rolling uplands with flattish tops standing like forested islands, particularly when seen from the north, in a sea of cultivated country that spreads up their southern slopes.

1.3.5 The Plains of Wallachia and Moldavia

Below the Iron Gates, the Danube flows across a broad plain developed on an old basement complex. South of the river lies the Bulgarian Platform, an undulating surface rising southwards to the Balkan ranges, varying in width from west to east from 25 to 100 km. *Loess* and alluvium cover the largely calcareous Jurassic and Cretaceous rocks that comprise it, with the platform terminating in bluffs above the marshy Danube valley, so that tributaries have downcut into the platform to the Danube level. A dry and fertile country, the woodland has been cleared from all but the steeper slopes for cultivation or for grazing in the drier parts. Settlement depends on springs in hollows or valleys. The eastern part, composed mostly of limestone, is generally less hilly, and dry and steppe-like.

North of the Danube lie the Wallachian Plains, over 300 km in east–west extent and from 100–150 km in width to the foot of the undulating and cultivated piedmont. The underlying Tertiary materials are masked by alluvium and *loess* and the land slopes south-eastward from the low Getic Plateau along the Carpathian foot towards the Danube marshes. On the north rivers have cut a corrugated relief into the soft Tertiary materials, but to the south, the plain is only gently undulating, with patches of blown sand on the eastern sides of valleys. Wallachia has become a great granary, though much drier than Pannonia, so that true steppe has been reclaimed in the south-east, in the Bărăgan, where saline encrustations on the soils reduce the country to a wilderness in some places.

Between the foot of the Eastern Carpathians and the Prut valley, the Moldavian Plain, 80–120 km in width, extends north–south over 300 km. Relief, particularly in the north in the Bîrlad Plateau, is stronger than in the Wallachian Plains, while a marked break of slope occurs south of Iaşi, separating the Bîrlad region from the *loess* and alluvium-covered Cîmpia Moldovei, one of the most fertile parts of Rumania, which merges on the west into the Suceava Plateau, a less-dissected version of the Bîrlad country. South of the Bîrlad, in the lower reaches of the Siret, the country is much like Wallachia. Everywhere woodland and steppe have given way to cultivation, though woods remain on the sharp rim of the Iaşi Basin. The soils—black earths and alluvial soils—are among the richest in Eastern Europe and their fertility has been retained inspite of bad farming and rural overpopulation—yet as a result of tenurial problems, poor administration and troubled history, the Rumanian plains have become a hearth of poverty.

Below Silistra, instead of flowing direct to the sea, the Danube makes a sharp turn north and follows a braided and meandering course to the north for almost 200 km along the western face of the ancient block of the Dobrogea before turning east near Galaţi to find its delta. The higher northern and southern parts of this massif rise to over 200 m, separated by a broad depression. The north is a broad hilly plateau where *loess* mantles an ancient planated granite surface, but the south, on calcareous rocks with karstic phenomena, is very dry and steppelike, which inspite of good soils, limits agricultural productivity, though this is an important grain area. The sunshine and the fine beaches along the coast have attracted substantial tourist development.

1.4 Climate (figure 1.2)

Many climatologists see east-central and south-eastern Europe as transitional between the Atlantic western European climate and the continental Russian plains. A narrow littoral strip along the Adriatic, in coastal Albania and in southernmost Bulgaria may be described as warm temperate western margin (Mediterranean). In actual temperatures, as a result of large mountain areas—in the Carpathians, the Dinaric mountains and the Balkan mountains—there is a tendency for an anomalous cold for the latitude, though a modest positive anomaly is revealed by sea level temperatures. The high concordant Adriatic ranges and the formidable Albanian and Bulgarian mountains prevent penetration inland of warm influences from the Mediterranean. The most continental conditions are found in the Pannonian Plains, particularly in winter.

The broader seasonal climatic features are related to major airstreams controlled by three great pressure systems. While the Icelandic Low and the Azores High play their part in this area, of more significance are the Asian summer Low and winter High pressure systems whose relative strength or weakness condition year-to-year variations. Even with these variations, however, the regularity of the yearly pattern of weather is far more marked than in Atlantic Europe, though naturally less than further east in the Eurasian landmass. The Azores high pressure system plays a significant role: in summer, when its pressure is highest, it extends not only over the Atlantic, with its centre about 35°N, but also over much of Western and Central Europe and into the western Mediterranean. In

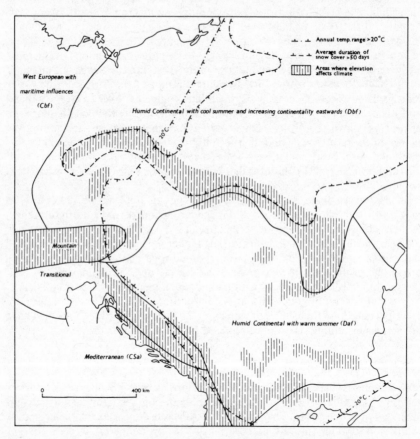

Figure 1.2. The climate of the Socialist bloc states of Eastern Europe shows a generally more continental character than Western Europe. In the mountains, elevation plays an important role in modifying the regime. The classification follows a slightly modified Köppen system.

winter the Azores high pressure is less intense and represents more a band of high pressure linked to the anticyclonic systems of Asia. Because at this time, the Mediteranean is warm and moist and conducive to low pressure, the high pressure belt lies across Central Europe at about 50°N, forming really a tongue of the Asiatic high. Kendrew describes this ridge as the barometric back bone of

Europe and points to its fundamental role in separating North European from Mediterranean climates.

Prevailing winds are mostly westerly, but are not so constant nor so strong as in Atlantic Europe. From the presence of the 'barometric divide', north and north-west winds are a common feature over Rumania, Hungary and the Balkans, often piercing and dry in winter. Nevertheless, cyclonic movement along the westerly air streams is important, particularly in the northern plains, and it also penetrates south of the 'barometric divide', though this is less frequent in winter.

Over the eastern part of Europe, winter is less variable than in Western Europe and becomes more stable and cold the further east one travels. In the Elbe basin, there is usually one month below 0°C; but in Poland, $3-3\frac{1}{2}$ months are below freezing, while one or two months of freezing temperatures are common in the Balkans. In Pannonia, 3 winter months are below 0°C and the desolate plains are swept by bitter winds. In the mountains of Carpathia 4–5 months are usually below freezing, but everywhere aspect and altitude play an important local climatic role. The Elbe freezes for about 31 days at Magdeburg and Dresden while the Oder at Frankfurt has 43 days on average frozen over. Ice covers the Vistula for 47 days. Though the Danube freezes in its upper reaches, it seldom freezes below Vienna, though it may carry floating ice. Under the influence of harsh Siberian weather, the Danube freezes over in its lowest reaches and in its delta with a frequency of about one winter in five. The Rumanian and Bulgarian Black Sea ports seldom freeze, but Baltic ports suffer from ice, usually insufficient to close them completely, though the more easterly ports may require ice-breakers.

Only on the Mediterranean fringes, the main rainfall comes in winter: elsewhere winter rainfall is inhibited by high pressure and the cushion of cold air wards away depressions that give winter rain to north-west Europe. Winter is, however, not dry, with precipitation mainly as snow, notably in the Pannonian Plains and in the mountains, though it is seldom deep. Eastwards the number of days with snow increases; for example, in the northern plains, Hanover has about 28 days, Berlin 37 days, Szczecin 47 days and Wrocław 44 days, though snow may last up to 80 days in eastern Poland. In the Hungarian plains, Szeged has 30 days with snow and a similar period is experienced in the Banat and Bačka, though in the north-east, it may lie for 40 days. In Wallachia and Bessarabia, however, the period is somewhat longer and in the mountains very much longer: the Tatra has snow from mid-October to late March and periods of 200 days are not unusual. Cold-air drainage with much inversion fog, an unpleasant feature in many plains and basins, means that the mountains often stand as islands of warmth in the winter. Especially cold as a result of such drainage are the *polja* of the karstlands, while cold air stagnated by anticyclonic calm in the Dinaric valleys flows over the mountains into the Adriatic trough as the bitterly cold *bora*. In the Vardar trough the icy *Vardarac* sweeps down to the Aegean, and similar winds occur in other parts.

As might be expected in continental conditions, spring is generally short and in much of Hungary and Rumania, precipitation is notably associated with late spring. Summer tends to be warmer than in Atlantic Europe and its continentality is reflected by thunder. Summer rain is particularly associated with thundery downpours, not uncommonly in late afternoon or early evening, with massive

Table 1.1   Climatic Data for Selected Stations

Station	Elev. (m)	Temp. (°C) Jan.	Temp. (°C) July	Coldest month	Warmest month	Annual precip. (mm)	Wettest three months
ALBANIA							
Berat	226	6.5	24.0	Jan.	Aug.	868.7	Oct. Nov. Dec.
Korcë	889	0.5	20.5	Jan.	Aug.	721.4	Oct. Nov. Dec.
Lushnje	19	7.8	24.5	Jan.	July/Aug.	1003.3	Oct. Nov. Dec.
Tiranë	126	6.4	24.0	Jan.	July/Aug.	1170.9	Oct. Nov. Dec.
Vlorë	1	8.9	24.5	Jan.	July	1089.7	Nov. Dec. Jan.
BULGARIA							
Burgas	17	2.0	22.8	Jan.	July	579.1	June Nov. Dec.
Kazanlik	372	0.6	21.8	Jan.	July	655.3	May June July
Kustendyil	525	−0.9	21.1	Jan.	July	607.1	May June July
Petrohan	1399	−4.9	13.6	Jan.	Aug.	1061.7	May June July
Pleven	125	−1.2	22.8	Jan.	July	599.4	May June July
Sofia	550	−1.7	21.3	Jan.	July	640.1	May June July
Varna	35	1.4	22.1	Jan.	July/Aug.	500.4	June Nov. Dec.
CZECHOSLOVAKIA							
Banská Bystrica	343	−4.2	18.7	Jan.	July	853.4	May June Nov.
Bratislava	133	−1.0	20.5	Jan.	July	655.3	May July Nov.
Česká Lípa	285	−2.2	17.6	Jan.	July	688.3	June July Aug.
České Budějovice	383	−2.1	17.4	Jan.	July	619.8	June July Aug.
Havlíčkův	455	−3.2	16.9	Jan.	July	711.2	June July Aug.
Jeseník	423	−2.9	16.9	Jan.	July	845.8	June July Aug.
Karlovy Vary	440	−2.1	16.9	Jan.	July	657.9	June July Aug.
Košice	216	−3.4	19.1	Jan.	July	662.9	June July Aug.
Liptovský Hrádok	648	−5.3	16.0	Jan.	July	744.2	May June July Aug.
Nitra	145	−1.9	20.1	Jan.	July	594.4	May June July
Olomouc	215	−2.7	18.5	Jan.	July	612.1	June July Aug.
Prague	183	−0.9	19.0	Jan.	July	475.0	June July Aug.
GERMAN DEMOCRATIC REPUBLIC							
Angermünde	45	−1.1	17.9	Jan.	July	551.2	June July Aug.
Berlin	55	−0.4	18.3	Jan.	July	594.4	June July Aug.
Brocken	1140	−4.8	10.5	Jan.	July	1483.4	July Dec. Jan.
Colditz	192	0.1	18.1	Jan.	July	662.9	June July Aug.
Eberswalde	14	−0.8	18.5	Jan.	July	563.9	June July Aug.
Frankfurt (Oder)	48	−0.9	18.3	Jan.	July	541.0	June July Aug.
Greifswalde	5	−0.4	17.3	Jan.	July	604.5	June July Aug.
Halle (Saale)	103	0.3	18.7	Jan.	July	508.0	June July Aug.
Hoyerswerda	119	−0.7	18.0	Jan.	July	662.9	June July Aug.
Leipzig	113	0.2	18.7	Jan.	July	546.1	June July Aug
Schwerin	52	−0.1	17.5	Jan.	July	627.4	June July Aug.
Wismar	1	0.1	17.3	Jan.	July	579.1	June July Aug.

Station	Elev. (m)	Temp. (°C) Jan.	July	Coldest month	Warmest month	Annual precip. (mm)	Wettest three months
HUNGARY							
Békéscsaba	88	−1.6	22.6	Jan.	July	563.9	May June July
Budapest	120	−0.8	21.9	Jan.	July	617.2	Apr. May June
Debrecen	146	−2.3	21.6	Jan.	July	591.8	June July Aug.
Hortobágy	95	−2.7	22.0	Jan.	July	523.2	May June July
Kecskemét	113	−1.8	21.9	Jan.	July	518.2	May June July
Magyaróvár	122	−1.4	20.4	Jan.	July	594.4	May July Aug.
Mohács	91	−1.0	21.7	Jan.	July	624.8	Apr. May June
Nagykanizsa	148	−0.8	21.1	Jan.	July	777.2	May June July
Szeged	90	−3.8	22.2	Jan.	July	574.0	May June July
Szentgotthárd	221	−1.9	19.8	Jan.	July	817.0	June July Aug.
POLAND							
Białystok	139	−4.1	18.4	Jan.	July	523.2	June July Aug.
Bolesławiec	201	−1.7	17.5	Jan.	July	655.3	May June July Aug.
Częstochowa	—	−2.5	17.8	Jan.	July	680.7	May June July
Hel	5	−1.1	17.2	Jan.	Aug.	487.7	July Aug. Sept.
Jelenia Góra	—	−2.7	16.8	Jan.	July	678.2	May June July
Kalisz	—	−2.0	18.9	Jan.	July	541.0	June July Aug.
Katowice	—	−2.5	17.7	Jan.	July	693.4	June July Aug.
Łodź	—	−2.4	17.8	Jan.	July	607.1	June July Aug.
Olsztyn	—	−3.4	17.3	Jan.	July	586.7	June July Aug.
Poznań	91	−1.1	19.4	Jan.	July	541.0	May June July
Przemyśl	—	−3.1	17.9	Jan.	July	708.7	June July Aug.
Świnoujście	6	−0.6	17.7	Jan.	July	627.4	June July Aug.
Szczecin	20	−1.1	17.8	Jan.	July	556.3	June July Aug.
Warsaw	120	−3.9	18.3	Jan.	July	558.8	June July Aug.
Wieliczka	248	−1.5	19.5	Jan.	July	665.5	June July Aug.
Wrocław	147	−1.1	18.3	Jan.	July	589.3	June July Aug.
Zakopane	838	−5.0	15.2	Feb.	July	1079.5	July Aug. Sept.
ROMANIA							
Arad	101	−1.1	21.4	Jan.	July	576.6	May June July
Bacău	167	−4.3	20.8	Jan.	July	543.6	May June July
Braila	15	−2.3	23.1	Jan.	July	439.4	May June July
Brașov	560	−3.9	17.8	Jan.	July	746.8	May June July
Bucharest	82	−2.8	22.9	Jan	July	579.1	May June July
Făgăraș	429	−4.6	18.7	Jan.	July	690.9	June July Aug.
Gheorghieni	804	−6.8	16.0	Jan.	July	602.0	June July Aug.
Hundedoara	243	−2.8	20.2	Jan.	July	627.4	May June July
Iași	100	−3.6	21.3	Jan.	July	518.2	June July Aug.
Paltinis	1405	−4.9	13.4	Jan.	July	909.3	June July Aug.
Satu-Mare	129	−2.4	20.1	Jan.	July	668.0	May June July

Station	Elev. (m)	Temp. (°C) Jan. July		Coldest month	Warmest month	Annual precip. (mm)	Wettest three months
JUGOSLAVIA							
Belgrade	132	−0.2	22.7	Jan	July	688.3	May June Aug.
Cetinje	671	+0.9	21.0	Jan.	July	4173.2	Oct. Nov. Dec.
Crvljivica	1031	−3.8	15.8	Jan.	July	1600.2	Oct. Nov. Dec.
Dubrovnik	20	9.0	24.7	Jan.	July	1272.5	Oct. Nov. Dec.
Jajce	341	+0.1	19.7	Jan.	July	1280.2	Oct. Nov. Dec.
Kosovska Mitrovica	521	−0.7	21.5	Jan.	July	561.3	May June Oct.
Kragujevac	175	−0.2	22.4	Jan.	July	678.2	May June Oct.
Krk	20	5.6	24.1	Jan.	July	1468.1	Sept. Oct. Nov.
Ljubljana	298	−1.4	19.7	Jan.	July	1618.0	Sept. Oct. Nov.
Nikšić	638	0.5	21.4	Jan.	July	2093.0	Oct. Nov. Dec.
Osijek	94	−0.8	22.2	Jan.	July	731.5	May June Oct.
Priština	630	−0.9	21.1	Jan.	July	607.1	May Oct. Nov.
Skopje	245	−1.7	23.3	Jan.	July	487.7	May June Oct.
Zagreb	163	0.0	21.7	Jan.	July	889.2	June Sept. Oct.

Source: Wernstedt, F. L. (1972). *World Climatic Data*, New York.

development of cumulo-nimbus clouds in summer. Although summer is the main rainy period in many parts, relative humidity caused by the active evaporation is moderate or low. In a rain shadow or where geological conditions are conducive, drought becomes a serious problem, as for example, in the Moravian Corridor and in the Hungarian Puszta. After a raw and cool spring in the northern plains, summer temperatures may leap to over 30°C—maximum July temperature at Ruse is about 42°C. In the mid-Danube, the July mean is about 18–20°, with the mean in some places over 21°C: certainly 18°C is exceeded for five months from May to September and the effect is increased by the relatively few rainy days. In sheltered Balkan valleys, July means may be 22–24°C, giving a markedly continental effect inspite of the proximity of the sea.

Special mention may be made of the Mediterranean regime found in a narrow belt backed by high concordant ranges that prevent penetration inland, but Mediterranean summer conditions may be spoilt by central European conditions spilling over the mountain rim, bringing rain or dull weather. Winters are notably mild, but broken by the bitter cold of the strong *bora*, which tends to frequent set paths between Trieste (up to 39 days per year) and northern Albania. The Albanian coastal plain, a broader belt of Mediterranean country than the narrower coastal shelf along the Dalmatian coast, is generally cooler in winter and less invaded by cold air drainage, but there is a high amount of sunshine in summer. A climate transitional from Mediterranean to the steppe is found in eastern Rumelia, which has winter rain but bleak winds from the Black Sea steppe that bring snow on as many as 18 days each year. The summer is nevertheless hot and comparatively dry.

1.5 Soils (figure 1.3)

The quality and intensity of soil survey varies considerably among the Socialist
bloc states of Eastern Europe, but everywhere most work has been done since
1945 and has consequently been strongly influenced by Soviet concepts. The
soils have mostly been much modified by man through long periods of cultiva-

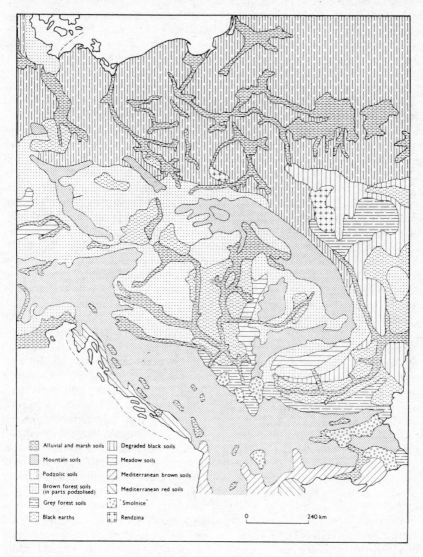

Figure 1.3. Podzolic soil types characterise the northern plains, while elsewhere brown
forest soils are particularly widespread, but over extensive tracts soil type is modified by
elevation, with extremely poor soil in the higher country, especially in the limestone areas
of the Dinaric mountains. Based on various sources.

tion and grazing, though this has not always improved the fertility. On the west use of fertilisers and more advanced methods of farming have generally maintained or improved soil fertility, but towards the east and south-east, much detriment has been caused to the soils through long use with inadequate fertilisation and bad husbandry.

The broad distribution is characterised by the podzolised soils of the northern plains, where the degree of podzolisation increases generally north-eastwards, whereas in the western parts of the plains, long cultivation has considerably modified them. Over large areas of the northern plains, the soils may be described as grey-brown podzolic soils, frequently with a gley character, associated with a natural vegetation of deciduous and mixed forest in which the coniferous element under natural conditions becomes more significant eastwards. The large quantities of glacial outwash material give the soils a frequently sandy character, while glaciated topography and its influence on drainage have resulted in swamp and bog soils; but in a few areas, true sands occur. The rather acid soils impoverished in humus have generally been markedly improved in German and former German territory and least so affected in the old 'Congress Poland', where heavy rural over-population in the nineteenth century put a severe pressure on the land. The southern parts of the northern plains, where a thin veneer of *loess* occurs, have the less leached and more fertile brown forest soils, also common in Bohemia-Moravia, in places round the Pannonian Plain and within the larger mountain basins. Various podzolic soils also occur.

Conditions of climate and parent materials have given the soils of the Pannonian Plains a distinctive character, marked by good potential fertility, derived in part from the large spread of *loess*, often of considerable depth. There are also contrasting areas covered with wind-blown sands that show only rudimentary soil formation, but where wind-blown sand overlies an earlier deposit of *loess*, careful ploughing has produced a workable and valuable soil (in the Tisza–Danube interfluve). To the west of the Danube and on the hill slopes, brown forest soils, with some evidence of podzolisation or leaching, are found and similar soils occur in the Sava–Drava basin, whereas east of the Danube is an extensive spread of black earths of various types, including degraded varieties that merge into the brown forest soils. These dark soils are usually associated with a natural cover of grass and a dry climate: there are some doubts, however, as to how extensive such a quasisteppe was before man's interference with the natural conditions. Provided these black earths can be effectively watered and properly cultivated, they are exceptionally fertile and maintain their fertility over long periods. Alkaline soils occur in the form of 'solonchak'—a limey-salty soil—and 'solonetz'—lime-free soil. These are generally infertile unless suitably treated, but incorrect farming practices may extend their area.

The Wallachian Plains have large areas of reddish-brown forest soils that merge southwards and eastwards into degraded and true chocolate brown 'black earths'. Similar soils occur in the Rumanian Banat, in central Transylvania, and in Moldavia, but there are large areas of podzolised soils on the Birlad Plateau and along the Carpathian foothills and footslope. In the Moldavian Plain, north of Iaşi, true black earths occur over a small area. Poor farming methods have robbed much naturally rich 'black earth' of a considerable amount of its nutrient and have also adversely affected its crumb structure, important for good aeration. In the Dobrogea 'black earths' of several types occur in the north, but much of the centre and south have light brown steppe soils.

The agricultural value of the 'black earth' soils—within a wide range of interpretation—is seen not only in the drier lands of Pannonia, Wallachia and Moldavia, but also in the southern parts of the northern plains, where some of the best farming country has developed upon them. One of the biggest and richest areas, largely achieved through the high level of farming technique and ample use of fertilisers, lies in the Saale basin, extending from Magdeburg to Erfurt in the shadow of the Hercynian uplands to the west. Another significant area of these soils forms the best Bohemian farming lands in the Elbe basin (Polabí) while they also occur in the drier conditions of the Moravian Corridor. Associated with *loess* deposits, they occur in Silesia south of the Oder and in parts of southern Poland. The richness of the soils of southern Poland developed on *loess*, whether of the 'black earth' group or not, has been an important factor in the ability of farming by quite simple methods to support a heavy rural population. Humus carbonate soils—*rendzina*—found in south-east Poland in areas of calcareous rocks are usually poor soils for farming, because they dry out easily.

The mountains and uplands are divisible into two groups—the northern Hercynian group and the Carpathian and Dinaric–Balkan group. The first group shows greater unity of soil type and less distributional complexity than the second, where southern types occur associated with the arid regime of Mediterranean climate and the occurrence of calcareous materials. The upland soils in the northern group are related to those of the northern plain, so that the Bohemian uplands, particularly in the Erzgebirge and the Krkonoše (Riesengebirge), have podzolic soils poor in humus and markedly acidic that are cold and infertile for farming and are notably under forest. On the highest areas, skeletal soils occur. In the Šumava, similar soils are also found, but tend to be less acid. Much of the acidity, it is suggested, derives from the parent material. Apart from the black earths of the Polabí, brown forest soils, with some traces of podzolisation but rich in humus in some districts, characterise the interior basins of Bohemia, though true podzols are found in the higher south and south-east. Soils similar to the upland rim of Bohemia are found in western Carpathia, where there are extensive areas of brown forest soils, but in some valleys *rendzina* is found and on higher surfaces, podzolisation becomes marked. In the higher areas of the Tatra, mountain meadow and skeletal soils occur and in the Eastern Carpathians, skeletal podzols are common, while on the often well-developed erosion surfaces soils are very wet. Similar features typify the Southern Carpathians. In both the Eastern and Southern Carpathians, larger areas at elevations higher than common in the Bihor Carpathians have given rise to extensive patches of mountain meadows with soils similar to their equivalents so well developed in the Western Alps.

South of the Sava and lower Danube, a considerable change in soil character takes place in a region of predominantly upland soils, and Jugoslavia has been described as the 'pedological museum of Europe'. The northern flanks of the Dinaric mountains are covered by brown forest soils and podzols, both generally poor in humus and with acidity varying from district to district. In the higher elevations there are skeletal podzols, mostly under forest cover. On the calcareous rocks of the karst, soils are particularly poor, often occurring in patches among bare rock. There is, however, great variety in the hollows: black earths or even grey and brown forest soils occur in many of the *polja*, and *terra rossa* is also found in hollows and valleys in the karst, moderately fertile but most valuable to the peasants of these poor lands, who go to great lengths to conserve soil by collecting it from small hollows in the hills. Skeletal *terra rossa* is widespread throughout the Dalmatian littoral. In Macedonia and in the Rhodope, cinnamon-coloured Mediterranean soils are weakly acidic, poor in iron and usually very stoney. Easily erodable and difficult to keep effectively moist, they pose serious farming problems. In Macedonia, there are areas of dark forest soil.

In Bulgaria widely varied soils reflect a close adjustment to climate. On the platform south of the Danube and in the central lowland basins, *loess* forms a major parent element and soils of the 'black earth' group occur, though these are usually degraded or poorly developed forms, including the *smolnica*, a highly degraded black earth of the central plains. On the southern side of the Danube platform, grey soils arising from degraded black earths merge into grey and brown forest soils along the mountain foot. South of the Balkan ranges, surrounding the degraded black earths of the central plains, are large areas of brown forest and chestnut soils, developed in conditions of hot dry summers and moderate winters. Such soils are also found in the dry basins within the Rhodope mountains where irrigation can usually help to improve their productivity.

1.6 Vegetation of Flora

Almost anywhere in Europe, it is unreal to speak of 'natural vegetation' (or climatic climax vegetation), because human influence has been strong enough to change the vegetation and affect climate and soil conditions. Furthermore, there is a natural poverty of flora in Central and Eastern Europe conditioned by the wholesale annihilation of species during the Pleistocene glaciations. Time has been too short for a full recolonisation by a rich flora of those areas from which the ice last retreated.

For the greater part of the study area, the climatic climax vegetation would be forest, though varying considerably in type north and south of the Dinaric ranges. In the extreme east, in the lower Danube and the Moldavian lands, 'natural' vegetation would have been an outlier of the southern Russian steppe. In the Pannonian Plains and possibly in Transylvania, a parkland of forest steppe was probably the home of early man: indeed, human influence has been suggested as a cause of turning these lands in open grassland. The effect of substratum and relief on drainage gives rise to large areas of wet land with typical bog vegetation in the northern plain and in Pannonia, though much original wet land has been reclaimed. Large reed covered marshes on the Danube, both in the area of the Great Rye Island and the delta, are now beginning to have commercial significance. Water-table conditions are also important in formation of saline and alkaline soils, which have distinctive plant communities of their own. Substratum conditions are particularly important in the calcareous Dinaric mountains in accentuating aridity, with consequent deleterious effect on vegetation. In Carpathia altitude and aspect affect vegetation, though the mountains are seldom high enough to rise above the tree line.

Over large areas clearance began very early and has continued into relatively recent times. In parts of Central Germany, on the *loess*, the possibly original deciduous forest may have been cleared by Bronze Age times, while the creation of the heathlands of Northern Germany may also have been the work of early man in clearing land for farming. Mediaeval clearance into the fourteenth century was common in the forests of the Sudeten Mountains, the mountain rim of Bohemia and the Hercynian uplands of Germany. In Southern Europe forests were invaded by grazing animals and shepherds who prevented rejuvenation of the forests after cutting for timber.

The present forest cover in many parts of the study area has a quite different composition to what might be expected in a natural condition. Policy in planting and rejuvenating forest has generally given preference to quick growing conifers, even where the original cover was deciduous or mixed. In parts of Germany and Poland heathland has been afforested and marshland and moor cultivated. Over much of the forest, oak would have been an important natural element and though it is a valuable wood, its slow growth makes it commercially unattractive. Nevertheless, soil conditions do markedly affect forest policy, so that pine is notably associated with outwash sands, while richer moister soil still retains stands of oak. In general, the conifers become an increasingly important element eastwards, but on the Baltic littoral, beech has been an important species in the climatic-climax vegetation and it is a significant tree on the lower slopes of the Carpathians, as well as on the northern flanks of the Dinaric mountains, besides parts of Bohemia and Thuringia. In Pannonia, Wallachia and other parts of the Balkans, oak and lime form important forest trees. In the mountains, mixed forest has been replaced by extensive stands of conifers, though the number of species of conifers is greater than the variety of deciduous trees. Spruce and fir are characteristic of the higher elevations.

Along the Adriatic coast, Mediterranean evergreen forest would form the typical climatic-climax vegetation. Southern varieties of oak and pine are the dominant species. Through the interference of man much of this potential natural forest land is now poor scrubland and has suffered serious soil erosion. A common tree cultivated in groves is the olive, but it has been introduced beyond its natural limits, as for example in western Istria, where it suffers not infrequently from sudden winter cold. In the mountains above 1000 m, beech forest is found, while there is also hornbeam in some parts of the higher littoral belt. Pine predominates in reafforested areas, but the extent of erosion makes many parts hard to rehabilitate. Throughout the Balkan lands, forest burning during internecine and punitive warfare in Ottoman times decimated the forest, as did the flight of people into the mountains to escape Turkish tyranny. The effect of added run-off from deforested lands is thought to have contributed to the swampiness and establishment of endemic malaria in the Albanian coastal plain that was first drained and reclaimed in the 1930s.

1.7 Fauna

The fauna of the study area falls between that of western Russia and of Western and Central Europe, while in the Balkan Peninsula the fauna contains some animals and birds of Mediterranean and even Asian origin. The large expanses of forest provide cover for the migration of animals, notably usually westwards in winter, hence the occurrence in hard winters of wolf and even bear in areas usually free of such beasts. Most striking is the occurrence in the study area of animals commonly regarded as extinct in Western Europe and much of Central Europe. For example, the wolf is sometimes present in the eastern Polish forests and Carpathia, these are usually animals driven westwards from the Russian forests by winter or by hunting programmes. In the Dinaric mountains and the Balkans, as well as in the Rumanian Carpathians, the bear is found. Other Carpathian animals include the marmot, lynx and the marten. The wild boar is a common denizen of the larger forests in upland and lowland, and it is also found in the Danube delta. Other animals include the ibex in the Dinaric mountains and the rare chamois in the higher parts of the Carpathians. Wild cat and mouflon are also found. The forests and mountains are the home of many different species of deer. The European bison is known only in reserves, of which the most important is on the Polish–Soviet border, while experiments to re-establish it in Rumania have been made. The elk is also preserved in reserves. Fox, squirrel, rabbits and hares as well as many species of mouse and bat are found throughout the area. Large numbers of migratory birds as well as permanently resident species are found. Pelicans live in the Danube delta. The beaver exists near Wittenberg on the Elbe, and it was found in Polesye until the last century.

The grasslands—particularly the steppelands of Wallachia, Moldavia and the Dobrudsha—have a native fauna of rodents, which often cause great damage to crops. These include the gopher, hamster, suslik, field mouse and ground squirrel, preyed on by polecats and foxes. Hares and badgers also occur. The steppe-dwelling wild horse and deer species have long since disappeared. Many of these species were also common in the Hungarian Plains, though the Hungarian white cattle, probably herded by the earliest inhabitants of the Puszta, are still found in the poorer parts. The rarer species such as the eagle and bearded vulture in Rumania are now generally under state protection.

Reptiles are common—grass snakes, vipers and coelopeltis (largest European snake) are found in appropiate environments. Lizards occur widely, particularly towards the south-east, where the tortoise and pond tortoise are found. Salamanders and newts are common in some places, but an interesting blind newt-like creature, the white olm, lives in the caves and subterranean waterways of the karst, where freshwater shrimps abound. Lake Ohrid is noted for its ancient and diverse fauna, while a rich fish life is found in rivers and lakes, so that in places, for example in southern Bohemia, fish 'farming' (notably carp) is important. It is interesting to note that the mongoose was introduced into Jugoslavia to kill snakes.

2 Historical Evolution from the Graeco-Roman Period to the Early Twentieth Century

2.1 Early Times

Greek civilisation exercised a peculiarly strong influence throughout the Balkans even into recent times. In political geographical terms Greek power was briefly expressed in the empire of Alexander the Macedonian, which extended from southern Albania across the Danube to beyond the confluence of the Olt, but after Alexander's death in 323 BC this empire rapidly disintegrated. 'Classical Macedonia' of this period has been invoked to claim exaggerated limits for Macedonian national dreams in modern times. The Macedonian Greeks nevertheless contributed to the colonisation and urbanisation of the Balkans—in 342 BC they founded Philippolis (Plovdiv), while thriving Greek colonies existed along the Adriatic and Black Sea coasts from the seventh century BC, trading with the interior. In the third century BC Celtic tribes from the north destroyed much Macedonian work, though they founded Singudunum (Belgrade) and probably Naisos (Niš).

Roman power held the Balkans for over three centuries, but its impact was quite different from the Hellenic, for in some respects its impress was shallower, though it spread over a greater area. Roman power emerged in the second century BC in the Greek Peninsula, in the Dalmatian coast and around the head of the Adriatic, where it had intervened somewhat earlier against Illyrian pirates. The first hold had been in the offshore islands and on the Albanian coast (including Epidamnus, 226 BC). The Romans moved into south Germany, Raetia and Noricum in 15 BC, while the Illyrian interior had been taken in 27 BC and Pannonia in 10 AD. The Rhine and the Danube thus became the northern limits of the Roman empire until Trajan (107 AD) incorporated Dacia and for a time the area known as Getia, between the Olt and the lower Danube (figure 2.1). Thrace had been incorporated in 45 AD, though it was resistant to Romanisation. Pannonia was regarded as particularly important because it was seen as the 'anteroom to Italy'. The Danube, with its bordering marshes, made an excellent military frontier, guarded by land forces and by naval patrols, though it had its weakness when frozen in winter. The push into Dacia and Getia had not only economic advantages, but also helped to command some of the routes from the steppe to the Danube basin. Roman dreams under Marcus Aurelius (161–180 AD) of extending the empire to the line of the Carpathians never materialised, though raids had been undertaken north of the Danube.

Raetia had been taken for the protection it gave to the important Alpine passes on the routes from the Rhine and Main basins that led into Italy, though it offered little other than timber and cattle. Noricum was rich in minerals and Pannonia had great agricultural possibilities, so that the growth of towns was stimulated and a healthy trade established with Italy. With the Danube lying along its

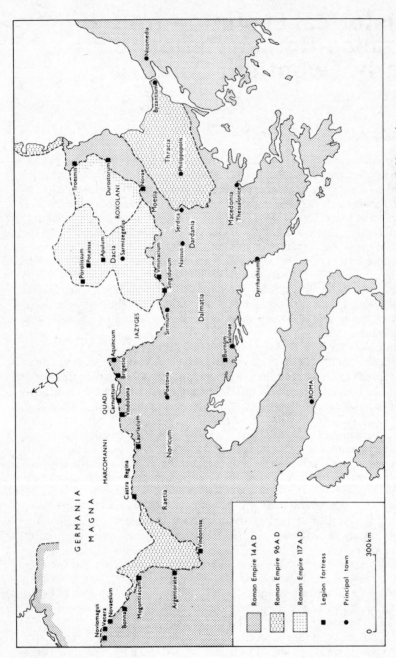

Figure 2.1. Europe south of the Danube fell under Roman sway, while a brief incursion was made north of the river in Dacia. On the ultimate division into an Eastern and Western Empire in 395 AD, the line of separation ran south from Sirmium along the line of the Drina river.

northern and eastern limits, Pannonia had all the military significance of a salient. Noricum, under Roman influence through trade long before it was incorporated, produced timber, salt and iron, but it was easily defended and its legionary fortress was established late (200 AD). Half of the eight to twelve legions stationed on the Danube were concentrated in Pannonia, as it could support a large population and on it converged routes from beyond the empire at a point where the Alpine barrier was weakest. Pannonia became a major granary and a wine producer, supplying many towns and the five large legionary fortresses of Augustan times. Carnuntum (73 AD), east of Vienna, was a focus of trade through the Moravian Corridor from the Baltic amber centres.

Moesia and Dacia consolidated and confirmed Rome as a Balkan power after the earlier incorporation of Dalmatia, Greece and Macedonia. Dacia had become a potential danger to Rome by its development of a strong political and military identity. Moesia was important because it covered the northern end of the Morava–Vardar corridor, which gave access from the Danube to the Mediterranean basin, especially in winter when routes across the Dinaric mountains were difficult. Upper Moesia (incorporated 29 BC) was a mountainous country peopled by mixed tribes of Thracian, Illyrian or Celtic origin that provided good fighting men for the Roman legions, while lower Moesia (incorporated 46 AD) was a granary for Thrace and Byzantium. In the second century AD Roman colonists began to found towns in Moesia, while a number of fortresses had been built during the first century.

The incorporation of Dacia came only after three trying campaigns, for the Dacians were better organised politically and economically than the tribes of the Balkan mountains. From incorporation in 107 AD until the legions withdrew in 272 AD, Dacia served the empire as a rich storehouse of metals, farm produce and timber and as a generous bulwark against the increasingly active steppe nomads. In this more marginal part of the Roman empire, the influence on language if not on culture has been more lasting than in other more closely integrated provinces, which, however, contributed much to Roman culture and power: the Illyrian provinces contributed five emperors from their native peoples. Diocletian's palace at Split was probably one of the largest and most luxurious edifices of the empire.

Tribes from beyond the Rhine and Danube had for a long time been allowed to settle in Roman territory, for several of the peoples living beyond the Roman frontier were far from 'barbarians' in the true sense, having absorbed much of the Roman way of life, often through contact with Roman traders. During the third and fourth centuries AD, the Roman frontier system began to break down under the persistent and growing pressure from these tribes and through an internal weakening of the empire itself. The great folk migrations generated by an unexplained restlessness, though apparently confused, came from three main centres of diffusion. The first was among the peoples—Germanic or Slav—in the northern plain from the basin of the Rhine to that of the Vistula. A second source was from the footslope of the Carpathians, while the third was from the steppe fringe of south-eastern Europe. The Germanic groups were farmers seeking land for settlement, but the nomadic groups from the steppe fringe were essentially pastoralists, like the Huns and Avars, more concerned with pillaging and looting.

In the slowly weakening empire Diocletian divided the Roman Lands into a

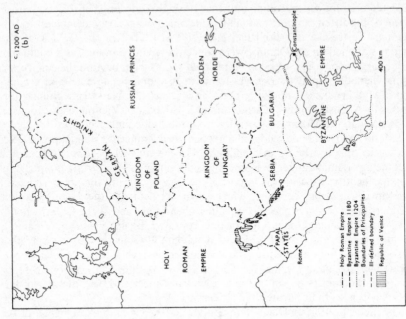

c. 1200 AD
(b)

GERMAN KNIGHTS

RUSSIAN PRINCES

KINGDOM
OF
POLAND

GOLDEN
HORDE

HOLY
ROMAN
EMPIRE

KINGDOM
OF
HUNGARY

SERBIA

BULGARIA

BYZANTINE
EMPIRE

Constantinople

PAPAL
STATES

Rome

Holy Roman Empire
Byzantine Empire 1180
Byzantine Empire 1204
Boundaries of Principalities
Ill-defined boundary
Republic of Venice

0   400 km

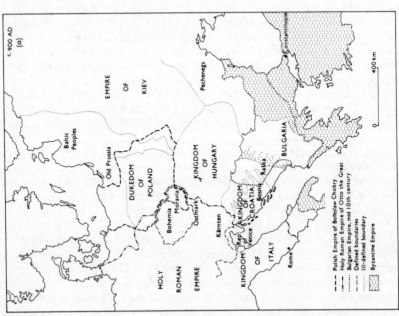

c. 900 AD
(a)

Baltic
Peoples

Old Prussia

EMPIRE
OF
KIEV

DUKEDOM
OF
POLAND

Pechenegs

Bohemia
Moravia
Ostmark

KINGDOM
OF
HUNGARY

HOLY
ROMAN
EMPIRE

Kärnten

Rep. of
Venice

KINGDOM
OF
CROATIA

Bosnia
Raška

BULGARIA

KINGDOM
OF
ITALY

Rome

Constantinople

Polish Empire of Bolesław Chobry
Holy Roman Empire of Otto the Great
Bulgarian Empire, mid 10th century
Defined boundaries
Ill-defined boundary
Byzantine Empire

0   400 km

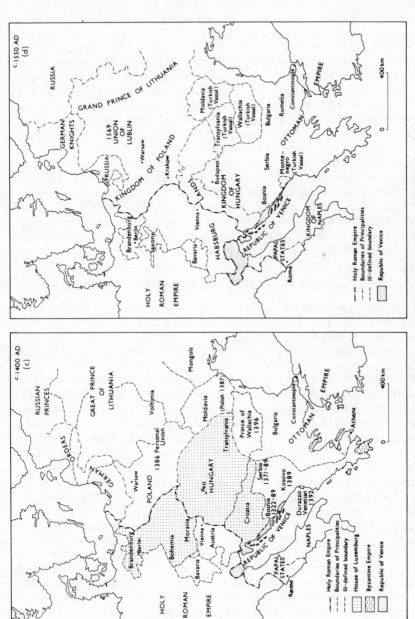

Figure 2.2. Several of the contemporary Eastern European states may have their origins traced back for nearly a millenium. A marked feature has been the fluctuating boundary of these states against the steppe and the Russian lands.

western and an eastern half in 285 AD, but after a brief reunification under Constantine, what had started as an administrative convenience became a more fundamental separation under Theodosius in 395 AD. The line of division ran north from Lake Scutari to the river Sava, the rough line of division that remains between Latin and Byzantine Greek Christianity. During the fifth century AD the rapidly disintegrating empire suffered a number of invasions in the Illyrian lands and the Balkans, when many Roman towns and fortresses were destroyed and the roads ceased to be safe for trade. The Romanised population was absorbed by the newcomers, except along the Dalmatian coast, where wealthy city states, largely dependent on sea trade, retained more of their Latin character. While the western empire merged into the vague concept of the Holy Roman Empire of the German Nation, the eastern empire, focused upon Byzantium (a Greek colony raised to an imperial city in 325 AD and renamed Constantinople), remained within fluctuating boundaries and fortunes until mediaeval times, when its Roman character had disappeared. After the sixth century it was little more than an administrative fiction, and by the thirteenth century AD only scattered remnants around the Aegean Sea (largely in Venetian hands) remained until the final fall of Constantinople to the Turks in 1453.

2.1.1   The Slavs and the emergence of the present ethnic structure (figure 2.3)

From Roman times onwards there is an increasing amount of documentary evidence of events in East Central Europe, which coupled to modern archaeological techniques and linguistic research, help reconstruct the changing ethnic pattern as the modern groupings emerge. It has been usual to distinguish between three main physical 'races'—the Nordic, the Dinaric–Alpine and the Mediterranean. Some anthropologists have classified several subgroupings (for example, the commonly described 'East Baltic' race). These physical types, however, bear no relationship at all to major political, cultural or linguistic boundaries, nor do they show anything more than an indifferent relationship to the major geographical division of the continent. It was once implied that these physical types had been at some stage in the distant past distinct and spatially defined racial groups. As the languages of Europe may be ascribed with few exceptions to the so-called Aryan or Indo-European (descended from Sanskrit), it was even suggested that the three major racial types might conceivably be derived from one original racial and linguistic type.

Such reasoning has been replaced by a theory of constant migration with mutation through natural selection (perhaps not completely divorced from basic Darwinism). It is thought, for instance, that round-headedness—the most economical way of containing a large brain in a small head—was a mutational change rather than a migrationary product. It is also now considered that blondness is very ancient and occurs so widely that genetic structures for it may be present in many different groups to varying degrees, although it seems—for inexplicable reasons—to be most pronounced in the Baltic lands. Rather than 'types', the view is now one of trends and tendencies that dismisses immutability of such traits as long-headedness and particular pigmentations.

The origins and aboriginal home of the Slavs is still uncertain. Proto-Slavic culture seems to have developed about the sixth century BC, though philological

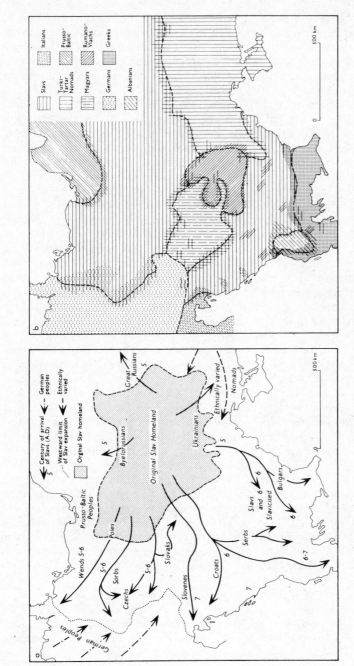

Figure 2.3. A most significant event in European history was the spread of the Slavs from their ill-defined homeland north of the Carpathians. By the end of the first millenium AD, the Slavs had been split by the Magyar invasion and were under strong pressure from the initial eastwards spread of the German peoples.

evidence in the form of the absence of early Slav words for certain forms of vegetation has been invoked by some scholars as an indication of much earlier origin. At its earliest stages, the distribution of the Slav tribes does not necessarily correspond to any of the recognised archaeological cultures. Although indisputably agriculturalists, the early Slavs were indistinguishable from many other farming groups.

A frequently close correlation between early Slav folklore, art and religion, with Indo-Aryan, Alanic and Turkic traditions suggests that the progenitors of these peoples lived in association with the Caucasian and Caspian areas at some stage. The Slavs may have begun their evolutionary process on the Pontic steppes, slowly migrating to the Polesye, regarded by some scholars as the *prarodina* of these people. There is, however, little archeological evidence to suggest a long sojourn by large numbers of people in this area and such a view of the Polesye as the cradle of the Slavs demands a population explosion for unexplained reasons about the fifth century AD that forced their outwards migration (figure 2.3). Other scholars have seen a wider early home in the western Ukraine or even in the Vistula basin and westwards therefrom; this latter view equates the Slavs with the late Bronze Age and Iron Age Lusatian or Urnfield cultures. If a wide distribution in the North European Plain is accepted, then the Slavs must have impinged on or even mingled with some of the early German tribes which, it is usually assumed, originated in the south Baltic littoral, possibly after a westwards migration in the early part of the first millenium BC. The Germanic tribes, with whom the Romans came into particular contact, were slowly spreading out from the Jutland Peninsula and the south Baltic littoral. For a time some of them (Goths) moved south-eastwards into the Black Sea steppe, possibly the result of taking advantage of weakened Slav groups recovering from the incursions of the Scythians (*circa* 500 BC). Germanic Bastarnes from modern Bessarabia raided widely into the lower Danube and the Balkans, while other tribes attacked Pannonia. Much of the Danube basin at this time was occupied by Celtic or Celticised tribes, such as the important Scordisi around the Danube–Sava confluence. In the third century BC Celtic tribes moved into the Maritsa basin and even raided Anatolia and the Greek Peninsula. The modern Czech lands were occupied by the Celtic Boii (in Bohemia) and the Germanic Quaden in southern Moravia, while Germanic Marcomanni were living in the Bohemian Polabi. About 200 BC, the nomadic Sarmatian Jazyges had entrenched themselves in the Danube-Tisza mesopotamia. In Transylvania Dacian peoples had a highly organised political and economic life by the time they came into contact with Rome. Illyria was still occupied by the people of that name who had migrated from the north possibly as early as 1800 BC, while the Thracians were probably a related people.

The Roman Imperium, under growing external pressure from the late second century AD, attempted unsuccessfully to 'dig in' on established frontiers. Peoples from outside ultimately became mercenary protectors of Roman lands against later raiders, a policy that encouraged adventurers to seek wealth and patronage within the Roman sphere and so perpetuate attacks. The first influence was felt in the strong pressure by Germanic groups that penetrated into Roman Danubia in the second century AD, notably the Goths in lower Danubia, the Vandals in Pannonia and the Langobards and Marcomanni in Noricum.

By the third century the ripples of a great movement from the interior of Asia began to be felt in the eastern marches of Europe, where the incursion of the wild Asiatic nomads, whose bizarre appearance struck terror into European peoples, was to make a far deeper impression on European tradition than its ultimate effect warranted. The Huns appeared suddenly and fearfully in 375 AD, driving before them Gothic tribes, and settling in the Tisza plains, an outlier of steppe-like country to which they were accustomed. From Attila's residence in the upper Tisza, devastating raids were made into the Romanised lands, inspite of tribute paid by Constantinople in return for a pledge of peace. Marauding Goths, driven away in front of the Hunnic onslaught, raided and pillaged in Moesia and in Illyria. After Attila's death in 453 AD and a defeat by an uprising of Germanic vassals, the Huns vanished into Asia. The power of the Goths tended nevertheless to increase and they took an ever thicker veneer of Roman culture. After 455 AD an important focus of Gothic power was in western Hungary and groups of Goths settled in Roman Pannonia, while Dacia fell to the Gothic Gepids. In 471 AD, Theodoric occupied Singudunum (Belgrade) and plundered Macedonia and Greece, finally settling at Novae (Svishtov) on the lower Danube in 483 AD. Ten years later Theodoric and his people moved into northern Italy.

In 566 AD a devastating invasion from the steppe came with the ruthlessly fierce Avars, who swept across the Carpathians and into Danubia, annihilating the Gepids and accelerating a movement of Slav tribes to seep slowly westwards, filling lands in the northern plains left sparsely settled by the strong movement of Germanic tribes against the failing power of Rome. In Danubia Slav tribes spread from their crossings of the Carpathians and settled in parts of modern Hungary. From about 500 AD the Byzantine empire had come under more frequent attack from these groups: in 518 AD Slavs were first reported to have crossed the Danube in strength. The loose congeries of Slav tribes were little real danger until they were linked to the power of the Avars, around whose periphery many settled, sharing in Avar trade. A combination of small forces of horse-riding Avars and large bodies of Slavs on foot began a great onslaught against the Byzantine empire in 559–60 AD, taking advantage of Byzantine preoccupation with a resurgent Persia.

The Slavs were a largely sedentary agricultural population, so that unlike the nomadic Avars, they settled in the Balkan Peninsula. The Avar empire, in the Plains of Pannonia, existed for about 200 years, though it played little part in events after its defeat by Byzantium in 626 AD and was finally conquered by the Franks in 799 AD. Much of the Slav penetration was unostentatious and peaceful, so that over Dalmatia and the Dinaric lands the Slavs spread and merged with the local people, slowly replacing the ancient Illyrian population. In the Greek Peninsula the same process took place, but here it was the Slav who merged into Greek culture. In Wallachia and in Dacia the Slavs also merged with local people, whose Latin tradition remained alive. By the end of the sixth century AD Slavs were found widely throughout the Balkan and Dinaric lands, though Albania and southern Thrace, both peculiarly difficult terrain to access from the north, were relatively little affected.

For a time after the collapse of the Huns, it had seemed that Danubia might become a Germanic land—the Gepids, later exterminated by the Avars, settled in Dacia, the Ostrogoths in Pannonia, while Rugians were on the north bank of the Danube opposite Noricum. The southwards and westwards movement of the Germanic tribes around the fringes of the Roman empire had given the Slavs much empty territory to fill. The Rugians were the first tribe to disappear from Danubia, while the Ostrogoths under Theodoric moved into Italy. The Lombards, originally from the Elbe basin, settled in Upper Pannonia (Austria) in the late fifth century, while under Lombard pressure, the Lech basin and the upper Inn valley were settled by Marcomanni and Quadi from Bohemia—this was to become Bajovaria (Bavaria). The Lombards under Avar pressure ultimately moved across the Alps into northern Italy.

In the Elbe basin left by the migrating Germanic tribes a Slav infiltration began as a thin veneer over a largely virgin land, spreading as far as the lower Elbe and even eastern Holstein (the Vagrians, Obodrites) while in the Lüneburg Heath, the Dreviane tribe settled. Slav groups also spread into what is today eastern Bavaria and to the Danube near Regensburg. In the fifth and sixth centuries Bohemia and Moravia were also colonised by Slavs 'as the Marcomanni and Quadi moved out. As they spread into Danubia, they fell for a time under Hun overlordship. These people were the progenitors of the Slovenes, who pressed to the Adriatic and raided Istria and Venetia about 600 AD. As noted already, Slavs had crossed the lower Danube in force about 518 AD and by 536 AD had reached the Adriatic, destroying the city of Salona. By 548 AD they had moved along the Adriatic coast to the area of Dyrrhachium (Durrës)—fierce invasions of Illyria are also mentioned around 550 AD. During the seventh century, all Dalmatia was occupied. The Slavs might have been successfully integrated into the Byzantine empire, but they turned to support the victorious Avars rather than become federates of Byzantium. Possibly Slav success against Byzantine forces came from their rapid adoption of Avar military methods. In contrast, the Antes, a Slav or Slav–Iranian people, in Bessarabia sided with Byzantium but were crushed by the Avars in 602 AD and the first clearly Slav empire disappeared from history.

The Slavs usually settled in the country they invaded and became a farming population instead of withdrawing with their booty. Thus by the seventh century, a countryside of Slav settlers lived in uncomfortable proximity to fortified towns held by the failing power of Byzantium, including Zadar, Trogir, Split, Dubrovnik, Kotor, Durrës and some of the offshore islands. In Moesia, Dacia, Dardania and Macedonia, the country was thoroughly Slavicised and big Slav settlements lay in Epirus. In the seventh century, there was also the migration of the Proto-Bulgarians, a people of originally Turki–Tatar culture from the Volga basin, who settled in nominally Byzantine territory in what is today northern Bulgaria and the Dobrudsha and established an overlordship over the onetime Slav vassals of the Avars. In a long struggle with Byzantium, the Bulgars fell under the influence of the Byzantine church and the use of 'Church Slavonic', so becoming identified with the Slavs. In contrast to the Bulgars who maintained a strong political identity under their own khans, the Slav colonists were unable to find a strong unifying political leadership and began to develop along different lines under differing historical influences. The obliteration of the Romano–Byzantine landscape of Macedonia, Thrace and the Dinaric lands by Slav colonisation brought the destruction of a unitary Christianity, established since the fourth century, that formed a 'bridge' between Roman and Byzantine. By the time Christianity returned it was unable to heal the emergent cultural separation.

Byzantine culture had been orientalised, while Roman culture had been Germanised: the great dichotomy of Eastern Europe had been wrought.

2.1.2 Emergence of the Germans (figure 2.4)

In the seventh century the Byzantine emperor Heraclitus had settled, on lands regained from the Avars, immigrant Croats and Serbs from Thuringia and Western Galicia, whose migration was set afoot by the growing Frankish supremacy in the north that was to start a German eastwards colonisation which continued until the fifteenth century. As a defence against Slav incursion the Franks had established 'marches'—in the north against the Polabian Slavs and in the south-east against Avars and Slavs, but their great expansion began under Charles the Great. Two early factors in Frankish strength were the support of the Saxons in the north (772–804 AD) and of the strong principality of Bavaria (788 AD) in the south, while about the same time, the Slavs of the Main basin were brought under Frankish domination. Frankish influence seems to have first spread into Bohemia under Samo, though he remained until his death in 659 AD independent head of the Slav Czech lands.

Charles the Great (768–814 AD) was rapidly to bring the Bohemians, Moravians and some Slovaks under his influence, while his powerful Saxon

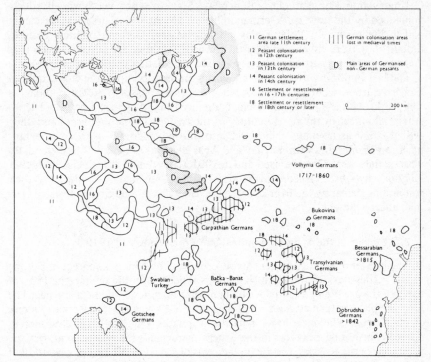

Figure 2.4. The mediaeval history of Germany was in summary a brilliant eastwards colonisation but a disastrous failure to form an effective national state. The map is based on research by Kuhn, Aubin, Krallert *et al.*

vassals controlled the Slavs between the Saale and Elbe (the Sorbian marches and the Daleminiziner) as well as Slavs on the lower Elbe. Episcopal seats were important springboards in the spread of Frankish–German power, though in the north a number of serious Slav revolts weakened the Saxons. In the south Frankish power spread into Carinthia and the Avar lands west of the Danube, especially after Pepin's capture in 796 AD of the main Avar base with immense booty. Some Slovenes and Croats were also pulled into the Frankish sphere. In 803 AD the *Ostmark*—the Eastern March or later Austria—was founded. Further Frankish spread was arrested by Bulgarian efforts to unite the Slavs against them. The more loosely controlled Frankish land rapidly fell away after the death of Charles the Great (814 AD), when the empire was divided among his sons on the failure of a powerful successor to emerge.

Though Frankish–German power was never again to reach comparable glory as under Charles the Great, German spread continued. A settlement, often organised and planned, of German peasants into empty or sparsely settled Slav lands expanded outwards until the Black Death, encouraged by the actions of aristocracy and by the clergy. As it progressed, many Slav groups succumbed to Germanisation, while on occasions non-German aristocrats sought German artisans to develop their lands. The eastwards spread began, however, to generate opposition from non-German princes, while peasantry became more resistant to Germanisation. For example, in Bohemia, a Slav peasantry was never effectively influenced by the powerful German influence among the aristocracy, the clergy and in the towns. In Poland Slav princes resisted German political designs, though they were otherwise tolerant towards German artisans and even used German mercenary troops in their mission to Christianise the pagan Balts.

The last major invasion to have a lasting impression upon the ethnic quilt of Eastern Europe occurred in 859 AD when across the passes of the Carpathians as well as through the plains of Wallachia poured the Magyars, a people of Ural-Altaic affinities. In the open country of the eastern Pannonian grassland, they settled—first as nomads, raiding far into Europe, and later as more sedentary pastoralists, merging with the Slav and Avar elements of their new homeland. By 970 AD they were Christianised and in 1001 AD by Papal agreement, a Magyar kingdom was established, having been tamed and made sedentary by their resounding defeat by the Franks at the Lech in 955 AD, though they resisted German encroachment.

2.2 Europe of the dynastic empires: late tenth century to 1918

By the late tenth century a more stable order was becoming apparent in Europe as the restlessness of the great migrations faded. Even the embryonic form of some of the great empires to develop in mediaeval times could be discerned. The German peoples formed the core of the grandiose if vague Holy Roman Empire of the German Nation, a loose congeries of princes with indifferent allegiance to a largely ineffectual emperor. In the eastern marchlands the Kievan state was the precursor of the Russian empire; in the ruins of the Byzantine empire lay the first identifiable Balkan state—Bulgaria; the germ of the later Polish–Lithuanian Commonwealth emerged in the Polish principality; but the brief glory of Svatopluk's Moravian empire had faded. The powerful empire-building

Habsburg in the Ostmark were gathering strength, though the Hungarian kingdom was already on the map, while the German dynasties of Hohenstaufen and Hohenzollern were yet to appear and the terrors of the Turks and the Mongols were to come.

2.2.1 The Holy Roman Empire

A loose confederation of mostly small states, the Holy Roman Empire was potentially the most powerful political organism, whose expansive political activities could be justified so long as a religious motive might be found: after all it was acting as the inheritor of Roman imperial traditions with the sanction of the Pope. Active consolidation of its position east of the Elbe was undertaken through campaigns against still unsubdued Slavs, as in Pomerania, or through Germanisation in the established marchlands held by German castles at strategic points and influenced by German bishoprics. Benefiting from the danger represented by the Magyars, German power was growing in the south-east—in Kärnten, Steiermark and the Ostmark under Habsburg management.

The Bohemians recognised Saxon overlordship but they had hopes of re-establishing the Great Moravian Empire of Svatopluk by including Silesia, Kraków and Slovakia. The Poles under Duke Mieszko (whose sudden appearance suggests he may have been a viking, though there is no concrete evidence) had welded, from the core at Gniezno, a powerful confederation of Slav tribes, Christianised by missionaries from the Bohemian court. This forestalled German moves to undertake the work from Magdeburg, while the Pope agreed to a Polish bishopric at Poznań in 968 AD, directly subordinate to Rome. The tendency for Polish power to increase was countered by a stronger German ecclesiastical hold in Bohemia through bishoprics subservient to Mainz. Although the Poles managed to seize Silesia and other territory from the Bohemians, the difficulty of expanding against the growing German strength on the west turned Polish endeavours eastwards and south-westwards.

With the baptism of Duke Stefan in 973 AD Christianity came to the Magyars and in 1001 AD, the Pope sent him a king's crown and an invitation to join the Holy Roman Empire. Contained by the Germans and Slavs on the west and north-west, the Magyars spread their power into Transylvania by the eleventh century, so becoming a bulwark of Europe against inroads of vicious nomads, the Pechenegs (1067–8) and Cumans (1071–2).

2.2.2 South-eastern Europe

South-eastern Europe was more unstable, with fluid allegiances in a society that had all the complexity of tribal and family groupings. The Byzantine authorities had pressed the Christianisation and Hellenisation of the Slavs over whom they exerted some control. The leading state had become Bulgaria, which had quickly accepted Slav culture through Slav Christian missionaries in the ninth century, but it is possible that the clash between Rome and Byzantine over dogmata helped to retard Christianisation. The Tsar Simeon (893–927 AD) played off Rome against Byzantium and the Franks and built a large but ephemeral Bulgarian empire that extended from the Tisza across Transylvania to the lower

Danube and into devastated and depopulated Serbia and Albania, while the Bulgarians also held Macedonia and the Maritsa basin. Bulgarian holdings north of the Danube were lost, however, to the Pechenegs. Kievan Russia sided with Byzantium against the Bulgarians, resulting in the loss of Thrace and Moesia. Gradually Bulgaria contracted westwards, apart from a brief resurgence, and by 1000 AD, the Bulgarian state lay across modern Serbia. In 1016 AD, Bulgaria merged into the Byzantine empire, when the capital at Ohrid fell, and until 1186 it had no existence as an independent state. During the eleventh century, Tatar tribes raided the Balkan peninsula, leaving groups of unwelcome settlers while Armenians and Wallachian Vlachs also settled. In whatever boundaries it sought, Bulgaria was ethnically diverse and comprised isolated basins and valleys in the rough Balkan terrain that each showed strong centripetal tendencies.

2.2.3 The Dinaric Lands

The Slovenes, present in the Sava valley from the sixth century, fell under Frankish influence and through Germanisation the area of Slovene speech was gradually reduced and they became part of the Duchy of Karantania, formed as a protective march against the raiding Magyars. The Croats had settled in the Dinaric lands in the seventh century and had been won to the Latin cultural sphere through the Roman church. Inspite of the great missionary work of the Slav clerics, Methodius and Cyril (early ninth century), that changed the eccelsiastical geography of the Balkans, the Croats remained true to the Latin world, but their loose tribal association gradually fell victim to Frankish intrusion and to Byzantine intrigue. Under Tomislav (about 924 AD) the Croats revoked their subjugation by Byzantium and for nearly 200 years an independent state (whose exact boundaries and nature are uncertain) existed. On the geography of the Croats in this period, there is disagreement between Magyar and Slav historians. The Magyars maintain that the main areas of original Croat settlement lay south of the Sava whereas nearly all Croat settlements north of the river resulted from poplation movements in the later Turkish period. The Croats maintain that at this period they occupied all the land from the Drava southwards to the Drina and Neretva. After 1089 internal confusion over leadership gave the Hungarian king a chance to interfere in Croatian affairs, creating a connection to last until the twentieth century. Through Croatian influence in the affairs of the Dalmatian coast as maritime traders and pirates, Hungary reached the Adriatic and the lingering Byzantine title to these lands was disputed by Croats, Hungarians and Venetians.

Slav settlement in the seventh century also marked Bosnia and Hercegovina, whose early history is remarkably obscure, though Hungarian historians look on Bosnia as the original core of the Croat kingdom. These territories changed their overlordship many times—the Croats, Serbs, Hungarians and Byzantium all holding some parts at varying periods. Without well-defined frontiers or a social organisation—largely autonomous tribal units—that allowed a collective identity, the Bosnian Slavs did not attain any cohesion until the twelfth century. The trade and life of the country was under Italian merchants from the coast, notably Dubrovnik. Bosnia lay in the border between Latin and Byzantine Christianity and was caught up by the puritanical Bogomil sect that rejected both interpretations.

Among the great seventh century migrations were the Serbs. According to some sources, the Byzantine emperor Heraclitus granted them territory, but this may have been just recognition of what they had taken. The five centuries after their arrival were occupied by internecine warfare and Bulgarian and Byzantine interference. In the latter ninth century some measure of unity among the southern Serbian tribes was achieved under the Bulgarian threat, but Byzantine influence was spread by the missionary work of Methodius and Cyril to separate the Serbs from the Croats and the Latin cultural sphere. From the late ninth to the early eleventh century, Serbia fell to a fluctuating degree under Bulgarian domination, though after the Byzantine defeat of the Bulgarians in 1018, the Serbs returned to the struggle for power. In the splits that occurred Montenegro emerged, able by its inaccessible mountainous nature to maintain its independence when the eastern Serbian lands, then known as Raška, were liable to domination from outside.

2.2.4 The Turkish Episode (figure 2.5)

By the fifteenth century a new force appeared in south-eastern Europe—the Ottoman Turks, a mixture of Turkish and Greek elements, successors to the Seljuk Turks since about 1300, when the Ottoman empire was a small area on the southern shore of the Sea of Marmara. These fierce, well-armed and organised warriors rapidly established themselves solidly in the Balkan Peninsula, leaving only small patches of territory and Constantinople itself in Byzantine hands. They were not exactly newcomers, since Ottoman mercenaries had helped Byzantium and the emperor Theophilus had established Turks in the Vardar area of Macedonia 500 years before the invasions began.

Thrace passed to the Turks in 1354–61; Rumania fell in the 1380s and they then spread forward to the Danube by 1394, making parts of Wallachia a vassal. Between 1371 and the early fifteenth century, Macedonia was reduced to Turkish overlordship, while after the battle of Kosovo Polje (1389), the Serbs became Turkish vassals. In the fifteenth century, Ottoman power spread into the remainder of the Greek Peninsula and Albania, Serbia and Montenegro were reduced to reluctant vassals. By the early sixteenth century, Bosnia and Hercegovina and much of Hungary were in Turkish hands, and Moldavia and Transylvania were vassals. The advance continued more slowly and uncertainly into northern Hungary until the decisive defeat before Vienna in 1683, after which the Turkish menace slowly receded. Through the seventeenth century, the Turkish empire moved slowly towards ruin, because like most rapidly expansive empires, once it lost its momentum decline set in.

The Ottoman empire was a mixture of subject Christian peoples and a ruling Moslem caste, dominated by highly trained soldiers—the corps of Janisaries—recruited largely from Christian boys taken forcefully from their parents. Bulgarians, Greeks and Albanians as well as Byzantine officials embraced Islam and rose to high rank, while Byzantine institutions were taken over. Unfortunately, relations between Christians and Moslems fluctuated between generous tolerance and gross intolerance, but the early liberalism was replaced

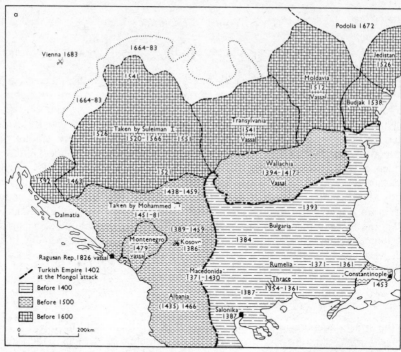

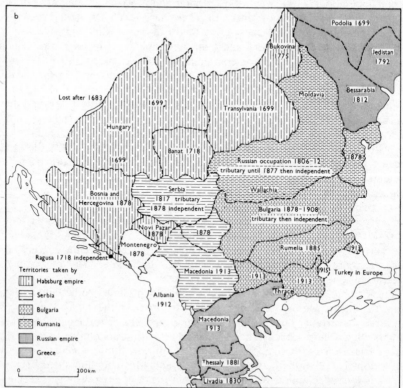

Figure 2.5. The long Turkish hold on south-eastern Europe has left its imprint even into modern times, while even the after-effect of the more tenuous hold on the Hungarian Plains and the Dinaric mountains may be traced. The defeat of the Turks before Vienna in 1683 was a vital point in European history—the victory of Christianity over Islam.

by vicious despotism and merciless exploitation of the common people. Outward expansion strained the administration and central control, so that local conditions varied widely and there was great financial and administrative strain because of neglect of some of the simplest actions of government and a disregard of adequate security for economic life, inspite of a liberal attitude towards trade. Oppression and usury were practised to offset these failings, but slowly everyday standards and levels of achievement fell further behind the rest of Europe.

The Turkish period left a deep imprint on the landscape, partly through a suggested view that the Turkish tradition as pastoral nomads led them to view their subjects as a nomad views his wealth in sheep and that like nomads they had little attachment to the territory through which they passed, while they were without skill or interest in commerce. To manage their human herds, the Turks

Figure 2.6. The rigours and terrors of Turkish rule drove many Christian Slavs to seek refuge in inaccessible mountain country or under the protection of other powers. These migrations—often led by the Church—have been plotted for the Serbs and Croats, based on the work of Cvijić. Based on *Shkolski Istorijski Atlas*, Belgrade (1965), p. 30.

chose and trained Islamised members of the subject peoples as sheep-dogs. Oppression of Christian populations, the loathed tribute of children, the ravages of the Turks for slaves, as well as brigandage, bad harvests, famine and drought generated much migration (figure 2.6). The abused and exploited 'rayah' left the *čifliki* estates and areas liable to raiding to flee to the mountains, but these barren lands quickly became overpopulated and generated further movements, often to areas beyond Turkish control. The general trend of movement, certainly in Serbia and Bosnia, was northwards, which was also marked in Bulgaria. A westward movement of Slavs into the Dalmatian coastlands also took place. Movement was of individuals, of families and of whole communities, often secretly organised by the Church.

Areas that accepted Islam were left with considerable freedom and exercised influence on imperial affairs, as in parts of Bulgaria, Bosnia, Macedonia and Greece. There was some colonisation by Anatolian Turks in south-eastern Macedonia, Thrace, north-eastern Bulgaria and the Dobrudsha, commonly into lands abandoned by Christian Slavs.

The Turkish invasion of Hungary after their victory at Mohács (1526) either exterminated much of the Magyar population or drove it away northwards and agriculture gave way to pastoralism. Vast tracts became virtually depopulated, with a scattered population (often descended from the pre-Magyar elements) living in the marshes or gathered into villages for easy defence: during the 150 years of Turkish overlordship, the number of villages was reduced by about half. When the Turks were finally expelled, the most extensively devastated parts in the south were resettled by Serbs, Rumanians and even Germans as well as Magyars. Turkish rule in Wallachia and Moldavia was exercised through Greek Phanariot 'princes' who sought to get as rich as they could in their short term of office, so extorting as much from the unfortunate peasants as possible. In Bulgaria conditions were generally better, with craftsmen often employed on Turkish government orders or accompanying Turkish armies in the field, while some Christian Bulgarians became guards along routes to the interior from Constantinople. But Bulgarian peasants in the Turkish-owned *čifliki* suffered most harshly. The spiritual and economic life in Bulgaria in Turkish times was in the hands of Greek clerics and merchants, while the Turkish element in towns was substantial. Even in the early nineteenth century, Sofia was still four-fifths Turkish and the remaining population comprised Jews, Armenians and Greeks as well as Bulgarians.

2.2.5 The Habsburg Empire (figure 2.7)

The Habsburg were originally obscure dukes of small territories, really large entailed estates, in the eastern Alps and upper Danube, successors to the German colonisation and formation of *Ostmark* and Karatania. In the fifteenth century, a Habsburg had been elected Holy Roman Emperor, as 'a harmless nonentity after previous turmoil'. Although the Habsburg empire was to grow until the eighteenth century, its dynamic period had ended by the late sixteenth century and thereafter it struggled to maintain its greatness until overwhelmed by nationalism in the early twentieth century. Its life was long enough and its

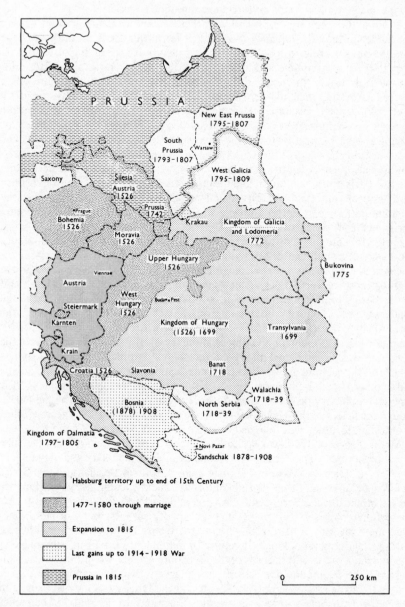

Figure 2.7. The Habsburg family and its scions built the classic polyglot empire, though attempts to expand northwards were thwarted by the emergent Prussia. The ethnic diversity of this empire can be seen in figure 4.3.

character distinctive enough to have left a deep impression on East Central
Europe in a kind of common culture and a common economy.

Although German by origin and with their empire firmly centred on Vienna
that made German the *lingua franca* of their territories, the Habsburg and their
several scions were cosmopolitans. The dynasty gave the polyglot empire its
character, for at no time could it find a truly satisfactory geographical descrip-
tion—it was merely 'the lands of the House of Habsburg' or the 'Empire of the
House of Austria'. Its lands were never bound together by geography, nationality or ethnography. Because the empire operated in the framework of German
language and culture, it has often been regarded as German—but the Habsburg
did not always support or foster the interests of their German population. The
Habsburg success against the Turks gave an impression of a mission as a Christian bulwark against Islam—such an image once established was fostered long
after the basis of the reputation had disappeared. In some respects the Habsburg
were less tolerant than the Turks and an alliance with the Jesuits cast the
religious pattern of Central Europe, while this also deterred some Orthodox
Christians from siding with them.

Early Habsburg expansion came from making Slavs in their eastern marches
into vassals through fear of the Avars and later the Magyars. After the Magyar
defeat in 955 AD relations between Hungary and the Habsburg improved and in
the fourteenth century, a permanent definition of boundaries in the March and
Leitha basins took place. The mixing of German and Slav peasants led to the
appearance of a linguistic boundary from Villach and Klagenfurt to the Drau
(Drava). By dynastic manipulation the Habsburg Archduke of Austria (1526)
became King of Bohemia and King of Hungary. In Bohemia the position of the
Habsburg was strengthened after the Czech defeat at Bila Hora on the religious
issue (1620), resulting in two-thirds of landed estates passing into German hands
and to other Habsburg supporters. For a long time the Habsburg, inspite of their
deputed missionary task, did little to clear Hungarian territory held by the Turks,
though the defeat of the Turks before Vienna in 1683 that marked the down-turn
of Ottoman fortunes was followed by more vigorous Habsburg action.

At the Peace of Karlowitz in 1699, most of central Hungary passed to the
Habsburg and they also received the Transylvanian Principality and Slavonia. In
1718 at the Treaty of Passarowitz, they gained northern Bosnia, northern Serbia
and Wallachia west of the Olt, though this was mostly lost in 1739. The lands in
the Banat and Bačka, Syrmia and Slavonia, in devastated southern Hungary, were
masterfully colonised by a polyglot collection of peasants, and a broad protective zone—the Military Frontier—to prevent further Turkish incursions erected,
with special rights for colonists in return for military service. From this zone was
to come most of the officer corps of the Habsburg armies, while a navy was built
to defend the Dalmatian possessions, using largely Croatian sailors.

Inspite of the loss of almost all Silesia and the Duchy of Glatz to Prussia in
1742, the Habsburg made gains at the Partitions of Poland in the richer
south—in Galicia and Lodomeria in 1772 and in the Bukovina in 1775. For a
time (1795–1809) West Galicia around Lublin, Radom and Sandomir, was held.
The reforms of Joseph II (1780) created religious freedom and gave the Jews a
new role in the empire, but the abolition of serfdom and the donation of peasant
security contributed substantially to problems of peasant farming in later times.

2.2.6 Prussia

The history of Prussia goes back to 928 AD, when Henry the Fowler reputedly established the Nordmark between the Elbe and the Oder. In the 1815 settlement at Vienna Prussia emerged—having been on the right side at the end—as a major power straddling the North German Plain.

The lands between the Elbe and the Oder had been colonised by Germans in the twelfth and thirteenth century. As the land filled with German farmers and villages, the territory was divided into further marchlands, out of which appeared the Mark Brandenburg. Raised to an electorate of the Empire, Brandenburg passed to the Hohenzollern family in 1411. The first Hohenzollern, the 'Toymaker of Nürnberg', began an unspectacular consolidation of these territories that lasted for 200 years. The Prussian or Borussian lands had been settled from the early thirteenth century by the Teutonic Knights under the will of the Polish King in order to Christianise the heathen natives, just as Livonia and Kurland were settled by German Brethren of the Sword under the Bishop of Riga. The German knights eventually were defeated by the Poles, for they had become unacceptably powerful, and the territory of Prussia was divided—West Prussia and Ermland went to Poland and East Prussia became the Duchy of Prussia, which was to pass to Brandenburg in 1618 though it was not relieved of suzerainty to the Polish king until 1657.

Brandenburg–Prussia was a poor country—thin glacial soils, much forest and swamp and a cool, damp climate fit only for rye and oats—whose resources did not compensate for its political precariousness surrounded by more powerful neighbours, though efficient and resourceful government was to win political power. Prussia emerged from the Thiry Years' War, champion of Protestantism and with territorial gains. Frederick the Great (1740–86) perfected the army and the administrative machine and added Silesia (1742) from the Habsburg and West Prussia, the Netze district and the Kulmerland from Poland in 1771 besides sundry territories. After his death further territories were to be added from the partitions of Poland.

2.2.7 Poland

The Polish–Lithuanian Commonwealth after the personal union in 1386 had been one of the powerful states in Europe until the end of the seventeenth century, only to disappear from the map in the late eighteenth century. German colonisation in the North European Plain beyond the Oder in the thirteenth and fourteenth centuries had pressed against the western marches of Poland and had penetrated into Polish crown lands, so that a tenuous Slavonic hold in these lands was weakened and the power of German aristocrats strengthened. By the fifteenth century, the border between Poland and the Holy Roman empire approximated to the alignment that was to separate German and Polish settlement areas for the next half-millenium. Contained on the west by the Germans and on the south by the Habsburg, Polish expansion from the thirteenth century turned eastwards and south-eastwards, into sparsely settled lands without truly effective political organisation.

Although never clearly legally defined, the Polish–Lithuanian Commonwealth spread over a vast area of White Russia and the Ukraine and reached even into Moldavia. To it belonged as vassals some Russian principalities, driven into association through fear of the Mongol–Tatars. In the early fifteenth century it was powerful enough to challenge the emerging Muscovite state and to extend its borders to the gates of Moscow. The Polish–Lithuanian state became ethnically diverse and under the leadership of Polish aristocracy, assimilated Lithuanian, White Russian and Ukrainian aristocrats to spread a veneer of Polish culture and usage. Economically, the state depended heavily on German and Jewish artisans and traders and on the labours of mixed Slavonic peasantry. The Polish aristocrats—the *szlachta*—carried a mission of Roman Christianity against the heathen Lithuanians and the Orthodox Russians as well as against the non-Christian Tatar–Mongol and Turkish hordes: Poland was the 'outer glacis of Christendom'.

The Polish–Lithuanian state in the century of the Reformation reached its zenith, with a wide spectrum of political freedom and a Golden Age in cultural and political power; but the long drawn out battles against Moscow had already brought some territorial losses. In 1569, in the Union of Lublin, the Lithuanian nobles sought equality with their Polish counterparts and as part of the deal, Lithuanian Ukrainian territory was transferred to the Kingdom of Poland. The end of the Jagiellon dynasty and the election of kings from 1572 created a battlefield of dynastic rivalries that weakened and divided the country, so that greedy neighbours began to threaten its very existence.

Two generations of economic difficulties and external pressures during the period of the elected kings sapped Polish strength, while internal disagreements tore apart the loyalties of society. Prussia, Russia and Austria all interfered for their own ends in the internal squabbles that reduced government to near anarchy by the misuse of the *liberum veto* in the *Sejm*. The election under somewhat clouded circumstances of Poniatowski to the kingship in 1764 was followed by his strenuous efforts to revitalise and reorganise Polish life. The threat of a resurgent Poland was, however, unacceptable to his sponsors, Prussia and Russia, especially as the Russians since Peter the Great had schemed to reduce Poland to a protectorate. The reforms Poniatowski introduced gave Prussia and Russia a chance to intervene through the opposition they generated. A short war in 1772 was followed by territorial concessions to the two powers and to Austria. A second demand for territory in 1793 further reduced the small landlocked Polish state, while a revolt by Kościuszko against the Russians in 1795 was followed by a third partitioning of Polish territory that swept the country from the map.

2.2.8 The Napoleonic Period and its Aftermath (figure 2.8)

Much of the old order in Europe fell victim to the far-reaching changes generated by the revolutionary armies of Napoleonic France. The Holy Roman Empire, long moribund, was swept away in 1806. The German states, except Prussia much reduced in territory, were gathered into a French sponsored Confederation of the Rhine, while some truly German territory was incorporated in an enlarged France. At the expense of Prussia and Russia, the French created the Grand Duchy of Warsaw in 1807, enlarged in 1809 by incorporation of Austrian territory, while between 1805 and 1809 the Habsburg lost their valuable Illyrian

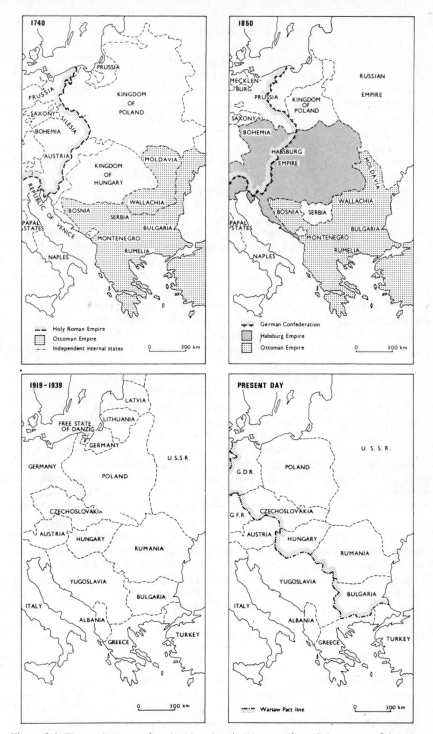

Figure 2.8. The settlements after the Napoleonic Wars confirmed the power of the great empires—Prussia, Austria–Hungary, Russia and Turkey. These were replaced, however, after the First World War by nation states—often termed the Succession States—whose boundaries were modified after the Second World War.

lands to France. The zenith of the French hegemony was reached in 1812 when the Grand Army and its allies, marched into Russia, only to be defeated by the evasiveness of the Tsar's armies and by the nature of the Russian lands. The debacle gave Prussia and Austria a chance to defect from the French camp and to join the Russians and British in events leading to Napoleon's defeat at Waterloo in 1815.

The Congress of Vienna was to impress frontiers on the map of Europe within which a century of technological and social change was to take place. The changes were nevertheless unevenly spread, making little impact in the Tsarist empire and in the rotting hulk of the Ottoman empire. Under the Treaty of Tilsit in 1807 and the aegis of Saxony, a Polish state—the Grand Duchy of Warsaw—had reappeared: this state—now the Kingdom of Poland—was retained within slightly modified boundaries, but fell under Russian domination and after 1831 became for all intents and purposes a part of the Tsarist empire. Prussia emerged with renewed strength and enlarged territory, particularly in the west, conceived as a possible check against a resurgent France. Prussia was now the most likely leader among the German states, whose number was reduced from 360 to thirty-nine—nevertheless, Germany still remained more a geographical than a political expression. In the considerable reshuffle, the Habsburg lands received the Illyrian kingdom of Dalmatia (held 1797–1805), along with Istria and lands in northern Italy, part of the former ecclesiastical territory of Salzburg and the Innviertel, besides the Tarnopol district, the fortress of Lemberg (Lwów) and the Bukovina, significant bastions against Russia. The city of Kraków, a small independent republic, passed to Austria in 1846.

The survival of the Habsburg empire, the new strength of Prussia and the Romanov domains confirmed that Europe was still dynastic—reflected by the Tsar's vague and mystic concept of the Concert of Europe—and the map took little notice of the ethnic pattern. From the mid-years of the century, awakening nationalism began to create particularly intractable problems in the Habsburg empire, while Prussia started a policy of Germanisation in its ethnically Polish territories, especially under Bismarck. In 'Russian Poland' the Poles were better off than any other non-Russian nationality in the Tsarist empire, where the position of minorities deteriorated throughout the nineteenth century, and Russian Poland prospered as the industrial base for the Tsarist empire. Most fortunate were the Poles of Austrian Galicia, who played on their value as a counterweight to embarrassing demands from the other nationalities in the polyglot Habsburg empire. With the awakening of Magyar national feeling and the weakening of the Habsburg hold that led to the creation of the Dual Monarchy in 1867, the non-Magyar peoples of Hungary suffered particularly through ruthless Magyarisation.

2.2.9 The Decline of the Turks

While the years after 1815 brought comparative peace in Western and Central Europe, the Turkish empire began to suffer a serious internal disturbance. Without interference from the other great European powers, it might well have disintegrated early in the century, but these powers, jealous of each other, were afraid that one or other might gain advantage at such a dissolution. Considerable alarm was generated by the growing Russian interest in the fate of Orthodox Christians and there was great interest in the control of the entrance to the Black Sea as well as in an influential hold in Asia Minor. While seeking to ease the position of the Christians, these powers were reluctant to see an alteration of the *status quo*, though they were unable to prevent the rise of national aspirations in the Balkans, some of which they supported either openly or undercover.

The first changes in the Turkish empire were heralded in Serbia by revolts that began in 1804. In Šumadija, the insurgents were in a strong position by their knowledge of a terrain ideally suited to guerilla warfare and inspite of large numbers of Turkish troops, many important towns and fortresses fell to the Serbs. In the Treaty of Bucharest (1812) between Russia and Turkey, there was vague wording about internal autonomy for Serbia. The reassertion of Turkish rule (with all its abuses and cruelty) when Russia was distracted by war elsewhere, brought further revolts in 1815 and 1817. From the second revolt, Serbia emerged as a small autonomous principality, though in 1833, its territory was extended slightly on the south. The awakened Serbian national feeling was now active not only in the political field, but also in studies of folk-lore, language and ethnology.

Although Serbia had managed to get rid of the Turks and Turkish garrisons in its territory between 1862 and 1867, a war with Turkey in 1867 ended in near disaster, saved only by Russian diplomatic intervention. When the Turks failed to carry out their promises, Russia—with Rumania, Serbia, Montenegro and the Bulgarian rebels—was victorious in a short war and under the Treaty of San Stefano, 1878, Serbia secured complete independence from Turkey and made territorial gains exceeded only by Bulgaria. Although the conflict caused by Turkish weakness was to the satisfaction of the great powers, they were still mistrustful of each other's ultimate aims. Consequently, the Treaty of Berlin, a few months after San Stefano, put a restriction on Russia's aspirations and sought to remedy Turkish misrule. Serbia received a considerable amount of territory excluding 'Old Serbia' (including Skopje), as the Austro-Hungarians were alarmed at the growth of Serbia. Greater Bulgaria was pruned, especially in the south-west. Serbia was separated from Montenegro by the Turkish territory of Novi Pazar garrisoned by Austria. Bosnia was occupied by Austria, as well as Hercegovina—though Moslems put up considerable resistance. Subsequently the Austrians colonised land in the north along the right bank of the Sava with Roman Catholics from outside the South Slav lands. Although strong criticism was levelled against the Austrian administration, considerable improvements in public security and material welfare took place.

The Montenegrins had maintained their independence inspite of many Turkish attempts to subjugate them, but during the eighteenth century, they had come to depend on Russian subsidies. In conflict with the Turks Montenegro had made some modest territorial advances, but its relations through the nineteenth century were very complex and involved much warfare. Even after the Treaty of Berlin (1878), Montenegro's boundaries remained in dispute up to the First World War.

Social and economic trends in Bulgaria in the nineteenth century were similar to Serbia, though the interest of the great powers played an even greater role than in Serbia. The geographical position of Bulgaria in relation to Constantinople and its strategic importance within the Turkish empire made independence more difficult to establish, and Russian participation in the Bulgarian freedom movement made the other great powers cool towards it. Unlike other Christian peoples of the Turkish empire, the Bulgarians were unfortunate in having no major pressure group in the outside world. An important stage in the Bulgarian struggle for independence was to be rid of the domination of the Greek element, stronger here than elsewhere, while national aspirations were increasingly associated with the commercial and artisan element. A late eighteenth century cultural rebirth played a role similar to the linguistic work in Serbia, but helped by generous Russian endowments. After the foundation of an independent Greek state in 1829, growing Turkish suspicion of the Greek Orthodox clergy helped the Bulgarian attempts to refound their own church. After initial moves in 1860 the Sultan issued a Ferman in 1870 creating a separate Bulgarian Exarchat, whose jurisdiction extended into many politically disputed districts.

The first insurgency in Bulgaria in 1875 and 1876 was unsuccessful, but vicious Turkish retaliation brought events to the notice of the West, reflected in Gladstone's 'Bulgarian horrors and the Question of the East'. Russian intervention—with a considerable growth of Pan-Slav feeling—resulted in war. Russian victory embodied in the Treaty of San Stefano (1878) created a Greater Bulgaria, *San-Stefanska Bulgariya*, which though transient was to become the long-standing aim of later policy.

After four months the pressure of the other great powers forced Russia into the Treaty of Berlin and a realignment of Balkan boundaries, directed by the 'honest broker' Bismarck. Bulgaria, established as an autonomous principality tributary to the Porte, with its own Christian government and national militia, was reduced from 164 000 km^2 at San Stefano to 64 000 km^2—from 4.5 million people to a mere 1.85 million. The southern Bulgarian districts of Eastern Rumelia (the Maritsa Plain and Plovdiv) again became Turkish provinces with administrative autonomy and a Governor-General acceptable to the great powers, but in 1885 joined the Bulgarian principality. Macedonia passed to the Ottoman empire, while to Bulgarian annoyance, the northern Dobrudsha went to Rumania in compensation for Bessarabia taken by Russia. In 1885 a Serbian–Bulgarian war over Eastern Rumelia ended in the former's defeat.

In 1903 a swing away from Austria towards France began in Serbia—first reflected in Serbian attempts to negotitate a customs agreement with Bulgaria and reluctance to renew an economic treaty with Austria–Hungary, whose mistrust of Serbian aims led to a ban in imports of all Serbian livestock, the country's main export, and the resulting 'Pig War' (1906–8) caused a switch to processed meat exports (with French capital) via Salonika. Final Austro-Hungarian annexation of Bosnia–Hercegovina worsened relations with Serbia, but no great power would support a war against Austria–Hungary for fear of Germany. Tension lessened when Austro–Hungarian garrisons in the Novi–Pazar Territory were withdrawn in 1908—partly a rethinking of strategy that switched from the military road to Salonika via Novi Pazar to the old route through Serbia itself.

2.2.10 The Balkan Wars (figure 2.9)

During 1911–12, various alliances between Bulgaria, Greece, Serbia and

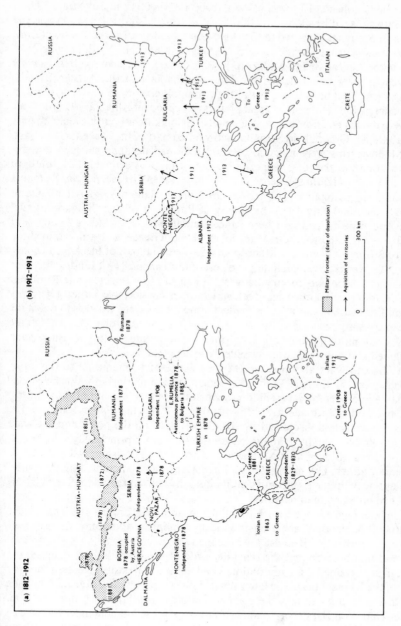

Figure 2.9. The Balkans, however defined, have been one of the most confusing areas territorially in Europe. Many old scores still lie dormant.

Montenegro were mooted. Disorders in Macedonia and Albania gave an excuse for war: in October 1912 some 800 000 troops (350 000 from Bulgaria, 250 000 from Serbia) faced less than 500 000 Turkish troops in poor condition and the Balkan troops quickly routed the Turkish army. In May 1913 the Treaty of London took away from Turkey all territory west and north of a straight line from Enos on the Aegean Sea to Midia on the Black Sea; Crete went to Greece, while the great powers could decide the fate of Albania and the Aegean islands. Bulgaria had been promised most of the captured territory, but Serbia, blocked in Albania by the action of the great powers (independent Albania, 1913), lost an access to the sea and now wanted an outlet at Salonika, thus putting claim to part of Macedonia. Greece held Salonika and wanted part of the Macedonian coast. The Montenegrins were irritated because they had no apparent gain and yet claimed one of the first victories, while Rumania claimed the southern Dobrudsha at Bulgaria's expense. Turkey now joined Greece, Serbia, Rumania and Montenegro against Bulgaria in the Second Balkan War. After fighting through June and July 1913 the Treaty of Bucharest obliged Bulgaria to surrender much of its gain: northern Macedonia to Serbia, including Skopje and Ohrid: Salonika and southern Macedonia went to Greece. Bulgaria retained the town of Strumitsa in eastern Macedonia and about 110 km of the Aegean coast west of the Maritsa river, including the port of Dedeagatsch (Alexandrupolis) but not Kavalla. Montenegro got the western half of Novi Pazar, while Rumania took the southern Dobrudsha. The Turks got a considerable piece of territory around Edirne (Adrianople) that made it impossible for the Bulgars to reach the Aegean coast by rail except through Greek or Turkish territory. This war left the states even more jealous of each other than before, with the Bulgarians humiliated and outraged, waiting sullenly to retaliate.

The Balkan wars also marked the emergence of Rumania on to the international scene in Europe. Early in the fourteenth century, both Wallachia and Moldavia had become Rumanian principalities, but by the end of the century, Moldavia had been made a Polish vassal and Wallachia was tributary to the Turks. Nevertheless, protected by the Carpathians on the north and the wide and impassable marshy Danube on the south, neither principality felt the full Turkish pressure, even after Moldavia had become a Turkish vassal in the early sixteenth century. Ultimately, Greek Phanariot princes appointed by the Turks had held sway. In the eighteenth century both the Habsburg and the Tsar had encroached on Rumanian territory.

Nominal Turkish overlordship continued until 1829, when the Tsar in the Treaty of Adrianople achieved practically complete autonomy for the two Rumanian provinces. Because they escaped the main force of Turkish domination and had been spared the religious strife of the other Balkan peoples, the Rumanians retained a greater national and cultural solidarity. Russian 'protection' of the Rumanians in the latter nineteenth century made Britain and France fear that Russia might take the place of Turkey in south-east European affairs. Under Napoleon III, France had begun to work for Rumanian independence to thwart Tsarist ambitions, so that French cultural influence, playing on the Romance tradition, became strong. The Treaty of Paris (1856) after the Crimean War freed Rumania from Russian influence and in 1861 the two provinces were united into one national assembly. The independent Kingdom of Rumania (declared in 1881) had been recognised by both Russian and Turkey after the Russo-Turkish war of 1877–8, when Rumania lost Bessarabia to Russia. Between the Congress of Berlin (1878) and the second Balkan War (1913), Rumania was too committed to putting its own affairs in order, especially to solving the land tenure problem, to be more than a spectator in Balkan affairs.

2.2.11 Mitteleuropa and the Great Empires

In the closing years of the nineteenth century, the eastern half of Europe appeared divided into three major political spheres, of which only one seemed dynamic. The core of Europe lay within the vague Germanic concept of *Mitteleuropa*—whose geographical boundaries were exceptionally ill defined but which supposedly represented those parts where German predominance was assured by German as the *lingua franca* and a cultural veneer of varying thickness. The concept of *Mitteleuropa* emerged in the early part of the nineteenth century and was to grow in strength as nationalism unfolded, to reach its climax in the early twentieth century.

The real focus of *Mitteleuropa* was the Second Reich, an ebullient and forceful union of German states under the vigorous and puritanical leadership of Prussia, growing at a striking pace and seemingly headed for the hegemony of Europe. The Reich overshadowed its older and weaker partner—after an initial struggle for leadership culminating in the Prussian victory of 1866—so that the Austro–Hungarian Dual Monarchy fell increasingly into the background in a continuous love–hate relationship with the German Empire. Austria–Hungary, far less thrusting and more introspective, was not a truly German empire like its younger rival, but a massive polyglot collection of peoples under a dynastic veneer of Germandom. Truly 'kaiserlich und königlich', since 1867 two monarchies under a single emperor, it was still an agglomeration of Habsburg estates and a club for Habsburg aristocrats, allowing free circulation from Lemberg to Triest and from Krakau to Subotica. Within were stirrings of national aspirations for at least autonomy, but it had stood worse shocks in the past and survived—the very recognition of the duality of the crown in 1867 was regarded as a sign that it was not yet atrophied enough to be unable to find some flexibility to cope with the new demands that time was throwing up.

The second great sphere was the enigmatic empire of the Tsar of all the Russias, an unknown force, backward but vast and potentially powerful. During the Napoleonic wars, the Tsar, fired by a mystic concept of the Concert of Europe, had intervened in the affairs of Western and Central Europe. His bizarre, ragged and 'oriental' troops had left as deep an impresion as had the early Mongol–Tatar hordes. Everyone wondered how long it would be before these strange armies would again pour out of their limitless plains: nobody had forgotten how they had destroyed the Grand Army in those empty spaces by their very reluctance to fight a conventional battle. Many Slavs in the Prussian, Habsburg and Turkish empires, looked upon the Tsar as their potential protector—*Mother Russia* would come to their aid if presssures became too acute, for the Tsar had built his image as a guardian of the oppressed Christian Slavs of the Turkish world. Some saw, however, that the hold of the Tsar was a deathly grip.

The third sphere was the complex, chaotic Balkans—a collection of small states which had won their independence in the latter nineteenth century and yet were locked in internecine struggles but unified in their opposition to the rapidly declining Turkish power. As their power waned and their self-confidence failed, the Turks became generally more oppressive, kept in being by the efforts of outside powers, who feared increasingly the advantages rivals might win in the will of a deceased Porte. The many independence movements and their conflicting and confusing demands led to a fear that such an illness might be contagious, spreading 'balkanisation', which came true in the assassination of a Habsburg prince that triggered off a conflict that embroiled all Europe.

3 Historical Development in the Twentieth Century

3.1 The New Europe: 1918–45

The collapse in 1918 of the Central Powers—Austria–Hungary, the German Reich and their Turkish allies as well as subsidiary supporters—ended four years of desperate warfare. Protracted peace-making lasting into 1920 produced a new map of Europe but left many problems, a breeding ground for new discontent. New states based on the principle of nationality were impressed on an existing pattern of society and economic relations. Before the new states had had time to mould themselves into viable organisms a world economic crisis opened economic and social wounds left by the surgery of the peace settlement. The settlement itself reflected a strange mixture of American-inspired self-determination and a French lust for revenge and eternal impoverishment of the vanquished, plus a dash of misguided 'fair-mindedness' from Britain. Many solutions reflected the work of minds steeped in history but leached of geography. In the end several solutions were by force rather than by reason. Eastern Europe bore the brunt of all these messy changes, to become the '*cordon sanitaire*' around the contagion of Bolshevism in Russia.

3.1.1 The Habsburg Empire

The Habsburg empire, described as 'a geographical nonsense explicable only by dynastic groupings and the accidents of centuries of history', was swept away in 1918. Six of the new 'succession' states were to share its onetime territories, each patched together on the basis of a vaguely defined 'self-determination'. When the test came, the Habsburg had shown themselves bankrupt of virility to adjust to new demands—to the surprise of many. Though forewarned of emergent nationalism, especially new images of national solidarity nurtured by Pan-Slavism, they missed the opportunity to channel it into constructive federalism. Instead, Viennese diplomacy had used national aspirations as a tool to divide and rule.

3.1.2 Austria

Austria was pruned of everything that could be stripped from its German core, though the German settled area of Burgenland was transferred to it from Hungary, making it the only enemy state to receive territory, albeit from another ex-enemy state. Burgenland, an old German marchland against Pannonia, guarding the way into the Danube valley and the Marchfeld, was in 1918 without doubt German in character and as German land passed to 'Deutschösterreich', though Sopron (Ödenburg), a major railway junction for the Magyar Kisalföld, stayed as a salient of Hungarian territory south of the Neusiedler See (Fertö).

'Deutschösterreich' was left a poor mountain country, with over one-third of its population in the majestic but shabby imperial capital, Vienna. Its access to the sea rested on international guarantees of its use of Trieste, once its major port but now in Italian hands. Austrian pleas for union with Germany were rejected by the Allied authorities, though such an *Anschluss* was to be forced on a later unwilling Austria by Nazi Germany.

3.1.3 Hungary

The haughty Magyar, remembered for his ruthless Magyarisation policy, received no quarter. The boundaries of 'Trianon Hungary' were drawn as tightly and as ruthlessly as possible, but from the outset the Hungarians repudiated the Treaty's terms. In fixing the boundaries of the new Hungary, the preference was everywhere accorded to neighbouring states and settled generally on strategic and economic grounds rather than on ethnic criteria. In the case of Czechoslovakia and Rumania, the need for adequate railway links was an overriding factor in the allocation of territory containing large Magyar populations. In 1914 the population of Hungary had been about twenty million, of whom ten million were Magyars. After Trianon Hungary was reduced to just over eight million (7.2 million were Magyars and 800 000 other nationalities). Consequently, about three million Magyars were left in other states of whom over 750 000 were in southern Slovakia, mostly in the plains between Bratislava and Mukačevo, and another large group comprised Magyars and related Szeklers in Rumanian Transylvania. The economic consequence for Hungary was that a carefully integrated industrial structure was torn apart by the new boundaries.

After the brief episode of the Soviet Republic of Bela Kun and the Rumanian invasion, experiments in socialism were not received kindly, so that even the monarchial constitution was preserved and the absent Crown represented by a Regent, Admiral Horthy. The process of economic recovery was first aided by the League of Nations, but later the country became increasingly dependent on foreign investment, notably from Germany. As a land-locked state, access to the sea depended on international guarantees, since the old ports of Austria–Hungary now lay under foreign control, a poor substitute compared to real ownership.

3.1.4 The German Reich

The German empire survived the First World War burdened with a heavy load of reparations, deprived of some territory, and with its international status reduced. The Weimar Republic, provided with a model constitution but inexperienced in parliamentary democracy, was a more centralised state than the Second *Reich* of 1871–1918. The power of the old states (particularly Prussia) was considerably limited. Territorial loss took place in both west and east; but in the west there was also the occupation of the Rhineland and a special semi-autonomous regime in the coalfield of the Saar under French control. In the east territorial loss included the Memelland to Lithuania and West Prussia, the Province of Posen (Poznań) and part of the Upper Silesia (after a plebiscite) to Poland. Danzig (Gdańsk) was made a Free City. The territorial separation of East Prussia from the *Reich* and the settlement in Upper Silesia in 1921, inspite of a majority vote for Germany, created immense resentment in Germany.

3.1.5 Soviet Russia

The Bolshevik Revolution of 1917 virtually removed Russia from the war through a peace enforced by the Germans, terrified of a spread of Bolshevism. The Baltic countries declared their independence but independence in the Ukraine was comparatively shortlived. Weakened by two major wars and by the Revolution and ensuing civil war, Soviet Russia was deprived of a broad belt of western territory to the advantage of Poland and Rumania. Suffering from an illness—Bolshevism—whose clinical nature and prognosis were unknown, it was isolated from the rest of Europe.

3.1.6 Poland

One of the largest and potentially most important new states, was Poland, conditions for whose existence had been laid down by President Wilson—all territories inhabited by Poles were to be part of the new state, which was to have secure and free access to the sea and its economic and political independence as well as its territorial integrity were to be protected. The general idea was apparently to define a state roughly within the boundaries before the first partition, with some modification in the east, where a clear case existed for a frontier based on the ethnic divide between Poles and Byelorussians and Western Ukrainians (then called Ruthenians), which had been carefully delineated by the British statesman Lord Curzon (figure 3.1). In the west all the Prussian Polish provinces, with a few small exceptions, were to be under Polish rule and the general line was to be the frontier before 1740. The core of this area was the Province of Posen (Poznań), where in 1910 30 per cent of the population was German. In the Netze (Noteć) valley and in the lower Vistula, there was considerable German population, but to the north, in poorer heath and morainic country, there was a thinly spread population of Slav Kassubians (related in language to the Poles), notably in the Tuchoła Heath (Tucheler Heide). Such an ethnic pattern was a help in creating a corridor to the sea that gave Poland a Baltic frontage on the low barren shore of the Bay of Danzig and the harbourless Pomeranian coast.

The undeniably German character of the port of Danzig at the mouth of the Vistula resulted in it being declared a free city under League of Nations' protection. Poland, however, enjoyed rights to guide Danzig's foreign policy and extraterritorial rights in postal, telegraph, telephone and railway services. The Free City was within the Polish customs administration and had a large Polish representation on its harbour board. In the southern morainic and lake country of German East Prussia, the Slav Masurians, like the people of the German Marienwerder district, were to decide by plebiscite whether they wished to remain German or become Polish. The Masurians regarded themselves as *Staroprusacy* (Old Prussians) rather than Poles, while they were Lutherans rather than Roman Catholics like the Poles. They possibly also feared Poland might go Bolshevik. Their vote and that in Marienwerder were overwhelmingly to remain in Germany. Throughout the western territories, the Poles began an active Polonisation campaign that fell particularly heavily on the rural population, many of whom were farmers settled under Prussian land schemes, and Poland was accused by Danzig of attempting to push this campaign in the Free City.

The Poles had sought possession of Upper Silesia on ethnic and historical grounds. Many observers imagined the inclusion in Poland of all the industrial and coalfield area, while others felt the district as a whole should remain in Germany in order to make possible the settlement of reparations. The outcry in Germany against complete inclusion of Upper Silesia was so forceful that it was decided (largely on British initiative) to hold a plebiscite in the area, which was occupied by French troops on behalf of the League of Nations. In the plebiscite of 1921, 59.6 per cent of the votes were cast for Germany and 40.4 per cent for Poland, though the allowance of a vote to all persons born in the area whether still resident there or not possibly favoured the Germans. The towns showed a clear majority for Germany, but the rural areas were markedly more Polish in sentiment, even though they did not necessarily have a Polish majority—in the northern and western rural districts, however, the German majority was quite clear. The final delimitation, fixed by an ambassador's conference, differed from

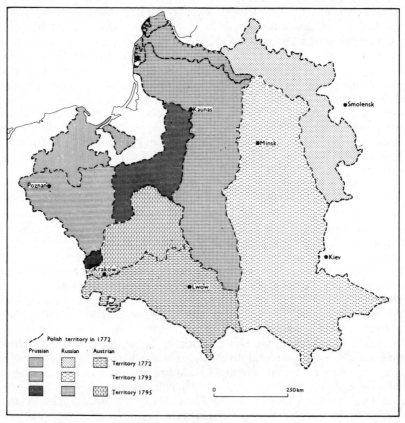

Figure 3.1. Many of Poland's contemporary problems are an inheritance from a century or more of foreign rule by powers of greatly differing character. After its mediaeval glory, it was eclipsed by the Partitions for the important formative period of the nineteenth century.

any of the lines proposed by the great powers and left about a quarter of the plebiscite area in Poland. The actual demarcation line was unfortunate in dividing a well-developed and integrated econmic unit. Poland received about 85 per cent of all coal reserves and 75 per cent of all industrial installations. Inspite of a Polish–German agreement (1922) on relations between the two parts of the coalfield, valid in the first instance for fifteen years and containing over 600 clauses, it was quickly apparent that even with the best will, the difficulties to overcome were virtually insuperable and relations deteriorated rapidly after 1935.

Many commentators have remarked on the greediness of the Polish demands for territory, particularly in the east, where Polish irredentism was thoroughly let loose (figure 3.2). Though the demands of the Polish delegation at the Paris peace conference were less extensive than many less official groups, they nevertheless claimed large parts of Byelorussia, the western Ukraine (Ruthenia), and the Polotsk district in the north along with most of Lithuania. To find a satisfactory military boundary was difficult and any such line in the Pripyat marshes generally lay too far east to be acceptable. Curzon's Line was a sincere attempt to divide Byelorussian and Polish cultural spheres, though many difficulties occurred, as Polish landlords spread far into areas of Byelorussian peasantry. The collapse of Germany and the revolution in Russia created a fluid situation resulting in confused fighting between the Poles and the Red Army. After initial successes, the Poles had to fall back, but before the gates of Warsaw, they counter-attacked and drove the Russians back beyond the Curzon Line and even beyond Minsk (the line offered by Lenin in January 1920). A peace was agreed at Riga in October 1920, but the Poles had been divided between those wanting a centralised Poland and those ready to give Byelorussia federal status, so that in the end, they gained less territory than might have been possible through a unified stand. Their hold in Lithuania could not be established because of German troops still in the country, though for a time they managed to hold Kiev in the Ukraine.

In the south they occupied Eastern Galicia, including Lemberg (Lwów), where the population was over 70 per cent Ukrainian and about 14 per cent Polish, inspite of Allied ideas that this territory would be a League of Nations mandate whose future would be decided by plebiscite. Late in 1920 Polish irregular troops seized the Lithuanian town of Wilno (Vilnius), where there was a large Polish and Jewish population. After futile attempts by the League of Nations to get agreement between Poland and Lithuania, even to the extent of a possible union, the matter was finally abandoned when the local *Sejm* (a Polish puppet) attached 'Central Lithuania' to Poland (1922). In early 1923 the Allied Council of Ambassadors agreed to the new eastern boundary of Poland as defined at the Treaty of Riga, to Polish occupancy of Wilno and of Eastern Galicia, but Lithuania did not recognise Polish rights to Wilno and relations remained exceptionally strained.

Poland emerged by the early 1920s twice as large in area as had been expected at the Paris peace conference. Its expansionist policy achieved by force of arms had skilfully played on the Western fear of Bolshevism and the French wishes to have a strong eastern counterpart to a possibly resurgent Germany. The new Polish republic founded its inauspicious inter-war career on ideas long outworn, of the Golden Age of the fourteenth and fifteenth centuries, with its new missionary role directed against Bolshevism, but its greedy expansionist policy

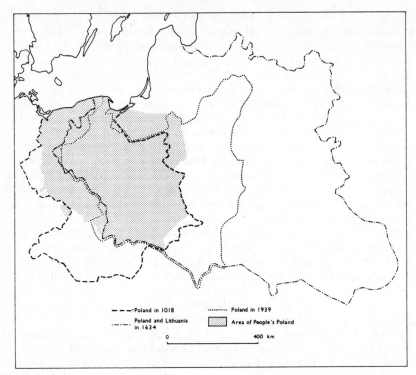

Figure 3.2. No study of Poland can ignore the country's widely shifting boundaries. After mediaeval expansion eastwards, modern trends have been to draw its boundaries westwards. Based on *Atlas Historyczny Polski*, Warsaw (1967), p. 54.

against powerful neighbours at their time of weakness had earned it only enemies. Even small Lithuania and the passive Czechoslovak state regarded the Poles with more than mistrust. Its main sponsor and friend in Europe was France, whose role and prestige were, however, in the descendent, while it was weakened by strong and dissident minorities: 68 per cent of its population was Polish, 14 per cent West Ukrainian, 10 per cent Jewish, 3.7 per cent Byelorussian and 3.7 per cent German. The Jews had grown to a position of power: in 1895, in then Russian Poland, Jews formed 14 per cent of total population but comprised 84 per cent of the merchants, 20 per cent of the literary men, 51 per cent of the educationalists and 24 per cent of the physicians. Jews comprised only two per cent of the farmers, factory workers and miners. The Jews had no strong national feeling, working for racial rights rather than for national aims, consequently antisemitic feeling on occasions ran high among Poles, inspite of a pact against antisemitism in 1925. Poland's respect of minorities was in general poor and deteriorated in the 1930s.

With long but poorly defensible frontiers, Poland was forced to maintain a large standing army, while internal strains among minorities demanded strong security forces. Economically relatively weak, such forces posed a substantial drain on its finances, especially as more sophisticated armaments were needed in the later 1930s. Even Poland's major industrial resources in Upper Silesia were strategically badly located and effort was given to building up industries less strategically vulnerable in the interior. An additional strain was created by grandiose attempts to become a Baltic power via its waterfront at Gdynia.

3.1.7 Czechoslovakia

Not since the earliest mediaeval times had there been a state representing both Czechs and Slovaks. Czechoslovak boundary problems were less difficult than those of Poland, but its internal problems were great since two contrasting peoples, with different economies, living in quite different landscapes, but bound together by a linguistic and ancient historical link, were to be moulded into a unified state. Application of self-determination within historical boundaries long blurred by ethnic patterns, left the new state with the most critical minority problem of all the Succession states.

Ideas of independence began in the Napoleonic period and came near to realisation in the revolutionary years of 1848–9. The more moderate Czechs were, however, wary of the young enthusiasts for the ideas of Pan-Slavism. Under the strict Austrian rule, moves towards any ideas of national autonomy were slow and much of the struggle was devoted to keeping alive a national tradition among the 'Bohemians'. Throughout the nineteenth century, the strength of the Czechs had grown against the German element by their far greater rate of natural increase. After the Austrian defeat of 1866 there was initially some Austrian inclination towards a tripartite monarchy—Austria, Hungary and Bohemia, an idea received with sympathy among the Czech population. During the 1860s and 1870s, Czech social, cultural and commercial bodies grew vigorously and Masaryk (1850–1931) emerged as the creative spirit behind the growth of a Czech and Slovak national consciousness, seen by him in a framework of a liberal Austro–Hungarian federation, since he was sceptical of both Pan-Slavism and Pan-Germanism. It was a period when Czechs were tending to penetrate into what had been overwhelmingly German settlement areas and occupational fields.

In general, the Slovaks were less articulate and pressing than the Czechs, while the Magyars were less liberal than the Austrians though they had made concessions to the Slovaks in the 1860s. Some observers maintain, however, that Slovak–Magyar relations were generally better than between the Magyars and Germans. It is even suggested that the Slovaks would not have left the Hungarian state without encouragement by the more nationalistic Czechs and émigré Slovaks in America. It might be truer to say that the Slovaks would have demanded their liberation at a later date.

The First World War and Habsburg reluctance to concede a confederation in place of a rigorously centralised dynastic monarchy lost Czech support and many Czech regiments in the Austro–Hungarian armies gave themselves up. In Russia a Czech legion of some 70 000 men was formed but during the Revolution it clashed with the Bolsheviks and fought its way to Vladivostok, where it was shipped home to Europe. In October 1918 a provisional Czech–Slovak government was declared in Paris and proclaimed the Czechoslovak Republic, while Czech and Slovak administrations took over at home.

The Treaty of St Germain (1919) established the new Republic, but gave little attention to its real problems by ignoring the large minorities' own claims to self-determination, for the acceptance of historical boundaries hardly fitted reality. Of its fourteen million inhabitants 35 per cent were neither Czechs nor Slovaks. There were about 3.2 million Germans, of whom 1.7 million lived in Bohemia. Some 750 000 Magyars lived in Slovakia (mostly in the south) and 460 000 Ukrainians (Ruthenians) in the easternmost part. There were also 75 000 Poles. The Germans, particularly active in commerce and industry, lived in western and northern Bohemia and in parts of Moravia and Czech Silesia in almost completely German districts, while large groups were found in most big towns and in places in Slovakia. Although the Czechoslovak state was among the most liberal in its policy to minorities, the Germans and Magyars as former ruling peoples took ill to the new situation. The position was worsened by the economic depression of 1929–31, when the industrial populations—among which was a particularly large German element—suffered more hardship than the rural population, which comprised almost entirely Slav elements. The Nazis encouraged discontent among the Sudeten Germans, and actions by the Czechs and Slovaks without reference to the minority people also damaged relations. The hoped for symbiosis between the different national elements and the emergence of a Swiss-type confederation did not come about, so that inspite of men of goodwill and vision on both sides, the gulf between the Czechs and Slovaks and their minority peoples tended to widen.

In many respects Masaryk created the concept of the Czechoslovak state before he had created the Czechoslovaks. With only relatively limited experience in administration inherited from the Hungarian period, the Slovaks felt inferior as numbers of Czech officials moved in to develop the machinery of government and Czechs tended to overshadow Slovaks in business and in the establishment of industry.

The boundaries of Bohemia and Moravia were the historical boundaries of the provinces which could be traced back to early mediaeval times, though a few districts such as Glatz which might have been claimed with some justification on historical grounds were not included. On the other hand, the district of Hlučín (Hültschin), a small territory, which before 1914 was a part of Germany, was added to the Czech lands, with about 50 000 people of whom about 80 per cent spoke a dialect of Czech. It was a poor and neglected part of Prussia whose people had depended on work in Silesia. At one stage, it was proposed to exchange the small finger of territory around Aš (Asch) in the Egerland (Chebsko) for the Glatz district, while the Czechs were also willing to modify the awkward territorial alignments near Frýdlant (Friedland) and Rumburk (Rumburg), but in the end no action was taken. On the Czech–Austrian frontier, there were some minor territorial modifications, notably at Gmünd and on the Thaya (Dyje).

The border with the new Polish state presented problems, with the main dispute over the Duchy of Teschen (Těšín, Cieszyn). Much of the western part of the Duchy, which was Czech speaking and also contained good quality bituminous coals, was assigned to Czechoslovakia but most of the town of Teschen was left in Poland. Through the Czech part ran the main railway link for this part of the coalfield, while the Czechs agreed to deliver a part of the coal output to Poland. Two small mountain areas were also in dispute—the Orava and Spiš districts. These were claimed by Poland because they had been used traditionally by mountain people from the Polish side of the Carpathians for pasture, so that some of the population permanently resident here were Poles. In the end the parts south of the main ranges went to Slovakia.

The tail of Czechoslovakia east to Užhorod, the Carpatho-Ukraine, was a remote and backward area, on the north a series of low Carpathian ranges crossed by historically important passes and on the south broad outwash fans dropping away into the Pannonian Plains, with Mukachevo as the principal centre. This territory was an important link between Czechoslovakia and Rumania, in case military action were to be needed against Hungary, of which it completed the encirclement on the north. The people in the mountains were related to the West Ukrainians, Orthodox or Uniate in religion, while there was also a strong Jewish and Gypsy element. The middle and upper classes were mostly Hungarian, and Magyar peasants were also found on the richer plains around Mukachevo. Under the St Germain treaty (1919), the Czech government agreed to grant ultimate autonomy to the Carpatho-Ukraine. Because the Czechs elected to make Ukrainian the approved teaching language, the support of the Orthodox clergy was lost, as they preferred Russian and consequently sided with the Magyar landlords, rigorously opposing the Czechoslovak authorities in one of the most effective land reforms carried out in interwar Eastern Europe. In the latter thirties, the official attitude towards the Ukrainians cooled as support for inclusion in a Greater Ukraine increased.

Throughout the inter-war period, as already noted, the Magyars continually stressed that the southern border of Slovakia had been fixed solely for transport and strategic reasons in favour of Czechoslovakia. It comprises a broad and fertile footslope and outwash plain along the southern edge of the Carpathians extending to the Danube, while east of Esztergom, the border follows the Ipoly valley and crosses more hilly country. In this belt of country lived the majority of the Magyar minority in the new republic, but the Slovaks claimed that 50 years previously the area had been largely Slovak and had been Magyarised by concerted policy from Budapest. The new capital of Slovakia, Bratislava, was a largely German and Magyar town.

Three Czech territorial ideas were not realised: a direct territorial connection to Russia—for this reason, the Czechs had opposed Polish control of Eastern Galicia in 1919—though later Czech enthusiasm for such an arrangement waned; a territorial corridor from the Danube to the Jugoslav territory in the Drava valley. The justification of such a concept was the presence of small Slav remnants in Burgenland. The third proposal was for some arrangement to include the Slav Sorbs of German Lusatia in the Czech state, but this also received no serious consideration.

As an inland state dependent on access to the world across other peoples' territories, the Czechoslovak republic clearly had important diplomatic and commercial problems. Although the Czechoslovaks had concessions in Danube and Elbe navigation and representation on the Oder Commission, as well as special rights in Hamburg and Stettin, their position was a precarious one. On the other hand, they held a trump card by controlling major north–south railway links in Central Europe and by their command of the vital routeway through the Moravian corridor. The long sausage-like territory of Czechoslovakia gave the country disproportionately long frontiers and a major problem of mobility along the major east–west axis, while the north–south distances were short enough to give concern, particularly in Moravia, that any attack might cut the country into two reasonably easily. With the large armaments plants of Škoda, the Czechoslovak army was, however, one of the best equipped in the inter-war years.

3.1.8 The Balkans

The collapse of Austria–Hungary and the Ottoman Empire left a power vacuum in the Balkans out of which appeared an entirely new political–geographical pattern, with old and new elements pressed into commonly unhappy boundaries. Of the new states Jugoslavia was by far the most complex and had the greatest internal strains, while a subdued Bulgaria smarted under the resentment engendered by a loss of face. The map of the lower Danube was greatly changed by the territories of an enlarged Rumania, while Albania was an apology for a state.

3.1.9 Jugoslavia

Union among the several South Slav peoples had been discussed throughout the nineteenth century, but the identification of a common Slav destiny had many difficulties. Scattered among different political spheres and administrative units, concerted action was difficult, while basic cultural antagonisms also hampered unity. Hungarian oppression in Croatia was a significant factor in cementing together South Slav feeling, while Serbian triumphs in the Balkan wars gave added impetus to the movement. A favourable concordat between Serbia and the Vatican in 1914 allayed fears by Roman Catholics of Serbian Orthodox intolerance, while in the same year moves by Montenegro to enter a fiscal and diplomatic union with Serbia was another step towards South Slav unity, inspite of fears of Pan–Serb aspirations.

By 1914 four possible solutions of the Balkan problem existed. A first but most unlikely solution might have been to preserve the *status quo*; the second might have been a Triple Monarchy by granting some form of autonomy to the South Slavs; the third possibility was a Greater Serbia, which had much support among Orthodox Christians although others feared it would fall too strongly under Russian control. The fourth solution was to realise the dream of a South Slav state, beset by so many difficulties that it seemed the least realisable.

The unfortunate secret Treaty of London (1915) that brought Italy's participation in the war on the Allied side, nearly drove the Jugoslavs back into the Habsburg camp, because it foresaw putting nearly 700 000 Croats and Slovenes on the Adriatic coast and in Istria under Italian control. By the end of 1915 the ranks of the Jugoslavs were once again closed, however, by the conquest of Serbia by combined Austrian, German and Bulgarian forces. The Declaration of Corfu (1917) betwen the Serbs and the Jugoslav Committee in Exile, favoured a union of all Serbs, Croats and Slovenes as a single nation under the Serbian crown, run as a constitutional, democratic and parliamentary monarchy. Whether the state was to be centralised or federal was left an open question.

Early in 1918 American views swung from 'autonomy' for the peoples of Austria–Hungary to an insistence on Jugoslav and Czechoslovak independence, encouraging organisation of a Jugoslav state. In December 1918 the Kingdom of Serbs, Croats and Slovenes was declared in Belgrade, by which time Montenegro had accepted incorporation into Serbia. Although there was support for a federation and even for a republic, the monarchial centralised state won the day under the pressures threatening from outside, particularly the hostility of Italy.

As the component peoples had eventually rushed headlong into the union, without any clear idea of how a Jugoslav state was to operate and without any defined contract, the future was bedevilled by frictions and tensions. The new Jugoslav state was built of small pieces—the core was Serbia and Montenegro to which were added lands inhabited largely by South Slavs that had been incorporated within Austrian and Hungarian territory, mostly on the north and north-west. Consolidation of the new state was hindered for some years by the lack of regulation of its frontiers and lengthy disputes with neighbouring states. Claims based on economic, strategic, ethnic or historical grounds had to be sorted out and whatever solution was decided invariably left dissatisfied minorities.

The settlement of the Adriatic frontier with Italy took nearly two years, with several proposals made on the Istrian frontier, but in the end all the Slav settled territory east of a line from Gemona to Trieste passed to Italy, including the Pola (Pula) naval base, a territory slightly larger than had been proposed in the Treaty of London (1915). The Fascists tried hard to Italianise Istria. Italy also received the island of Cres (Cherso) and Lastovo (Lagosta), as well as the port of Zadar (Zara). Original suggestions for a buffer state in Rijeka (Fiume) were wrecked by the Italians' seizure of the port, to which the Allies meekly submitted. In 1924 Rijeka (Fiume) was incorporated into Italy and the Jugoslavs had to be content with the suburb of Sušak as a port for the northern part of their country. In Steiermark, the frontier line ran roughly along the linguistic divide, but in Kärnten (Carinthia), the boundary was settled by an Inter-Allied Commission in Klagenfurt. As voting in the most southerly zone was solidly in favour of Austria, no vote was taken in the northern zone, suggesting that some 10 000 Slovenes had voted to remain in Austria. The line of the Karawanken mountains became the new frontier.

The border with Hungary was fixed by the Treaty of Trianon in June 1920. The Banat, except for a small Magyar triangle south of Szeged, was divided between Rumania and Jugoslavia, while Jugoslavia got the Bačka (apart from a small area around Baja) and part of the Baranja. In the north-west two small Hungarian districts, the Prekomurje and Medjumurje, also passed to Jugoslavia. In the Bačka the frontier was pushed north to include Subotica with its large Serbian population. The Jugoslavs occupied and claimed the coalmining district of Pécs, but under pressure from the Supreme Council in Paris had evacuated it in August 1921. Rumania had been promised all the Banat under a secret treaty of 1916 by which the country had entered the war on the Allied side, but the final frontier, forced through by the French, tried to equate the ethnic pattern. An important Jugoslav consideration was to gain sufficient territory to be able to protect Belgrade in depth.

Under the Treaty of Neuilly (1919), the large gains made by Serbia in the

Balkan wars were recognised and in addition some small strategic areas of Bulgarian territory were transferred to Jugoslavia, notably a small Bulgarian salient near Strumica that threatened the security of the Vardar valley railway. Albanian settlement had been spreading north-eastwards towards Pećs and Priština since the late seventeenth century, while the Turks had encouraged Albanian colonisation after 1878 in the Kosovo, Metohija and Novi Pazar districts. Although the frontier with Albania had not been determined by the time of the 1921 census, there were nearly half a million Albanians living in Jugoslavia. The frontier line was eventually fixed approximately at the alignment of 1913, though the Jugoslavs did not withdraw from some Albanian areas until 1926.

The first census of 1921 revealed the new Jugoslav state as formidably mixed in ethnic and religious terms. Of nearly twelve million people, 83 per cent spoke Serb, Croat and Slovene. There was a slight predominance of Orthodox adherents over Roman Catholics, but the country also contained over a million Moslems, mostly in Bosnia and the Albanian districts. People were essentially rural dwellers and peasants—only three towns had more than 100 000 people: Belgrade, Zagreb and Subotica. After more or less continuous warfare since 1912 conditions were chaotic and there was grave suspicion between different regional and religious interests, while the peasantry suspected the aims and interests of the townsfolk and middle classes. It is not surprising that with so much inner conflict, progress was slow and conditions deteriorated after the great depression arrived a little later in Jugoslavia than elsewhere.

Few people in any walk of life really understood the concept of Jugoslavia, but King Alexander did much to lay its foundations against great odds and even hostility from his own Serbs. There was the long standing particularism and parochialism—not surprising in a country with such diverse standards and cultural ideas. Basically, the Croats and Slovenes suspected the Serbs, who for historical reasons were still supplying a large part of the army and administration, in a belief that Serbia sought a hegemony over all the country. The Serbs, on the other hand, felt that the Croats were often disaffected, looked down on Serbs from their higher standard of living, and were still steeped in Austro–Hungarian ideas. Within the country there was a struggle between the centralists, who believed that strong central control was vital if the Jugoslav idea was to be moulded; and the federalists, who wanted large measures of autonomy so that local ways might be preserved. Though on several occasions it came perilously close to disintegration, it was really the latent hostility of Hungary and Bulgaria and the open hostility of Italy that held the country together in the fateful 1930s. At the root of so many difficulties, the cultural dichotomy between north and south was aggravated by the physical character of the country, with its bare, inhospitable Dinaric backbone, a useful refuge from persistent foes, but a divisor between the Adriatic world and the great Pannonian basin.

The large non-Jugoslav minorities lived in strategically critical peripheral areas, particularly dangerous when even the allegiance of its own South Slavs might be suspect. A constant threat to Jugoslav links with the outer world was posed by the Italian holding on the Adriatic coast and the Italian–Albanian command of the entrance to the Adriatic, a problem that became critical with the growth of Italian naval power and the idea of *Mare Nostrum* in the mid-1930s. Even the access to the Aegean via Salonika was threatened by a hostile Albania on the west and by a not particularly co-operative Bulgaria on the east—there remained the unsolved question of Macedonia, though superficially the Jugoslav–Bulgarian *rapproachment* of 1934 settled this. The same year a *Balkan Entente*, comprising Jugoslavia, Rumania, Turkey and Greece, was founded and efforts made to draw it close to the *Little Entente* of Jugoslavia, Rumania and Czechoslovakia. From 1935 Germany began increasingly to influence Jugoslav affairs through an expanding horizon of trade, which was followed by relaxation of relations with Italy.

3.1.10 Bulgaria

Bulgaria had on occasions been a great Balkan power; its nationalism was clearly defined and united, but because of its support for the Central Powers, it had been trimmed to relatively meagre dimensions and was sullen in defeat.

Under the Treaty of Neuilly (1919), Bulgaria lost small pieces of territory, as already described, to Jugoslavia; the corridor to the Aegean Sea between the Mesta and Maritsa rivers, including the useful port of Dedeagatch (Alexandrupolis), and also the territory around Adrianople (Edirne) taken in 1915; while in the north, the southern Dobrudsha was handed to Rumania. The territory surrendered to Jugoslavia contained largely Bulgarians and the surrender of the Tsaribrod and Bosilegrad areas pushed the frontier closer to the Bulgarian capital, Sofia. The Greek–Bulgarian treaty (1919) foresaw the exchange of populations to simplify the ethnic quilt and it was perhaps regrettable that such a policy was not pursued in other instances in the Balkans, because many of the discontents arose from the complex distribution of ethnic groups.

The Macedonian Problem, one of the contentions of the nineteenth century, remained latent and after 1934, apparently solved by agreement between Bulgaria and Jugoslavia. The defeat of the Bulgars in 1918 was perhaps the most important factor in its quiescence, since it had formed part of the programme for Greater Bulgaria. The geographical limits of Macedonia were as ever vague—from Lake Ohrid in the west to the Mesta river in the east; from Skopje in the north to the Bistrica river and the Aegean coast in the south. Throughout history it had never existed as a single unit, though it had been the core of a great if ephemeral empire in Classical times. In 1919 its population had been estimated at about two million, more than half Christians and the bulk of the remainder Moslem, with some Jews in the towns. Ethnically, it was extremely mixed—in harmony with its position at the meeting point of many different peoples. While little doubt could arise over the Greek, Gypsy, Albanian and Vlach elements, much debate took place over the real affinity of the Slav population, though ethnic studies revealed gentle gradations from Bulgar to Serb usages. Greek influence was everywhere strong, conveyed mainly through the church and education, notably among the more wealthy townsfolk, while after 1878 the Bulgarian Exarchat had also tried to strengthen its hold. Bulgarian claims rested upon one-time possession of the country and on the character of its peoples: Serbian claims were also based on one-time ownership but also on the deep impress in its architecture and literature. Greece could point to the Greek culture and religion in the region, especially in the towns, while Rumania had an interest in the 75 000 to 100 000 nomadic Vlachs. The Macedonians had seldom produced leaders of ability and the diverse ethnic character of the population made a common public opinion impossible. None of the proposals formulated for the country in the early twentieth century could be implemented because of wars; after 1918 the country was divided between Jugoslavia and Greece. A Macedonian Revolutionary Committee sponsored from Bulgaria tried to stir up disorder, but many Macedonians of Bulgarian sympathies emigrated to Bulgaria. In Greek Macedonia large numbers of Greeks from Turkey (300 000 townsfolk and 116 000 agricultural families) were resettled.

3.1.11 Albania

Albania emerged out of the Balkan wars, having been declared an independent state by the Council of Ambassadors in London in July 1913 following a proclamation by Albanians in Vlorë. Its limits included, however, barely half the Albanian people. An independent Albania upset the plans of the Balkan states for the division of territory after the first Balkan War and was a direct cause of the second conflict. As early as 1914 Italy had established considerable influence in Albania, which was to remain throughout the subsequent inter-war period. The population of this mountainous country was about 800 000 of whom 66 per cent were Moslem, 12 per cent Roman Catholic and 21 per cent Greek Orthodox. The smaller Christian groups had, however, a political power greater than their numbers suggested.

The boundaries suggested for Albania in 1913 had varied from very tightly drawn limits—proposed by the Balkan Allies—to very generous limits claimed by the Albanian provisional government. Nearly all were conceived in terms of international strategy rather than economic or social grounds. Further proposals were made in the secret treaty of London (1915), while in 1917 Italy declared a protectorate over Albania and began a policy of Italianisation and colonisation in southern Albania, but the Peace Conference refused recognition of the protectorate. The Italians then demanded a mandate over the country and a reserved area around Valona (Vlorë) and offered Korçë (Koritsa) to Greece and the Shkodër (Scutari) area to Jugoslavia. The Albanians took matters into their own hands, established a capital at Tiranë, and drove back the Italians who withdrew to Saseno (Sazenit) island, having realised that the coastal districts were too malarial for Italian colonisation. The League of Nations, fearful that the Albanians had not sufficient financial resources or experience of government, agreed that if self-government failed, the task of 'restoring independence' should be entrusted to Italy, a decision that no doubt gave the Albanians every encouragement to put their house in order. In mid-1920, the French withdrew from Korçë and their 'independent republic' joined the Albanian state. The Serbs held on to strong positions in the north and only powerful pressure from outside prevented them advancing on Tiranë. In 1921 the League of Nations confirmed the boundaries of 1913 and so left the Albanians of Kosovo and Metohija in Jugoslavia, but final definition of the frontier lasted until 1926 and left many people separated from their pastures and their markets. In finance and defence, Albania in the 1920s began to fall under growing Italian influence.

3.1.12 Rumania

Before the First World War, the Kingdom of Rumania embraced only those Rumanians living in Wallachia and Moldavia and in the Dobrogea (Dobrudsha), but considerable numbers also lived in Bessarabia, Transylvania and the Banat, while groups of Rumanians and related Vlachs were found south of the Danube. As a result of the settlements at Paris, a much enlarged Rumania appeared on the map and added to its territory by the seizure of Bessarabia from a weakened Russia. The population was largely rural and numbered about 16 million; of this number some 3.75 million were non-Rumanians—1.5 million Magyars and Szeklers, 400 000 Germans, 1.1 million Ukrainians and 750 000 Jews. The Rumanians enjoyed cultural and national solidarity centred around the Romance tradition in the language that brought Rumania much under French and Italian influence in the inter-war years. They were, however, predominantly Byzantine Christians.

Having joined the Allied powers in 1916, the Allies were ready to agree to Rumanian acquisition of all territory where there was a substantial Rumanian minority. The largest territorial acquisition lay west of the Carpathians in Transylvania, a rolling hill country barred on the west by the forested Bihor Massif, that gravitated towards the Pannonian Plains rather than across the Carpathians ranges towards the Old Kingdom. Central Transylvania contained a large Magyar minority, including the Szeklers, ancient frontiersmen whose task had been to guard the approaches to Hungary. There were also considerable colonies of Germans. Of a Transylvanian population of 2.7 million, about half were Rumanians. In the north were some Ukrainian and Slovak colonies and everywhere in the towns there were Jews.

In the north Rumania gained the Bukovina (10 250 km²), a former crown province of Austria. Of its population of 800 000, about 275 000 were Rumanians and other elements were Ukrainians (300 000) and Germans (170 000). Bukovina west of the Czeremosz river went to Poland, because of its important railway link in the security of south-east Poland. It was a rich territory but suffered from serious rural overpopulation and was thus poor. In the east the land between the Prut and the Dnestr, Bessarabia, had a population of 2.7 million, with Rumanians comprising one million, Ukrainians 900 000, numerous German colonists and a considerable Jewish population. The Rumanians were mainly in the north, while the bare, open and marshy plains near the Danube mouth were mostly peopled by Ukrainians and Tatars. The Rumanians claimed that when Bessarabia was taken by Russia from Turkey in 1812, its population was predominantly Rumanian and had been subjected to Russification and colonisation by Ukrainians. The Rumanian Bessarabians were commonly described by the Russians as Moldavians, claimed to be culturally distinct from Rumanians. For a time in 1918 Bessarabia established its autonomy, but had been occupied by Rumanian troops following a resolution of its Diet for representation in Rumania. The Rumanian claim *de jure* was never recognised by Russia. The Soviet Union organised on its bank of the Dnestr a Moldavian Soviet Republic in 1924. Because of Rumanian fear that the U.S.S.R. might use force to retake Bessarabia, treaty obligations were entered into with Poland and France.

The southern border in general followed the line of the Danube, except in the east, where Rumania held the ethnically diverse Dobrogea, including the southern part with a predominantly Bulgarian population. Since the Dobrogea had passed to Rumania in 1878 there had been a continuous colonisation by Rumanian peasants at the expense of other peoples, who had had to pay for land left them after expropriations. In the south-west Rumania had an interest in the Banat where there were also Jugoslav and Hungarian interests. It seemed at the peace conference impracticable to assign the whole Banat to any one of the powers and yet to separate it ethnically would disorganise its commercial life; nevertheless, separation was agreed, though agreements between Rumania and Jugoslavia were made to maintain and develop the irrigation canals.

A short-lived Bolshevik regime in Hungary tried to grab back Transylvania in the hope of establishing direct contact with the Soviet Union. The Rumanians retaliated by driving back the Hungarians to Budapest and then, according to the Hungarians, looting their occupied territory in compensation; but the Rumanians regarded this a justifiable reward for saving Central Europe from a Bolshevik *coup*.

Internally, the Rumanians had a major task of economic development and solution of a long-standing problem of land ownership that had held the peasants as virtual slaves. In some ways Rumania's internal problem bore some relation to the Jugoslav situation, because it had to overcome the divisive effects of topography. Transylvania looked to the middle Danube basin, but Wallachia and Moldavia looked to the lower-most Danube and to the Black Sea. While the great bow of the Eastern Carpathians was a valuable 'fortress' into which the Rumanians had commonly sought refuge from invaders, it did pose a serious problem of contact and mobility. The question of defence made Rumania a keen member of the Little Entente and encouraged the development of strategic railway links with friendly neighbours such as Poland and Czechoslovakia.

3.1.13 The Simmering Pot Boils Over

The settlements made after 1918, whether by negotiation or force, left vast discontent. The rise of powerful dictatorial regimes in Italy and Germany, clamouring for 'rectification', set an explosive chain alight, while reluctance of the other great powers to act decisively and of the League of Nations to do more than declare ineffectual 'sanctions', encouraged demands to grow. The opening was the *Anschluss* between Germany and Austria—which Austria had sought after 1918 but by 1938 was less enthusiastic to complete with the National Socialists. Throughout the mid-1930s the Germans had been building up influence and political relationships wherever possible in Eastern Europe through the medium of trade, which countries were glad to accept in an atmosphere of general depression, especially as the Germans were often prepared to pay above the general world price level.

The demand for the secession by Czechoslovakia of the German minority areas (a territory larger than the common use of *Sudetenland* warranted) revealed German intents. It had been clear after about 1935 that Czechoslovakia had failed to win the allegiance of its German minority, with influence from Berlin growing steadily. Direct action against Czechoslovakia had to be avoided by the Germans, since the Czechoslovaks had guarantees of security from the

French and the Soviet Union, later joined indirectly by the British. They were also quite well prepared themselves and an armed conflict could have involved the yet unperfected *Wehrmacht* in a nasty clash. A demand to set up a virtually autonomous German province within the Czech state made in 1938 was rejected by Prague and an armed conflict seemed imminent. The Czechoslovak government was persuaded by Britain to give the necessary concessions to the German minority, but these were rejected by the Germans, who now insisted that the *Sudetenland* must be surrendered to Germany on the basis of self-determination. Britain and France, unprepared for war, made a determined effort to avoid conflict by edging the Czechs into acceptance.

In the autumn of 1938 German forces moved into the German minority districts around the borders of Bohemia and Moravia, though the line of demarcation was not strictly according to ethnic principles. Shortly after the Germans agreed to Hungary taking its minority districts in southern Slovakia, while the Poles seized Teschen. Some 2.8 million Germans were incorporated in the *Reich* as well as the larger part of Czechoslovak industry, besides complete disruption of railway and other communications. The final blow came with the establishment of a protectorate over Bohemia–Moravia in March 1939, and the confirmation of the autonomy granted to Slovakia in October 1938, as full independence. The Carpathian–Ukraine (autonomous since October 1938) was occupied by Hungary in March 1939.

In early 1939 German propaganda switched to the long-debated concept of *Lebensraum*. The Germans were *Volk ohne Raum* but in parts of Eastern Europe there was an immense extent of *Raum ohne Volk*. Relations worsening for years with Poland rapidly deteriorated, so that it was clearly the next victim. German demands included the incorporation into the *Reich* of Danzig and the abolition of the Polish Corridor. Attempts to get effective German–Polish negotiations failed, possibly because the Germans sensed the Western powers would not go to war. After events in Czechoslovakia, British and French guarantees to Poland sounded rather hollow. The German position was greatly strengthened in the summer of 1939 by the signing of a non-aggression pact with the Soviet Union after the British and French had failed to win Soviet support. On 1st September, 1939, the German armies moved into Poland and little more than a fortnight later the Russians entered Eastern Poland. By the end of the month the war in Poland was over, though fighting continued into October. Most of western Poland, west of a line from Warsaw through Łódź to Kraków, was incorporated into Germany, while the country around Suwałki was incorporated into East Prussia. The area around Warsaw as far as the river Bug and then across to the upper San was made into the Government-General of Poland under German administration. East of the Bug and San, Polish territory was taken into the Soviet Union.

Italy seized Albania in the spring of 1939 but had declared neutrality at the outbreak of war. By 1940 the war had switched to the Balkans where the Rumanians were in a particularly vulnerable position. The Soviet Union occupied Bessarabia and north Bukovina, while the Germans forced the surrender of the southern Dobrudsha to Bulgaria and the return of northern Transylvania to Hungary. Pressure was applied throughout the Balkans to drive countries into the Axis camp: Rumania, Slovakia and Hungary agreed, while Bulgaria and

Jugoslavia were undecided at what point to surrender. Greece did not respond and the Italians attempted unsuccessfully to take the Greeks by force. In 1941 Bulgaria joined the German camp, while Jugoslavia—under massive pressure—also succumbed but popular pressure forced repudiation of the agreement and precipitated a successful German attack. By spring, 1941 the Balkans had been reduced and a territorial carve-up followed. Parts of Slovenia in Austria before 1914 were taken into the *Reich*, while southern Slovenia and territory along the Dalmatian coast were annexed by Italy, which also controlled Montenegro. Albania was enlarged by territory in the north and north-east. Macedonia was taken by Bulgaria, which detached Thrace from Greece. Hungary annexed the Prekomurje, Bačka and Baranja, but had a dispute with the newly created Kingdom of Croatia (Croatia, Bosnia and Hercegovina) over the Medjumurje. Within particularly tight frontiers, Serbia was made a puppet state by the Germans, who also controlled the Banat.

The declaration of *Grossdeutschland* in 1942 made much of Central Europe an integral part of the Third Reich. The success of the attack on the Soviet Union, made in June 1941, had been marked by the rapid retreat into the interior of the Red Army, which had left a wake of its 'scorched earth' policy. The *Wehrmacht* had been lured into the immensity of Russia, where its strategic and logistic problems multiplied, without the critical decisive victory before Smolensk, 'Gateway to Moscow'. Though the Germans had probably come nearer to victory than Napoleon, their fortunes began to ebb after the summer of 1942.

Early in 1943 the *Wehrmacht* began a slow retreat from Russia after failing to take the strategic key of Stalingrad. By mid-1944 the Red Army had crossed the pre-war Soviet borders on two fronts—the northern, where resistance on the direct route into the *Reich* was stiffer, and the southern, following ancient routes through Wallachia and Pannonia. During 1944 Rumania had been virtually taken and Bulgaria 'liberated', forcing the Germans to pull out of Greece, while Serbia and Montenegro were held by local partisans or Red Army units. The Soviet forces had cleared almost half of Hungary, though Budapest remained beleaguered. In the north tough fighting brought the Red Army to the Vistula by late 1944, though most of East Prussia was still German-held. In early 1945 Soviet armies took Slovakia and western Hungary, and in May, with Berlin beleaguered, Germany capitulated. Bohemia and eastern Austria and part of Slovenia were still in German hands. Western armies held some territory later to pass under Soviet control, for the British had advanced deep into Mecklenburg and the Americans had reached the Elbe at Torgau in Saxony and had moved into Czechoslovakia, but this did not compensate for the Soviet victory in capturing Berlin and Vienna.

There had been considerable divergence of British and American opinion on strategy in the closing stages of the war. The British reflected Clausewitz's dictum that war is a continuation of policy by other means, whereas the Americans saw war and politics as separate. The British had pressed for operations in the Balkans with Turkish involvement on the Allied side, or for operations in the Baltic. The Americans preferred to concentrate efforts in Western Europe for a hard knockout blow. The Russians were clearly in favour of the American view, not so much because it might shorten the war but because it left them a free hand in Eastern Europe. Roosevelt believed the United Nations Organisation would make spheres of influence and regional balances of power superfluous. Consequently, he left the Russians more than enough room in which to develop those very mechanisms, about whose continuing validity they—like Churchill—had no doubt.

Chester Wilmot points out that 'the prospect of a Russian advance deep into Central and South-Eastern Europe dismayed Churchill, and was one of the main reasons for his unflagging advocacy of those Balkan operations which Roosevelt . . . so persistently vetoed'. Without American knowledge Churchill proposed to the Russians that the 'controlling interest' in Rumania and Bulgaria should be exercised by the Soviet Union, and in Greece and Jugoslavia by Britain. If America had had its way, even Greece would have been surrendered to the Soviet sphere of influence. Roosevelt never seemed to see any imperial dreams in Stalin's attitude and failed to take the many rebuffs he got as evidence of true Soviet aims.

3.2 An even newer Europe: Aftermath of The Second World War

3.2.1 Territorial Change

Whereas after the First World War, new nations based on principles of nationality had arisen from the ruins of collapsed dynastic empires, the changes after the Second World War concerned the form and organisation of society and government. The free hand established by the Soviet Union opened the way to sovietisation of the states and their interrelations on the principles of Marxist–Leninism.

3.2.2 Germany

Various solutions of the German problem had been canvassed during the war—from plans to reduce Germany to a pastoral country to less severe solutions to carve it into a number of petty states. It was agreed that 'unconditional surrender' was to be followed by a long military occupation, strict payment of reparations from existing installations and German assets abroad, as well as territorial concessions, notably to Poland, the Soviet Union and France. Ethnic German population outside Germany was to be repatriated. With no German government after the capitulation, the country was put under four-power military government and for military and administrative convenience, divided into four zones of occupation—British, American, Russian and, after the Potsdam Agreements, French. In theory at least Germany was to be treated as an economic unit.

The occupation zones, formed along the boundaries between units of local government, comprised groups of the new *Länder* (states) on which an ultimate federal structure was to be built. The Soviet occupation zone, therefore, was composed of the Land Mecklenburg in the north, composed of the old states of Mecklenburg–Schwerin and Mecklenburg–Strelitz (united since 1934), and part of Pommern west of the Oder. The central part was formed by Land Brandenburg, a former Prussian province and the Land Sachsen–Anhalt, comprising the Prussian province of Sachsen and the former Anhalt state, while in the south-west lay Land Thüringen, an amalgamation of many small territories made in 1920. In the south the old state of Sachsen was enlarged slightly by addition of Silesia west of the Görlitzer Neisse. Stettin and some surrounding territory on the west bank of the Oder estuary passed to Poland, and the new Polish frontier then ran south along the Oder and the western or Görlitzer Neisse. The western boundary with the British occupation zone was modified slightly from previous local government boundaries to simplify definition. Berlin, former *Reich* capital, was divided into four occupation sectors administered by a four-power *Kommandatura*. Somewhat vague agreements existed over the right of access by land by the British, American and French armed forces and authorities to their sectors from the west.

The early intentions to regard the country as a whole quickly began to fail as relations between the Western powers and the Soviet Union deteriorated. Whereas in the British and American zones, the emphasis was on close co-operation, the Soviet authorities increasingly followed their own line. Although in the early stages the Soviets appear to have been ready to work for the economic management of Germany on a unified basis, the French opposed such action, perhaps discouraging the Soviet authorities from their early co-operativeness. During 1946 and 1947 the four-power Council of Foreign Ministers discussed a settlement in Germany, with the main disagreements in the economic field and on the form of the future German state. The general Western view was a decentralised, federal state, while the Soviets wanted a centralised state, with the major powers' right to veto any unacceptable development. There was also no agreement on what form of peace treaty should be concluded with Germany, once it had its own representative government. In late 1947 these negotiations finally broke down, followed by a breakdown in four-power government, marked by a clear division between the Soviet zone and the three Western zones as well as the growing isolation of the Western sectors of Berlin.

The Western powers decided to concentrate their efforts on the economic and political rehabilitation of their own zones of occupation, as far as possible without prejudice to a future peace settlement. Raising of the levels of industry, the currency reform of 1948 and the impact of Marshall Aid were accompanied by emergence of German organs of higher administration and by autumn 1949, the German Federal Republic had emerged under Western guidance. These events were used by the Soviet authorities to isolate their zone further and to try to force the Western powers out of their sectors of Berlin by a ruthless blockade for over a year, when a airlift to the beleaguered city on a scale unknown before won for the Western powers a major prestige victory.

The creation of a West German state was paralleled by the formation of a Soviet-sponsored German Democratic Republic modelled on the People's Democracies then evolving in Soviet-dominated Eastern Europe. The new Democratic Republic had a population in 1946 of 18.5 million—compared to 16.7 million on the same territory in 1939. Probably about 25 per cent of these people were refugees from former German territories east of the Oder–Neisse or from German ethnic groups elsewhere in Europe. It had, however, been carved out of a much larger organism and its territory had never been conceived as supporting an independent nation-state, in which one part of the German people now found themselves.

For the Red Army it was strategically valuable—large garrisons could live more easily off the defeated Germans than the liberated Poles or Czechs. It gave an important western salient: from the south-west, a forward position in Thüringen could threaten the middle Rhine, while in the north, western Mecklenburg lay only 50 km from Hamburg and a threat could be posed to the narrow entrances to the Baltic. Soviet garrisons in central Germany and in eastern Austria covered the flanks of Czechoslovakia.

3.2.3 Poland

Poland was affected by a major territorial shift westwards that substantially altered the whole nature of the country. The Allies had agreed that Poland should be cómpensated territorially at the expense of Germany, but the early views of small modifications to give Poland better access to the sea and a larger share of the potentially rich Silesian lands quickly grew, inspite of Churchill's warning that 'it would be a pity to stuff the Polish goose so full of German food that it got indigestion'. The problem of Poland's territory was viewed not only from the country's immediate interests but also in the context of permanently weakening Germany. In the debates the Russians generally showed a much sharper view of the political geography of eastern Europe than the Western statesmen. The Poles in London and Washington remained throughout the negotiations firmly opposed to the surrender of any of their 1938 territory east of the Curzon Line, whereas the Soviets made plain their demand for German Königsberg and the Polish lands east of the Curzon Line. In the Soviet view Poland's future was not just a matter of Russian honour but also of Russian security.

The new Poland shifted bodily westwards by the western addition of German territory and the amputation of its prewar lands east of the Curzon Line, had been reduced from 388 600 km^2 in 1938 to 312 700 km^2 in 1946, but its coastline had increased from 140 km to 694 km. Its western boundary lay from the western bank of the Oder at Stettin (Szczecin) upstream and along the western—Görlitzer–Neisse to the Czech border at Zittau. The eastern border followed the general alignment suggested 30 years earlier by Lord Curzon, though on the south it lay just east of Przemyśl, leaving Lwów in Soviet hands and in the north, merged with the arbitrarily drawn border straight across former German East Prussia, so that the south around Allenstein (Olsztyn) was in Poland. The Free City of Danzig (Gdańsk) also passed to Poland but the border with Czechoslovakia returned to its 1937 position. The Soviet Union had vigorously opposed an American attempt to claim Lwów for Poland, because the Russians claimed it was ethnically and historically Ukrainian. Soviet interest in German East Prussia was in its valuable naval ports and in the valuable Amber Coast: the territory became a detached portion of the Russian Republic, while Wilno (Vilnyus) was incorporated into the Lithuanian S.S.R.

The German lands taken by Poland were 'under Polish jurisdiction until such time as a final German peace treaty should define their ownership'. This uncertain legal status caused veiled remarks about the future to be made on both sides, but the Poles set about integrating them fully into their state. The German population had fled before the Red Army or had been later expelled, so that a massive Polish resettlement began, many coming from former Polish territories taken by the Soviet Union.

Although the population of Poland had fallen from 34.6 million in 1938 to 23.7 million in 1946, it was a far less ethnically diverse state: in 1938 only 69 per cent of the population were ethnically Polish, and east of the Curzon Line only a quarter of the population had been indisputably ethnically Polish. To absorb the Germans who had neither fled nor been expelled, notably in Upper Silesia where allegiances were more complex, a new concept of 'autochthonous' population was created. This designation covers most of the 800 000 Germans believed to have remained in the 'recovered territories', the German population of which had been estimated at 8.6 million in 1938.

The new Poland was economically a potentially stronger state than pre-war and now had resources to rival Czechoslovakia as the industrial focus of East Central Europe.

3.2.4 Czechoslovakia and Hungary

Territorial change in Czechoslovakia was the surrender of the Carpathian–Ukraine, because of its strategic importance as a foothold on the Pannonian Plains, to the Soviet Union. Elsewhere Czechoslovakia returned to its boundaries of 1937, except for a slight favourable modification opposite Bratislava. It seized the opportunities presented to get rid of its unwanted minorities. The Ukrainian (Ruthenian) element had already been lost to the Soviet Union, while expulsion reduced the number of Germans from 3.3 million in 1930 to 165 000 in 1950 (from 23.6 per cent of the total population in 1930 to 1.3 per cent in 1950). Magyars fell from 596 861 (4.3 per cent) in 1930 to 367 733 (3.0 per cent) in 1950. The Czech and Slovak population, 69.4 per cent of the total in 1930, comprised 94.2 per cent in 1950.

Hungary returned to its 1938 boundaries, since it withdrew from gains made immediately pre-war and during the war years. Although the Hungarians lost their German minority, they were forced to receive displaced Magyars, notably from southern Slovakia and from Transylvania.

3.2.5 The Balkans

Bulgaria returned to its prewar boundaries, but retained the southern Dobrudsha, while Rumania again took possession of northern Transylvania lost to Hungary under the Vienna award (1941), although it did not regain Bessarabia which remained in the Soviet Union as did northern Bukovina. Albania re-emerged in its pre-war boundaries, though it appeared in the immediate post-war years that it might become a satellite of Jugoslavia. Considering the strategic importance of Albania in covering the entrance to the Adriatic, it seems surprising that the Soviet Union was prepared to make such a concession.

Jugoslavia returned in general to its 1938 boundaries, but it tried to reopen the question of the Klagenfurt area with the Allies, though inspite of a considerable propaganda barrage, no move was made to meet Jugoslav wishes. Indeed, the deteriorating relations between the Western Allies and the Soviet authorities marked a hardening in attitude towards the Jugoslav case. Jugoslavia did, however, retain all the Italian holdings on the Adriatic coast, but a dispute with Italy developed over Trieste, the major northern Adriatic port for both Jugoslavia and Italy, as well as Austria (two-thirds of its trade in the 1950s). North of Trieste, the Italo–Jugoslav boundary was aligned so that some Slovene areas remained in Italy, including the disputed town of Gorizia. A final settlement was not reached until 1954, when a small strip of territory around Trieste linking it to Italy remained in Italian hands, while the rest of Istria, predominantly Slovene, including an area south of Trieste originally in dispute, passed to Jugoslavia.

3.2.6 People's Democracies in Eastern Europe

In 1939 few people imagined that the war would end with the emergence of a politically strong Soviet Union on the threshold of great economic power: equally unexpected in the early years of the war was that this new colossus would win a dominant position across Eastern Europe. Only a most far-sighted clairvoyant could have imagined that the century-old concept of *Mitteleuropa* would be split down the middle and reduced to a zone of confrontation between two opposed ideological camps. Red Army troops were only an outside sign of the great changes that Marxist–Leninist ideas brought by Soviet advisers and Moscow-trained 'native' Communists were to make. The simplification of the ethnic map and the relatively limited territorial changes hid far deeper and fundamental changes in the society, political organisation and economy of Eastern Europe than the more cataclysmic territorial changes after the First World War. These lands had been tied closely to the Third *Reich* for its own economic aggrandisement and the German war effort had left them impoverished, while the Germans had behaved clumsily in their relations with the Slavs, so that the Russians appeared as liberators, if not very attractive ones. In several countries the right and middle wings in politics had compromised with the Germans in an attempt to maintain some freedom, while the left of all shades had been ruthlessly hunted down, and commonly the more educated and articulate groups had suffered elimination, so that local leadership of society was weakend. The carefully schooled East European Communists who had sought Soviet asylum before the war now came into their own.

In Jugoslavia the Communists under local leadership—particularly Tito—had already established themselves through the partisan movement. It was therefore harder for the Soviet authorities to infiltrate, since the Jugoslavs had their own established usages and their own undisputed leader. In Czechoslovakia the Communists also enjoyed respectability, since the party had taken an open and active part in the inter-war democratic government, while democratic, parliamentary government was quickly re-established and the Communists were ultimately forced to gain supreme control by a *coup d'etat* in 1948. In the Third *Reich* Communists had been efficiently 'eradicated': the Soviet authorities quickly introduced Moscow-trained German Communists, (*Gruppe Ulbricht*) plus new recruits from the prisoner-of-war camps. The liquidation of the pre-war Polish Communist party left only a weak organisation dependent on Moscow-trained Poles who moved in with the Red Army to set up the Lublin National Committee before Polish politicians in Western Europe could get home. The Bulgarian party used to illegality, violence and clandestine operations, was hardly fitted for government and intially needed support from a large Soviet pro-consular reticule. In Rumania the Communists struggled for power until late 1947, when the king was finally deposed.

The final step in the building of a reasonably reliable Soviet Imperium was the creation of the idea of a people's democracy, conceived by Marxist–Leninist theorists. In 1954 the Great Soviet Encyclopedia stated that 'the experience of history has shown that the system of People's Democracy successfully fulfils the aims of the dictatorship of the proletariat, even when there exist several parties and social and political organisations, on the one indisputable condition that the only leading and directing force of all political life is the Communist Party, which does not and cannot share leadership with anyone'. In many ways the new state organism fits the wishes of the people in principle if not in detail, since few would wish to return to a great many of the ways and systems operative before 1939.

From an early date polycentrism began to develop, for with such a varied cultural, historical and economic background it was not surprising that national elements began to enter into the interpretation of Communist ideology. As early as 1947 the Bulgarians had made it clear that inspite of their long friendship with the Russians, they did not wish to become an integrated Soviet republic but to follow their own course as a people's democracy, so remaining a 'free and in-dependent state with its own national and state sovereignty'. A little later, Poland announced its rejection of agricultural collectives because its democracy was not similar to Soviet democracy, just as it claimed to be a society structured different-ly to the Soviet system. Such independent and nationally-oriented statements ran contrary to Soviet hopes that the new people's democracies would become vir-tually union republics within a broader Soviet framework.

By 1948 it had become apparent to the Soviet Union that the new satellites were following all too independent lines of development and were even con-templating their own political groupings, such as a union between Jugoslavia and Bulgaria (even perhaps with Rumania), which even though it might have been true to Communism in content and philosophy, was unacceptable to Moscow, because new policies in Western Europe were making the further expansion of Soviet influence in Europe increasingly unlikely. There followed a purge of all un-reliable elements in the Communist party leadership in the new people's democracies, resulting in the expulsion of the Jugoslavs from the 'fraternal fami-ly of Communist parties'.

The process of Sovietisation—agricultural collectivisation and industrialisa-tion and new territorial-administrative systems—was accelerated and economic plans were co-ordinated with the Soviet plans. From 1948 to the latter part of the 1950s the period of the 'Cold War', relations between the Soviet Union and the Western powers were at a low ebb. The 'iron curtain' kept the Soviet satellites effectively isolated from developments in Western Europe and during the lifetime of Stalin, they were under strong pressure to contribute to Soviet economic reconstruction at the cost of improvements to their own living standards. After the death of Stalin a more conciliatory line was taken and the countries were given a greater measure of decision over their own doings.

A crisis arose in the late 1950s through Khrushchev's liberalisation policy and the 'debunking' of Stalin. As the rigorous centralisation policy was eased, *Comecon* (chapter 8) began to appear as more than mere Soviet *bloc* window-dressing. Many observers had seen the initial role of *Comecon* as a means of isolating Eastern Europe and particularly of ostracising Jugoslavia. Up to Stalin's death economic development in the satellite countries had been based on self-sufficiency and limited trade with the Soviet Union: after his death the emphasis changed and the countries began to trade more with each other. Nevertheless, Marxist theory was against supranationalism and continued to respect 'national economies and sovereignty', no doubt arising from Lenin's views on the 'national question' within Russia. Such an interpretation was a safeguard against the formation of multinational and regional coalitions and associations, which might challenge Soviet authority or make it more difficult to play one country off against another. Because these moves towards decentralisation and the easing of the Soviet grip did not move particularly fast, pressures developed in some countries, spilling over into disorder and revolution—notably in Poland and Hungary—with a necessity to reinforce and emphasise the continued Soviet presence.

The political geography of the Socialist *bloc* countries of Eastern Europe emerged in the mid-1960s, transformed into people's democracies but preserving their national iconography, though classical Marxist theory held that nationalism would ultimately wither away. In the meantime, however, the deep-rooted nature of nationalism and nation states had to be faced, to which a new concept of 'Socialist' nationality was applied, being referred to in a number of new constitutions. Concepts put forward by Stalin in his 'Marxism and the National Question' were still used, though no longer credited to him. Nations were, according to those ideas, historically conditioned and stable communities of people evolved on the basis of community of language, territory, economic life and culture. The new nationality would arise from the old bourgeoise nationality as a result of the collapse of capitalism and would be transformed to the new spirit of Socialism and ultimately true Communism. Such a proposition made it possible to retain the old nation states and to accept national iconography, whose abandonment might otherwise have serious repercussions on the stability of society. Consequently, national Communist parties often continued to support policies opposed by Communist parties in adjacent countries, though such division helped the Soviet Union maintain its supremacy. Such divergencies were tolerated until one or other party was called to adopt the policy decided by Moscow—in fact, absolute loyalty to the Soviet Union as the Socialist fatherland remains the basis of so-called 'Socialist nationalism'.

3.2.7 Germany

The Soviet-held part of Germany had been promoted to a carefully steered satellite in the 1950s, following the need to have a counterpoise to the West German Federal Republic. In the 1960s the German Democratic Republic became a fully-fledged people's democracy and in 1968 received a new constitution for 'a Socialist state of the German Nation'. The German Democratic Republic, for long not recognised by the Western powers, has had its international status questioned by many legal arguments, not least the assertion that the West German state is the legal inheritor of the continuity of the German *Reich*. Both German states have sought to avoid any action which would clearly, in the eyes of international law, split the German people into two nations, though effective separation for twenty-five years has created many subtle differences.

Under four-power government Germany had been divided into large states (*Länder*), envisaged as members of an ultimate Confederation (figure 3.3). As effective centralisation of the German Democratic Republic developed, these no longer fitted the needs of the new state, whose territorial-administrative structure was brought into line with other 'people's democracies' by replacing the *Länder* with fifteen *Bezirke* modelled on the Soviet *oblast*. Measures such as these confirmed people's worst fears and the more Soviet ideas were introduced, the stronger became the flight of people to West Germany, particularly from the younger, more economically and demographically productive age groups. So bad had the flight become that in 1961 an end was put to *Republikflucht* by the building of the Berlin Wall and other restrictive measures. Population fell from a maximum of 19.1 million in 1948 to 16.9 million in 1964, with little recovery since. Economic questions have dominated the eastern republic's life—the building of a more balanced economy from the wreckage of the Third *Reich*, the vicious reparations policy of the early occupation period, and such critical difficulties as water supply for the large chemicals industry. Nevertheless, its

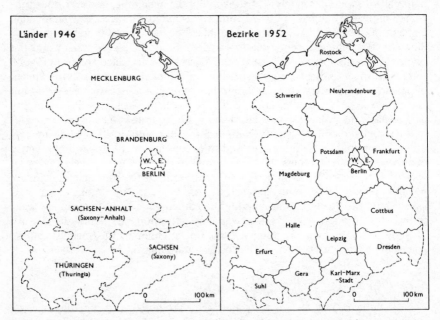

Figure 3.3. The changes in the territorial–administrative structure of the German Democratic Republic reflect the wide reorganisation that has taken place in Eastern Europe. The historically conditioned Länder created in 1945 as possible units for a larger German Confederation were replaced in 1952 by Bezirke modelled on Soviet criteria.

comparatively sophisticated industrial structure compared to the other satellite countries has given it an importance as great as its strategic and political role.

The unhappy history of German–Slav relations over a long period put the German Democratic Republic in a special position among the predominantly Slav satellites in East Europe, which emphasised the country's one minority group—the Slav-speaking Sorb population of Lusatia. Sorbian and German everyday life and culture have been closely linked since later mediaeval times, so that the distinction has become a primarily linguistic one, though monoglot Sorbs have been unknown since the eighteenth century. The number of Sorbs is uncertain—attempts were made after the Second World War to inflate it to over 100 000. The 1946 census claimed 32 000; in 1957 the homeland organisation *Domowina* claimed 38 000, though some authorities have put the figure in the 1960s as low as 25 000. For a long period Sorbs and Germans have lived peacefully side by side, while Sorbian organisations developed under German influence, particularly under the philosophical ideas of Herder and the romantic revival of the mid-nineteenth century. Under the Nazi 'racial' policy, attempts were made to disprove the Slavonic origin of the Sorbs. Sorbian nationalism was seldom forceful and mostly generated by slavophile groups in Prague—the Czechs had tried to establish an autonomous Sorbian republic in 1919 and pressed for the same again after the Second World War. Application of Soviet ideas on the nationality question introduced a subtle 'reslavification' and a need to recognise 'nationality' on the basis of the Soviet-style multi-national state. Some Marxist theorists have called for the assimilation of the Sorbs into the German community on the basis of the withering of nationality under Communism, but others have dismissed this as contrary to the view of the resistance of language and consequently national feeling against forcible assimilation. The law passed by the Saxon *Landtag* in March 1948, to guarantee the rights of the Sorbs to their own culture was later extended to Brandenburg and to the national constitution. Undertones of Pan-Slavism, though never overtly referred to, have been rejected as contrary to classical Marxism. An attempt in 1952 to create a separate Sorbian *Bezirke* was opposed by the Sorbs, so that their 'national district' is now divided between the *Bezirke* Cottbus and Bautzen. It suffers from the problem seen in the national districts in the Soviet Union: immigration of outsiders with industrial expansion and emigration of local people in search of better opportunities elsewhere. The development of the Lusation lignite fields poses a real threat to the survival of the Sorbs.

Political pressure brought to bear by the Soviet Union led in 1950 to an agreement being signed between the German Democratic Republic and Poland to establish the Oder–Neisse line as an internationally recognised frontier and an 'immutable frontier of peace and friendship'. The West German government constantly restated its view that the frontiers of Germany should only be fixed by a final German peace treaty with a united Germany, but in 1970 a treaty between West Germany and Poland recognised the Oder–Neisse border and described both states as having no territorial claims against the other.

Berlin has remained a constant problem for the German Democratic Republic, with West Berlin entirely isolated by the 'Wall' built round it in 1961, though in the early 1970s some relaxation of the tension has been achieved. In the late 1950s Khrushchev suggested that the Western powers should withdraw from West Berlin and the Soviet Union would hand over East Berlin to the German Democratic Republic, followed by proposals for a German Confederation, in which Berlin would become a 'demilitarised free city'. These proposals were rejected by the Western powers. Early in 1959 the Soviet Union proposed a draft peace treaty with Germany and threatened to go ahead with this even if the Western powers did not join the suggested talks. Ultimately, a foreign ministers' conference was agreed and the immediate danger of a confrontation receded, but negotiations failed to find agreement on how free elections could be guaranteed from outside interference and on what degree of German participation there should be in the process of reunification, besides the questions of giving the Germans security after the peace treaty. A main Western proposal was to start German reunification by reunifying Berlin, but on how this should be done no agreement was reached. The negotiations were continued through 1960 and 1961 with virtually no progress. After the building of the Berlin Wall, relations between East and West deteriorated and remained at a low ebb until the new West German *Ostpolitik* at the end of the 1960s. The agreement on Berlin between the Western powers and the Soviet Union in December 1970 secured transit from the German Federal Republic to West Berlin by land against interference, but West Berlin remained as before not a constituent part of the Federal Republic. It was also agreed to ease movement between West Berlin and areas bordering on it, while the possibility of an exchange of territory to eliminate unworkable exclaves was also considered.

3.2.8 Poland

The emergence of the German Democratic Republic as an independent state within the Soviet empire gave Poland a neighbour on equal terms instead of a military occupation zone. In one way the Poles wished to reduce their dependence on the Soviet Union and yet in other ways, this was impossible. First, it might have swung the Russians in favour of the German Democratic Republic; second, it might have left Poland without a strong guardian against German resurgence; and third, by all indications, Soviet intentions were not to loosen the grip on Poland without a struggle to Poland's disadvantage. A small comfort was the 1950 agreement with the German Democratic Republic on the delimitation of Poland's western frontier, but no concessions could be wrung from the West Germans, while the Western powers kept a somewhat ambivalent attitude towards Poland. For nearly a decade the Soviet authorities had treated Poland almost as a colonial possession: 'Muscovite' Polish Communists, more dedicated to Moscow than to Warsaw, ran the country, while the armed forces were commanded by a Soviet general of Polish origin. Living conditions deteriorated rather than improved and contributed to revolts that preceded a major change of government in 1956—the New Course—when the skill of Polish leadership gave the Soviet Union no pretext to act directly against it, while there was an important improvement in the relations between the state and the Roman Catholic church.

The promise of the New Course was not maintained and Poland slowly lapsed back into economic difficulties and even to supporting the Soviet Union against more adventuresome and progressive elements in Eastern Europe. Some relaxation of tension over the western frontier was brought by the agreement signed with the German Federal Republic in 1970, which at last codified West German acknowledgement of the Oder–Neisse line. It also proposed to ease relations between the two countries, notably in trade and the repatriation of the remaining Germans back to Germany (though some ambiguity appears to have arisen over the definition of 'Germans' in this last issue).

3.2.9 Czechoslovakia

The 1950s in Czechoslovakia were occupied by training a new labour force and trying to get industry back into full production after the loss of the Germans. Although Czechoslovakia's standards were generally higher than the other Eastern Euopean countries, the quality of living improved little and dissatisfaction and social malaise spread. From the early 1960s the growing economic achievement of the German Democratic Republic began to give concern, particularly as the Czechs found it hard to revitalise their flagging economy. The Stalinist interpretation of Communist dogma that had influenced the Czechs longer than most other East European countries, fell into increasing disrepute and a new liberalising movement began to appear. Unfortunately, by the later 1960s the Czech reformers began to liberalise too fast for Soviet liking, with the fear that the move to a Western-type market economy might encourage other Eastern European countries to open themselves to strong Western influence. When the Czech reformers failed to heed a Soviet demand to slow the pace and alter the course, the Red Army occupied the country in the late summer of 1968, and in the subsequent reforms, a federal state of Bohemia–Moravia and Slovakia was created in 1969, but this was emasculated by the return to centralised planning of the economy.

3.2.10 Hungary

After the riots of 1956, Hungary settled down to revitalise its economy and at the same time to prevent overpopulation by limiting natural increase after the 1960s. Internal problems arising from economic and demographic geography have kept the Hungarians occupied, though they have shown a high degree of co-operation in the economic field with other Eastern European countries, notably the German Democratic Republic and Poland, but relations with Rumania have been perhaps more cordial than might otherwise have been expected from their earlier history. The Red Army, generally less in evidence, has kept a careful watch from its garrisons in the country and from its commanding position on the southern edge of the Carpathians.

3.2.11 Rumania

Until the early 1960s Rumania remained a model of orthodox Stalinism and subsequently Khrushchevism, because the Rumanian leaders owed much to Soviet support and tutorship and consequently showed their gratitude and their dependence. Even more so than Poland, Rumania had become very much a Soviet colony and had supplied vital raw materials at a critical stage in the rebuilding of the Soviet economy. In 1962 there appeared the first rift: Rumanian objection to *Comecon* plans for an international socialist division of labour which appeared to perpetuate Rumania's role as the producer of raw materials and semi-manufactured products and which took no cognisance of plans for rapid industrial development. In retaliation, Rumania speeded up the negotiations with Western countries over outstanding compensation for confiscated industrial assets and began to introduce Western help into its development plans. Rumanian determination to develop its economy in its own way forced *Comecon* to modify the plans and accept 'national independence and sovereignty, full equality of .rights, comradely mutual assistance and mutual benefit'. Nevertheless, there are limits imposed on how far Rumania can press its independence, since it has one of the longest borders directly with the Soviet Union (over 800 km), though it has been one of the few East European states to raise old territorial issues by reminding the Soviet Union of its claims to Bessarabian Moldavia. To demonstrate its independence Rumania has co-operated with Jugoslavia in the large Iron Gates hydro-electric project without the support of *Comecon*. Rumania has also pursued a more tolerant and friendly policy towards China, again doubtless as an act of defiance to Moscow and has described itself as a Socialist Republic rather than a people's republic. The cultivation afresh of the old Romance tradition emphasises the view that Rumanians are different to their Slav and Magyar neighbours.

3.2.12 The Balkans

Albania has openly aligned itself with China in the struggle for dogmatic supremacy in the Communist world and since 1962 has not participated in *Comecon's* work. Stalinist policies have remained operative in Albania. Bulgaria has shown a loyal support of Moscow's Communist dogma, though it has opened contacts with the West, notably to earn foreign currency through tourism.

In the late 1950s conditions began to improve in Jugoslavia, though its economic problems were by no means solved. In the form of the Socialist Federal Republic of Jugoslavia, it seemed that the intractable inter-war problem of regional jealousies and mistrust had been overcome, but the new constitution of 1963 did not eliminate the age-long contrasts. The constitutional trends have been towards a restriction of the competency of the Federation to those matters common to the interests of all nationalities within the country—the assurance of the socio-economic foundations of the state; safeguarding individual rights and the social security of the people; the co-ordination of economic and social development; the safeguarding of the nationalities' interests; and defence and international relations. Discontent has been reflected in 1969 in a dispute over language in Slovenia and the limitations of the autonomy received under the new trends have been shown by events in Croatia in 1971.

By the early 1970s the pattern of political geography of people's democracies was well established in Eastern Europe. After the Czechoslovak crisis of 1968, it was obvious, however, that change was not going to be so rapid as it had been in the mid-1960s.

Part Two
The Demographic and Economic
Framework

4 Population

The eight Socialist *bloc* countries of Eastern Europe have a combined population of 125.3 million (1972)—about 28 per cent of the total European population without the Soviet Union.

The states themselves are all small—the largest, Poland, has a little over 32 million people, while in Albania there are only two million inhabitants. In general, they have shown a surprising growth, mostly above the average for the continent.

4.1 Distribution of Population (figure 4.1)

The contemporary regional distribution of population reflects not only the relative 'carrying capacity' of the different terrains, arising from factors of the physical environment, but also from different socio-economic conditions, and from variations between the several national development policies, while even some long-term historical influences may be perceived. In Western Europe a longer history of industrialisation and more intensive urbanisation has blurred the relation of population density to the agricultural potential of any given area, whereas in Eastern Europe the long continued heavy dependence of the major part of the population on farming has left the relationship between population density and agricultural potentiality more clearly discernible. Until the industrialisation of recent years, the distribution of town population in these countries often bore a marked relationship to agricultural conditions, as most towns were agricultural markets. The centrally planned industrialisation based on developing the most advantageous sites has brought the growth of urban and industrial population largely unrelated to the older—agricultural—pattern of population distribution, although the older patterns have been far from obliterated.

4.1.1 North European Plain

The North European Plain lies across much of Poland and the German Democratic Republic. Although population is generally only moderate, two large towns—Berlin (3.1 million) and Warsaw (1.3 million) lie in the Plain. The Baltic coast is lined by small and medium-sized ports; most important are Rostock–Warnemünde (195 450), the *Trójmiasto* (Gdańsk–Gdynia–Sopot) (554 000) and Szczecin (337 000). In the morainic country behind the coast, densities are generally around 50 persons per km^2 but are less east of the Oder (20–40 persons per km^2), with large expanses of forest and lake. In the belt of the *Urstromtäler*, sandy, heathy and marshy country, densities fall in places to less than 50 persons per km^2, though Berlin and its fringing satellites form an exception. In the Polish sector densities of 60–80 persons per km^2 occur in the rurally overcrowded parts of central Poland, a legacy from past political conditions. Throughout there are many small market towns.

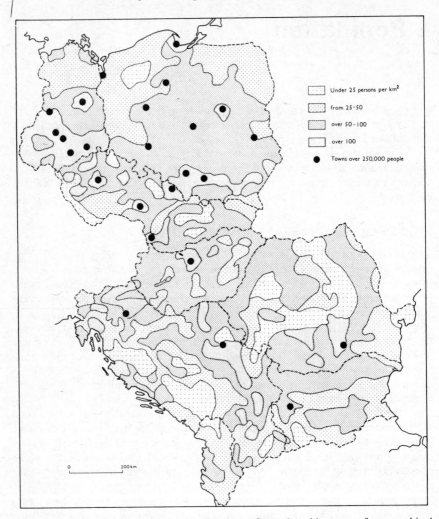

Figure 4.1. The map of population distribution reflects the wide range of geographical conditions in Eastern Europe. Various sources.

Towards the south, soils are better and the more rewarding farming is reflected in higher densities. In the *loessic Börderland* of Magdeburg and Saxony, densities of over 100 persons per km² occur in open, treeless farming country interspersed by large nucleated villages, but in places mining and industrial developments complicate the picture. Large towns include Magdeburg (269 700), Halle/Saale (289 700) and Leipzig (585 500). In the more sparsely populated heaths of Lusatia, Cottbus and Neu-Hoyerswerda have grown through mining development. Before the war comparable densities were found in Lower Silesia, on the rich soils along the Sudeten foot, but nowadays densities are somewhat lower as a result of the flight of the Germans and the relative slowness of Polish recolonisation, though it has been more intense here than elsewhere in the 'recovered territories'. Rural districts remain less populated than pre-war, but most towns are now larger, except where there was heavy damage (Wrocław, 1970: 523 000; 1939: 615 000). In Upper Silesia a large proportion of the original population remained and has been strengthened by a vigorous Polish immigration, so that densities of over 200 persons per km^2 are common in this major cluster of towns—including Katowice (303 000), Zabrze (197 000), Bytom (187 000), Gliwice (171 000), and Chorzów (151 000). The *loessic* belt extends eastwards from Kraków (583 000), with densities of over 80 persons per km^2 and in some places over 100 persons per km^2. This great granary in Austro-Hungarian times became a belt of rural overpopulation in the nineteenth century, with a pre-war population reputedly 50 per cent above its carrying capacity. The post-war period has seen the development of various industrial projects, as at Nowa Huta and Rzeszów.

4.1.2 Hercynian uplands

These comprise much of the southern German Democratic Republic and south-west Poland (Sudeten Mountains) and also Bohemia–Moravia. In this dissected upland country broken by fertile basins and corridors, there is usually a clear relation between population density and relief, so that widely different densities occur in close proximity. In Saxony and Thüringen the lower and broader valleys and basins carry considerable densities of rural farming folk and many industrial communities, while the higher valleys have long fingers of settlement extending up to considerable elevation. This is characteristic of the former mining area of the Harz, where the smaller and higher places are now holiday centres, with a seasonally shifting population. The higher surfaces are sparsely peopled and covered by extensive forest. High densities occur in the industrialised and urbanised country around Karl–Marx–Stadt (Chemnitz) (298 000) and Zwickau (127 400), with densities in the *Kreise* of 150–250 persons per km^2. The northern Sudeten country in Polish territory, with broad vales between the ranges and the broad embayment of the upper reaches of the Nysa, has densities of up to 60 persons per km^2, still less than pre-war, except in the Wałbrzych coalfield.

4.1.3 Bohemia

Bohemia is a broad, undulating and dissected plateau, which dips to the north to the broad fertile basin of the Polabí. Higher and rougher country forms the margins of the province. The most thickly settled parts are the north and centre, notably in Polabí with its rich soils and important waterway of the Elbe (Labe). Here densities are generally about 100 persons per km^2, with many important industrial towns. On the southern edge lies Prague, a million-city. A belt of dense settlement lies along the Ohře depression, with its lignite mines and towns such as Ústí-nad-Labem (73 000), Teplice (51 000), and Most (55 000), but Bohemia is generally characterised by numerous small towns. In southern and western Bohemia population is markedly sparser, with commonly less than 50 persons per km^2 and below 20 persons per km^2 in the forested Šumava. Two main concentrations of population occur around the industrial town of Plzeň (146 000) and its nearby mining communities and in the upper Ohře around Sokolov, while in western Bohemia are the world famous spas of Karlovy Vary and Mariánské Lázně. The main centre for southern Bohemia is České Budějovice (75 600). The frontier districts of Bohemia have been repopulated since the expulsion of the Germans.

4.1.4 Moravia

Moravia, with good soils and a long vegetative period that provide a basis for a rich agriculture, has densities well above 60–80 persons per km^2 in the valley of the Morava and in the basin of Olomouc. Another important concentration is in the Svitava valley around Brno (337 000). In the Sudeten ranges in the headwaters of the Morava and Oder, densities fall to under 40 persons km^2, but in the Czech Silesian coalfield high densities occur, with the main towns of Ostrava (247 000), Karviná (75 800) and the new town of Havířov (80 800).

4.1.5 The Carpathians

These are populated mainly in their valleys and basins, with sparse population in their forests and often only a transhumant population on the uppermost alpine meadows. In the High Tatra, the higher Beskids, the Fatra ranges and the Low Tatra as well as the Slovak Ore Mountains, there are broad open upper surfaces where densities fall below 20 persons per km^2. The main concentration of population is in the Váh valley, around Žilina (40 700) and Trenčín and in its upper reaches around Ružomberok, in a series of broader basins, which are also found along the Nitra and Hron, and provide attractive settlement areas, for example around Banská Bystrica (38 800), Zvolen (24 700) and Prievidza (17 000), where densities may exceed 100 persons per km^2. In Eastern Slovakia, there are lower ranges amid broad basins, often with densities of more than 100 persons per km^2 around Spišská Nová Ves, Prešov (40 500), Humenné, Michalovce and Košice (136 900). Many old mining towns have become spas and resorts. A broad zone of low hills and broad vales on the Polish Carpathian flanks has similar densities wherever there is warmth and shelter on better soils.

4.1.6 The Rumanian Carpathians and Transylvania

The great eastward-facing bow of the Rumanian Carpathians consists of high ranges, often rising above the tree line, dissected by deep valleys and large interior basins, which provide routeways through the mountains. Within the bow, Transylvania is a rolling, partly dissected landscape blocked on the west by rougher massifs. Within the mountains large areas have less than 20 persons per km^2 whereas in the basins densities of over 60 persons per km^2 are common, with 30–40 persons per km^2 on the lower slopes where forest has been cleared. Densities of over 100 persons per km^2 occur on the southern and eastern flanks of the mountains and on the inner flanks. In the mountains, settlements are mostly small scattered groups of houses but more marked agglomeration is found in the basins, with markedly compact villages around Brasov, Petroșeni, Mercurea

Ciuc and Gheorgheni. Modern development has created numerous small industrial settlements, while in some mountain areas resorts have grown round mineral springs or in recreational areas. Few towns are of great size—the main cluster is around Petroşeni (31 000) with Lupeni (32 000), Vulcan (23 000) and Petrila (28 000). The largest town is Braşov (137 000), while Piatra Neamt has 38 000 and Sighet, 28 000.

The massifs separated by narrow depressions on the western flank of Transylvania show somewhat higher densities than in other Rumanian mountains. Broad valleys and unglaciated open surfaces allow settlement to penetrate up to elevations of over 1000 m, but the extensive limestone tends to keep densities moderate, mostly about 30 persons per km². Richness in metallic ores has in places attracted small mining communities, and the picturesque limestone scenery has brought tourist developments. The western part of Transylvania with good soils has been more prosperous and better settled, particularly the Tirnava and Mureş basins, with densities of 60–100 persons per km² and numerous towns, including Cluj (167 000), Sibiu (103 000) and Tirgu-Mures (75 000). In places large villages with fortified churches date from German 'Saxon' settlement, notably in the south.

4.1.7 The Pannonian Plains

These have varied soils and moisture conditions that exercise great influence on settlement. The general density is between 50–100 persons per km², though there are marked agglomerations and patches of sparsely settled country. Around Budapest (slightly over two million inhabitants), up to 150 persons per km² may be found, whereas south of Lake Balaton densities seldom exceed 70 persons per km². In the eastern part of the Alföld, however, densities below 50 persons per km² occur in the drier parts, and similar low densities are found in the sandy country between the Danube and the Tisza. In contrast, there are more than 100 persons per km² in parts of the sandy Nyírség in north-eastern Hungary. Similar densities occur in the westernmost parts, in the Kisalföld and around Zalaegerszeg and Szombathely, while such densities are found in the northern plain (now in Slovakia) where the main centre is Bratislava (260 000).

An unusual feature of the population geography of the Pannonian Plains is the giant Puszta village, so that a third of the population lives in settlements of 1000–5000 people and only 8 per cent in communities under 1000 people. Several communities of over 10 000 people do not have town status. Some people live in scattered farmsteads (*tanyák*) outside the village nucleations. The administrative area of many Hungarian towns is abnormally large in relation to their population.

The southern Pannonian Plains, in the Banat and Bačka, form rich farming country, with dense rural population in large planned villages dating from resettlement after the Turkish devastations. Here, 60–100 persons per km² is a common density and there are many thriving market towns, but in areas liable to flood, densities fall below 50 persons per km². Belgrade is the main town, with over 600 000 people. The ethnic complexity of this country is often reflected in the form of villages, while high natural increase and substantial migration in the last twenty-five years have resulted in marked growth. Further south the plains merge into the hills and riverine plains along the Sava and Drava valleys. Liability to flood in parts of the valleys of the Sava and Drava, in the Baranya and the Srem, has restricted density, while the old 'military frontier' of Habsburg times is felt in a marked belt of lighter settlement. The north-west is densely settled in the valleys and hills of Croatia, with Zagreb (460 000) as the main town, and densities of 60–75 persons per km² may rise in places to over 100 people per km².

4.1.8 The Plains of the Lower Danube and the Plains of Moldavia

The Plains of the Lower Danube as well as the more dissected Plains of Moldavia (a western extension of the plains of southern Russia) have densities generally of 50–100 persons per km², locally higher in some favoured places. More sparsely settled areas occur where there is liability to flood or in extremely dry areas (Bărăgan Steppe). A marked agglomeration occurs around Bucharest (1.5 million) and in the rich agricultural and industrially developed Ploiești oilfield, where densities are generally well over 100 persons per km². Other well-settled areas include the Olt Basin, the Moldavian Plains around Buzău, Bacău and Roman and the upper Siret valley. In the lowest parts of the Danube valley and in the Dobrogea, densities seldom exceed 60 persons per km² and are well below 20 persons per km² in the Danube delta. Aridity has restricted settlement in the Dobrogea and the highest densities are on the Black Sea coast where resorts have developed. Important towns are Galati (112 000) and Brăila (123 000) and the Black Sea port of Constanța (155 000). Urbanisation in Rumania has been slow: about 40 per cent of the population is now town-dwelling, but this seldom exceeds 20 per cent in the plains of the Lower Danube and Moldavia, except for the Ploiești and Buzău areas, while around Bacău and Roman, 35 per cent of the population is town-dwelling. Agglomerated villages typify the plains and often serve as market and service foci. Rural overpopulation has been a critical phenomenon in the twentieth century.

4.1.9 The Bulgarian Tableland

The Bulgarian Tableland south of the Danube has between 50–100 persons per km² in the better watered areas with good soils. Towards the south, on grey forest soils along the mountain foot, and in the drier east, density falls to below 50 persons per km². Settlement is mostly villages of 800–1000 people and the principal towns include Ruse (128 000) and Pleven (79 000).

4.1.10 The Dinaric and Balkan mountains

These form most of Jugoslavia, Albania and Bulgaria, with extensive tracts of dry limestone and numerous large intermontane basins, particularly in the Balkan mountains. Modest to low densities are characteristic, though in the eastern parts densities are higher than might be expected, a legacy of Turkish oppression when many sought refuge in the mountains. In the north, in the Karawanken mountains, population clusters in the valleys above which rise forested slopes and barren summits. In the mountains of Slovenia, the fertile northern basins and valleys have densities of more than 60 persons per km² rising to over 90 persons per km² around Ljubljana (160 000), with well-developed industry and agriculture. The Slovenian population is dispersed in farms with few large villages and small towns. Less than 50 persons per km² are found in the Istrian Peninsula, except in the more favoured coastal areas. Along the Adriatic coast, wherever there are good harbours, population has clustered, usually in small, typically Mediterranean towns. Where these have access across the mountains, they have grown to considerable size—for example, Rijeka (101 000) and Split (85 000)—while tourist development has encouraged growth in other coast towns. Wherever the mountains come sheer to the coast, densities of less than 25 persons per km² are found, as along the foot of the Velebit range or the Popovo Planina, but in contrast, favoured areas (Ravni Kotari with Zadar as main town, and the Bay of Kotor) are well settled. The islands strung along the coast generally have lower densities than the mainland, but tourist development has stimulated population growth.

The largest area of scanty population in Jugoslavia is the barren and lofty limestone karst, where density seldom exceeds 25 persons per km² with the lowest densities in the south-east. The moister basins provided by the *polja* or the major valleys are the foci of population, and the high and barren surfaces are virtually deserted except for shepherds' summer huts. Towns are few and small, mostly in basins as route centres. Because of lower altitudes, the north-west is more favourable to settlement and is crossed by several ancient routes. Some *polja* are thinly settled because they suffer from cold-air drainage or inundation in winter. The main settled area is the Neretva valley, with the town of Mostar (56 000), an ancient bridging point, though the stoney karst to the south-east is particularly sparsely settled.

The inland flank of the karst is a broad belt of mountainous country containing relatively little limestone, consequently not so dry and more forested, with greater population density above 30 persons per km², though density drops in the higher country with its narrow gorge-like valleys along the edge of the karst. The fertile basin around Sarajevo (227 000), has many small towns and industrial communities besides a dispersed rural settlement that give densities of over 100 persons per km². In the northern Šumadija, high densities of rural population occur in the fertile lowlands amid the hills, with over 100 persons per km² living in small communities. In places infertile Tertiary marl is thinly peopled. Most small towns date from after the coming of the railway and the urban scene is dominated by Belgrade (over 600 000) and by Niš (98 000) in the Morava valley. Densities in the valley of the middle and upper Morava are generally about 75 persons per km², but drop appreciably towards the hills. To the southwest in the fertile basin of Kosovo Polje, Priština (46 000) is the main town of a countryside in which extensive Serbian colonisation has taken place this century. In the Metohija basin densities are lower and the population is strongly Albanian. In both these intermontane basins, densities are between 60–100 persons per km². Throughout these eastern uplands, particularly in north-east Serbia, there are many mining communities, some little more than villages; where there is mining, density is usually about 60 persons per km², but elsewhere only 30 persons per km².

The Vardar basin, roughly coincident with Macedonia, contains much poor crystalline country, so that densities under 30 persons per km² are common, but in the fertile basins and valleys densities rise to over 100 persons per km². Macedonia still has a strong seasonal movement of population, though transhumance to the mountains in summer has tended to decline. Ethnic contrasts play a part in the pattern of population distribution in this complex country. There has been a long tradition of town dwelling, for safety rather than economic reasons, with a surprising number of towns for the population. The main centre is Skopje (228 000), while Bitola (55 000), in the far south-west, serves the basin-studded mountains towards the Greek and Albanian borders. A pocket of better settled country lies around lakes Ohrid and Prespan.

4.1.11 The Balkan and Rhodope Mountains

In the Balkan and Rhodope mountains, the main ranges have densities of 30–50 persons per km² on their lower slopes, but in the higher parts densities may drop to below 10 persons per km². The main areas of population are in the wide basins and broad valleys, though not all are particularly fertile: in the Sofia basin, with about a quarter of the total Bulgarian urban population (Sofia, 801 000), agriculture is not especially fertile. The Maritsa valley, with better soils and warm climate, has densities of 50 persons per km², rising to over 100 persons per km² in places, as around Plovdiv (222 500), while other areas of denser population are around Stara Zagora and Khaskovo. Together the Maritsa valley and the Upper Thrace Plain are a most thickly settled part of Bulgaria. The high densities of rural population in the sheltered basins and valleys reflect the intensive 'garden' cultivation. In contrast the Pirin and Western Rhodope have below 50 persons per km², but the Eastern Rhodope has about 50 persons per km². In the Strandzha mountains, poor soils and aridity more than elevation result in low densities, often not more than 20 persons per km². During the Turkish period many people sought refuge in the mountains, but since Bulgarian independence there has been continual migration from the mountains, apart from modern mining communities developed in these areas. Urban population is mainly in the west and south-west, dropping to 20–24 per cent in the east and north-east, where Várna (180 000) and Burgas (106 000) are the main towns.

Apart from the coastal plain, until recently malarial, Albania is a mountainous country, with population in small clusters arising from a need for defence where blood feuds have long been practised. It is one of the least urbanised countries in Europe, with some towns little better than villages, usually located between the uplands and the plain. The largest town is Tiranë (152 000), the capital. The coastal plain and foothills have densities of over 100 persons per km², but in the mountains there are seldom more than 30 persons per km². The better settled mountain country is the basin around Korçë (42 500) and the middle valley of the Black Drina, while the most sparsely peopled is the northern Prokletije.

4.2 Population Growth

Though in general the Eastern European countries have followed a similar pattern of demographic development to Western Europe, the timing of the several stages has been later and, in some instances, different time spans have distinguished these stages. A basic difficulty in detailed study is the lack of adequate census material for several countries, especially if a study is projected back into the nineteenth century. At the same time, the varying quality and different statistical measurement among the several countries also make the task more formidable.

In the nineteenth century Western European countries had shown a rapid growth of population, especially in the second half of the century and much of the impetus had been carried into the first decade of the present century. In Eastern Europe there was also a marked increase, tempered by substantial emigration from certain areas. In the inter-war period, it was the countries of Eastern and South-eastern Europe that had twice the continental average growth, whereas much of Western and Central Europe fell well below the average; consequently, the share of total population in Western and Central Europe diminished and that of Eastern and South-eastern Europe increased. Since the Second World War, the Eastern and South-eastern European countries have had to make good substantial war losses, but since 1950 their performance has been little better than that of Western Europe (table 4.1).

Table 4.1   Eastern Europe — Population 1850–
2000 AD

(within the boundaries of the period)

1850		*c.*50.0 million
1900		*c.*80.0
1920		90.0
1938		111.6
1955		93.8
1965		120.4
1970		124.7
1975	est.	137.0
2000	est.	170.0—180.0 million

Source: Various yearbooks.

Inspite of substantial war losses in some Western countries, the impact of both world wars on overall demographic characteristics was greater in eastern (notably in Jugoslavia and Poland) than in Western Europe. In the First World War, the more mobile eastern front had a greater impact on the civilian population than the virtually stagnant western front, while epidemics, starvation and the postwar 'flu pandemic were of particular significance in Eastern Europe. The immediate post-war years also saw much adjustment by migration to the new political territorial pattern. A factor in population growth in Eastern Europe in the 1920s was the cutting off of emigration to the United States that had reached large proportions before 1914. By the second decade of the inter-war period, population growth in Eastern Europe had slowed appreciably, while Czechoslovakia and Hungary had come close to the demographic patterns in Western Europe.

Losses in the Second World War were particularly high among the civilian population, while genocide policies almost eliminated certain elements, like the

Jews and Gypsies, and there was also considerable migration, notably the mass exodus of the Germans. The decade 1940–50 marked an absolute loss of population, with notably large declines in Poland and Czechoslovakia. In the decade 1950–60, a generally high rate of increase was recorded, except as a result of migration from the German Democratic Republic and through a relatively low rate of natural increase in Hungary. During the 1960s rates of increase tended to decline, though Albania maintained a remarkable rate of growth at the head of the European table (table 4.2).

Table 4.2   *Growth of Population in Eastern Europe*

Country	Percentage Growth for Period				
	1920–39	1940–50	1955–65	1965–70	1960–80 (est.)
Albania	32.3	12.0	33.8	16.2	87
Bulgaria	30.0	8.8	8.6	3.5	18
Czechoslovakia	14.0	−15.8	8.1	2.2	16
German Democratic Republic	13.9†	9.5*	−5.0*	1.1*	2*
Hungary	14.2	0.6	3.5	1.6	7
Jugoslavia	31.0	−0.5	10.7	4.4	24
Poland	29.9	−23.3	15.5	3.1	28
Rumania	28.2	1.3	11.9	6.4	21
	A	B	B	B	B

Boundaries: A—Inter-war boundaries († Figure for *Reich*); B—Post-1945 boundaries (* excluding West Berlin).
Source: Various national yearbooks.
Kosiński, L. (1970). *The Population of Europe*, London.
Kirk, D. (1945). *Europe's Population in the Inter-war Years*, Geneva.
Notenstein, F. W. (1945). *The Future Population of Europe and the Soviet Union*, Geneva.

4.2.1 German Democratic Republic

Before 1939 the population history of the German Democratic Republic was part of the story for the *Reich* as a whole. In the Prussian census of 1907, the area described as 'Mitteldeutschland' (roughly coincident with the present Republic) had a population of 16.4 million—at a time when industrial growth was beginning to accelerate. In 1933 the population of the area of the present Republic was 15.8 million and 16.7 million in 1939. The census of 1946 (of rather doubtful accuracy) showed a population of 18.0 million and by 1948, population had risen to over 19.0 million—the result of strong immigration by expellees. From 1948 population began to fall, as a strong movement began to West Germany. This was particularly composed of young people in the economically and demographically most productive age groups, so that a deep impression was made on overall population movement. This so-called *Republikflucht* had reduced population in 1961 to only 17.1 million. Even stern measures against this exodus did not stem the downward drift, for in 1964 the bottom of the curve was reached at 16.98 million, after which a slight upward trend appeared. Natural increase has, however, slowed markedly since 1963 and by 1970 had fallen to a marginal natural decline. The demographic problem for the future is one of the most intractable and serious problems faced by the German Republic, with serious implications for its international role in the Socialist *bloc*.

4.2.2 Poland

Growth of population in Poland before 1918 is difficult to estimate, since the country was divided between three empires. The estimated population in 1900 in the inter-war area of Poland was 25.1 million; by 1921, it was 27.2 million; in 1931, 32.1 million; and by 1939, 34.8 million. In the twenty years between the wars it is claimed that 96 per cent of total increase was from natural increase and four per cent by migration: there was, however, a compensating outward migration to Belgium, France and even the U.S.A.

Territorial change, frightful war losses, as well as the expulsion of the Germans from the annexed western territories left Poland in 1945–6 with 23.6 million people. Only in the late 1960s had the total population climbed back to the figure of the early 1930s. The early post-war years were marked by a rapid rise in the birth rate and the greatest natural increase was recorded in the early 1950s, since when the birth rate has fallen fairly sharply. By 1965 natural increase had fallen to little above the average for 1936–8. With population at 32.5 million in 1969, by 1980 it will have reached 35.6–36.0 million and 38.8–40.1 million by the year 2000.

4.2.3 Czechoslovakia

The Czechoslovak lands had been fairly intensively colonised in the thirteenth and fourteenth centuries. This included immigration of foreign settlers, most intensive in Bohemia and Moravia, where the Bohemian Premyslides were more active in encouragement than the Hungarian Arpad kings in Slovakia. During the Thiry Years War (1618–48) there was great human and material loss, not fully made good until the mid-eighteenth century, when the Czech lands were again comparatively well settled (average density 42 persons per km^2) for the period. Even Slovakia at this time, inspite of large forests and extensive mountain areas, had a density of 34 persons per km^2. In the feudal period, employment opportunities were fairly evenly spread through Bohemia–Moravia and Slovakia, while mobility was reduced by feudal laws and poor transport. From the middle nineteenth century, economic conditions began to change and population in Bohemia–Moravia grew more rapidly than in Slovakia, where Hungarian policy was more conservative, though considerable migration took place from Slovakia and from Bohemia to Vienna and Budapest. By 1910 8 per cent of the total Czech population lived in Vienna—there were as many Czechs in Vienna as in Prague. Budapest had about five per cent of the total Slovak population, while Slovaks formed a strong element in migration to the U.S.A. In the 60 years before the First World War, one-third of the total natural increase had migrated from the Czech lands and two-thirds had gone from Slovakia. Large scale migration ended with the First World War, while natural increase also slowed in the inter-war period. Between 1938 and 1945 2.7 million people left Czechoslovakia and large numbers perished in concentration camps. In order to avoid deportation, many women turned to child-bearing, so that there was an extraordinarily high natural increase. In 1945 the Czechoslovak population structure was also affected by the flight and expulsion of minorities, notably the loss of well over two million Germans. The early 1950s were a particularly favourable period for natural increase, since when the rate has fallen, though still comparing favourably with the inter-war period. Slovakia is still growing by natural increase more rapidly than the Czech lands and has among the highest natural increase in Europe.

4.2.4 Hungary

In Hungary the depredations of the Turks left a deep scar on population, so that during the eighteenth century growth was achieved in considerable measure by immigration of non-Magyar peoples. Within present-day Hungarian territory population has risen from four million in 1840 to just on ten million in 1970. The greatest annual increase in Hungarian population had been during the emergence of modern capitalism between 1880–1910, inspite of strong emigration to North America. There had been at this time, however, a substantial migration from the border lands of the then Kingdom, particularly into Budapest and other emergent industrial districts. After the First World War, growth was caused chiefly by immigration by Magyars who had found themselves left in foreign territory by the Treaty of Trianon. Once this flow ceased, growth slowed down, especially in the uncertain economic conditions of the 1930s. In spite of war losses and the elimination of non-Magyar nationalities, natural increase between 1949 and 1955 was comparable to the best decades of the later nineteenth century, but during the 1960s, growth of population slowed appreciably, with a marked fall in natural increase.

4.2.5 Rumania

In Rumania the present territory had a population of 8.6 million in 1869, 11.1 million in 1900, 14.3 million in 1930, and 15.8 million in 1948. In 1970 the population was just over 20 million. As a result of territorial changes, the country has, however, shown wide swings (table 4.3).

Over the inter-war period, annual natural increase had tended to fall: in 1930, it had been 14.8 per thousand but by 1939 it had fallen to 10.1 per 1000. In the immediately post-war years, natural increase was at 8.3 per 1000 and rose into the 1950s (1956, 14.3 per 1000) only to fall again (1963, 7.4 per 1000). It currently lies at a level similar to those of the more advanced countries of Europe. Wide regional variations in natural increase are concealed within the overall national figures: particularly high natural increase (1960–3) occurred in Moldavia, notably around Hirlau, in the Moldova basin, in the Dobrogea and the Danube delta, as well as in parts of Transylvania. In contrast, very low natural increase or even natural decline marked the south-west, around Arad and Timisoara.

Table 4.3   Population and Territorial Change in Rumania

	Area (1000 km²)	Population (million)	Year of estimate
Rumania before the First World War	129.6	7.235	1912
gain from Bulgaria, 1913	7.5	0.282	1913
from Hungary, 1919	103.1	5.257	1910
from Austria, 1919	10.4	0.800	1910
from Russia, 1919	44.4	1.935	1897
Greater Rumania	295.0	18.057	1930
lost to Bulgaria, 1940	7.4	0.367	1930
to Soviet Union, 1940	50.1	3.409	1930
Rumania after Second World War	237.5	15.873	1948

Source: Arbeitsgemeinschaft Ost, Wiener Quellenhefte zur Ostkunde, 1960, vol. 1.

4.2.6 Bulgaria

Population growth in Bulgaria was affected in the nineteenth century by the country's political fortunes and later by its fluctuating territorial extent in the Balkan Wars and the First World War. Population was also affected by ethnic changes—notably the decline of the Turkish, Greek, Armenian and Jewish elements. Continuous improvement in public health and hygiene have been factors in boosting natural increase, particularly through the reduction of the death rate. Between 1948 and 1952, Bulgaria had one of the highest rates of natural increase in Europe, while it had shown considerable growth in the inter-war years, exceeded only by Jugoslavia and Greece. In the decade 1940–50, an 8.8 per cent increase in population contrasted with the general low level of increse or even decline in most Eastern European countries, but it was below the increase (+ 12 per cent) in Albania, though more recently the rate of growth has tended to slacken.

4.2.7 Jugoslavia

A reasonably accurate calculation of the population of Jugoslavia can be dated back only to 1910, when the country within its inter-war boundaries had a total of 12.3 million people; even by the 1921 census, population (11.6 million) was still five per cent below the pre-war figure. War-time losses had, however, been much higher in some parts of the country than others—Serbia and Montenegro having suffered particularly heavily. Only the Vojvodina had a slight increase (+ 2.0 per cent). There had also been a heavy loss of potential births, estimated at 1.2 million for the whole country, but falling most heavily on Serbia. By 1931 population had risen to 13.93 million (table 4.2).

The recovery of Jugoslav population has been remarkable after 1.7 million deaths in the Second World War. Considerable changes have been shown in annual natural increase, but it has generally remained high. In 1880 natural increase was estimated at 15 per 1000; in 1931, 16.0 per 1000; but by 1938, it had fallen to 12.0 per 1000. In 1948, natural increase was again at 16.4 per 1000 and thereafter declined: in 1953, it was 14.3 per 1000 in 1964, 12.8 per 1000 in 1968, 10.3 per 1000 and in 1970 stood at only 8.4 per 1000. This fall in natural increase has taken place in spite of a greater decline in the death rate than in the birth rate, while overall growth has remained below natural increase because of a tendency to continuous migration. With a high rate of natural increase in the less developed south, in spite of patterns of migration within the country, there has

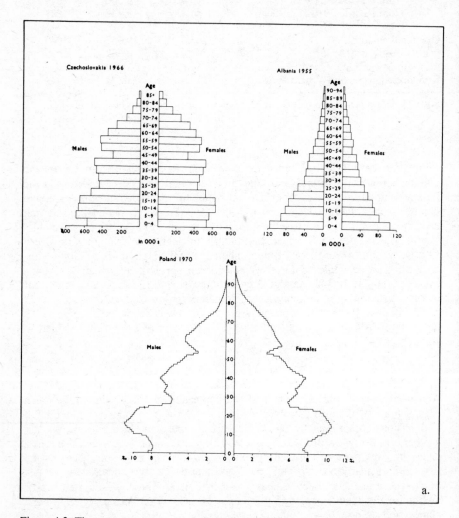

Figure 4.2. The contemporary population pyramids of the eight Socialist bloc countries show considerable diversity. Where sufficiently detailed data are available, the loss of population through two world wars is clearly marked. The less detailed data for Albania does, however, reflect its still rapidly growing population, very much in the pattern of the 'developing countries'. Based on various national statistical yearbooks.

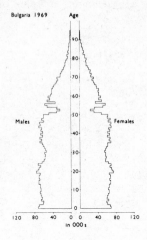

Bulgaria 1969

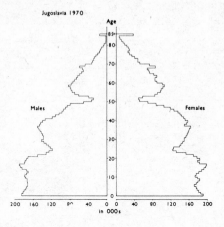

Jugoslavia 1970

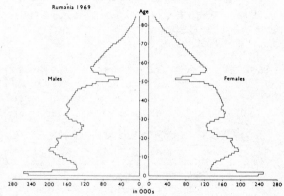

Rumania 1969

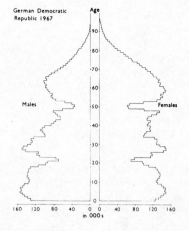

German Democratic
Republic 1967

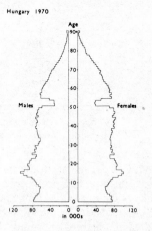

Hungary 1970

b.

been a considerable shift of the centre of gravity of population towards the south and south-east.

Table 4.4   Population in Post-1945 Area†
of Jugoslavia

Year	Population (million)
1921	12·545
1931	14·534
1948	15·842
1953	16·991
1961	18·549
1970	20·527
Projection on basis of 1961 census results:	
1980	22·834

† Area = 255 804 km²
Source: *Statistical Pocket Book of Jugoslavia*
(1971). Belgrade.

4.2.8 Albania

Albania shows some of the demographic characteristics of countries of the 'Third World'. In 1900 the present Albanian territory had a population of about 500 000; by 1920, 800 000; and by 1930 it was on the million mark; in 1940 the population was 1.1 million and 1.6 million a decade later. In 1970 the population

Table 4.5   Annual Natural Population
Increase in Albania

Year	Annual natural increase per 1000
1939	12.9
1942	18.6
1946	11.8
1950	24.5
1961	31.9
1963	29.1
1967	26.9

Source: Straszewicz, L., (1970). *Geografia gospodarcza europejskich krajów demokracji
Ludowej*, vol. 2, Warsaw.

of Albania was 2.1 million (table 4.3). The industrialisation of the country and the stability introduced by the centralisation of power have been significant factors in the rapid population growth that has accompanied a modest improvement in living standards. In the inter-war period birth and death rates in Albania were high and gave a high rate of natural increase, though in 1939 natural increase was less than twice the present level.

4.3 Age and Sex Composition

Graphical representation of the age and sex structures of countries in the form of pyramids gives valuable guidance to their economic and social fortunes. By their shape these pyramids represent past development of the population and may give some clues for future prognosis. The height of the pyramids is much the same, with a life expectancy difference of five years on the male side to eight years on the female side between the eight Socialist *bloc* countries (table 4.6) However, levels are a little below equivalent figures for Western Europe. In Europe as a whole, there is about a decade difference between the highest and lowest expectancies, while the Eastern European countries lie close together in the lower half of the spectrum.

Table 4.6   Life Expectancy in mid-1960s
(Age in Years)

Country	Male	Female
Bulgaria	67.8	71.4
Czechoslovakia	67.5	73.4
German Democratic Republic	67.1	72.0
Rumania	65.4	70.2
Hungary	65.2	69.6
Poland	64.8	70.5
Albania	63.7	66.0
Jugoslavia	62.2	65.3

Based on assorted data.

A rapidly growing population shows a pyramid with a wide base and gently sloping sides; a stagnating population has a pyramid of sugar-loaf shape, while a declining population shows a pyramid with a base narrower than its middle altitudes. War, catastrophe and disease can eat indentations into the sides of the pyramid, though usually, war and civil commotion affect the male side more seriously than the female flank.

4.3.1 German Democratic Republic

In the German Democratic Republic the upper age groups show a serious imbalance between the sexes reflecting the substantial war losses between 1914 and 1918 and subsequent premature male deaths from war wounds. In the mid-fifties age groups there is a marked constriction arising from the small classes born during the First World War and the immediate post-war years of hardship. Another, if smaller, indentation occurs in the classes born during the economic depression, 1929–33, although the larger classes born in the Nazi-sponsored 'baby boom' are also represented. Losses in the Second World War are marked by a severe pruning of the male groups and the loss of potential births is marked by a further constriction representing the small classes born in 1947–50, followed by larger classes during the 1950s. A marked swell can be attributed to the larger groups born since 1961 when the Berlin Wall reduced the exodus to the West, but from the mid-1960s, a gradual contraction of the classes born each year has taken place. The pyramid has characteristics of a stagnating and potentially declining population, in which the older age groups are uncomfortably well represented. With large year to year fluctuations in the age groups, planning in economic and social terms is made difficult (table 4.7).

Table 4.7   Age Structure in the German Democratic Republic

Year	In working age groups %	Children (below 15) %	Pensioners (over 65) %
1939	67.5	21.4	11.1
1950	64.1	22.1	13.8
1960	61.3	21.0	17.6
1970	57.8	22.8	19.4

Source: Statistisches Jahrbuch der DDR, Berlin, various years.

4.3.2 Poland

The population pyramid for Poland shows deep inroads caused by the two world wars and a marked imbalance between the male and female sides. Compared to 1950 the pyramid in 1970 showed a contraction in the classes below 15 years of age, whereas in 1950 the youngest classes, notably the 5-year-olds and younger, have been particularly large. Again compared to 1950 the pyramid in 1970 shows a considerably larger proportion of people in the age groups over 55. Compared to 1950, however, the working age groups in 1970 are without the serious bottleneck in the 30–35 year-old group, while limited numbers in the 50–55 year-old group in 1970 at least simplified promotion prospects for many. Although the proportion of young people (below 17 years of age) improved between 1950 and 1965, it has been below pre-war levels, just as the proportion of people over 60 was markedly above the pre-war level. By 1970 there were many indications in the Polish population pyramid of an ageing population, which may in part derive from better medical care and an improved expectancy of life. The population pyramids of the new western territories show a generally large number of young people in the working age groups, whereas the eastern districts have pyramids of a more 'sugar-loaf' form suggesting an ageing and stagnating population.

4.3.3 Czechoslovakia

In Czechoslovakia the Czech and Slovak lands need separate examination: both parts in 1900 had typically broad-based pyramids of rapidly expanding populations, but by 1960 the situation had changed radically. In the Czech lands the pyramid had the characteristic 'sugar-loaf' form of an ageing population, whereas the Slovak pyramid still had some evidence of continuing growth. In Slovakia there was a considerably smaller proportion of people in the older age groups than in the Czech lands, and the younger classes were markedly larger. The classes of young people in the Czech lands contracted rapidly after the post-war 'baby boom'. In the Slovak lands the proportion of children substantially exceeds the proportion of old people, while the reverse is true in the Czech lands. In both Czech and Slovak pyramids the effects of the two world wars are apparent, although this impress is more clearly seen in the Czech lands, where population was notably affected by the economic depression of 1929–32.

4.3.4 Hungary

The population structure and development in Hungary resembles in several respects the more developed Western European countries. The pyramid shows a phase of rapid growth passing into a period of comparative stagnation or, at best, very slow growth. Throughout the earlier part of the century, the proportion of children under 15 has declined and the share of age groups over 60 has increased, though the total proportion in the age groups 15–59 has remained fairly constant. There has, however, been an increasing share in the upper brackets. National policy produced considerable fluctuations in the post-war birth rate: in 1953 policies aimed to stimulate growth were introduced, only to be reversed in 1956. The pyramid is broken by the abnormally large classes born under the stimulation policies while the economic revival in the latter 1960s is also reflected.

4.3.5 Rumania and Bulgaria

The population pyramids of Rumania and Bulgaria show more clearly evidence of continuing growth in their markedly triangular form. The Rumanian pyramid shows growth up to the early 1960s and a sudden expansive tendency a decade later. Both world wars are marked by small classes and there is some trace in the uppermost age groups of the Balkan Wars of 1913. Rumania shows a large proportion of people in the economically and demographically productive age groups—some 62.5 per cent are in the age groups 15–59 and less than 10 per cent of the population is over 60 years old. The Bulgarian population pyramid shows long continued growth with an easing in the last decade. The pyramid from the 1956 census displays clearly the first and second world wars as well as the turbulent period at the start of the century. The effect of these inroads is generally less unbalancing than in other Socialist *bloc* countries. There is the clear effect of a plunge in the birth rate from 40 per 1000 in the 1920s to 15 per 1000 in the 1960s, though there was a corresponding collapse in the death rate from 21 per 1000 to eight per 1000 in the same period. It has been suggested that the removal of the Turkish population, with a high rate of natural increase, has effectively slowed overall growth.

4.3.6 Jugoslavia

The population pyramid of Jugoslavia shows a structure of growth eaten into massively by two world wars. A general trend towards larger classes marked the post-war years until the mid-1950s and there was undoubtedly an influence of better prenatal and maternity facilities offsetting a decline in birth rates by reducing infant and child mortality. The northern parts of the country, with the highest standards of living, show lower birth rates but higher death rates than the south and consequently natural increase has been lower. Slovenia and Croatia reflect the northern pattern of population, with a marked sugar-loaf form of pyramid, suggesting stagnation, ageing and possible ultimate decline. In Macedonia and Montenegro the population pyramid has more characteristics of growth—a more truly pyramidal form, most pronounced in the Kosovo and Metohija—a product of large families, high birth rate and modest death rate.

4.3.7 Albania

Albania occupies a very distinct place. Its population pyramid shows clear evidence of an expanding population and a slightly concave form to its limbs suggests accelerating growth. According to Straszewicz 44.4 per cent of the population is under 15, 46.6 per cent is between 16 and 59 and 9.0 per cent is over 60 years of age.

4.4 Migration

There is a long historical record of migration in Eastern Europe as the complex ethnic quilt indicates, but this section deals only with the modern period from the late nineteenth century, when three distinct periods can be distinguished. The first was the late imperial stage—lasting until the First World War—influenced by the socio-economic organisation of the great dynastic empires. The second marked the readjustments in population demanded by the new political and economic map created by the inter-war succession states. Finally, the third is the period of Sovietisation since 1945.

The imperial stage was marked by migration from Eastern Europe to overseas destinations, chiefly to North America—a move for economic betterment from oppressive social and political conditions. The Germans were among the first migrants—starting in the Rhinelands in the 1830s and 1840s, spreading eastwards as railways allowed easier access to the North Sea ports. The crest of the migration from central Germany was in the 1860s and from eastern Germany in the 1870s and 1880s, but thereafter the rapid industrialisation absorbed many who might have otherwise joined the stream. In Austria–Hungary, emigration began from Bohemia before 1850—affecting the more progressive German and Czech populations, but by the 1870s, a rising tide of Slovenes and Croats was beginning to move, while in the north Poles were joining the emigrants' ranks. By 1900 emigration from the Habsburg lands was principally of Poles, Jews and Galician Ukrainians, though soon Magyars began to move to America. These migrationary trends had begun to affect Rumania, Bulgaria and Serbia just before the First World War, when the Russian empire also became a major contributor of emigrants to the American continent—a large part from the 'Pale', for Jews formed over half the emigrants from Tsarist Russia, while Baltic peoples and Poles and Ukrainians from the *Kongresówka* were also significant.

A substantial migration after 1860 began within the Reich to the newly industrialising districts in the Ruhr, Saxony and the great cities, particularly Berlin. Migration from eastern Germany to the Ruhr, encouraged by scouts sent by the industrialists, gained momentum after the Franco–Prussian War. It was not only Germans from the Reich's poorer rural areas who were attracted to the industrial towns, but also Poles and Masurians from within Prussian territory and Czechs, Poles and Galicians from the Austro–Hungarian empire. Between 1880 and 1910 over a million foreigners settled in Germany. Czechs and Germans from Bohemia went mostly to Saxony; Poles from Russia, Austria–Hungary and even Prussia moved to the Ruhr or to Silesia. A Polish source claims that over 600 000 Poles went to industrial areas in Germany (500 000 to Westphalia and the Rhineland) between 1870 and 1914. Many Prussian officials were settled in strongly Polish districts and there was migration of Saxons and others into industrial Silesia. Habsburg German officials were found in all parts of the Austro–Hungarian empire, while Magyar officials were commonly found in Slovak, Croat or Rumanian parts and Russian officials were also present in Russian Poland. Budapest attracted Slovaks and Croats, while Czechs, Slovaks and Magyars flocked to Vienna. Jews from many parts of Eastern Europe also began to move westwards into the towns.

The First World War curtailed drastically such mobility, for the great empires were replaced by jealously guarded national states. Prussian and German Austrian officials left Poland, while many Austrian Germans returned from the new Czechoslovak state, just as Magyars gave up their official duties in Croatia, Slovakia or Rumania to return to Trianon Hungary. Internal migrations of pre-war times became international movements after 1918 as a result of the new boundaries. As German rearmament got underway, Sudeten Germans began to seek employment in the Reich, while many German minority groups had always sent their children to German universities. Inspite of desperate attempts to change its course, migration from country to town in Germany grew in the 1930s—in East Prussia, between 1933 and 1939, ten per cent of the rural population was lost. The strength of migration from the German East became a political issue, because it left areas with declining German population when official policy claimed that the Germans had insufficient *Lebensraum*.

Emigration from the Habsburg empire had generally been to industrial areas in Germany or to America—after the First World War, both these possibilities dried up. The internal movements had been from countryside to towns, but even these streams were broken by the new frontiers—Slovaks and Croats could no longer move to Budapest, nor Czechs and Magyars to Vienna, not that any incentive remained to go to these cities, now the impoverished capitals of small states.

The Czechoslovak state deflected much internal migration to its towns, notably to Prague, though German and Hungarian minorities tended to leave for their own countries. Many Czechs, mostly from southern Bohemia, began to settle in chiefly German districts and towns, while Czech officials also began to move into Slovakia to replace former Magyar officials. The high level of natural increase in Slovakia and the relatively limited economic opportunity continued to make emigration attractive for ambitious Slovaks, who now sought work in Bohemia and Moravia rather than in Hungary. Czech Silesia and the Těšín (Teschen) district, once a focus for Polish settlers from Galicia, began to attract Czechs and Slovaks. Even the division of the large estates did not stem the flow of peasants from the countryside and some major development schemes—like the Bat'a plants at Zlín—were designed to improve opportunities in the more crowded rural districts.

In Hungary migration focused on Budapest and a few industrial towns such as Pécs and Baja or agricultural areas where spaces were left by emigration of minorities, as in the Baranya, while there was a substantial inflow of Magyars from adjacent countries. Much of the internal migration was supplied by peasants from areas with very small holdings.

In Poland movements were complex: the early years of the 1920s were marked by considerable repatriation of war refugees into eastern Poland and Galicia, but this concealed a flow from these areas into other parts of Poland, especially into the former Prussian lands. The Polish element in the population of the eastern districts constituted the main migration into towns and the bulk of migrants to other parts of the country. A strengthening of the Polish element took place on the Baltic coast with the development of the port of Gdynia, while Polish officials moved into the coalfield of Upper Silesia.

In Rumania, Bulgaria and Jugoslavia inter-war migration was limited because the peasants were generally reluctant to move, but late in the inter-war period industrialisation and urbanisation began to exert some influence. Census material, where available, showed that the population was predominantly in the same district as place of birth. In Jugoslavia Belgrade was the main focus of migration, at least for Serbs, while Croats moved to Zagreb, their own regional capital. Some dispersion took place from the poorer mountain districts, notably in Montenegro and Macedonia. The major cause of migration in Bulgaria was population exchange, mostly of Greek, Rumanian and Turkish elements, though Sofia became attractive to migrants within the country. Some of the migration from the Balkan uplands may be seen as a continuing process of readjustment after the long and disastrous Turkish period. Little attention was paid in Rumania to migrationary trends. Largely through migration, Bucharest trebled in size between 1912 and 1939, to become one of Europe's boom towns. The other area of growth was in the oilfields of Ploiești. Migration took place from the 'Saxon' and Magyar districts of Transylvania, while similar movements of Bulgarians and Rumanians took place in the Dobrudsha.

4.4.1 The New Migrations (figure 4.3)

The problems created by large minorities in the succession states after the First World War made governments determined to rid themselves of unwanted people after the Second World War. As one group has moved, the empty space it has left has been filled by another people, though not without considerable delay in some cases. By far the largest group affected has been the 18 million Germans involved in these migrations.

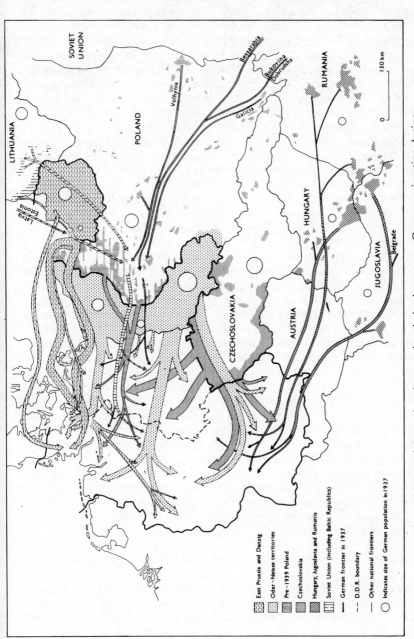

Figure 4.3. One of the major elements in ethnic change was German migration during and after the Second World War. Based in part on a map from W. Essen. *Europa und die Deutschen Flüchtlinge*, Institut zur Förderung öffentlicher Angelegenheiten, Frankfurt am Main (1952).

The *Zurück ins Reich* programme was sponsored by the Nazis to bring back to Germany ethnic German groups initially from the Baltic countries, Bessarabia, Bukovina and Soviet-held Poland. These people (over 450 000) were resettled largely in annexed Polish territory—Westpreussen, Wartheland, eastern Upper Silesia or the Zichenau area. The resettlers arrived in carefully planned transports under specific treaty arrangements and were generally settled in accommodation sequestered from Poles forced to move into the General-Government. Reputedly 1.2 million Poles and 300 000 Jews were so affected. After the German invasion of the Soviet Union other ethnic German groups from southern Russia were also repatriated. Between 1939 and 1941 some 50 000 Russians, Ukrainians and Lithuanians in the areas of Poland and Memel taken by German troops were returned to the Soviet Union, while reputedly two million Poles from Soviet-occupied Poland were sent to Central Asia and Siberia. Under the Vienna Agreement of 1940 160 000 Magyars in southern Transylvania were moved to the Hungarian held part of the historic province in return for 220 000 Rumanians; some 15 000 Magyars were sent to Hungary from south Bukovina and a small number moved from Moldavia to the Hungarian Bačka. A considerable but uncertain number of Rumanians found in the Ukraine were sent home by the *Wehrmacht*. Important adjustments in population followed the German occupation of Jugoslavia: 70 000 Croats were moved to Croatia from Serbia; 6000 Croats were moved from Lower Styria to Croatia, while 300 000 Serbs were moved to Serbia from various parts of Jugoslavia. Some 60 000 Bulgars were also moved from north to south in the Dobrudsha and others were sent home from the Soviet Union. About 1.5 million Jews from Western Europe were despatched to extermination camps in Eastern Europe.

In 1939 about 18 million Germans lived in East and South-east Europe beyond Germany's 1937 boundaries and in the German territories annexed by Poland and the Soviet Union in 1945: the annexed lands east of the Oder–Neisse rivers contained 9.6 million of these people. A further 1.4 million (est. 1939) lived in the Soviet Union. By 1950 when the major period of flight and expulsion ended, almost eight million German people from these areas were resident in the German Federal Republic and about four million were in the German Democratic Republic; at least 380 000 had found homes in Austria and another 100 000 were in other Western European countries or overseas. Excluding the Germans living in Russia, about 3.1 million Germans in the affected territories were unaccounted for. Although many of these people perished in the privations of the 1940–50 period, others certainly have been absorbed by the non-German people among whom they lived.

The mass movement of Germans was triggered off by the declining fortunes of the German armies in Russia as large numbers fled before the advancing Red Armies. The main flight and expulsion came in 1945–6, following the Potsdam Agreement (Article XIII). Many Germans already moved during the war years into Polish territory incorporated into the *Reich* were also swept into the mass movement, though some were actually forced to return to the U.S.S.R. by the Soviet authorities.

The frontier of consolidated German settlement has been pushed westwards by the expulsion of German population from the territory annexed by Poland to the line of the Oder–Neisse, while the extensive area of predominant German

Table 4.8   Ethnic Composition of Eastern Europe c. 1930–9*

Date	1933	1930	1930	1930	1930	1934	1931	1938
Country	German Reich	Poland	CSR	Hung.	Rum.	Bul.	Jug.	Alb.
Total population	65 219	31 916	14 730	8688	18 057	6078	13 934	1064
Germans	64 603	741	3318	479	761	4	602	—
Poles	438	21 993	100	—	38	—	18	—
Czechs	} 6	} 38	}9757	} 108	} 43	_	} 138	_
Slovaks								
Sorbs	57(?)	—	—	—	—	—	—	—
Magyars	—	—	720	8001	1555	—	557	—
Rumans	—	—	14	16	13 181	} 16	} 276	13
Vlachs, etc.	—	—	—	—	—			
Bulgarians	—	—	—	3	364	5275	73	—
Macedonians							‡	‡
Serbs	—	—	} 6	} 55	} 48	_	}10 257	—
Croats								
Slovenes	—	—	—	5	—	—	1159	—
Montenegrins							‡	
Ukrainians	—	4442	—	—	641	—	31	—
Byelorussians	—	1697	—	—	—	—	—	—
Russians	—	139	569	1	451	12	25	—
Gypsies	—	—	33	8	101	81	54	—
Jews	—	2733	205	—	519	—	—	—
Turks	—	—	—	—	} 288	} 622	180	} 30
Tatars	—	—						
Greeks	—	—	—	—	21	10	—	37
Armenians	—	—	—	—	—	23	—	
Italians	—	—	—	—	—	—	15	†
Gagauses						‡		
Karakatchans						‡		
Aromunians						‡		‡
Albanians	—	—	—	—	4	—	524	984
Islamic Serbo-Croats							‡	
Lithuanians	2	83	—	—	—	—	—	—

Source: Kirk, D. (1946). *Europe's Population in Interwar Years*, Geneva, Table 17.
* Figures given in thousands.
† No figure given for Italians.
‡ Not separately distinguished.

character in Bohemia has also disappeared. In the northern plain the pattern of settlement between German and Slav has been put back 750 years and to a somewhat earlier date in Bohemia. The parts of Poland from which the Germans were expelled have been resettled by Poles, either from the crowded rural lands of the *Kongresówka* or Galicia or from eastern Poland annexed by the Soviet Union. In Czechoslovakia many Slovaks and Gypsies (about 1.8 million in total) are found in the former German Bohemian towns.

Table 4.9   Ethnic Composition of Eastern Europe c. 1960*

Total population	GDR 17 125	Poland 29 965	CSR 13 776	Hung. 10 028	Rum. 18 567	Bul. 7943	Jug. 18 607	Alb. 1660
Germans	16 975	†50	165	200	400	—	60	—
Poles	—	29 540	85	—	8	—	—	—
Czechs	—	—	9050	—	12	—	30	—
Slovaks	—	20	3830	60	25	—	86	—
Sorbs	120	—	—	—	—	—	—	—
Magyars	—	—	425	9520	1700	—	505	—
Rumans	—	—	—	15	15 960	—	60	—
Vlachs, etc.	—	—	—	—	—	—	80	—
Bulgarians	—	—	—	—	13	6980	62	—
Macedonians	—	—	—	—	—	—	1040	10
Serbs	—	—	—	20	43	—	7800	—
Croats	—	—	—	25	5	—	4290	—
Slovenes	—	—	—	5	—	—	1590	—
Montenegrins	—	—	—	—	—	—	515	5
Ukrainians	—	150	70	—	65	—	40	—
Byelorussians	—	100	—	—	—	—	—	—
Russians	—	20	5	—	40	12	13	—
Gypsies	—	30	100	60	115	210	90	10
Jews	—	30	18	100	100	7	5	—
Turks	—	—	—	—	15	670	165	—
Tatars	—	—	—	—	23	7	—	—
Greeks	—	—	—	—	11	9	—	40
Armenians	—	—	—	—	7	23	—	—
Italians	—	—	—	—	—	—	25	—
Gagauses	—	—	—	—	—	10	—	—
Karakatchans	—	—	—	—	—	3	—	—
Aromunians	—	—	—	—	—	—	—	10
Albanians	—	—	—	—	—	—	915	1580
Islamic ⎫ Serbo-Croats ⎭	—	—	—	—	—	—	980	—

Source: *Atlas Narodov Mira* (1964). Moscow.
* Figures given in thousands.
† Excludes 'autochthonous' German–Silesian population.

Migration has continued since the mid-1950s on a more modest scale, with a steady stream of people leaving the German Democratic Republic up to the building of the Berlin Wall in 1961. Many of these people have been from expellee groups which found themselves in the German Democratic Republic. Up to 1961 over 2.5 million people had undertaken *Republikflucht* to the western German Federal Republic, mostly from the economically and demographically productive age groups; consequently the impact has been greater than numbers suggest.

Migration in the territory annexed by the Soviet Union included the expulsion of the German population (1939 = 1.7 million) from the Kaliningrad *oblast* (that is, northern East Prussia) and their replacement by about 300 000–500 000 people from the interior of the Soviet Union (reputedly many Tatars from the Volga). Over 1.5 million settlers were also brought from other parts of the country to eastern Poland incorporated into Byelorussia and the Ukraine: somewhere between 1.5 and 2.0 million Poles were moved into Poland. In Czechoslovakia about 33 000 Czechoslovak citizens were repatriated from the Carpathian Ukraine and some 100 000 Slovaks were returned from Hungary, compensated by a counterflow of Magyars to Hungary. About 80 000 people were interchanged between Hungary and Jugoslavia and some 200 000 Rumanians moved into northern Transylvania, though ethnic minorities have suffered generally less in the more liberal Rumanian policy. In 1950 some 157 000 Turks left Bulgaria, but when the action ended in 1955, only a little more than half the original number expected had gone. There had been a considerable return flow of people from Western Europe, either from various 'free' armies or from 'slave labour' in the Reich.

Such international movements were taking place as internal movements began to get underway. In Rumania some 50 000 Germans, Serbs and even Rumanians were moved from a 50 km security zone along the Jugoslav frontier into the Bărăgan steppe. The accelerating pace of urbanisation and industrialisation in all countries set up streams of migrants into towns—in Hungary, this was a drift towards Budapest and into new industrial towns; new towns in Poland, as well as the deserted industrial towns of former German territories, attracted many migrants, though the 'repopulation' of Warsaw also attracted country folk. Similar streams are discernible elsewhere, though in Bulgaria the drift from the country became so great in the late 1950s that it caused critical labour problems in agriculture. In the Hungarian riots of 1956 some 190 000 people fled the country, though reputedly 42 000 have returned, while many Czechs had left before the Russian occupation of 1968. Jews from several countries have migrated to Israel and there has been a steady drift of Germans back to Germany, notably from Upper Silesia.

4.5 The Ethnic Quilt (figure 4.4; tables 4.8, 4.9)

No study of Eastern Europe can omit reference to the diverse ethnic structure and the complex interrelationships between the various peoples. Some reference has already been made (chapter 2) to the emergence of the major ethnic groups, but this section deals with the position from the later nineteenth century. Many unsolved ethnic questions remain in the fields of language, cultural patterns and the history of migrations, while the romanticism of the eighteenth and nineteenth centuries coupled to the chauvinistic nationalism of the late nineteenth century also clouded the issues. Throughout the mediaeval period, religious issues and dynastic problems were more important than language or ethnics in community and territorial problems. In the Habsburg empire the resettlement of lands taken from the Turks appears to have been carried out with whatever peasants were available. Such tactics were to confuse further the ethnic pattern and ultimately 'nationality' when these became major issues of everyday life. In the Ottoman empire the basic division was between Moslems and Christians, but once Islam had been embraced ethnic origin played no part and Slavs, Greeks, Albanians and others found their way to the highest levels of authority. Until recent times the

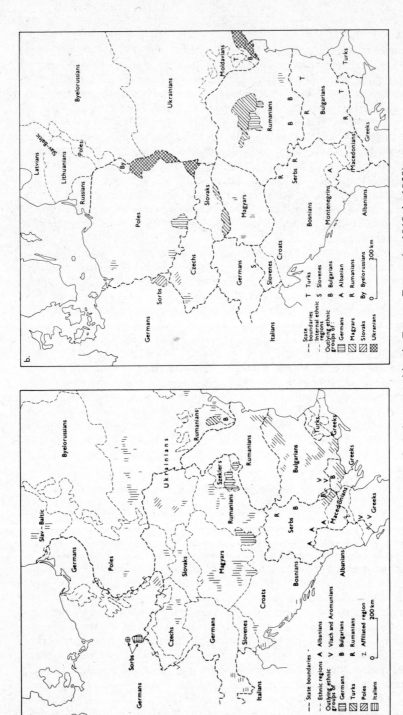

Figure 4.4. The two maps of ethnic composition in Eastern Europe (a: 1910; b: 1950) reflect the great changes that took place after the Second World War which substantially simplified the pattern. Various sources.

highly stratified nature of society allowed elites and aristocracies to rule with in- difference to the languages and traditions of their underlings.

The decline of Latin and the increasing use of printing from the sixteenth cen- tury gave importance to vernacular languages and the first seeds of nationalism. The ethnic or 'national' question began to be a serious issue from the eighteenth century under the influence of thinkers concerned with the racial and ethnic differentiation of man and a romanticism that aroused keen interest in the past and in folklore, while the study of physical anthropology grew with the new scientific approach to medical problems. The result was an amalgam of scientific method and fact with imagination and romanticism that built mysticism and iconography around the different groups. Such views as Pan-Slavism and the great Teutonic myths aroused popular interest. In the German empire growing national sentiment brought attempts in the later nineteenth century to convert its non-German subjects to *Deutschtum*; but in the Habsburg empire it was among the several different peoples that national feelings grew, pressing the dynasty to recognise them. The Magyars, however, pursued an active policy of trying to convert to the Magyar language and way of life subject Slavs and Rumanians. Pan-Slavism, vague and ill-defined, was a potent factor in awakening national identity among the Czechs and Poles and even the Slovaks under the leadership of a small core of intelligentsia, while similar forces were at work among the South Slavs. The triumph of nationalism came in the concept of the national state in the settlements after the First World War, guided by President Wilson's 'self- determination'. It became extremely difficult in the confusion to reconcile territorial demands and ethnic boundaries, making the definition of uninational states almost impossible. The minorities had their rights protected by legal guarantees which in most instances proved ineffective. The inter-war years were a time of acute nationalism worsened by the emergence of racialism in National Socialist philosophy.

The draconic ethnic solutions practised by the Nazis and the experiences of the national states with large minorities encouraged a desire to simplify the ethnic pattern within the political–territorial framework of Europe after 1945, with the success of the Greek–Turkish exchange of population in the 1920s taken as a model. But there were also serious undertones of power-politics notably in the changing balance between Teuton and Slav in Eastern Europe to the advantage of Soviet Pan-Slavism.

The ethnic groupings can be described on the composite basis of language, religion, custom and historical association or even cultural artefacts, though the groups are affected by a wide range of outside influences. Ethnic affinity and sub- sequently 'nationality' have come to be measured generally by language, which became the common indicator of national allegiance in census returns. Where such methods were used, however the questions were formulated, there was a tendency for the results to be weighted in favour of the dominant group. Out of fear or hope of economic advantage or just not to appear an outsider, people in the borderline tended to assess themselves, at least for official purposes, as members of the dominant group. Vociferous minority groups also tended to make extravagant claims of their own strength.

In the Austrio-Hungarian census, language was usually regarded as the 'customary language' (used in everyday work and dealings) because this favoured

German or Magyar, the main vehicles of trade and official communication. The succession states favoured, however, 'mother tongue' because it tended to magnify the local idiom against the former official languages. In the German census of 1933 the number of German speakers was inflated by asking for particulars of knowledge of German. Problems arise where bilingual or multilingual groups exist, while elevation of dialects to separate distinction also allows manipulation of results. The Prussians played down the Poles in their eastern territories by separately distinguishing between Kaschub, Masurian and Polish: the Poles did a similar exercise in their Byelorussian and Polesye lands in inter-war times, while the Hungarians tried the same ruse before 1914 in their Serbo-Croatian districts. Austria manipulated tabulation before 1914 by classing all Yiddish speakers as German speaking, so inflating the German element in Galicia and Bukovina. Response was often open to partiality by insinuation, duress or fear of reprisal, as in inter-war Jugoslavia, where forms were filled in before an official.

Language has become the primary determinant of the national groups and the major family in Eastern Europe is the *Slavonic*. It has been said that 'there is at the present time no specifically Slav civilisation, common to all the Slavs and to none of the other peoples; and in all probability there never has been and never will be'. A Soviet calculation in the *Atlas Narodov Mira* (1964), claims 29.6 million Poles, 9.1 million Czechs, 7.8 million Serbs, 6.5 million Bulgars, 4.3 million Croats, 4.0 million Slovaks, 1.6 million Slovenes, 1.3 million Macedonians, 0.7 million Ukrainians and 0.5 million Montenegrins, as well as small numbers of other Slav peoples, within the study area. The number of different groups listed is suggestive in itself of the diversity among these people, who have been markedly influenced from outside—from the German and even French cultural sphere on the west, the Russian cultural sphere from the east and the influence of Islam from the south-east, while among some groups Venetian–Italian influences can be traced and there is also among the southerly groups a long Greek tradition exercised through the Church. The influence of the Roman and Byzantine churches is still clearly seen in the use of the Latin or Cyrillic alphabets.

Numerically, the largest Slav group is the *Eastern*—the Great Russians, the Ukrainians and the Byelorussians, with the expansion of the Russian state as a function of their dynamic eastwards spread, but poorly represented in the study area in contrast to the *Western Slavs*, whose main contact has been with the eastwards expansion of the Germans and the spread around the periphery of Pannonia by the Magyars. They form the economically most advanced Slav group. Numerically most important are the Poles and the related Kaschubs and Masurians; second most important are the Czechs and Slovaks, the case for whose union is convincingly demonstrated. A small group in the limelight since the Second World War has been the Sorbian (Wendish) community of German Lusatia, the remains of a once more extensive scatter of Slav peoples westwards across the North European Plain.

By far the most diverse group is formed by the *Southern Slavs*—the Serbs and the Croats, the Slovenes, the Montenegrins and the Macedonians. The Bulgars represent a people of Asiatic origin, slavicised in their wanderings from the Volga basin. The enigmatic early history of the Slavs is discussed in chapter 2. In morphology, phonetics and syntax, the Slav languages are related, but it is more difficult to decide what other characteristics the Slavs have in common; certainly, music and dance play important roles and there is a possible common thread of concept and design in folk art and in folk lore. Until modern times the Slavs remained largely a backward peasantry (though this can only be applied relatively among the several peoples) that accepted cultural artefacts of other peoples and were dominated by 'foreign' elites or Slav aristocracies. Perhaps it was this backwardness and 'subordination' that have identified them as a major family of peoples. Under the philosophical influence of Herder, there emerged a new awareness of Slavdom and the concept of a common interest and inheritance in the Pan-Slav movement. Inspite of the many conflicts between the groups, in times of strain there is often a semblance of a closing of the ranks. There is no doubt, however, that Pan-Slavism, with its mystic undertones, suited well the Russian cause of guardian of the Slav world—*Mother Russia*. The national awareness of the different groups of Slavs is generally historically deep-seated, but it was allowed to crystallise only at a late stage and emerged most forcefully in the nineteenth century struggle against the over-riding dynastic will of the Habsburg and Hohenzollern or somewhat earlier in the struggle of the South Slavs against the Turks, where the issue was more of Christian against Moslem. Modern Slav nationalism has in many instances called heavily on early Slav history and myth for its 'iconography'.

4.5.1 Poles

Numbering over thirty million in the early 1970s, the Poles represent a remarkably closely knit people whose awareness of their own nationality is unmatched. The first appearance of a truly Polish state—the use of the name *Polska*—comes in the tenth century AD under the reign of Mieszko. The name suggests *the people of the field* or *plain*. The Poles embraced Latin Christianity and became missionaries for the Church of Rome in the Christianisation of their eastern marches, as well as a bastion against heathen incursions into Europe. Through the towns, strong German influences entered Polish life. The great Polish–Lithuanian Commonwealth inaugurated under the Jagiellon dynasty was a golden age that enriched Polish traditions, but was undermined by social weaknesses. No truly independent Poland existed from 1795 until after 1918, but the identity of the Poles was preserved and their language survived intensive pressure. The three different levels of material well-being and education that emerged in Poland made the welding together of the nation after 1918 a difficult task. There was also powerful French influence among the intelligentsia. The historical view of their country was potent in keeping Polish national identity alive, though it contributed to what many foreign powers regarded as excessive territorial demands after 1918. Though Polish society has great finesse and elegance, its leadership suffered in the years of foreign domination. Poles made a substantial contribution to art, literature and music, but had been deprived of experience in government and much of the economic life had fallen into non-Polish hands; consequently effective economic and political organisation seemed to escape Poland during the inter-war years. Sandwiched between Protestant

Prussia and Orthodox or atheist Russia, the Polish missionary view of the role of the Church of Rome was well entrenched.

The heavy loss of its intelligentsia during the Second World War has left the problem of economic and political organisation no less acute than the inter-war period. The consequences of the war as much as the introduction of Marxist-Leninism have forced the Poles to build a new socio-economic structure since 1945. The trauma of a bodily shift westwards has demanded creation of new regional consciousness: much of Wilno's Polish community has been moved to Olsztyn in former German East Prussia, while the fabric of Upper Silesian society has been shaken by the expulsion of the German element and the playing down of the German influence in local culture and dialect. With large Polish communities in Western Europe and North America, Poles at home have successfully kept in contact with the Western world, while acceptance of many of its artefacts have become symbols of Polish resistance to complete submergence in a sovietised Eastern Europe.

The Polish language, more formal and polite in form than other Slavonic tongues, preserves many archaic Slav forms, such as palatisation and nasal vowels, while it contains many early loan words from Latin, Czech and German. The literary language is based mainly on dialects of Great Poland. One of the greatest difficulties in the codification of modern Polish was a standardised orthography. Kaschub in the lower Vistula and Masurian in the Lake Plateau of East Prussia were distinguished by Prussia as separate languages, while a mixed dialect of Polish and German formed the colourful and expressive *Wasserpolnisch* of industrial Silesia.

A German army manual published in 1939 described the Polish character as 'sanguine, vivacious, impulsive, very hospitable but irresponsible and inconsistent. Under good leadership, the Pole is a good soldier . . .'. Polish national sentiment seems centred around an historical concept and a way of life more than around a territorial core.

4.5.2 Czechs and Slovaks

The Czechoslovak state was essentially the creation of the Bohemian patriot Masaryk. Historically, only Bohemia could look back on a golden age: Slovakia had been a mere tributary of greater states. While Poland was a clear historical image, there was no equivalent for the Czechoslovaks. Czechs and Slovaks had tended to grow apart in language and pattern of life and came together after 1918 almost by default. The Czechoslovak state created in 1918 was a multinational conglomeration of peoples—in the census of 1930, 53.0 per cent were Czechs, 16.4 per cent were Slovaks, 23.6 per cent were German, while Poles, Ukrainians, Magyars and others made up the remainder. The Czechs, the dominant element, were the 'people of state', while the Slovaks formed the senior partners, though numerically less than the powerful German element, and had little more than an apprenticeship in the new state.

A truly Bohemian dynasty ended in the fourteenth century, and in the fifteenth century Czech national sentiment and language had become identified with the Hussiste movement, whose defeat at Bilá Hora in 1620 signalled the end of national independence and the growing suppression of language and culture.

Although under the Habsburg the Czechs had become largely peasant farmers or industrial workers and the aristocracy and entrepreneurial classes had been German, a strong 'cultural nationalism' had begun to develop before the revolution of 1848—reflected in the study of Slav languages and the collection of Slav music (Šmetana, Dvořák) as well as the *Sokol* sports movement. The Pan-Slav movement was ardently cultivated by Czechs. By 1882 a Czech University had been founded in Prague, the cultural and national centre, though Czechs had absorbed much German culture.

As a result of Austrian easy-going policy and their own national awareness, the Czechs were well organised and able, while Slovaks under the less tolerant Magyars had become less aware of their identity, lacking organisation and an effective leadership, though a Slovak national organisation, the *Matica*, had existed since 1862. The lack of a developed intelligentsia and of experience in government brought an influx of Czech officials in 1918 into Slovakia and its heavy dependence on Prague. Material wealth was generally higher among the Czechs in the inter-war years than among any of the other Slav peoples, while the country had a stable, parliamentary government.

The Czechs and Slovaks are less elegant and polished in manner than the Poles, but the Czechs have shown much greater aptitude for organisation and economic management. Aristocratic tradition and the existence of a petty aristocracy, strongly marked in Poland, have been virtually absent in Czechoslovakia.

As languages, Czech and Slovak, harsher, less elegant and polite than Polish, were originally closely related, but vowel mutation differentiated Czech from other Slav languages from the fourteenth century. Early orthography of Czech was much influenced by Polish usage, but from the fifteenth century a Czech phonetic spelling developed, notably with the increasing use of the printed word. During the seventeenth and eighteenth centuries, German influence grew, but a reaction brought a linguistic revival and an attempt to replace German loan words. It was not until 1894 that modern literary Czech was finally stabilised. Had the use of Moravian instead of Bohemian dialects been chosen, it is likely that Czech and Slovak would have drawn closer together again, making the creation of a separate Slovak literary language unnecessary. In Czech Silesia, the dialects are transitional from Czech to Polish and possibly reflect a very old stage in development. Slovak is more musical and less forceful than Czech and could form the basis of a Slav *lingua franca*. From the fourteenth century, Czech was the literary language of the Slovaks until the emergence of their own literary language in the nineteenth century, which has many borrowings from Czech and Russian. Since 1918 Slovak has had full rights as a language in the Republic, inspite of agitation for the creation of a unified Czechoslovak literary language.

4.5.3 *The South Slavs*

The South Slavs in Jugoslavia and Bulgaria form a diverse collection of peoples, descendents of Slav immigrants, pre-Slav stock and slavicised immigrants, with names of ancient origin that can in some instances be traced back along their migration routes. The Slovenes and Croats fell under Roman Catholic and Latin influence and the later domination of the Austro–Hungarian empire. The Serbs in contrast came under the Greek Orthodox church and the cultural influence of Byzantium, as did the Slav peoples who settled in Bulgaria and slavicised the immigrant Ural–Altaic Bulgars. The Turkish period spread terror and migration widely through the South Slav peoples to complicate further the ethnic relations and left its impress in the acceptance of Islam by some Slav peoples (for example Pomaks in Bulgaria and Moslem Bosnians).

The intermixture is reflected in the diversity of physical types found among these groups. Inspite of the many social and economic divisions and the diverse cultural patterns, language has been the constant factor of identity among the South Slavs and has often overridden otherwise deep clefts. The separate languages of the South Slavs began development quite late and appear to derive from a language still represented by the oldest extant Bulgarian texts. In Jugoslavia over 80 per cent of the population speak Serb or Croat but there is such close affinity and mutual intelligibility in the two languages that they may be regarded as one, though Serb is written in Cyrillic characters and Croat in the Latin alphabet. Direct transliteration phonetically and character-by-character is, however, possible. Serbo-Croat has been described as the most beautiful and yet most manly of the Slav tongues. Croat orthography is based in Czech. The languages are rich in dialects, the major distinction being made in the use of the words *kaj, ča* and *što* for 'what'. The *što* form is spatially predominant and the basis of the literary language, while extension of the educational system has generally encouraged a trend to uniformity.

Slovene, separated from Serbo-Croat in the seventh to ninth centures AD, with consequently archaic forms, is spoken by 1.5 million people. Of nine dialects that of Ljubljana was chosen for the literary tongue. The language, first encouraged by Protestant reformers in the sixteenth century, had its grammar codified in the eighteenth century and its orthography based on Czech, but there has been strong resistance to attempts to merge it with Serbo-Croat. Although the Slavs' first literary language, Macedonian was one of the last recognised in its own right (1943), often being claimed with strong political undertones as merely a dialect of Serbian or Bulgarian. Since that time great progress has been made in the development of an effective literary language using the Cyrillic alphabet.

Bulgarian emerged from the Macedonian Slav language in the tenth century among the immigrant Ural–Altaic Bulgars, who retain little or no trace of their original Turkic speech. Modern Bulgarian, developed during the sixteenth century, is notable for its distinct structure, particularly the loss of cases and use of a definite article. The church long opposed attempts to bring the literary language into line with popular speech: from the mid-nineteenth century, the eastern dialect became the basis of the literary Bulgarian, with a strong Russian influence, but attempts to simplify it in the 1920s were not successful until after 1945.

The intrigue of the great powers often worked contrary to South Slav nationalism and independence, while lack of internal unity also hampered achievement of effective nationhood. As elsewhere, the Romantic movement and the growth of nationalism intensified self-consciousness and encouraged study of language and folklore. South Slav nationalism triumphed in the creation of Jugoslavia, in which by tradition and experience, Serbia became the effective core, but the more advanced economic communities of Croats and Slovenes mistrusted the reality of Serbian goodwill. Jugoslav nationalism represents a joint action of widely divergent Slav societies as a counsel of desperation to gain freedom from the greater evils of domination by neighbours. Strains and stresses remain great and no real Jugoslav nation and people yet exists.

The emergence of modern Bulgarian national identity extended over more than a century, beginning with the appearance of a materially well-endowed intelligentsia from the predominant peasant stock in the eighteenth century, and was based upon the idealised image of Bulgarian history and folklore, as well as the creation of a Bulgarian literary language. Russian encouragement contributed to the strength of Bulgarian national feeling, particularly in the struggle with the Greek Orthodox clergy. The germination of Bulgarian nationalism took place in the Bulgarian trade guilds (*esnafi*), which contributed to the printing and dissemination of nationally-orientated vernacular literature. By 1870, the Bulgarians had established their own church (*Exarchate*). Modern Bulgaria, with its Slav identity, still shows sympathy for Russia and mistrust of Turkey, while in the earlier part of the century, Bulgarian nationalism was built around dreams of territorial expansion based on the Golden Age of Tsar Boris in the ninth century. The Bulgarians maintain that ethnic discrimination plays no part in their life and that they are without religious fanaticism.

4.5.4 The Sorbs

The Lusatian Sorbs, a remnant of a once widely spread veneer of Slavs in the German sector of the Northern European Plain, have retained much of their language and culture, inspite of deep German influence. They have come into the limelight since the Second World War with the growth of the stature of Slavdom. Estimates of the number of Sorbs range from over 100 000 to as low as 25 000 (the lower number is the most probable). The Lower Lusatians, whose language has marked Polish influences, live in the Spree valley, while south of Hoyerswerda are the Upper Lusatians, a more prosperous group, whose language is more like Czech. Sorbian has, however, many structural influences from German, particularly in sentence construction, but also retains plentiful archaic features. It was first codified in the mid-nineteenth century, when newspapers and books were printed, and its cultivation has generally received strong support from Prague, where a University chair of Sorbian studies was established in 1933. With industrial development in Lusatia, the future of these people, inspite of government assurances of protection of their cultural autonomy, is not bright, particularly as they are all bilingual with German.

4.5.5 The Ukrainians

In Poland, Czechoslovakia and Rumania small groups of Ukrainians remain, whose dialects are marked by West Slav influences to a greater extent than the literary language based on the dialect of Kiev. Many are Uniates (an Orthodox rite in communion with Rome) who under post-war pressures have suffered more than the truly Orthodox or the well-organised Roman Catholics. Ukrainian identity and literary language suffered suppression under the tsars and received little encouragement from the Austro-Hungarians or the later succession states. For obscure political reasons, the Western Ukrainians were often termed Ruthenians in the inter-war years. Small numbers of *Byelorussians*, mostly Roman Catholic, are found in eastern Poland—linguistically related to the Ukrainians and much tainted by Polish culture. Large numbers of Soviet citizens of various ethnic origins form the Red Army garrisons and vast proconsular reticule in the people's democracies.

4.5.6 The Germans

In 1939 in the study area there were nearly 34 million Germans, of whom a little over 26 million were in the Reich. In the mid-1960s, there were some 17 million in the German Democratic Republic and about 875 000 outside its boundaries. Possibly up to another 800 000 might be added for the 'autochthonous' population of the Polish western territories (mostly in Upper Silesia). The influence of German culture and language is widespread in Eastern Europe, while Slav words have also been absorbed into German. The various German ethnic minorities in Eastern Europe spoke dialects that often reflected from what part of Germany they had originally come, though markedly influenced by local non-German words. Under the Austro-Hungarian empire and the Second Reich, German was a lingua franca throughout Eastern Europe, particularly in commerce and education. While the German Democratic Republic and much of the pre-war German territory east of the Oder–Neisse were traditionally Protestant, most German groups elsewhere, including even Upper Silesia, were Roman Catholic.

4.5.7 The Jews

Before the Second World War Jews were an important element in Poland, Rumania, Czechoslovakia, Hungary and the western parts of the Soviet Union, as well as in modest numbers in the Balkan countries. They moved into the Balkans and even into eastern Galicia and Volhynia from the Black Sea littoral from the eleventh century, while at an early date, Jews from Western Europe had penetrated into Hungary and the Sudeten country. The main drift of Jews from the west came in the twelfth and thirteenth centuries, notably into Poland and Lithuania. The Jews who had migrated with the German eastwards colonisation brought their own German dialect mixed with Hebrew, old French and Slavonic words to form 'Yiddish'. Under privileges given by the Polish–Lithuanian state, Jews came to have a virtual monopoly of commercial and financial life. In the seventeenth century and the onset of troubled times in Poland, many fled to the west, while those remaining found life increasingly difficult, particularly under the spread of Russian power, when they were deprived of many of their former privileges. In those areas of Poland that fell to Prussia Jews quickly absorbed German culture and often migrated to Berlin and other German towns. From Polish areas under Austrian control Jews moved into Bukovina, Transylvania and even into Wallachia and Moldavia. From 1880 to 1914 a massive Jewish migration to the United States took place. Antisemitism during the Second World War led to the death of several million in extermination camps and ghettoes, while most survivors fled to Israel. The relatively small number of Jews in the Balkan lands were mostly descended from 'sephardic' communities driven from Iberia after 1492 and still use a language derived from Old Castilian.

4.5.8 The Magyars

The Magyars or Hungarians are quite apart from the Slavs and a common European tradition. The bulk—about 10 million—live in Hungary, but are also found in Slovakia, Rumania and Jugoslavia. There is a large Hungarian community in the U.S.A. (about 650 000). The Magyars, a nomadic people of Ural–Altaic origin (Ugrians), appeared in the Pannonian Plains late in the ninth century AD. After a catastrophic defeat at the Lechfeld in 955 AD, they began to abandon their nomadic way of life and their raiding for a sedentary colonisation and accepted Christianity after 970 AD. Although they mixed with earlier Slav elements and other peoples such as the Jazyges and Cumans, they preserved their tongue and much of their culture, but in the growth of towns and the development of sedentary farming there were strong German and Italian influences. After troubled times during the Turkish conquest, the Magyars became part of the Habsburg empire in the eighteenth century, until a strong national movement led to the creation of the Dual Monarchy in 1867. The use of Magyar as an official and school language in place of Latin after 1844 and the strength of its position in the Dual monarchy after 1867 brought an active programme of Magyarisation. Although Hungarian society developed an élan and finesse, the overbearing and oppressive Magyar earned a dislike among subject peoples, so they had few friends when the Treaty of Trianon drew exceptionally tight boundaries around the country after 1918.

The predominantly Slav nature of the new Soviet Imperium has ill-fitted Magyar tastes and has allowed nothing of the revanchist nationalism that flourished in the inter-war years. The Magyars take much of their national iconography from looking back nostalgically either to the early Hungarian kingdom under Stephen (997–1038 AD) or to the Age of Enlightened Absolutism. Stephen's crown remained a key to Magyar iconography until 1945.

Magyar, a Finno–Ugric tongue, is an agglutinative language without genders but with an elaborate system of prefixes and suffices, pleasant in sound, but its literature has made less impact than the markedly different Slavonic languages. The study of Hungarian music in the nineteenth century has been reflected in the world renown established in this century by Bartok and Kodály. Although there is a strong Calvinist tradition, the country has had a Roman Catholic majority.

In eastern Transylvania a distinctive community of *Szeklers*, closely related in language and custom to the main body of the Magyars, is obscure in origin, but they seem to have colonised the Carpathians to defend important passes. The Szekler communities appear to have been successful in absorbing Rumanians to their culture, while they have received some recognition of their distinctiveness by a measure of autonomy granted them in Rumania after the Second World War. Tirgu Mureş is their cultural centre.

4.5.9 The Rumanians

The bulk of the Rumanians is found in their titular state—Rumania (about 14 million)—but nearly two million live in the Soviet republic of Moldavia and small numbers (as well as the related *Vlachs*) are found scattered through the Balkans. The Rumanian language has strong structural and vocabulary similarities to the

Romance tongues, though it contains many words derived from Slav and other south-east European languages. The Rumanians may represent descendents of romanised Dacians, who retreated into the mountains as invaders from the steppes spilled across the plains, but they later returned to colonise Wallachia and Moldavia. Alternatively, the Rumanians may be descended from romanised inhabitants from south of the Danube who migrated into the Carpathians, perhaps during the great Bulgarian state in the ninth century AD. Such a view would help to establish the relationship between the Vlachs and Rumanians. It is possible that the migrants from the south came into contact with small pockets of romanised people still hiding in the mountains. A Hungarian thesis, which suggests that movement from the south took place after the Magyars had becomes established in Transylvania sometime in the eleventh century, was used to strengthen Hungarian claims to Transylvania.

'*Vlach*' is of Slav derivation from an old Germanic generic word for Roman provincials, latinised in Wallachia, though this regional designation is not known in Rumania, where the corresponding area is called *Tarà Româneasca* (the Rumanian Land), which comprises Oltenia (the Land of the Olt) and Muntenia (the Land of the Mountain). The Moldavians in the Soviet Union speak basically the same Rumanian language but under Russian influence use the Cyrillic alphabet.

The Rumanians throughout almost all their history have been controlled or influenced by other peoples—the Hungarians, the Turks and the Phanariot Greek princes, or the Russians. During the First World War and in the inter-war period, Rumania came under growing French influence and the Rumanians cultivated their relations with the Romance world of Europe. Byzantine culture has supplied the religious background and Church Slavonic was used not only in church but also as an internal written language until the seventeenth century. Rumanian nationalism developed first in Hungarian Transylvania and spread later to the rest of the Rumanian settled land. Though strong and emphatic in its Romance traditions, Rumanian nationalism has been liberal towards the other nationalities of the country. In the Soviet period, the Rumanians have not surrendered their views and have been resolute in the defence of their identity in a largely Slav imperium.

4.5.10 Minor Peoples

Closely related to the Rumanians are the small and scattered groups of *Vlachs* or *Aromunians*—mostly shepherds or simple farmers—found in Jugoslavia, Albania and Bulgaria. In general, they have tended to merge with other peoples and slowly be absorbed to the Slav world. Similar Greek-speaking groups are the *Karakatchans* (3000) of Bulgaria, though they are reputedly also found in Jugoslavia and Greece as well as Albania, where their number is too small to warrant separate enumeration. Despite attempts to stir up national feeling among these peoples, they seem to live peacefully with their neighbours. The *Gypsies* entered Europe across the Bosphorus in the eleventh century and spread across the Balkans and Pannonia towards the north and west. Their language originated in India, from which they came, but it is now much augmented by Greek words. Gypsies who lost their own speech have been usually counted among the people whose language they have adopted. The Gypsies were usually reluctantly tolerated and during the Second World War large numbers were exterminated in concentration camps.

The *Albanians* have shown a strong natural increase since the Second World War. Nearly two million live in Albania and almost another million in Jugoslavia, mostly along the Albanian border, with small numbers in Bulgaria and Greece. The Albanian language, one of the least known in Europe, appears to be a survivor of the Illyrian tongues spoken throughout much of the Balkan Peninsula and Dinaric lands and even north of the Danube before the coming of the Slavs. The first written literature in Albanian appears in the mid-sixteenth century, but attempts to codify the language were hampered by lack of agreement among scholars on its orthography. The Turks tried to suppress Albanian literature and education in the eighteenth and nineteenth centuries. There is considerable variation between the languages of north (*Geg*) and south (*Tosk*), but the dialect of Elbasan, intelligible to both, forms the standard literary tongue. Until recent times Albanian society has been dominated by strong tribal loyalties, while women have had few rights. Turkish influence was strongest in the south and centre rather than in the more inaccessible north. In the north, Roman Catholicism was common and in the centre, many Albanians turned to often radical interpretations of Islam. The south was much influenced by Greek culture and the Greek Orthodox church, though the church in Albania became autocephalous in 1937. Albanian culture survived largely because the country was off the mainstreams of European life and was not generally under pressure from outside. Albanian national feeling, however, awoke at the same time as Slav and Greek nationalism developed in the Turkish empire. Its eventual independence owed more to a desire to create 'neutral' territory than to recognise the Albanian national aspirations. In the inter-war period with French, Italian and British help, much was done to modernise Albanian society, but the country came under growing pressure from Italy and Jugoslavia. After the Second World War Albania came under strong Jugoslav surveillance and might well have been absorbed by the Jugoslavs if they had not defected from the Soviet camp. More recently Albania has switched to the Chinese camp and this action may be seen as an attempt to maintain its identity.

5 Town and Village

5.1 Towns: A general survey

Although some Slav historians claim that the Slavs developed towns of their own, the overwhelming influence on urban development in Eastern Europe has come from outside. Until twentieth century industrialisation the town played a smaller part in everyday life in Eastern Europe than in Western Europe. In so many instances it represented a foreign influence, even foreign population, amid rural peasant economies. In the contemporary scene the most urbanised part is in the west—in the German Democratic Republic, in Bohemia–Moravia and in western Poland. The large town-like villages of the Puszta give an anomalous character to urbanisation in Hungary. Small towns are well developed in northern Jugoslavia, but the southern part has a low level of urban development, like Bulgaria and Rumania. Few real towns have existed until recently in Albania. In nearly all these countries the urban scene is dominated by the large capital city, yet only five of Europe's thirty-nine 'million cities' lie in Eastern Europe.

5.1.1. Classical Tradition in Towns

Some towns may be dated back to Classical times, though many Greek foundations have disappeared and in the turbulent conditions, none attained the splendour of the cities of the Greek Peninsula. The Romans diffused town life, but their towns were primarily part of an effective political and military organisation. The main Roman settlements lay at route intersections, mostly in the lowlands south of the Danube, but a few existed briefly in Dacia. Although inhabited by local people, these towns did diffuse Roman speech and habits to the surrounding countryside. Some of the largest and best equipped towns were the big legionary fortresses of the frontier, like Acquincum and Carnuntum. Towns in the mountains were usually garrison centres. Along the Adriatic coast port towns gave access to the interior, like Salonae, Narona and Dyrrachium, the latter at the western end of the *Via Egnatia* that crossed to Thessalonice.

As the Roman empire declined, the town lost its economic and administrative importance. The dating of walls around towns suggests a slow spread from the frontier districts of instability, but in the turbulence of the sixth and seventh centuries AD Roman towns were devastated, though some form of occupancy continued in many towns. What remained of the Roman urban tradition, preserved in large part through the Christian church, seems to have been more successful in the Western empire than in the Eastern, where the luxury of urban centres seems to have been more of a burden. In some instances settlements shifted their sites: the people of Salonae fled to offshore islands when the Avars attacked and destroyed their city but later returned to found a new community in the vast ruins of Diocletian's palace at Split, while the citizens of Epidaurus (Cavtat) fled to the safety of the island of Dubrovnik. Coastal settlements in general survived better than inland centres, since Byzantine or Italian sea power was more readily able to protect them. Beyond the protection of the Byzantine emperors the town almost vanished, though Justinian tried a virtual last ditch attempt to preserve the Roman urban tradition and even fortified villages. The landscape of the sixth century Byzantine empire was seemingly one of towns as fortified *hedgehogs*[1] in a countryside increasingly in the hands of Slav and other immigrants, but many settlements listed at the time cannot now be identified. The continuity of occupancy of certain towns is seen from records of bishoprics. In the seventh century these were reduced almost entirely to the littoral of the Aegean Sea, but later bishops began to appear from sees in the Rhodope, the Maritsa basin, Thrace and Macedonia, which no doubt points to some town-like settlement as their seat.

5.1.2 Early Towns in the Slav Lands

The invading Slavs and Bulgars contributed little at first to town foundation, but once they began to create principalities, seats of government with something of the character of a town emerged, doubtless influenced by the Romano-Byzantine tradition. These communities were usually large enclosures surrounding huts for craftsmen and farmers as well as churches and market places: in some a special enclosure indicated a princely residence. The churches were sometimes built from stones quarried from abandoned Roman buildings. The first Crusade in the eleventh century visited some of these places—Zemun near Belgrade and Niš were described as fortified, with mills and bridges, but the paucity of town life is suggested by the long marches made by the Crusaders between these 'towns', especially outside the Byzantine boundaries.

North of the Danube many settlements may be dated to Iron Age 'proto-urban nuclei', tribal centres, fortified religious sites and princely seats, which provided a refuge and were commonly sited in good defensive positions. In the plains, such sites were usually on lake islands or amid marsh, and Czech investigations have suggested a rough correlation in density with soil fertility. Evidence suggests that they were built between the seventh and tenth centuries, though some smaller ones may be earlier. All were surrounded by wooden stockades, strengthened by earth and masonry, within which lay permanently inhabited huts for craftsmen, workshops and often a stone built church. By the late ninth century, the most important settlements dominated large areas of country and were often bishops' seats and princely castles, a relationship still reflected in the cathedral within the bounds of the Hradčany at Prague and in the Wawel at Kraków. Gniezno, Poznań and Wrocław have similar associations, though from the late eighth century a separation began to take place between the princely and ecclesiastical functions and the trading and artisans' quarters. The separation was usually well defined by the eleventh century. For example, in Kraków, a separate monastic and clerical settlement grew up; in some cases it was also fortified (for example Poznań). Usually a separate enclosure, the *Podgrodzie*, had grown up outside the castle, where craftsmen, retainers, traders and artisans lived. Until about the twelfth century, the embryonic Slav towns north of the

---

[1] *Hedgehog:* derived from German usage in the Second World War—a highly fortified position or settlement held in territory otherwise dominated by the enemy or his partisans.

Danube appear to have been largely native effort with some outside influences from traders and the church.

History textbooks often give the impression that the wave of town foundation that swept across Central Europe from the Rhinelands created towns essentially German in style and in population amid a Slav population without important settlement foci. It seems more likely that the embryonic Slav towns were settled by small groups of German merchants and traders before German colonisation turned to founding new towns, so that many 'German towns' rest on pre-existing agglomerations of Slav population. The 'German town' was essentially a jurisdictional and social concept, in which the Germans came to form an élite, giving the leadership to a large Slav population; for example, at Danzig (Gdańsk), Germans never rose above 30 per cent of the population in the fourteenth century, though in some towns (notably in Bohemia, particularly Prague) this proportion was higher.

5.1.3 The Age of Planned Towns in Central Europe

The twelfth century became the age in Central Europe of the planned town, which in some instances replaced existing settlements, but in other cases was put down on green-field sites chosen for their potential in sparsely settled areas as a form of mediaeval pioneering. Many were little better than villages, though they usually attracted settlers by offering urban privileges in spite of their rural character. These towns did not imply any change in the nature of the local economy and they served largely as means of enhancing trade, because they were often on or near the site of an existing market. By regulating trade and providing a guild structure for the encouragement of handicrafts, they provided secure and reasonably fair conditions in which commerce might develop. After 1400 these towns were commonly the product of entirely non-German initiative though they preserved German legal forms and were carried by Poles and Lithuanians deep into the western lands of Russia. They are also found in Bohemia and Transylvania, parts of western Hungary, Slovenia, Croatia and in Slovakia. Differences in urban laws from district to district depended on the German towns from which they were taken. Along the Baltic coast, Lübeck law was common, but over much of the northern plain east of the Elbe and across Poland, Magdeburg law was typical. Nürnberg law was found in southern Bohemia, but there was the use of Leitmeritz (Litoměřice), Olmütz (Olomouc) and the mining law of Iglau (Jihlava) in Bohemia; in Slovakia, Schemnitz (Kremnica) law was used and a special local law was devised for the mining communities of Spiš (Zips). Viennese and the locally variant Stuhlweissenburg (Székesfehérvár) law was common in Hungary and northern Jugoslavia. Many towns founded in south-eastern Hungary were later destroyed by the Turks and had to be refounded in the eighteenth century Habsburg colonisation. It has been estimated that between 1200 and 1400, over 1500 towns were founded.

The classical theological idea of Jerusalem found in many early manuscripts was the basis of the concept of the 'Gothic ideal town' (Schinz), represented as a circular wall enclosing a town divided into four 'quarters', with a central market place and four gates, one of which is slightly displaced in position. It is usually possible to distinguish two street patterns—the main through streets and the central market associated with long distance trade and the more confused pattern of streets, cul-de-sacs and the small market for local trade. Adjacent to the main market place were the town hall, the cloth hall and warehouses, the guild houses and the Jewish quarter. Thorn (Toruń) and Frankfurt an der Oder are good examples of this layout, distinguishable in the early street plan of Berlin. While large rectangular markets were common in the northern plain, many south German towns had long, broad axial street markets (particularly in Bohemia). The successful growth of these towns is seen in the creation shortly after foundation of a new town, almost a separate legal entity, retained in the names *Altstadt* (*stare miasto*) and *Neustadt* (*nowe miasto*)—the foundation of the Altstadt in Magdeburg in the twelfth century was followed by the Neustadt in 1230; in Prague the corresponding dates are 1230 and 1348 or 1237 and 1340 in the 'colonial town' of Elbing. In the northern plain, the planned towns were laid out at generous intervals of a day's journey of six to eight hours.

5.1.4 *Mongol–Tatar and Turkish Incursions in South-eastern Europe*

It has been suggested that the Mongol–Tatar invasion of the thirteenth century and later Turkish incursions may have stimulated town growth by demonstrating the security of living in a community protected by a defensive wall. While some of the largest towns in the northern plains and in Bohemia may have reached 10 000–12 000 people in the thirteenth century, towns of even 5000 people were extremely rare in South-eastern Europe. Under Turkish rule many smaller towns decayed through economic stagnation, but sites selected as main seats of Turkish administration certainly grew in importance. Sofia, Bucharest, Novi Pazar and Skopje flourished in Turkish times, while the Turks actually founded Sarajevo as a governor's residence in 1462 and by the mid-sixteenth century it had a population of probably 50 000. The trading towns of the Adriatic littoral also flourished—some, like Dubrovnik, with considerable autonomy or others, like Šibenik, under skilful direction of the Venetians.

5.1.5 *Towns in Post-Medieval Times*

From the late fourteenth to the nineteenth century there was little change in the number and distribution of towns in Eastern Europe (figure 5.1) In eastern Poland and the westernmost parts of Russia, a few small towns were created in the fifteenth and sixteenth centuries. In the Ottoman empire apart from the main seats of administration, stagnation marked most towns. While eighteenth century ideas of town planning and creation of princely *Residenzstädte*[1] penetrated through the Habsburg empire and the German lands, these had no impact in the Ottoman empire, though they were slightly felt in Poland, particularly in Warsaw. The great burst of town growth in Western Europe in the nineteenth century was not felt until the lattermost part of the century in Eastern Europe, marked in the industrial towns of central Germany (German Democratic Republic) and the Silesian coalfield, while in the Habsburg empire, the industrial towns of Bohemia formed a striking contrast to the stately country towns. One of the least attractive

[1] *Residenzstadt* (pl. *Residenzstädte*): A German term for the elegant capitals of small principalities from the seventeenth century onwards.

examples is the soulless textile town of Łódź in Poland. In Bulgaria during the nineteenth century, Turkish interest encouraged some villages to develop as primitive industrial towns producing textile and other domestic goods. The growth in shipments of foodstuffs and raw materials from Eastern Europe, especially from the Danube and Black Sea, to Western Europe stimulated the development of markets, transport facilities and agriculturally orientated industries that gave impetus to town growth, for example at Brăila, Galati and later Constanta, while after 1857 oil working at Ploiesti accelerated growth.

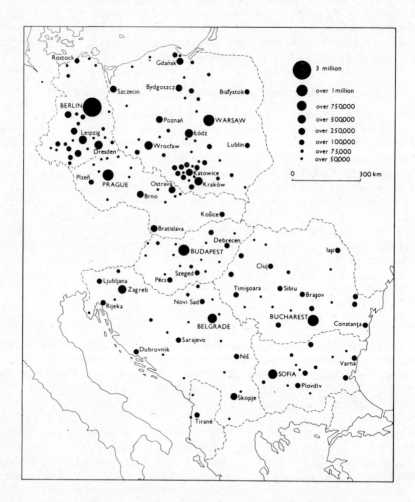

Figure 5.1. Eastern Europe is marked by considerable intraregional levels of urbanisation. The southern parts of the German Democratic Republic, western Bohemia and the now Polish Upper Silesia stand out. The lowest degree of urbanisation is found in Carpathia and the Balkans. Based on various national statistical yearbooks.

5.1.6 Towns between the World Wars

The inter-war economic conditions did not encourage formation of new towns nor, to any great extent, town growth. There was, however, some growth in the capitals of the new succession states and in towns vital to their economics. In the territory now the German Democratic Republic, towns grew slowly, apart from new centres of the chemical industries under the Nazi development plans. The need for a port completely under Polish control led to the establishment of Gdynia, and growth of towns marked the attempt to develop a strategically safe central Polish industrial area. In Jugoslavia there was a feeble attempt to encourage industrial towns away from the strategically vulnerable northern periphery. In Czechoslovakia the foundation of the new town of Zlín (Gottwaldov), with its massive shoe and rubber factories, sought to relieve unemployment and poverty. In Hungary urban growth centred on Budapest, while a similar situation was found in Bulgaria and Rumania. Italian investment in Albania brought some growth in the capital, Tiranë, in Elbasan and the port of Durrës. In Poland during the inter-war period the towns were focal points of efforts to overcome the differences in living standards between the former Prussian, Austrian and Russian sectors of the country. A not dissimilar situation was found in Jugoslavia, though the problem was attacked less resolutely than in Poland.

5.1.7 The Town since 1945

Towns in Socialist Eastern Europe have been affected by Marxist–Leninist dogma. As a 'proletarian centre', the town should be the spearhead of Communism. Though town status is measured in economic terms, the town is an administrative and planning focus around which the whole territorial–administrative structure is hung. One aim, whose priority appears to have been reduced, has been to even out differences in living standards between town and country. Strong central planning control and executive authority make it possible to mould the town in ideological ways unknown in the Western countries.

Elimination of unlimited speculation in land and the tight control on urban land use are used to build a new pattern that reflects the classlessness of the Marxist–Leninist society. The town is regarded as a unit and planning aims to integrate functional land uses rather than create separate zonal uses. The central business district of the Western town is more a cultural and administrative focus in the Socialist town. There are usually only limited commercial functions—the contrast in the number of shops between, say, Warsaw or Budapest and Vienna is striking. In the decentralisation of the commercial functions the neighbourhood unit plays a part, discouraging shopping trips to the town centre and so releasing the burden on public transport. There is a lack of the facilities in Western towns that revolve around the motor car. The importance attached to mass demonstration marches has commonly brought the development of a *Prunkallee*[1] and vast square (as seen in East Berlin) or the provision of a vast sports arena as in the Park of Culture outside Katowice.

[1] *Prunkallee*: a German term used to describe the wide and ostentatious main thoroughfares of many Soviet cities and, more recently, of East European capitals.

The neighbourhood units, inspite of disappointing progress, are commonly associated with a specific industrial plant. Each unit should contain dwellings of different sizes (usually in blocks of flats), the necessary shops, schools and other amenities. They should, therefore, theoretically be remarkably self-contained and have a population of about 2500 people.

Marxist–Leninist town planning is best seen in the new 'Socialist towns', associated with major industrial developments and usually designed to achieve a single objective. In Poland Nowa Huta was planned to house workers of the large new Lenin steelworks and to attract labour from rurally overpopulated districts around, while Nowy Tychy was an attempt to ease congestion in the Upper Silesian industrial area. In Jugoslavia Titograd was, in contrast, designed as a regional administrative centre. The form and content of 'Socialist realism' is best seen in these towns, which basically consist of groups of neighbourhood units, and a central administrative core, all focused on the main plant. The designs are based mainly on views current in the early fifties when the plans were formulated, while the basic idea of the architecture was to be 'Socialist in content, national in form'. Until the mid-1950s architectural style was strongly influenced by Soviet tastes and revealed little of being 'national in form'; Leipzig, Warsaw, Berlin and Sofia contain many examples. Now, architecture in new towns is more functional, with the stark rigidity of form seen in the new towns of the West.

In the latter 1960s there was growing criticism of the earlier towns and it is recognised that errors were made. Too great a compactness was attempted in order to give the so-called 'big-city effect'. This produced monotony and overcrowding of buildings that were too high and lined overwide streets. Many plans are now regarded as having been too geometric and wrong to focus the town solely on its main plants, even if separated by a park or lake.

The great changes in the economy and society wrought by the new dogmata have left some towns without their former *raison d'être*, such as by a shift of functions from one town to another: for example, Nowa Sól in Poland has taken over functions formerly performed by Głogów which was almost completely destroyed. In the Sudetenland the expulsion of the Germans left towns almost uninhabited and some remain with populations much below pre-war levels and in a state of decay. This is also true of market towns in parts of the Polish 'recovered territories' that today serve still sparsely repopulated rural areas, notably in Pomerania and former East Prussia. Historic towns have, however, been preserved: in Poland, the old towns in Warsaw and Gdańsk have been painstakingly restored and in Czechoslovakia, over fifty towns have particular quarters selected for preservation—in a few cases, whole towns are so classified—whereas in the German Democratic Republic, a number of the finer buildings in devastated Dresden have been carefully restored. In the German Democratic Republic and in Poland, however, industrial developments, particularly mining extensions, have been allowed to swallow up existing towns and their populations resettled elsewhere.

5.2 Examples of Selected Towns

5.2.1 Berlin (figures 5.2, 5.3)

Slav settlements on the sites of Berlin and Kölln before the twelfth century were

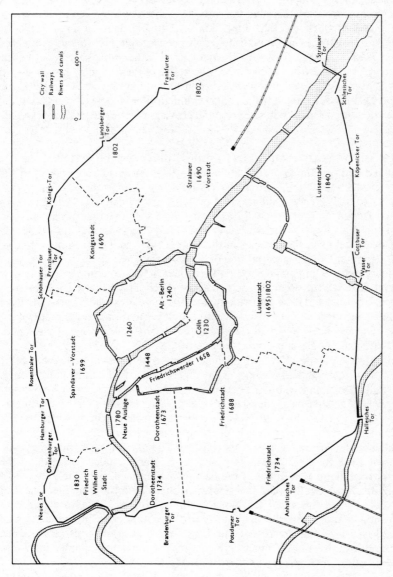

Figure 5.2. Natural water features formed an important element in the original site of Berlin around which later 'Suburbs' were laid out to the line of the customs wall.

taken over by the first German settlers, attracted by a crossing place of the Spree on the trade route from the Amber Coast to the Middle Rhinelands, readily defensible amid the lakes and rivers of the Havel–Spree *Urstromtal* system. The two communities were united in the early fourteenth century and their markets came to rival Brandenburg, seat of the *Markgraf*, as well as rising as the leader of a league of towns in the Mark Brandenburg, exercising considerable influence on the *Hanse*. Some setback to their fortunes came with the control of the Hohenzollern in the fifteenth century, who stripped them of many privileges. In 1443 a castle had been built at Alt–Kölln to keep order, while in 1451, the 'prince's court' was moved from Tangermünde to Berlin. The conversion of the castle into a roomy palace in 1538 and the provision of new defences marked the emergence of Berlin as a true capital and as a financial centre for Brandenburg–Prussia.

The Thirty Years' War was disastrous, with most of Berlin's buildings destroyed and two-thirds of its population lost. Its fortunes were revived by the Great Elector (1640–88), who improved the defences and founded new 'towns' adjacent to it. With the establishment of gardens and new buildings, the town gradually changed into a typical *Residenzstadt*. Up to this time Berlin had had only small handicraft industries, serving a purely local market, but in the late seventeenth century, the opening of the Havel–Oder canal linked it to Breslau and to Hamburg. Gradual expansion of the municipal area in the eighteenth century increased Berlin's population and reflected its growing importance in new suburbs. In 1738 the original core and seven outer suburbs were enclosed by a customs wall around an area twice that of thirty years earlier. The walls were eventually removed in the mid-nineteenth century, but the names of many of the wall's gates remain—the most famous is the *Brandenburger Tor*. By the mid-eighteenth century Berlin's population was almost 100 000.

Frederick the Great (1740–86) sought to make Berlin a capital worthy of its status. New government buildings, a new opera house and a number of palaces were built, though in the suburbs housing remained low, single-storied buildings. Industry was also encouraged, especially for the state needs: a foundry was built to make armaments, followed by other undertakings supplying a wide range of government needs. To serve the growing luxury demand of the capital, a porcelain and a silk industry were established. The markets were moved outside the town since their space was required for military drilling squares and the process of making Berlin a massive barracks continued, with the addition of further fortifications. It is said that Frederick changed Berlin from the Athens of the North to the Sparta of the North. Much of the architecture of the later eighteenth century and the early nineteenth century was monumental and ordered in a way that expressed the disciplined nature of the Prussian state. Nevertheless, even into the nineteenth century there remained immediately outside the central area, a remarkably rural character.

Prussia's brief eclipse in the Napoleonic wars had a serious effect on Berlin, where artificially stimulated industries quickly collapsed and population fell by 10 000 between 1801 and 1810. Development began again with renewed vitality when Prussia emerged more powerful from the settlement of 1815. Industry now began new growth, encouraged by road building and later railway construction. A milestone was the opening of the Borsig metal works in 1836.

Between 1816 and 1846 the population rose from 197 000 to 397 000 and Berlin outgrew its old walls. By 1861 population exceeded 500 000. While plans were developed for various parts of the town, it was not until the 1860s that an overall plan for development was designed, whose conception owed much to trends in Paris, unsuited to the Berlin situation. Some observers see 'English influences' in the design of the squares. The concept of the *Mietskaserne*, soulless barrack-like tenements, was first incorporated into this plan, with the view of building such blocks inexpensively to cater for the rapid growth in population. The massive rise in speculative land values increased the tendency for the less expensive accommodation to be pushed away from the street frontages and to create the problem of the *Hinterhof* (rear courtyard flats) in which about half of Berlin's population was to live by 1900.

Berlin's growth had been accelerated by the creation of the Second Reich in 1871 and its increased importance as the capital of one of the world's most powerful states. As the focal point of the new German empire Berlin's administrative, financial and commercial functions were to grow energetically. Industrial growth was also quick, notably in electrical and railway engineering, besides the luxury consumer durables, all much encouraged by its emergence as the focus of the Prussian railway system in the 1850s.

Until the middle nineteenth century Berlin had expanded mainly to the north (Reinickendorf, Rosenthal), but thereafter expansion was more to the west, where the growth of 'rent barracks' was most striking (Wedding, Gesundbrunnen, Moabit, Hanseviertel, Tiergarten) (figure 5.3). There was also some growth towards the south, notably in Schöneberg and Tempelhof. The old town remained the home of the lower civil servants and craftsmen, while in Dorotheenstadt, Schöneberg and Friedrichstadt were the higher classes of civilian and military officials. The north and west were largely working-class districts that remained rather isolated and without strong corporate feeling. As central Berlin became increasingly concerned with administrative, governmental and commercial operations, people migrated to the outskirts and satellite communities, particularly as suburban railways and tramways were built. Population was swollen by a steady influx of migrants from other parts of Germany or even Jews from Poland and Russia. The growing wealth of Berlin encouraged the development of villa districts, new town-like communities, in Westende (1866), Lichterfelde (1869), Grunewald (1889) or Nikolassee (1905) and Frohnau (1909), attractively sited amid woods and by lakes.

In 1912 in an attempt to co-ordinate the development of Berlin and the rapidly growing residential districts and towns around, a Planning Association for Greater Berlin was set up, followed in 1920 by a massive expansion of the city boundaries to take in a population of over four million. Greater Berlin was simply an agglomeration of communities of different character and origin—the old mediaeval communities merged into Berlin in 1709; the old towns extant before the early eighteenth century; the old villages that became towns in the nineteenth century; other planned communities laid out in the seventeenth and subsequent centuries; and the new communities laid out after 1871.

After the First World War, considerable new working-class housing replaced the worst of the *Mietskasernen*. One of the first new districts was at Neu-Tempelhof, followed in 1930 by the adventurous Siemensstadt (Gropius) and

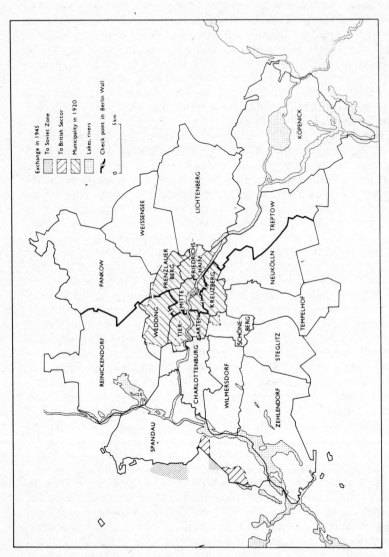

Figure 5.3. The boundaries of the city were greatly expanded in 1920 by the creation of Greater Berlin, which had a population exceeding four million during the Second World War. Divided among the four occupying powers in 1945, the three western sectors—British, American and French—were completely isolated by the erection of the famous Wall through the city heart in 1961.

between 1925 and 1931 the famous Britz settlement. After 1933 experimentation was stopped by the Nazi planners, who sought to return to the absolutist style of *Preussentum*, examplified by the project for Charlottenburg Nord (1937–9). A massive general plan to create a capital for the Thousand Year *Reich* was drawn up based on the vague concept of the *Führerprinzip*, and included vast avenues for parades, immense monumental government buildings and an assembly hall to hold a million people. War ended the initial preparations.

After heavy wartime bombing and the Red Army attack into the centre of the city in 1945, Berlin was in ruins: from a maximum population of almost 4.5 million in 1943 there were a little over three million people in 1946. Berlin was divided between the four occupying powers—the western part was in British, American and French hands, while the eastern part and the central districts east of the Brandenburger Tor were under Soviet occupation, and a four-power *Kommandatura*[1] coordinated its government. In 1946 a new 'collective plan' for the redevelopment of Berlin was devised to create a townscape with careful separation of the confused pattern of land use. There were to be no residential areas with more than 250 persons per hectare and arrangements were foreseen to prevent concentration of traffic at a few bottlenecks, which the pre-war Plan would have failed to achieve. The new plan for a population of 3.5 million was conceived in the belief that Berlin would remain capital of a united Germany that would consequently require all the necessary higher governmental functions and that it would remain a major industrial centre, in spite of wartime shifts in industry.

The split between the Western Allies and the Russians in 1948 made hope of a unified redevelopment fade. Berlin West and Berlin East, with separate adminstrations and working in different political and economic conditions, began to go their own ways. The plan for East Berlin retained much of the pre-war Speer Plan in the centripetal focus of its streets, the centralised organisation of the town and the radial axes extending into main residential areas. In contrast West Berlin's plan has been to distribute the urban functions more evenly, with effective fast traffic links. The various districts are separated by amenity areas and green belts and there is not the clear focal concentration of the 'city functions' in the centre seen in East Berlin. Such decentralisation prevents the problems caused by large commuting flows into a restricted areal core of a largely non-residential character, a situation not avoided by the East Berlin plan.

Since 1961 West Berlin has been effectively sealed off from East Berlin and from the German Democratic Republic. The impact of the 'Wall' through the centre of the town has been to discourage development in a broad strip along the boundary between the Western and Soviet sectors, leaving a dead zone in the core. In West Berlin the suburbs have become more important than the former core through a conscious planning decision, but the same thing has happened in East Berlin, almost contrary to planning decisions. In the Western sectors striking new suburbs like the Hanseviertel have emerged, though some of the new residential areas are not particularly successful designs (for example Märkisches Viertel). The long street frontage and gloomy rear courts of the *Berliner Miljö*[2] of

[1] *Kommandatura*: a Russian word devised to describe the four-power headquarters and administration in occupied Berlin in 1945.
[2] *Berliner Miljö*: the German mis-spelling of the French *milieu*; it suggests the rather tawdry nature of society in the squalid tenements of the Prussian capital.

pre-1914 have, however, largely disappeared. In East Berlin the main axis has become the *Prunkstrasse* of the Karl-Marx-Allee (Stalinallee, Frankfurter Strasse), while the demolition of the old royal palace provided space for a main saluting base at the Marx-Engels-Platz. The governmental functions have shifted to an inner suburb, Pankow.

The isolation of West Berlin disrupted the railway system of the Greater Berlin. The only railway still operating for traffic across the town from the German Democratic Republic is the international express route. In order to be able to divert trains from the western parts of the German Democratic Republic to Berlin East station, a ring railway was completed in 1957 that had been in spasmodic construction since 1902. It now serves commuters from the towns around the periphery of West Berlin travelling daily into East Berlin. The urban railway system operates as two separate networks for East and West Berlin and some new construction has made West Berlin more self-contained. There is little road traffic between the two halves of Berlin and access from Western Germany to West Berlin is limited to the autobahn from Hanover for military traffic. Air services are also separate—for West Berlin to Tempelhof and for East Berlin to Schönefeld.

The position of the two parts of Berlin in international law is much disputed. Western observers maintain that the establishment of East Berlin as the capital of the German Democratic Republic is contrary to the agreements made among the Allied powers in 1945, while Eastern observers dispute the legality of West Berlin as a federal state in the German Federal Republic.

The age structure of West Berlin shows a very much larger proportion of old people than in the Federal Republic and the German Democratic Republic, while there has been little success in attracting young people to settle. The economy, because of the isolation of West Berlin, has had to be geared to reducing the problems of transport to a minimum by avoiding the import of bulky raw materials and the production of bulky low value articles. Industry in West Berlin

Table 5.1   Population of Berlin 1740–1970

Year	Population (in 000s)
1740	90
1785	147
1820	185
1861	521
1890	1560
1919	1900
1939	4300
1943	4470
1946	3060
1959–60	West: 2200/East: 1090
1970	West: 2122/East: 1079

Source: Schinz, H. (1964). *Berlin–Stadt-schicksal und Städtebau.* Brunswick. Statistical handbooks of the two German republics.

depends increasingly on high value in relation to weight and size. West Berlin has also tried to become a major focus of congresses and meetings as well as film making, television programmes and the theatre. East Berlin with free access to the countryside around, has not faced such problems, but it is, however, questionable whether it has the best site for the capital of the new Republic.

5.2.2 Prague—Praha (figure 5.4, 5.5)

The dramatic quality of the site of Prague is given by the great incised meander of the Vltava immediately north of the oldest parts of the town. Prague, on the flank of the plateau of Bohemia before it dips northwards to the plains of Polabí, grew on the lower valley benches within the meander at a point where the incised valley of the Vltava begins to open out. A ridge of somewhat higher ground commands islands and fords in the river from its bluffs on which defensive works might be erected. Prague has benefited as a point of interchange between the contrasting environments of the Bohemian Plateau with its once extensive forests,

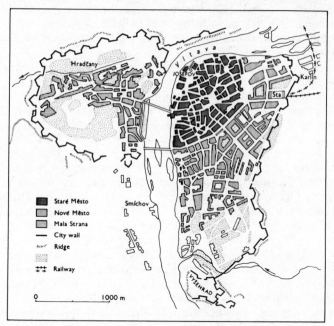

Figure 5.4. The political history of Bohemia is reflected in the small change in the area of Prague between its mediaeval golden age and the mid-nineteenth century, although numerous stately buildings were erected in the seventeenth and eighteenth centuries.

and the open and fertile country of Polabí, centrally located in the heart of the settled part of the Bohemian 'diamond'.

Well before the ninth century AD settlements existed at Vyšehrad and at Levý Hradec (a little to the north); in 873 AD a bishopric was established. With the founding of the Hradčany on a more commanding bluff the bishopric and the princely seat moved to this site around which the communities that came to form

Prague began to grow, developing on both banks of the river, so that late in the tenth century a wooden bridge was reputedly erected.

Charles IV (1346–78) enlarged and beautified Prague from his *burg* on the Hradčany alongside the St Vitus cathedral. At the foot there had grown a quarter for courtiers and servants, the Menši Město (later Malá Strana—the Little Quarter), where there were also German colonists. On the east bank, on a broader site provided by the slip off slope of the meander, there was a merchants' and Jewish quarter, the Staré Město (Old Town), whose centre was the Týn church, where there was a merchants' staple, and it was surrounded by a wall, extended in 1235, when a largely German quarter, the Havelské Město, was built. In 1357 a stone bridge was built across the Vltava, but on the east bank, a strip of land subject to floods was left without buildings. In 1348 a new settlement, the Nové Město came into being south of the Staré Město and extended as far as the old fortress of the Vyšehrad, with its own wall and its own town hall: it was also a merchants' quarter, with a cattle and horse market. The same year also marked the building of the 'Hunger Wall' around the Malá Strana as a measure of relief for the population, while the Carolinum University, one of the earliest in Europe, was also founded. With between 40 000 and 50 000 inhabitants, a university and the seat of the Holy Roman Empire, Prague in the fourteenth century was one of the most important towns in Europe.

Although there were periods of sporadic growth that absorbed the nearer out-lying settlements, Prague generally stagnated after the battle of Bílá Hora in 1620, until after the arrival of steam railways in 1845. Even in the mid-years of last century Prague was still contained within defences closely following the line of the old mediaeval walls, though the fortifications were now Vauban-style bastions and glacis. Removal of the wall between the Old Town and the New Town allowed the building of a spacious thoroughfare (Na Příkopě) to become the main shopping street. A broad rectangular street plan laid out on the former vineyards became the suburb of Vinohrady, east of the New Town. With Austrian and German capital and entrepreneurial activity, industrial districts emerged on the north by the river in Karlín, Vysočany, Libeň and Holešovice. In the south, in the Botič valley, the first area industrialised became the port of Prague. West of the river Smíchov grew as an industrial and railway settlement. The town developed as the focus of the Bohemian railway system but the roughly dissected site presented many constructional problems, including a lengthy tunnel under the centre of the town to the main railway station. Fortunately, the character of the Malá Strana and Staré Město was preserved.

A new impetus came with the formation of the Czechoslovak republic in 1918. Many modern residential districts such as Dejvice, Spořilov and Košíře were built in the inter-war years and included some advanced 'garden city' concepts. At the same time well-designed modern buildings, such as the Ministry of Pensions, received acclaim throughout the world. Prague missed the worst of 'Stalinistic' architecture after the war and many post-war residential areas are in clean, functional styles, such as Novodvorská, that combine the best of Eastern and Western planning.

In the eighteenth century Prague was reported to have a population of about 70 000; by the 1870s the population was 117 000, when the small majority of the population was Czech and the remainder German and Jewish. In 1908 the pop-

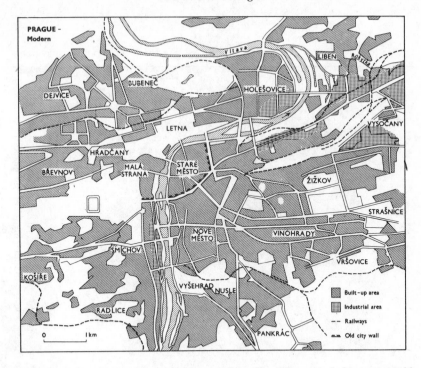

Figure 5.5. Modern Prague has grown around the still well-preserved old core, notably in the Old Town (Staré Město) and the administrative focus of the Malá Strana.

ulation was 229 571; in 1930 849 000 and almost a million by 1939. In 1950 population was 931 000 and by 1955, 1 020 300, since when there has been little increase, following a policy of deconcentration of population and industry to develop the smaller towns of Bohemia and to encourage industrial development in Slovakia.

5.2.3 Warsaw—Warszawa (figure 5.6)

The first references to Warsaw occur in early mediaeval times, when it was one of several small communities in the neighbourhood. It is first referred to as a town, a river port and a castle of the prince of Mazovia in the fourteenth century.

The site of the original town was on the western bank of the Vistula (Wisła) where bluffs, some 30 m high, came close to the river. For a long time there was little or no settlement on the easily flooded low eastern bank. The Old Town (Stare Miasto), laid out rectilinearly immediately above the bluffs, focused on its market place (Stary Rynek) with the Town Hall and was surrounded by a strong brick wall with the castle on the south-east. From an early date most buildings appear to have been built in brick. In the fifteenth century on another bluff a little further north, the New Town (Nowe Miasto) began to grow. Between the two 'towns' lay the crossing point of the Vistula. The New Town was also compactly

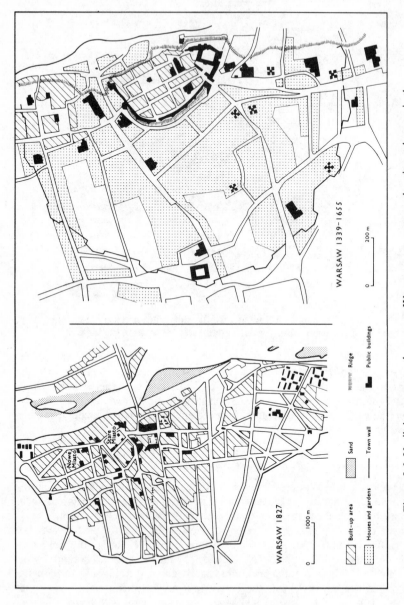

WARSAW 1339–1655

0   200 m

WARSAW 1827

0   1000 m

Built-up area   Sand   Ridge

Houses and gardens   Town wall   Public buildings

Stare Miasto

Nowe Miasto

Figure 5.6. Until the seventeenth century, Warsaw was very much as it can be seen in the Stare Miasto today. In the early nineteenth century, the main elements of the modern street pattern were laid out, though development was later restricted by the constraints of Russian defence needs.

built, but most of its buildings were wooden. Beyond the New and Old Towns lay a loose scatter of farms and town houses, several monasteries, convents and churches and large open spaces used as markets. In 1621 a wall was built round this area, mostly for customs purposes as the town had become a major trading focus in the Polish kingdom. In 1596 Zygmunt III had moved the capital from Kraków to Warsaw because the latter was geographically more central for the state at that date. The effect was considerable growth, particularly of fine town houses and palaces and of less affluent quarters for servants and government officials.

Warsaw suffered a severe setback in the wars of the mid-seventeenth century, but in the eighteenth century under the Saxon kings there was considerable growth and much of the present character of the town was formed. To help beautify the town, architects were brought in from Dresden. By the end of the eighteenth century, Warsaw had nearly 100 000 inhabitants and by this time the Krakowskie Przedmieście and the Nowy Świat were thoroughfares of palaces and town houses extending south towards the royal palaces at Łazienki and Wilanów.

From 1815 to 1830 Warsaw enjoyed a brief time as capital of an autonomous kingdom, but thereafter the power passed to the Tsar. Inspite of the Tsarist oppression and stagnation Warsaw continued to grow in the nineteenth century, becoming an important commercial and industrial centre for the westernmost parts of the Tsarist empire, as well as a major junction on the politically and strategically important St Petersburg–Warsaw–Vienna railway. A large Russian citadel on the north-west side tended to limit growth in this direction and the town spread more to the west, where the large Jewish suburb of Muranów and the railway suburb of Wola developed. On the south were residential districts and numerous barracks, while new and generously planned streets had been laid out like the Marszałkowska and Jerozolimska. The outer ring of Russian forts, however, tended to keep the centre of the town concentrated and congested, because buildings erected near the forts could be torn down whenever the Russians felt inclined. The Vistula was trained within its banks, so that on the east bank, the industrial suburb of Praga began to grow. By 1914 Warsaw had well over 750 000 inhabitants but it was a badly overcrowded town, lacking any coherent planning as the result of piecemeal growth. A new impetus to growth was given by the Polish Republic after the First World War, so that it reached and exceeded the million inhabitants mark. The Russian citadel was demolished and replaced by the suburb of Żoliborz; on the south Mokotów was developed and much growth took place east of the river.

In 1939 Warsaw was badly bombed and damage was also done later by partisan warfare. After the 1943 rising the Germans razed the walled Jewish quarter of Muranów and in 1944 great damage was done in guerrilla warfare as the Red Army watched impassively from the opposite bank of the Vistula. In 1945 the population within Warsaw's boundaries was only 162 000—only 22 000 people were left on the west bank where three-quarters was in ruins. In rebuilding Warsaw emphasis was put on restoring historical buildings, using old sketches and paintings. As examples are the successful restoration of the Stare Miasto and the Krakowskie Przedmieście, unfortunately at a cost the country could ill afford. The replanning of Warsaw was much influenced by the ideas of the 'town of

Socialist realism', well illustrated by the Stalinistic style of the Marszałkowska Dzielnica Mieszkaniowa around Constitution Square. Elsewhere, crowded slums like Muranów have been replaced by generous residential accommodation. The immense skyscraper of the Palace of Science and Culture presented to Poland by the Soviet Union now looks out-of-place. Links across the Vistula have been improved by new bridges and a new east–west road, partly in a tunnel under the Old Town.

Table 5.2   Population of Warsaw 1860–1970
(*within its boundaries at given date*)

Year	Population (in 000s)
1860†	158
1880†	383
1897*	594
1914†	781
1921*	937
1931*	1172
1939†	1289
1945†	162
1946*	479
1950*	600
1960*	1139
1970*	1308

Based on *Rocznik Statystyczny*, various dates.
* Census.
† Estimate.

Further industrial development has taken place, especially in an attempt to diversify the pre-war pattern. Heavy engineering, motor vehicle manufacture and metallurgy now overshadow the traditional consumer goods. These developments have been mainly on the east bank of the Vistula, where a new river port has been built downstream, though the bulk of traffic handled is small. To cater for the growth of the town, its boundaries were greatly extended in 1961.

5.2.4 Budapest (figure 5.7)

Budapest dates from the Roman legionary fortress of Aquincum, one of the main strongholds guarding the Pannonian frontier, situated roughly on the site of modern Óbuda, one of the easiest crossing points of the Danube. After the arrival of the Magyars, this site maintained its importance as a major trading focus and there were also health-giving mineral springs.

The site is flat to gently undulating, apart from the steep and isolated hills of Buda on the west bank of the river, and on the east bank, the gently undulating Gödöllö hills in the outskirts of Pest. The plain opens out southwards and the change in gradient of the Danube is marked by a number of low sandy islands. In former times the river in the plain section flooded a broad, wet and often impassable lowland. The site of Buda–Pest thus lay at a point of easy crossing between the deep channel of the river in the gorge section and its broad, shallow but marshy reaches below this point, while small eminences provided sites for defence works to cover the fords.

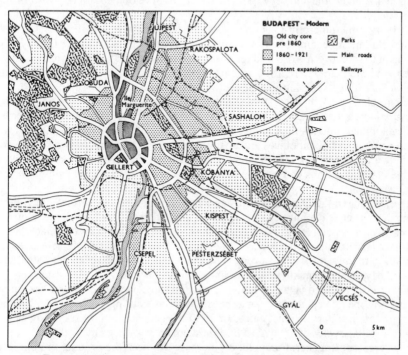

Figure 5.7. Budapest still shows the core of the modern town in Pest on the open east bank of the Danube, while Buda nestles beneath the slopes of the Gellert Hill. Loose, open building lots characterise many of the outer suburbs of the modern town.

The early Hungarian capital was at Esztergom, later at Székesfehérvár and finally at Óbuda. With this royal function Óbuda and Pest grew in importance, with the latter becoming an important commercial focus in the Pannonian plains. Both were devastated in the Tatar invasion of 1241, but Bela IV returned to the site and chose a long, narrow limestone ridge opposite Pest, the Várhegy, as an easily defensible position. This focus of Buda is still marked by the castle at the southern end, while much later (1849) defence works were built on the Gellért-Hegy to the south. The castle on the Várhegy unsuccessfully resisted the Turks in 1541 and the Austrians in 1686; thereafter its importance declined and the precincts within the walls became part of the governmental area of Buda.

The Turkish hold from 1541 to 1686 was a time of slow development when the settlements took a marked Turkish character, lost in the devastation during the struggle to free them from the Turks. As Buda and Pest were repopulated and rebuilt in the eighteenth century, a strongly Austrian baroque town began to emerge, while many new citizens were German. During the nineteenth century, Pest—on its more level site east of the river—grew more briskly as a commercial focus than the hillier Buda, spreading north and eastwards from the old centre opposite Buda of the Belváros and the line of its walls. In 1849 a British engineer built a suspension bridge over the river to replace an earlier bridge and ferries and tunneled under the Várhegy to facilitate urban development on the western side of the hill.

During the nineteenth century there was considerable growth of river traffic and Budapest became one of the main Danube harbours. In the 1850s railways began to radiate out from Budapest, but it was not until after 1873 that a railway crossed the Danube. In 1896 a short underground railway was built, one of the first in Europe. The latter nineteenth century was a time of rapid growth and great change, with the establishment of industry financed by German and Austrian capital (figure 5.7). Csepel Island became the main site for industrial development and also the main river port. Buda could no longer contain the increase in government offices and an imposing parliament building was erected on the waterfront in Pest. Of the new streets laid out the Kiskörút was built on the line of the old walls of Pest, the Belváros, while further out, following a former river channel, the Nagykörút formed an imposing semicircular boulevard from the Danube to the Danube, enclosing what became the commercial and government quarter of the joint city of Budapest created in 1872. Buda has remained in many parts a quiet town, while Pest is the creation of the ebullient nineteenth century. The ornate, plaster-faced buildings of this period are similar to towns elsewhere in East Central Europe. The use of land was, however, generous, particularly in the outskirts, where single storied houses with large gardens or generously planned villas (notably on the Buda side) were built. The poorer areas are now being replaced by neighbourhood unit housing planned in a manner common in other Socialist cities. In 1950 by incorporation of seven towns and fifteen villages closely related to Budapest, an enlarged area of Greater Budapest was created. In general, population increase has been the product of migration from other parts of Hungary. Unfortunately, Budapest overshadows the country, containing almost a fifth of the national population and is equal in population to all the other towns of Hungary added together.

Table 5.3   Population of Budapest 1830–1970

Year	Population (in 000s)
1830	119
1869	312
1900	863
1920	1230
1941	1710
1945	1590
1960	1810
1970	1940

Various sources.

The industrial districts lie in part along the river where there is much barge traffic. Other districts include Angyalföld, Köbánya, Kispest and Pesterzsébet in the south-east. A new industrial district on the west bank is Lángymányos. Budapest is the major focus of industrial activity in the whole country, with major engineering plants (Ganz railway equipment, Ikarus buses and river boats up to 1500 tons), chemicals, textiles and food industries.

5.2.5 Bucharest—București (figure 5.8)

The Rumanian capital, Bucharest, with a million inhabitants, stands out striking-ly as the primate city far in excess of the other towns. Little is known before the fifteenth century when it was first mentioned as a fortified site by the small river Dimbrovița, in the central part of Eastern Wallachia, where rivers draining from the mountains had cut broad, shallow but steep-sided valleys into the *loess* cover. The process of down-cutting had left well-developed terraces, which overlooked the rivers and their moist meadows in low bluffs. The riverine meadows here were less frequently inundated than those in the Danube floodplain, while the site lay between the true plain—dry and open—and the forests of the mountain footslope, at a point where the valley of the Dimbrovița narrowed and some low islands made crossing easier. Water supply here was also easier than on the more exposed interfluves.

The growing resentment to the Turks in the sixteenth century gathered Wallachian opposition in Bucharest, which was devastated in the fighting. With Rumanian national aspirations increasingly associated with the town, the Turks gave the Rumanians some encouragement to use Bucharest as a capital, since it was easier to control from the Turkish bases on the Danube than the old capital, Tirgoviște. At a time of Turkish strength, in 1659, Bucharest became the real capital, now also a most important trading town on the routes south to Constan-tinople. In the late seventeenth century, it was large and prosperous and roads were built leading out of the town, while several caravanserai-like hostelries opened, as well as the first schools, hospitals and even a printing press. Street names in the old part of the town still recall many of the craft industries which flourished. Trading contacts were established early in the eighteenth century with the great fairs of Leipzig and under the Turkish Phanariot rulers the growth of Bucharest continued. There was a marked spread of housing—mostly low buildings in large gardens, notably on the higher terrace levels in the north, where water supplies were available from the late eighteenth century. In common with the other steppe towns in South-east Europe and southern Russia, it had a large area in relation to its population and preserved something of a rural character. As a garden city, its greenery and spaciousness impressed travellers. There was no wall and well-sited churches and monasteries served as defensive points. Buildings tended to avoid moist hollows and also the higher terraces and in-terfluves wherever water supply was problematical. Growth was piecemeal and confused, but it was a remarkably cosmopolitan town, with German and Jewish groups, as well as Albanians, Arabs, Bulgars, Greeks and Serbs and others from within the Ottoman empire. A population as high as 100 000 has been suggested for the early nineteenth century, but this is doubtless an overstatement.

Its identity with Rumanian nationhood made it an ideal capital, while it had a convenient geographical location for the two united principalities in 1859. The Moldavian capital, Iaşi, was away in a remote part of the country and uncomfortably near to the growing power of Russia, nor was a capital feasible in Transylvania held by the Habsburg. The town remained, however, semi-rural in appearance, with shops, bazaars, workshops and hostelries mixed amid houses and gardens, along streets that radiated from the banks of the Dimbovita. Between 1860 and 1870 the first major improvements began to be made, though railway development came in 1869, later than elsewhere, and the first line was to the Danube ports, with which trade was quickly growing. The several railways into the capital were later joined by a ring railway, so that the North Station became the main passenger terminus.

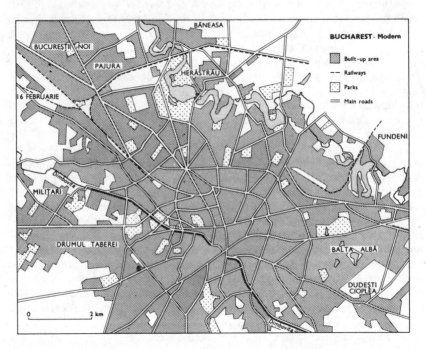

Figure 5.8. Modern Bucharest lies on the interfluves along the Dimboviţa and Colentina rivers. The main focus is between the main station and south-eastwards towards the Dimboviţa, while on the north, towards the Colentina, is a large suburban area laid out in the last century by the Russians.

Industrial development took place under careful tariff protection, though several craft industries succumbed to competition from Rumanian factory industry and even from imports. Like many capital cities strategic industries became important: in 1863 an arsenal was built and subsequently engineering developed. The main industrial expansion has come since the Second World War (figure 5.8). Mechanical and electrical engineering have further expanded and manufacture of chemicals has started. Industry has been grouped particularly in the vicinity of the railways and since 1945, the industrial districts in the southern part of the town, though a large metallurgical plant has opened on the eastern flank. The new industrial plants have been carefully co-ordinated with residential schemes. The choice of the south for industry has been partly to avoid driving smoke over the town when the strong north-east *crivaţ* wind blows in winter.

Table 5.4   Population of Bucharest 1831–1970

Year	Population (in 000s)
1831	70
1860	121
1878	177
1914	362
1918	382
1941	992
1948	1042
1960	1355
1970	1554

Various sources.

The development since 1945 has done much to remove the older housing, with insanitary conditions and unpaved streets, though much remains to be refurbished. In the central parts pre-war buildings, often with strong French and German architectural influence, mix with heavy Stalinistic styles erected in the immediate post-war period and with more functional styles erected since the 1950s. Redevelopment in the central area took place after wartime bombing. Much residential development has taken place on the outskirts as the public transport system has been improved. In 1950 to cater for the enlarged town, the muncipal boundaries were substantially expanded.

5.2.6   Belgrade—Beograd (figure 5.9)

Belgrade—Beograd (the White Town)—has an impressive site on bluffs 65–70 m above the Danube where outliers of the Sumadija hills reach the river, looking more impressive than their modest height warrants above the surrounding plain. The town has spread south-eastwards across the flat top of the ridge, directly at the confluence of the Danube and the Sava. In recent times Belgrade has also begun to spread on to the low flood plains of the Sava and Danube on the west and north.

During the Roman period, it was an important fort—Singidunum—guarding the Pannonian frontier. Later the migrating Slavs used the site, apparently frequently destroyed by barbarian invaders from across the river, as they spread out from the Pannonian plains. The settlement, though inhabited by Serbs, was part of the Bulgarian empire until the eleventh century and then fell to Byzantium. In the thirteenth to fifteenth centuries Belgrade was fought for by both Serbs and Hungarians in the struggle for what became known as the 'Key to Hungary'. The Serbs eventually moved their capital to Smederovo and left

Belgrade in Magyar hands. The Turks besieged the town without success in 1444 and 1456: it was not until 1521 that *Darol-i-Jehad* (Home of wars for the faith) fell to Suleiman the Great and became the seat of a Pasha—one of the four pashaliks formed in Serbia. Smederovo had fallen to the Turks in 1459.

Belgrade fell to the Prince of Baden for two years (1688–90) and the Prince Eugene held it from 1717–39 when it was heavily fortified. The Turks again held it from 1739–89, when it passed to Austria until 1792. The Serbian leader Kara George took it in 1806 and held it until 1813. In 1815 another revolt caused the town to pass to a Serbian administration, though the fortress remained garrisoned by the Turks and a Pasha retained his seat in the town. This peculiar dual administration lasted until 1867. In 1869 it became the seat of government and royal residence of the Kingdom of Serbia and grew into a typical European capital.

The core of the old town at the head of the promontory is the former Turkish fortress—the *Kalemegdan* or Town Field—occupying an area sloping down to the Danube. To the south extends what was formerly the walled town, but the heart of the modern town lies beyond the line of the one-time walls. North of this core, nearer to the old fortress lies the Dorcol, the Turkish town which was inhabited largely by Turks into the 1860s. To the east and south-west of the town are wooded hills—Zvezdara, Topčider and Košutnjak—into which urban development is beginning to spread.

Belgrade was badly damaged by Austrian artillery in the First World War and by air attack in the Second World War, so that parts have had to be extensively rebuilt and little remains of the character imparted by the Turks. Considerable building since 1945 means that much of the town has a most modern character (figure 5.9). Belgrade is an important railway junction and has quays along the

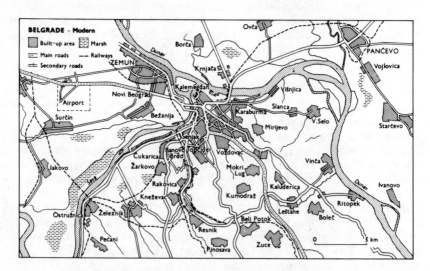

Figure 5.9 Belgrade lies on commanding bluffs at the Sava–Danube confluence. Modern development has stretched south into hillier country and has also taken place on low terraces above usual flood level on the north bank of the Sava.

Sava adjacent to the main railway. The ancient fair is still continued in a modern exhibition area set aside by the Sava. The industry in the town is on the east along the Danube, but the major modern industrial plants are outside the town in Zemun, Rakovica and Železnik. In the period since 1945, a large new area of administrative buildings and residential quarters has been built north of the Sava on an alluvial tract between Zemun and the capital. The airport has also been expanded here. Eventually this new community of Novi Beograd will have a population of 250 000. North of the Danube, Pančevo is growing and has a new oil refinery, but much of the country along the river is liable to inundation. In Turkish times Belgrade had about 20 000 people, but by the end of the nineteenth century it had reached 50 000. It was well into the period between the two world wars until a population of 100 000 was reached, though in 1939 this had grown to 250 000. The half-million population was exceeded in the early 1960s, partly the result of extension of the city boundaries.

5.2.7 *Sofia*

The Bulgarian capital, Sofia, has been a settlement since before Roman times, when it became a flourishing town and tribal centre for the Thracian *Serdi*. The later Slav immigrants perpetuated the name as *Serdec*—'the Centre'—reflecting its nodality as a route focus. The remains of a Roman bath and an early Byzantine church may be seen, as well as the sixth century church of St Sofia, from which the modern name is taken. Sofia lies in a high elongated mountain basin, some 80 km long and 75 km wide, at an altitude of 550 m. On the south the town is overlooked by the striking Vitosha Massif, rising to 2290 m. Sofia is the point of intersection of the east–west route via the Dragoman Pass to the valley of the Maritsa, a major route in Byzantine and Turkish times, while this is crossed by a north–south route from the Danube via the Iskar gorge and Botevgrad Pass. Routes also lead south-westwards into Macedonia and the Morava–Vardar corridor, or to the east to the Tundza basin. The actual site is fairly flat, with two small streams that drain to the Iskar flanking the central area of the town.

The modern town has wide streets and some good modern buildings in the central part. Much effort has been given to clearance and improvement in the central part of the town, where a few old churches and mosques remain and where there are a number of carefully tended historical monuments. The centre leaves, however, an impression of rather confused and incoherent planning, with few grand views or impressive squares, despite much greenery. In 1910 Sofia's population was about 134 000; in 1934, it had reached 235 000 and in 1946, 427 000. The population in 1970 was 973 400.

5.2.8 *Tirana—Tiranë*

Tiranë, the Albanian capital, a town of little over 150 000 people, was chosen as capital in 1920 to supersede Vlorë and Durreš. Its population rose from 11 000 (1923) to 25 000 in 1938 and there were 60 000 inhabitants in 1945, outstripping Korçë, Shkodër and Elbasan. Development has come largely through the centralisation of government, but Tiranë is also the main industrial centre, with over half the total capacity of light industries and metal-using industries. Tiranë lies on the inner margin of the coastal plain in an area of good soil, overlooked by the limestone ridge of the Mali i Dajtit. The urban morphology is characterised by very loose development, with a great many houses standing in large gardens. The centre, largely a product of Italian town planning in the 1930s, is more clustered, with fairly wide streets and large public and governmental buildings. On the out-skirts, rather narrow lanes, often in poor condition, give the town an oriental appearance. It dates only from the seventeenth century, owing its origin to Turkish initiative.

5.3 Villages: A general survey (figure 5.10)

With relatively modest urbanisation in most countries of Eastern Europe, the village still plays a major part in settlement but varies widely in form, size and in spatial distribution, adjusted to local conditions, though often influenced from areas outside. The villages show the influence of local building materials, water supply, terrain conditions, land use patterns and general agricultural conditions. Artistic tradition also plays a part, while historical changes may be imprinted in the village. The new economic and social conditions created by socialisation and collectivisation are also producing new forms of rural settlement, changing the visual countryside. The contemporary scene still appreciably retains, however, the pattern developed with the collapse of feudal institutions, because until recent-ly change has been slow. Little is known of the origins of several types of settle-ment, while the historical evolution of other forms remains in dispute. The com-paratively simple thesis of the ethnic affinity of village types popular in the late nineteenth century has not in general stood the test of time.

It can be seen that the Carpathians, the Dinaric and Balkan mountains are largely distinguished by small hamlets or dispersed settlements, while the northern plains and Pannonia, the lower Danube and Moldavia are characterised by nucleation. A few areas stand out because of distinctive types of rural communities: the planned settlements in the resettled areas of the Banat, Bačka and Baranya; the *čiflik*[1] villages of Bulgaria and Macedonia; the immense 'village towns' of the Puszta; or the unusual *Rundling*[2] villages of onetime Slav marches in the northern plain. Some crude relationship exists between quality of land and degree of nucleation, for the richer farming lands all show nucleated settlement. In the mountains the pastorally based economy generally displays dispersal or only loose nucleations.

5.3.1 The Northern Plain

The Northern Plain is characterised by linear villages which may be of the remarkably regular plan laid down by 'locators' in areas of German colonisation. Here the *street village* is most common, with subtypes of the *green village* or the modified older *Rundling* (figure 5.11). Eastwards, the highly regular German

---

[1] *Čiflik*: an estate held by a Turkish *bey* on a temporary tenure and worked by Christian labourers in a virtual state of slavery.
[2] *Rundling*: German term for a small, round defended village or hamlet, usually associated with Slav settlement in marshlands with German tribes.

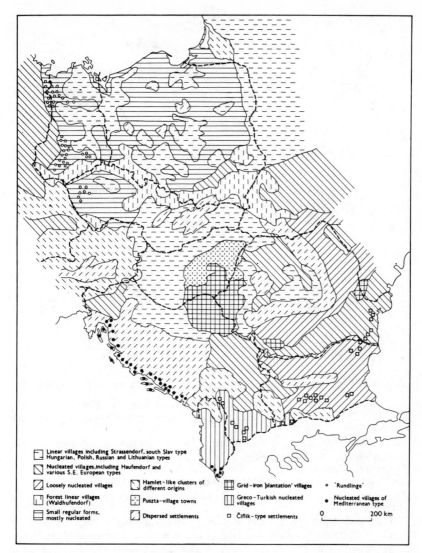

Figure 5.10. Most research on village types has been based on morphology, from which
this map is compiled. Such a classification, however, draws together widely different
types of social and economic organisation. In the north and west, German influence has
been strong, while great diversity of ethnic influence is found in the south-east. Various
sources.

villages change in central and eastern Poland to straggling lines of houses along
wide muddy roads. In the westernmost German Democratic Republic, there are
nucleated villages of irregular plan, the older *Haufendorf*[1], while intermingling,

[1] *Haufendorf*: German term and one common in settlement geography for an irregularly shaped,
nucleated village.

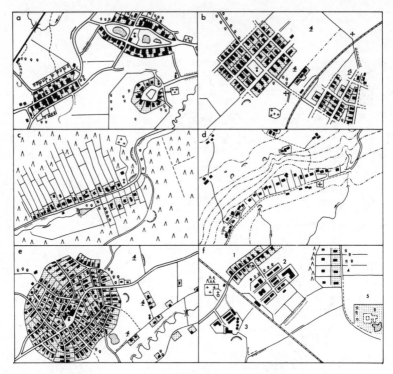

Figure 5.11. Villages show various arrangements of street patterns and house lots.

(a) *Strassendorf, Angerdorf* and *Rundlinge* of the North European Plain.
(b) Grid-iron plans of 'planted' villages characteristic of parts of Silesia and the Banat and Bačka.
(c) *Waldhufendorf* found along valleys in the forested central uplands (for example, Sudetenland and the Erzgebirge).
(d) The polye village of the Dinaric karstlands—houses are sited above the winter-flood level of the polye floor but below the barren limestone hills.
(e) The large townlike villages of the Hungarian Puszta with their outlying *tanyák* settlements.
(f) The socialist landscape: (1) the original villages; (2) new housing—often small blocks of flats; (3) new farm buildings of the collective; (4) small holdings carved from the initial land reform of the original estate; (5) the former manor house and home farm.

particularly in western Mecklenburg and in Thüringen, are the small round villages (*Rundlinge*) usually taken to have a Slav origin, designed for easy defence in a marcher region. Whereas the German villages were associated with the *Gewannflur*[1], heavy plough and three-field rotation, these Slav villages were probably linked to small square fields and relatively simple techniques of farming. In the Oder and Warta basins, Silesia and East Prussia, highly regular

---

[1] *Gewannflur*: an old German system of land tenure in hides, associated with a three-field rotation and a heavy wheeled plough.

villages, often with a cross-shaped street plan, set in forest areas, originated from the Frederician colonisation in the eighteenth century. Of late origin are the linear dyke villages in the reclaimed marshland of the Vistula and Noteć basins. In Mecklenburg, Pomerania and East Prussia, villages were usually associated with estates of the landed nobility.

There is also regional difference in the form of houses and the layout of farms. The Baltic region has house types based on the long, single structure of the Low German house, associated even with fishing communities of the Pomeranian coast. These houses, usually built of timber framing, with clay filling or bricks, are single-storied. South of the Baltic lake plateau, the Middle German farmstead (usually two-storied) becomes common and extends into the uplands, consisting of one or more buildings grouped round a courtyard, with an imposing gateway giving access to the street. It may be half-timbered or built in brick or stone, depending on date and place of construction, adopted throughout the 'colonial' lands of eastern Germany, while in various modified forms it is found among non-German communities, so that it is not unusual in parts of Poland and is particularly charcteristic of Bohemia and Moravia, in both Czech and German settlement areas. East of the Oder a long house with an arched verandah occurs in several forms, from the rich and large types (*Vorlaubenhäuser*) of Silesia and East Prussia to more modest types in the poorer areas. In central and eastern Poland low thatched huts in brick or logs are usual, generally built with their gable to the street with a yard and small outbuildings at the side. A feature of parts of the Baltic uplands and country immediately to the south is the manor house (*Gut, dwór*) of the former landed estates. In the German Democratic Republic since 1945, villages have been rebuilt with the housing (often two-storied or small blocks of flats) separate from the farm buildings.

5.3.2 The Southern Uplands

In the southern uplands—the Saxon hills, the Thüringer Wald, the Erzgebirge, Sudeten mountains and the Beskids—late colonisation cleared their once massive forest cover. Here the village characteristically straggles along valleys, following forest paths or small streams and the holdings stretch back into the forest. This *Waldhufendorf*[1] is usually associated with colonisation in the fourteenth century before life was disrupted by the Black Death. In western Bohemia and the upper Vltava, small nucleated villages, fairly evenly scattered, are typical. The richer agricultural lands of Bohemia and Moravia have large villages, usually of the street or green type with courtyard farms, but irregular and round forms are also common, though the industrialisation has given many villages a partly urban and industrial character.

5.3.3 The Pannonian Plains

West of the Danube in the Pannonian Plains, there are large linear villages of remarkably regular plan, though along the frontier with Austria there is some scattered settlement. The most distinct form occurs in the *Puszta*, notably

---

[1] *Waldhufendorf*: German term for a straggling village along a road or stream, which stretches back in long strips into forest clearings.

between the Tisza and the Körös where Turkish raids were common in the sixteenth and seventeenth centuries. Here, immense villages (many of almost town-like character) arose from the peasants seeking safety in large communities for effective defence. After the defeat of the Turks, many people moved back into the open Puszta to small scattered farmsteads (*tanyák*)[1]. In Pannonia, villages mostly favour *loessic* interfluves above the river meadows and likely flooding where there is a variety of land and wells may be sunk easily: the beam well is found throughout Hungary and in southern Slovakia as well as in Jugoslav territory. In the sandy Tisza–Danube interfluve and the Nyírség, villages are usually small and relatively widely scattered. The Pannonian Plains have a long house with the gable to the street and a verandah along one long side. There is usually a small croft with outbuildings. In the Banat, Bačka and Baranya, Habsburg initiative recolonised devastated land with settlers drawn from many peoples, but accommodated in chessboard pattern villages. Within *Transylvania* nucleated villages, usually of a regular pattern are common. In the south, German 'Saxon' villages are often distinguished by their fortified churches, which usually date from the fifteenth century, though the villages, commonly in the form of a cross, are earlier (thirteenth century). The farms are commonly of the Middle German type and housing more substantial than in the villages of other ethnic groups.

5.3.4 The Carpathians

In the Carpathians settlement is marked by strong site controls and by the smallness of the groupings, while altitude is also a factor in size and type. Settlements seek sunny slopes and the largest are found in the broad warm basins. The houses occur in small clusters in loosely dispersed groups or in long straggling lines. In the highest parts temporary settlements used in summer are found. In spite of local variations in house types, certain features are common like high pitched roofs, and use of wood—either in shingle or log form, with wooden roof shingles. In the richer parts, long houses of the Pannonian type or substantial houses of the *izba*[2] variety are found, but in the poorer areas, meagre one-roomed huts are common. Elaborate decoration of houses is not unusual. In Slovakia and the Carpathian–Ukraine as well as on the Polish northern slopes, elaborate and skilfully built wooden churches are frequent, often standing some distance from the villages. In the piedmont belt, there is often an abrupt change to much more dense settlement, while house types from the plains are often found well up the larger valleys.

5.3.5 Wallachia and Moldavia

Wallachia and Moldavia have generally loosely nucleated settlements, with patches of planned settlements, including some of recent date, as in the Bărăgan Steppe. The most strongly agglomerated settlements are in the plains south of a

[1] *Tanyá* (pl. *Tanyák*): Magyar term for a small isolated farmhouse or cottage in the fields outside the village. Originally occupied only in summer, but nowadays commonly inhabited throughout the year.

[2] *Izba*: a Russian log cabin or peasant house, commonly of one or two rooms.

line from Craiova to Galați and in the Prut basin north of Iasi. In the Dobrogea remains of Turkish *čiflik* villages occur. There is evidence that the nucleated settlements have evolved as a result of population growth from an earlier type of dispersed hamlet. House types vary considerably, but the frame house with plastered walls or mud brick house (rather short-lived) are most common. Verandahs are a common feature of the houses. In some of the poorer steppe areas the older houses are very low, roofed with turf and sometimes set partly into the earth.

5.3.6 The Dinaric Lands

South of the Sava–Drava rivers, a more diverse pattern of villages emerged than in the Pannonian Plains. Much of Croatia and Slovenia comprises small villages and hamlets, usually loosely grouped. Mediterranean influences are seen in Istria and near Rijeka, whereas towards the Alpine foothills the appearance is more Central European. In parts of Dalmatia traces of Roman centuriation[1] suggest an ancient origin for some villages. Compared to lands that fell under Turkish control the northern settlements are usually old, representing early Slav sites or later forest clearings. In the rougher mountain terrain a higher degree of dispersion occurs than in the agriculturally richer plains and aspect becomes important in village siting. In some areas where forest clearing took place in mediaeval times the *Waldhufendorf* type of village occurs. In the more open country of the Prekomurje and the Sava–Drava plains Pannonian influences are found. In the Sava plains single-cross or double-cross shaped villages are common, merging eastwards in the Bačka into the regular grid iron forms of the Habsburg colonisation, though the influence of the 'military frontier' can be still seen through much of the Jugoslav–Magyar borderlands, with large and substantially built villages in the Voivodina left by former German settlers. The houses in the Sava–Drava lowlands are much influenced by the Pannonian long house with verandah and outhouses around a yard.

The *Šumadija country* has loosely nucleated villages, the result of an increasing population and intensified land use that caused hamlets to grow into irregular, moderately-sized villages with various ground plans, spreading in the nineteenth century into the lower Sava and the Drina basin. Long winding street villages are common in the Bilo Gora. In the Ibar basin, straggling villages, comprising several hamlets, stretch along ridges or are clustered on the brows of several hills that allow some cultivation. In *southern Serbia and Macedonia*, notably in the Vardar basin, and found also in Bulgaria, are the villages created by the large Turkish estates, the *čifliki*, which consist of one or more squares of small cell-like houses dominated by the *bey's* residence and sometimes surrounded by a wall. Many of these settlements were modified or disappeared when the *čifliki* were dissolved. The southern *Adriatic littoral* and the Greek border regions are marked by tightly nucleated villages of small stone houses, often two-storied, with low angle roofs, also found in *southern Albania*, though in that country the common settlement is a loosely grouped collection of small houses of

[1] *Centuriation*: a Roman system of land division, usually producing a grid iron pattern of land parcels.

simple design. In the more fertile parts of *Bulgaria* nucleated villages of various kinds and sizes occur, but in the south and south-west are notably small hamlets.

Dispersed settlement, most characteristic of the higher *mountain areas*, may be the original type of settlement of the migrant Slavs. Any villages may consist of several scattered hamlets, so that a single village may extend over several kilometres and each hamlet may be one or more kilometres from its nearest neighbour, found over much of western Serbia, Bosnia and Hercegovina as well as in western Croatia. In the Slovenian Alps there are long lines of scattered houses. In the karstlands, villages are small and their houses commonly strung round the edges of the more fertile hollows in the limestone, but they may also cluster on low limestone outcrops that rise from the floors of such hollows. In the least fertile limestone countryside, settlements are well-spaced small clusters or strings of houses, little better than low stone sheds. In the highest parts of the *Stara Planina*, there are scattered huts and farms, while small hamlets and groups of farmsteads are common in the Rhodope and on the Bulgarian–Jugoslav frontier. Wooden huts with steep shingle roofs are more common in the forested mountain areas, while 'alpine' influences in design spread south into Bosnia. In parts of Bulgaria and Jugoslavia under Turkish influence, the more prosperous village houses show marked Turkish design: two-storied houses with an overhang of the upper floor, the lower part often in stone, the upper floor in wood. In turbulent areas a stone fortified house (*kula*) was common (for example in Bosnia). Crude huts are found on the highest summer pastures, sometimes simple pyramid-like shacks of the older pastoral peoples, with the simplest and poorest of all in the Albanian mountains.

5.4 The impact of socialisation on the village

The introduction of various interpretations of Socialist agriculture into Eastern Europe has had a varied impact on the village. In some parts the countryside is dotted by villages with new houses and farm buildings, even schools and tractor stations, while in other parts, there seems to have been little change, with old style housing and a marked lack of new construction. Generally, the changes have been most striking where collectivisation in any of its forms has been stringently applied. The common trends have been to separate dwellings and farm buildings, to nucleate settlement, to provide new amenities (*Kulturhaus, Dom Kultury*[1]) and to reduce the contrast in life style between town and village.

In the German Democratic Republic, in Mecklenburg and Brandenburg, a land reform in 1945 broke up big estates and gave peasant holdings of their own. New groups of farms and patches of small fields mark this process, which was soon reversed when the estates were turned into state farms, often in the same boundaries, which tended to preserve the old settlement pattern. While many mansion houses had been destroyed, others became the *Kulturhaus* for their farm. In Czechoslovakia collectivisation has tended to attract settlement into the farm centres, where there is usually much new housing, more hygienic if less picturesque than the older styles. The contrast in field size between the large collec-

[1] *Dom Kultury*: Soviet term rendered variously in Slav and other languages (for example, German *Kulturhaus*) in Eastern Europe for the club and social focus of collective and state-farm villages.

tivised fields on the Czech side of the border and the small strips of the non-collectivised Polish peasants is a vivid impression of the border area. Although *labour brigades* and the other methods of the collective farms have tended to encourage nucleation, dispersed settlement has often been remarkably resistant to change, as seen in the Hungarian Puszta. Where nucleation and village growth have taken place, new streets and functional separation has often been attached to the old core, seen in villages in the German Democratic Republic. It has been pointed out that buildings form a major item in the fixed capital assets of collectives and state farms amounting to as much as forty per cent, according to Rumanian statistics.

Several observers have suggested that, while a 'Socialist landscape' has appeared in the countryside over wide areas, it remains strongly national in form, in the layout of the new village communities and in housing, while acceptable standards are higher in the German and Bohemian lands than in the south-east.

6 The Economic Landscape before the Second World War

The eight Eastern European Socialist countries have been drawn together since 1945 by the application of Marxist–Leninist dogma to their economic and social life, though the ways in which this has been done have varied in detail between these states. The considerable variation in their economic structures and levels of development, which they now seek to even out, arises not only from their different endowment with natural resources, but also from differences in their historical experience.

The strongest and most influential are the German Democratic Republic and Czechoslovakia, with advanced economies based on an extensive pre-war industrial base. Poland also has an industry with a wide variety of manufactures and a relatively high level of urbanisation, but the country has been industrialised through territorial shift rather than the process of industrial growth. Hungary follows closely behind Poland, but its industry suffered heavily in inter-war times by territorial disruption brought by the collapse of the Habsburg empire. The other countries have generally lower levels of urbanisation and higher proportions of their labour force in agriculture. Some observers have pointed to a similarity between their state of development at the end of last century and that of the developing countries in the contemporary world. In the inter-war years along with Poland and Hungary they were commonly termed 'Agricultural Europe'. They had been heavily dependent on foreign investment which had tended to keep them as producers of raw or semi-processed materials. Inspite of Italian participation, Albania, with its antiquated social system, remained the most backward part of Europe.

The adjustments needed to the economic infrastructure of Eastern Europe after the emergence of the succession states from the wreckage of the old dynastic empires had not been completed before new changes began in the late 1930s that heralded those of the Second World War. New territorial alignments after 1945 began the process again on a still imperfectly balanced system: the adjustment now had to be made within a fundamentally new organisational and conceptual framework.

The German Democratic Republic emerged in 1945 as the Soviet Occupation Zone within arbitrary boundaries carved from a highly developed and elaborately integrated economic structure of the Third Reich that had been adjusted surprisingly well to the territorial changes caused by the First World War. Poland had been hung together in 1918 from remains of three empires at considerably different levels of development: the comparatively well-developed Prussian lands contrasted strikingly with the very modest levels of the onetime Russian lands, while former Habsburg lands had somewhat intermediate conditions. In 1945, without full adjustment having been achieved, Poland was shifted bodily westwards. The absorption of an elaborate industrial infrastructure developed in the annexed German lands 'industrialised' the country, the root, paradoxically, of most Polish economic and social difficulties since 1945. The Czechoslovak state in 1918 inherited economic problems arising from the different levels of development in the former Austrian Bohemia–Moravia and the Hungarian-dominated Slovakia, while there was also a problem of the unequal division of economic activity between the Czechoslovak element and the powerful German minority. In Hungary economic difficulties arose from the disruption of the spatial pattern of the economy by the tightly drawn boundaries defined by the Treaty of Trianon. Jugoslavia, perhaps the most artificial of all the Succession states, comprised territories with widely different levels of development and potential and the consequent problems of uneven regional development are still a dilemma. The Rumanians faced problems not dissimilar to those of the Jugoslavs.

The strong influences exerted on economic life in Eastern Europe by Germany before 1914 were slowly re-established after the First World War. Danubia and the Balkans were increasingly orientated towards Germany by Nazi economic policies in the 1930s, though the political influence of France on economic life in-spite of its waning power cannot be ignored for, as a significant exporter of capital for investment, it was often a serious competitor with Germany and Britain. The importance of such foreign capital investment was reflected in the greater encouragement given to transport facilities and to the production of raw or semi-processed materials rather than to industry likely to compete with the in-vestors' own home manufacturing industries.

The succession states, notably Poland, showed considerable inter-war étatisme, state intervention and direction in industry, generally at a level higher than in Western Europe. In some respects such intervention helped to offset the high level of foreign participation in investment that conditioned the spatial and infrastructural pattern of their economies in ways not always in step with the best national interests. Étatisme also helped to direct adjustment to the new territorial situations. In Jugoslavia, attention was paid to shifting industry into the interior away from vulnerable peripheral areas, while similar trends were seen in Poland, where major transport and harbour facilities were felt to be necessary as part of the adjustment process. Even the industrial growth of 'Mitteldeutschland' in the 1930s, so important in the economic geography of the new German Democratic Republic, can be seen in this light.

6.1 Agriculture

Traditionally, agriculture has played an important role in the employment structure of Eastern Europe, though expectedly least important in the more industrialised countries, where its share began to decline in the latter part of the last century. Elsewhere it remained the mainstay of economic life until after the Second World War, when industrialisation began to reduce its significance. It has been one of the most problematical sectors of economic life and unless solutions are found economic and social progress is unlikely to be sustained. From region to region there are, however, wide variations in the natural conditions and consequently the pattern of agriculture.

In the landscapes of the North European Plain, the open, rolling surface makes possible relatively easy use of large scale machinery. Climatic conditions permit the cultivation of most arable crops and grains, especially winter wheat and roots, while broad moist river valleys are significant hay producers. Unfortunately, soils are not outstandingly good—the north and central areas are marked by glacial clays and sands that give heavy moist soils or very light dry soils liable to wind erosion. Where the soil becomes exceptionally sandy, it is usually given over to forest, though the 'natural' vegetation was probably heath, which is still found. The clay soils require intensive manuring and liming, as well as adequate fallowing, though these practices have not always been adequately carried out in the past. Wet soils—clayey and peaty—occur in hollows and these can be rich in nutritive value and fertile if properly drained.

South of the ancient glacial meltwater valleys are wide areas of rich *loessic* deposits weathered to fertile dark soils, forming usually the richest lands, with some areas of highly calcareous soil in southern Poland. The natural condition of the soils in the west has been changed considerably by skilful husbandry, whereas in the east, primitive farming methods have tended to damage the natural soil structure. Some of the best soils occur in the *Börderlands* of Germany, where steppe-like soils developed under climatic conditions different to the present, mostly in the rain shadow of the Harz and Thüringen Forest, so that in these areas drought is often a hazard.

In the North European Plain there is a tendency to greater continentality towards the east. Rainfall shows a more marked summer distribution and occurs commonly in heavy thunder downpours, sometimes destructive to crops. Over this section of the Plain, there may be up to one month's difference in the start of the harvest between north and south and east and west. The relatively long and cold winter has always been a problem for livestock, especially in the eastern districts where winter fodder has been more difficult to provide from the lower yields and poorer methods of storage.

Once a great cattle range and then a vast granary east of the Danube, the Pannonian Plains have a distinct character. Climatic conditions are markedly more continental, though elements of East European continental, West European maritime and Mediterranean climates may be detected. In any one year, one or other of these elements may tend to predominate and so affect agricultural output. The basin character of the Pannonian Plains tends to lead to massive quantities of inward moving air sinking, warming and dessicating. The result is that plants which demand much light and warmth with relatively modest moisture flourish. These include fruits, vines, vegetables and medicinal plants. Drought however, is, a serious and constant threat, particularly in the eastern part of the plains, when rain does not fall for many weeks. It is reckoned that almost every other year must be considered a drought year. Nevertheless, great heat—60–85 days with over 25°C—each year does allow crops such as rice, groundnuts and figs to do well. On the other hand, winter cold is important for crops such as apples and pears. The main problem of the Pannonian climate is its variability and considerable annual variations act detrimentally on different sectors of agriculture—hot summers notably damage fruit crops while moist summers are adverse to vine cultivation. Poor winter snow cover in a dry year can cause freezing of seed, but a wet year may drown it. Dry springs with high winds cause serious soil erosion.

The soils of the Pannonian Plains are generally fertile, related to steppe forms, with patches of woodland soils or calcareous rendzina on higher ground. In many areas, partly the result of bad farming methods, surface salt makes soils little use. The presence of *loess* over large tracts of country helps soil fertility, but in the Tisza–Danube mesopotamia there are big areas of sands and sandy soils, some of which overlie *loess*. Through works to prevent flooding by straightening the gradients of some rivers such as the Tisza in the late nineteenth and early twentieth centuries, lowering of the water table led to the drying out of wet ground but also to further drying of areas already too dry.

The steppe influence is strong in the Moldavian and Wallachian plains, while it is also marked in the northern plain along the Danube in Bulgaria. Climate is more extreme than in Pannonia. Strong winter winds expose the soil to deep frost penetration and erosion, while the summer is dry, with rainfall in thundery downpours, mostly in the early part. Aridity and gullying are serious problems of the Rumanian farmer, particularly in the driest areas such as the Bărăgan steppe. Fortunately, the soils are generally fertile and steppe-like in character, but poor farming in the past has done much damage to them. Like the Pannonian *Puszta* this was once great cattle country that attracted nomads from the steppes, but in the nineteenth century, it became a major granary for wheat and maize. More recently, farming has tended to be diversified and more emphasis again put on animals.

The Hercynian lands have mostly podzols developed on gneiss, granite and related rocks. These are not generally fertile soils, which coupled to the raw moist climate, makes farming unattractive. Aspect and elevation are important factors, and much land is meadow or forest. The warmer and more fertile lowlands and basins will produce a wide range of arable crops and where their soils have developed on *loess*, they are particularly rich. Rich dark soils occur in Polabi and good soils are found in the Moravian Lowlands, though drought is a danger here. These lands became centres of sugar beet cultivation during last century.

The Carpathians, with their dependence on livestock and patches of poor farming, are a contrast to the fertile plains, and forestry is important over large areas. Aspect, elevation and angle of slope exercise strong influence over farming. The higher surfaces, with poor podzols, are often too humid for crops other than potatoes, the hardier cereals and grass. The best conditions are in the warmer and drier basins and broader valleys, where good forest soils occur, so that these and the lower mountain slopes have generally been extensively cleared of forest. One of the richest areas is the Transylvanian Tertiary hill country, where even degraded chernozem is found. Unfortunately, poor farming methods in the past have done much to lessen the value of soils and have caused serious soil erosion.

Föhn effects help to bring early springs to mountain basins and allow early movements of stock up the mountain sides. Such phenomena are particularly common in Rumania, where, for example, the *Vîntual Mare*—the Great Wind—blows in the Făgăraş and Sibiu basins. The eastern Carpathians suffer in summer from instability conditions that cause heavy thundery downpours, so that deforestation and bad husbandry have resulted in acute soil erosion. Over three million hectares are reputedly affected, particularly in the Bîrlad Plateau, Jijia basin, the Pre-Carpathians, the Oltenian hills and parts of Transylvania, though nearly a million hectares have been reclaimed since 1960.

In the Dinaric and Balkan mountains the diverse agriculture shows a close adaptation to climate, soil and terrain conditions, though some historic factors have also affected the pattern. The emphasis is generally on livestock, notably in the higher mountains of the south and in the extensive karst. Large areas of karstland are almost devoid of soil and support few animals. Cultivable land occurs in the floors of basins and depressions (*polja, doline*), often with reasonably good red soils. Past overgrazing has done great damage by accelerating soil erosion. In alpine Slovenia, the crystalline areas of Bosnia–Hercegovina and central or southern Serbia, podzols give poor yields and there are few basins with flat floors as in the karst. There is much pasturage, but it gives a poor hay. On the Adriatic littoral, Mediterranean climatic conditions allow characteristic crops such as the vine and olive. As in the mountain basins, cold air drainage from the high cold winter air of the mountains can have serious effect on farming.

The mountains of Bulgaria are characterised by woodland soils, but the southern mountains are generally very dry in summer and extremely cold in winter. Over considerable areas in the mountains, terraces are used to help prevent soil erosion and to overcome the problems of slope. To overcome aridity the area irrigated has been increased tenfold since 1945. Some of the most important farming areas are mountain basins such as those around Sofia and Kyustendil and Plovdiv. The Bulgarian sector of the Balkans is climatically a transitional zone between the continental steppe influences from the north-east and the Mediterranean influences from the south to bring heavy winter snow in the mountains. Consequently, agricultural patterns show some relation to both these major climatic zones.

6.1.1 Historical Development of Agriculture

Agriculture has extremely ancient origins in Eastern Europe, with the early development of peasant cultures in the south-east, influenced by Middle Eastern groups. From these areas agricultural methods were gradually disseminated to the hunting and collecting peoples of the north, where sedentary agriculture seems to have become widespread in neolithic times. Until mediaeval times, in Slavonic settlement areas, agricultural methods remained simple, with small, square fields, simple ploughs and even shifting cultivation, notably in forested lands. Forests, preserved for defence, provided berries, honey and wax to augment the simple village economy. Simple rotations provided grain and fallow, while animals were grazed on village commons, on the fallow or in the forests. Sheep, cattle and pigs were kept, but geese and poultry were also important. It was not until the fifteenth and sixteenth centuries that the three-field system was introduced into the more easterly areas. The Slavs who moved into southern areas came into contact with fruit and vine cultivation, but in many mountain areas pastoralism remained mostly in the hands of Vlachs, Albanians and other older groups. In the Carpathians both Slav and Ruman groups were pastoralists. In the Pannonian, Wallachian and Moldavian plains immigrant nomadic groups from the steppes imprinted their economy for various periods, though usually the more sedentary farming of the subservient Slavs outlasted this imprint. Nevertheless, large scale cattle herding remained a feature of the Puszta until the nineteenth century, although the Magyars had relatively quickly adopted the more sedentary ways of their Slav underlings.

Between the ninth and sixteenth centuries, the period of feudalism over much of Europe, considerable changes took place in agriculture in Eastern Europe. From the west came the pressure of German colonisation and influence which made greatest progress in the North European Plain, but was also felt in Danubia. Change was also wrought by the stultifying influence of the Turkish spread from the south-east—forcing many peasants to seek refuge in the hills, ravaging and devastating once fertile lands, such as the southern parts of the Puszta, while introducing new organisational forms such as the *čiflik*.

The German colonisation, which included absorption of the sparse Slav population as well as the introduction of immigrant German peasants, brought the establishment of villages and the clearing of land for the three-field system of cultivation. The Germans also introduced a heavy plough, well-suited to the glacial soils, while large strip fields replaced the small, square field of the Slavs. The Slavs, with their simpler methods and ploughs, had favoured the lighter *loessic* soils and drier diluvial platforms. The Germans with their better equipment spread on to the heavier soils and sank wells that released villages from location near to streams, for the Slavs never seemed to use the well. The German colonisation brought clearing of the woodland—the *Rodungszeit*—notably in the Erzgebirge and the Sudeten mountains, while they also engaged in clearing marsh (sometimes using immigrants from the Netherlands—for example, *Bugholländer*). There is evidence from place names that Slav lords also imitated the clearing activities of the Germans, in Poland, Bohemia and even in Slovakia. Monastic foundations, notably Cistercians, did much to improve farming techniques and conditions, as well as using their expertise in forest clearance, particularly in Silesia, the Ostmark and in Hungary. The main forest clearance ended in the second half of the fourteenth century and could be traced up to the upper limit of cultivation.

The main crops at this period were wheat in favourable areas, barley and some spelt or similar crops, while autumn rye, spring oats and buckwheat were important throughout mediaeval times. Vegetables were grown by many Slav villagers, and vines were cultivated on a large scale, sometimes in unsuitable places because of the demand for liturgical wines. Flax and hemp were the main fibres grown. Livestock was fed on common grazings and in the heaths and forests, but this did not provide manure for arable cultivation and often other means were used to maintain the fertility of the soil in a primitive manner. The lack of winter feed made it necessary to slaughter many animals each year. The rise of towns increased the commercial element in farming in the German lands and in Bohemia, though basically it remained a subsistence economy. In the Slav lands of the Vistula basin and eastwards, the demand from the few towns was small and a simpler economy, including gathering of fruits, honey and wax in the forests, existed, only indirectly influenced by the German improvements in the west.

The agricultural history of the Pannonian Plains has been influenced strongly by forces from outside. In the ninth century the early sedentary Slav population was displaced or enslaved by the semi-nomadic Magyars, who moved into a landscape of light woodland or even wooded steppe, and it is suggested that some areas, such as the Danube–Tisza mesopotamia had been cleared by peoples such as the Cumans (*Great Cumania*). There were also large areas of seasonal marsh or permanent swamp where wildfowlers or fishers lived, mostly drawn from the earlier peoples, who were also found in poor, dry dune country, like the Nyírség. Generally, the western plains, especially the Kisalföld and Transdanubia, seem to have been distinguished by arable and fruit cultivation or by extensive forested uplands such as the Mecsek and the Bakony. The destructive onslaught of the Turks from the late fifteenth century was to leave a more lasting impress than earlier marauding attacks and the landscape of small villages and scattered settlements disappeared from large areas. Recurrent destruction discouraged arable cultivation, so that pastoralism became more important, for stock could be driven away whenever danger threatened. Large numbers of cattle were driven to markets in Austria. The smallest dispersed settlements, apart from those of wildfowlers and fishers in the marshes, disappeared and villages grew into massive agglomerations, still characteristic of the southern Puszta, as people clustered together for defence against the Turks.

The Balkan lands suffered from neglect and stagnation, because Turkish policies tended to lead to ruination through careless and thoughtless land use. Even in Byzantine times much of the Dinaric and Balkan mountains appear to have been well-wooded, though considerable inroads had already been made. Wood was voraciously consumed throughout the mediaeval period for shipbuilding, housing and fuel, while forest was deliberately burned to destroy cover during warfare. In Istria, Dalmatia and Croatia forests had been mercilessly exploited by Venetians and Ragusans. Mediaeval travellers describe great forests in the Balkan Peninsula that are today represented only by meagre stands of timber. Reseeding was hampered by the extensive grazing of goats and pigs, while the tendency for many people to escape into the mountains put a human pressure on the land that reduced the rate of natural rejuvenation of forest. The deforestation caused soil erosion and material washed from mountains led to growing marshiness in the coastal lowlands, with the spread of malaria. Even in the more fertile farming country, Turkish policy encouraged the decline of agriculture, when land was expropriated for Turkish officials who held estates for some time before they were moved to other places and positions—a system not conducive to anything other than ruthless exploitation of the land. An oppressive landlordism coupled to a growing mismanagement of local affairs as the power and virility of the empire waned brought uprisings and depopulation as peasants melted away into the mountains.

In the Dinaric and Balkan lands pastoralism was singularly important. Pigs were kept in the beech and oak forests and elsewhere sheep and cattle were herded. Salt pork for Venetian or Genoese ships was a major item. On the Adriatic littoral citrus fruits were introduced and the vine and olive grown, while the demand from the Turkish market encouraged cultivation of such things as attar of roses and, from the sixteenth century, tobacco. The mountain basins and lowlands became granaries, though mediaeval Byzantium had obtained most of its grain from the northern shore of the Black Sea. Moldavia and Wallachia also became suppliers, but there were great areas of good grain-growing land unused. Bee-keeping for mead was encouraged, while flax and hemp and various beans were grown. The cultivation of mulberry for silk rearing introduced by Justinian died out under the Turks.

The decline of Turkish power in Pannonia was followed from the latter part of the seventeenth century by the slow rehabilitation of farming in the devastated lands. In the Banat and Bačka immigrants of various ethnic origins were settled in planned villages laid out by the Habsburg administrators. Through the eighteenth century and into the early nineteenth century, Pannonia became increasingly a granary, especially in the Puszta, but in the second half of the century, the inflow of cheap extra-European grain undermined its position. There was increasing use of machinery and the proportion of fallow land also fell, while land reclamation increased the arable area. Throughout the nineteenth century, notably in the south, there remained reserves of land to be occupied and pastoralism held sway in considerable areas: in 1839 it was claimed that a quarter of the agricultural land of Hungary was uncultivated. In the Wallachian and Moldavian Plains crushing taxation and shortage of labour caused neglect of cultivation well into the nineteenth century—in 1820 a British observer estimated that only a sixth of the land was cultivated. Even after the Rumanians gained their freedom colonising the plains with immigrants from other parts of Europe was proposed.

In the Habsburg empire agrarian policy was generally enlightened, notably the *Urbarium* of Maria Theresa in 1767. With subsequent legislation, although feudal duties were not abolished, at least peasants were protected from gross exploitation by definition of the serfs' rights and obligations. Peasant land was defined and so guarded against encroachment by the landowners. Where the *Urbarium* was not applied, as in Transylvania, peasant conditions were generally poor, as was also the case in Croatia. In the Military Frontier special tenurial rights produced large peasant holdings against the liability for military service. There was encouragement—generated by the eighteenth century physiocrats—for intensive cultivation and quality production, and a great deal of reclamation and land improvement carried out.

In the 1830s after three centuries of oppression and paralysis, Turkish land reforms were introduced, effectively in some parts of their empire. The reforms followed riots against Turkish land-grabbing and brought the abolition in several areas of tithes and labour service as well as changes in tenurial patterns. While Turkish landownership could be swept away, the legacy of privilege and corruption was harder to eradicate, notably in Rumania. The Turkish tithe on field crops had discouraged arable cultivation but had encouraged livestock holding, and consequently over-grazing and deforestation.

The Carpathians remained backward, as poor peasants eked out a living from transhumant herding and working in the great forests. In the valleys, small patches of arable were tilled by simple methods for modest yields, though more advanced farming was found in the broader, warmer basins. The main products for market were meat, milk, cheese and sour cream. Woodworking provided domestic industry and a marketable surplus for cash.

Over much of Central and Eastern Europe, the late fourteenth to mid-eighteenth centuries had been a time of strife that made social and economic change difficult. In the countryside a basically subsistence economy had produced a small surplus that generally satisfied the modest demands from the small towns which anyway produced considerable amounts of their own food. The eighteenth century however, brought great philosophical awakening of ideas in social and economic spheres, that had first taken root in Western Europe and were to penetrate into Eastern Europe after Napoleon. Unfortunately, from the changes they brought to the countryside were to arise the great problems of rural-overpopulation, land hunger and land reform that reached crisis level in the years between the two world wars. Emancipation movements began in the latter part of the eighteenth century—in the Habsburg's Austrian lands and then in the Napoleonic period in the German states and in Poland. Reforms followed in Serbia, Hungary, Rumania and Bulgaria, with the years 1830 to 1880 particularly important in South-east Europe. Nevertheless, the major problems were not solved and a struggle against the landowners was to continue well into the twentieth century.

The emancipation movement in Central and Eastern Europe, where true feudalism had existed, freed the peasants from their enserfment that had been generally extended in range during troubled mediaeval times: in much of South east Europe, the concept of 'fief tenure' implied by Central European feudalism was less clearly defined, with the element of obligation weak or lacking, either having lapsed or never having existed. The land reforms did not, however, generally give the peasants land or even break effectively the power of the land-owners. Many emancipation laws, while apparently generous, were slowly watered down by 'interpretive' legislation; their legal interpretation and the disbursement of justice was often left to the landowners in the countryside, meaning that peasants with grievances were hardly likely to receive fair hearing. As late as 1908 it could be said of East and West Prussia, 'though the name serfage is no longer used, this condition exists in spirit and to some extent in fact'. In real terms the old order hardly changed, inspite of whatever the law might say. At least within the German *Reich* after 1870 many peasants were able to escape the rigours by migrating to the new industrial towns, but in other parts of Europe—in Hungary or Rumania, for example—such a channel was not so readily available.

Large Junker estates, a common feature across Mecklenburg and Pomerania, in Brandenburg and Silesia, as well as in East and West Prussia, treated their workers paternally and conditions on many were good, while their owners, using skilled factors, ran them efficiently, with machinery and often their own sugar mills or distilleries. Elsewhere in central Germany, a healthy peasant class with medium or small holdings existed, freed in the nineteenth century from the last vestiges of feudalism but still closely bound to the soil. In Russian Poland, in spite of Napoleonic reforms, pressures and chicanery made the peasants' life hard, with small holdings, little capital and large families. In Austrian Poland the situation was little better, though the Austrians were less malevolent, but the small peasant proprietors saw their dwarf holdings gradually subdivided as population grew. In Bohemia–Moravia small peasant proprietors were a vigorous class who had won many rights in 1848, though the large estates still existed. In Hungary reforms and emancipation had made little impact and large half-cultivated *latifundia* worked by quasiserfs remained common into the twentieth century, though there were some efficiently run estates owned by the Jewish *sugar barons*. The peasants of Moldavia and Wallachia were also badly off as the landowning *boyars* were a rich unstable absentee class without attachment to their land and paternal feelings for their peasants found among estate owners elsewhere. The peasants were commonly victims of extortionate rents, high taxes and other impositions. Some relief came through Cuza's reforms of 1864, though their basic liberalism was spoilt by injustices in their execution. In a similarly bad position were the Bosnian peasants exploited by tyrannical and petty *agas* and the abuses of the Ottoman system in decay, so that grievances were not settled until 1910.

The Serbian land reform of 1830 has been described as 'a conscious choice of peasant proprietorship in preference to a new form of fief tenure' and produced a remarkably successful result. The peasants were not encumbered with debt, so common elsewhere; there was sufficient land available to give adequate holdings; and there was a readily expandable Austrian market for pigs. The large family farms had generally sufficient capital, labour and livestock to give a fair return, though there was some technical backwardness. National independence, as in Serbia, underlay Bulgarian reforms, though many peasants had already bought out Turkish landowners, divided the land into small holdings and indebted themselves fairly substantially. Nevertheless, because of the difficulties this had caused, both peasants and government attended more to agricultural organisation, notably in credit and marketing, than the Serbs. The Bulgarian smallholders were also skilled market gardeners with a highly intensive use of land.

6.1.2 Peasant Farming in the Twentieth Century

In the land reforms after 1918 peasant farming tended to gain at the expense of the great estates. While such a move had much to commend it socially ⌐nd politically, it was not always good economically. The new peasant farmers hau to face the problems of rural overpopulation that had arisen through a failure to check population growth, since empty land had been filled towards the end of the nineteenth century. They had to cope with a market that had been eroded by the late nineteenth century inflow of cheap extra-European grain and foodstuffs. Rural overpopulation was neither accurately recognised nor understood: worsening market conditions were often aggravated by conditions created to combat them. High levels of subsistence farming and the division of inheritance in many districts concealed the real gravity. Large landowners accepted worsening market conditions by taking lower prices, depressing the wages of their workers and leaving important tasks on their estates undone. Few recognised that changes in their methods and cropping patterns were one salvation. Fewer still saw investment in industry as a possible solution and hardly any recognised that demands for protection by tariff barriers aggravated the situation. Economic nationalism as well as autarky of the inter-war years, notably after the Depression in 1929 prevented free trade in agricultural products, limited markets to the small national units. The Germans might have provided the great market for East European crops, but failed to take full advantage of the possibilities until too late, while at the same time the heavily protected German peasant, so favourably regarded by the Nazi government, was also a stumbling block. In several countries, little attention was given to co-operatives or adequate peasant finance and education, possibly because there was a reluctance to change peasant life, of which far too rosy a view existed.

Extensive grain cultivation had continued when prices fell to unrewarding levels inspite of a strong demand for livestock products. Peasants had failed to see that co-operation in livestock farming or in fruit farming offered them better prospects with limited capital input. Investment opportunities in food processing industries had been overlooked. The promise of the great Danubian plains to become as rich and promising as the American Corn-Hog belt had failed to get the impetus to materialise. The possibilities were, however, reflected by the industrial crops and highly intensive market-gardening style farming that had saved Bulgaria from the worst effects of the Depression. The break-up in Hungary and Czechoslovakia of large estates integrated with beet-sugar or distilling industries had often brought a decline in these promising industries and left peasants without the chance to augment their income in winter. In itself, peasant farming offered effective ways of using an existing labour force. By its intensive methods it tended to increase output per head and was well-suited to any but extensive crops and it tended to encourage savings and to maintain a more equable distribution of income with consequent social stability.

Except in a few especially backward regions, the breakdown of the old communal tillage had left peasants free to cultivate their scattered strips as they wished, with little capital but usually much labour. Yields compared to those of Western Europe were generally low but often better than in competing areas outside Europe. Relatively little fertiliser was used and some of the most productive areas, such as the rich black soil lands of Danubia, depended on the natural fertility and rejuvenation of the soil. Livestock was kept on a restricted scale, partly because of the lack of a strong demand from towns over much of the study area, while the primitive system of cultivation often made keeping livestock over the winter hazardous, when there was sometimes not enough food for humans. Animals were allowed to graze only on the edge of fields or patches of fallow, and inadequate control of breeding was undertaken. The lack of rich pasture and the general dryness of much of Eastern Europe discouraged dairy farming. Where animals were kept in numbers, stall-feeding from local coarse grains or sugar beet waste was most common. Peasants tended to favour poultry and pigs, more 'flexible' animals than cattle. Cattle, oxen or buffaloes (in the south-east) were kept as draught animals: it was only estates and richer peasants that possessed horses. Most peasant farms sold a third or more of their output in local markets, while estates sold a much larger part of their output.

The North European Plain was distinguished by a mixture of large estates, particularly in the Baltic littoral and poorer northern areas, and peasant farms of various sizes and levels of efficiency in the centre and south. On the whole, yields in Germany were better than in Poland, while those areas that had passed from German to Polish control after 1918 had shown a decline in yield. The German high tariff barriers made intensive manuring profitable and there was a large chemicals industry to supply fertiliser needed. Such conditions were not found in Poland, where the intensiveness of farming was less and there was little difference in the levels of cultivation between peasant farms and the large estates. The crops were notably rye—the major northern bread grain—that accounted for a quarter of all German and a half of all Polish grain output. Wheat, however, was more important than rye in western Mecklenburg. Some oats and barley were grown in rotations with rye and potatoes. The potato, like rye, was very important in central and western Poland and grown by farms of all sizes. The potato was used either for alcohol or starch production or as feed for pigs, one of the main forms of livestock. A major problem in central Poland was that the ground offered little opportunity to cultivate anything other than potatoes and rye, the prices of which fell fairly consistently during the inter-war years.

In the large inter-war eastern provinces of Poland, farming was exceptionally poor. Where soils were either too wet or too dry, major capital investment, usually lacking, was needed either to drain or to irrigate. Rye and potatoes followed by fallow was the usual inadequate rotation. Poor cattle were grazed on extensive but meagre pasture. Farms were about 7–10 ha but were inadequate, because of the low yield, to support a family. Even the estates were badly farmed and poor.

The better soils and climate of the southern part of the North European Plain provided an improved living for the farm population. In the German Reich, the *Börderland* was a country of medium and large farms with estates, notably in Anhalt and in Silesia. Soils on the *loess* were naturally fertile, but areas of clay and alluvium were also worked for the same level of 'high farming'. There was generally less forest and pasture than in the north and over four-fifths of the area was arable land. Wheat and sugar beet were major crops, with barley and root crops. Sugar beet was in many places the crop around which the farm economy revolved: waste from sugar refining was an important feed, so that beef cattle rearing and milk production were undertaken. Pigs were widely kept, while sheep were more important here than in most parts of the *Reich*. Machinery was more commonly used here than in corresponding parts of Poland.

Southern Poland, with better natural conditions than elsewhere in the country, had a more intensive farming system with more livestock. The cropping system was generally good, but yields were lower than in central Poland and tended to decline in the inter-war period. Half the arable area was under grain; a quarter was devoted to meadows and green fodder crops and less than a quarter to root crops and potatoes. A cause of the falling yields was over-emphasis on grain in rotations with inadequate and improper manuring; it had been proposed to make correct manuring enforceable by law. The livestock side of farming provided milk that was marketed through effective co-operatives, but improvement could have been made by better management of the pastures. Here large farms were being broken up by selling parcels of land at high prices, but this made little difference since they were no better performers than the smaller peasants. A few large estates survived the land reforms by turning to activities such as fruit growing. The subdivision of land for inheritance and the chaotic system of purchase of scattered parcels meant wasted effort by peasants, with a five-hectare farm split into thirty or more pieces, so that problems arose less from technical levels than from land fragmentation. Attempts at betterment were hindered by the growing population pressure on the land and the falling yields. Towards the Carpathians, conditions were generally worse, as they were towards the east.

Western Czechoslovakia was primarily a countryside of large or medium-sized peasant farms, of between 25 and 75 ha. Over three-quarters of the farmland was arable. Farming was generally intensive, with cattle fed on hay, roots and sugar beet waste. Pigs were usually kept in considerable numbers. With fairly large farms, the Czech peasants used quite a lot of machinery, but like southern Poland there was weakness in the use of manure and pastures were neglected. The Czech peasant was also fortunate that the State supported his price levels, especially for grains. The major grain-producing areas were the fertile Polabí, with sugar beet cultivation as well (this was also important in the Olomouc basin) and the drier lands of the Moravian corridor. Some areas existed on special cultivation, such as hops around Žatec. Potatoes were most important in the higher parts of Bohemia.

In Slovakia, notably in the eastern parts, a far less advanced level was practised, though the plains of southern Slovakia belonged to the farming type of western Hungary. The main feature of mountainous Slovakia was greater emphasis on livestock, notably sheep in the higher parts, though in many upland basins cattle were important and were moved on the hoof to market. Where arable cultivation was possible, yields were commonly below Bohemia–Moravia and the potato was generally cultivated. Peasants augmented their living by working in the forests, while in summer many of the men moved up to the summer pastures.

One of the potentially richest areas and yet an area where standards of production were disappointing was Pannonia. Good performances were found in western Hungary and southern Slovakia (where there was a large Magyar population), but farming suffered badly in the inter-war period because of the depression in the wheat market, though in Hungary there was an attempt to produce more lucerne for seed and export to Germany. The large estates were often little better managed than the peasant farms. Farms of all sizes depended heavily on wheat and maize with relatively little livestock, while conservative attitudes prevented change. Some more progressive estates tried to develop new methods of cultivation and species of crop to raise their yield. A particular weakness was the little use made of manure to maintain soil fertility. Even the medium-sized peasant farms had low yields and relatively low intensity of cultivation, though the best performances were on farms of the German minority, where more interest was shown in livestock. The large landless farming population of the estates was the core of the critical rural unemployment that forced the Hungarian government to discourage use of machinery on the land.

The plains of the Alföld, Banat and Voivodina, with their rich dark soils of remarkable fertility were marked by bad farming methods. Maize followed wheat year after year without a proper rotation or the use of root crops, while manure was not used. The high soil-nitrogen content allowed fair returns even with bad methods, though yields were beginning to falter; and lucerne, which could have restored the health of the soil, was not used. A major hazard was the tendency to drought and to consequent large fluctuations in yield from year to year. In the Alföld wheat and maize were generally sold if prices were high, but when prices were low, maize was usually fed to pigs (for lard), bred on small farms and then sold to the estates for fattening on hay, lucerne or sugar-beet pulp. Few cattle were kept and these were mostly draught oxen, so that little manure was available, consequently less than a fifth of the arable land got stable manure and under a tenth had artificial fertiliser. The conservative farmers of the Alföld farmed at a low intensity, tending to become more extensive in their methods, while the effect of the new economic alignments and tariff system was reflected in a fall in the density of livestock. To offset this some of the progressive larger peasant farms in the south turned to fruit and poultry production. Rural unemployment and acute poverty existed, notably in the least fertile areas, such as the Nyírség.

The Banat and Voivodina were more prosperous and progressive, although physical conditions were much the same. The medium-sized farms of about 10 ha, laid out in the colonisation of the eighteenth century, remained adequate to support a family into the twentieth century, while social habits kept the size of the families limited and living standards were generally better than in the Alföld. Farming generally depended too much on wheat and maize, but the rotations were more advanced and yields high. Machinery was used, but there was a reluctance to change methods in spite of new conditions in European markets.

The plains of Wallachia and Moldavia were particularly backward farming areas in inter-war times. There was good soil but frequent drought, but peasants farmed primitively and wheat followed maize year by year with little subsidiary cropping. Because maize had to be planted early if it were to develop adequately before the late summer drought, it failed in many years. Peasants generally farmed their strips as if communal cropping were still practised and did nearly everything by hand. Animals were grazed on the stubble in autumn, though little livestock was generally kept. Many families did not even possess a cow; consequently little manure was available and much was wasted as fuel or for brickmaking. A critical problem appeared in the inter-war years in the gradual decline in yield from exhaustion of the remarkable soil fertility, while animal health was poor and peasants suffered malnutrition from a diet too heavily dependent on maize. There was, however, not such an acute problem of overpopulation as in many parts of Poland.

Towards the Carpathian mountains, in the foothill zone, conditions were poorer and the density of population higher. Peasant farms usually had sheep which were pastured on land away in the hills, but about half the families owned no animals. In the valleys there was vine and fruit growing and some peasants created wealth by owning vats for storing wine and plum brandy or providing simple machinery to comb the wool. It was usually the larger holdings that produced wheat and the better wines, for which little market outside Rumania had been found. The government tried desperately to stimulate interest in better methods and in co-operatives, as well as to make machinery available and to encourage animal husbandry.

The acid podzols of much of Transylvania gave poorer yields than generally found in Wallachia and Moldavia, though areas of degraded black soils and brown forest earths were more rewarding, and the standard of farming was less primitive. With a high density of farming population and not infrequent crop failure, this was a land from which there was considerable migration. The three-field system with a fallow was followed in parts of Transylvania even into the twentieth century. Though animal manure was not used heavily, there was use of artificial fertiliser on the soils poor in calcium. Equipment was simple, with wooden ploughs drawn by water buffalo in many villages. Wheat was grown in place of maize, though on some poorer soils, rye was the main cereal, while potatoes were also cultivated along with hoe crops, oats and some maize. Pigs and the buffaloes (for a rich milk in small amounts) were the main livestock.

It was not uncommon for the peasants in Bulgaria to farm in a most intensive fashion a small plot on the plain or in a mountain basin and to graze sheep on the open pastures of nearby hills. On the plains between the Danube and the Balkan mountains, however, farming was similar to the plains of Wallachia, with maize and wheat growing on small farms using primitive methods. Nevertheless, lucerne was being grown on an increasing scale and much done to improve the quality and number of livestock. In the basins and valleys of the Maritsa drainage system, there was an emphasis on 'garden style' cultivation—around Plovdiv there was vine cultivation and vegetables, while around Karlovo and Kazanlik rose cultivation was important. Over a thousand villages were concerned in tobacco production, which flourished with German purchases in the late 1930s. The inter-war years marked a very rapid increase in the area sown to potatoes. An unfortunate trend was that the smallest holdings were tending to multiply, while the concentration in the south on labour-intensive crops left a large pool of labour without adequate earnings in the off-season. Investment in processing plants to use vegetable and fruit crops was reduced in effectiveness by the tariff barriers raised by some European countries against imported fruits and processed foods, while the cost of foreign aid in developing such necessary things as irrigation was prohibitive.

The Karst and southern Serbia were dependent on imports of grain and might have been regarded as overpopulated had it not been for the fact that the peasants were often able to augment their income by work in the forests or as shepherds. In the mountains simple farming was carried on in the valleys and the great inter-montane basins, while in the hills themselves there was only a sparse pastoralism. The red residual soils were generally fertile when properly cultivated, but peasant farming methods too commonly encouraged soil erosion. The usual pattern was of crops raised on small patches of fertile ground near the meagre huts, with poor yields and little facility to store grain crops properly. Livestock was poor, with few cattle or pigs but many sheep, while goats were slowly destroying the vegetation and accelerating soil erosion. In the inter-war years, the government had begun to take measures against destruction of remaining forests, but with little success under the prevailing population pressure. The exceptional poverty forced the government in the worst districts to provide relief meals, at least for children, during the 1930s. In the Bosnian forests where some Islamic usages remained, the poverty-stricken peasants did not even possess the simple wooden ploughs used elsewhere but only a crude digging stick (*ralo*).

In Albania conditions were similar though more primitive, with some of the best potential land unusable because of malarial infestation of the coastal lowlands. Many peasants, heavily indebted to landowners and merchants, had developed the unfortunate practice of share-cropping. Agrarian reform was the most vital problem if economic progress were to be made, but unpopular with the powerful *beys*. Italian initiative, however, showed what could be done in improving land and raising the miserable level of productivity. Women did most of the field work while men were more concerned with livestock. No idea of rotations existed and the same ground was sown to the same crop until yield became worthless, so that a kind of shifting cultivation on open fields trampled by beasts was practised. Maize was the main grain, with some barley, rye, oats and wheat as well as rice. Sugar beet was grown around Korçë where a small sugar factory was built. Fruit and vegetables were for family use or sale in local markets, while olives were grown up to 80 km from the coast in favoured places. Tobacco was grown for local use, as well as flax and hemp until the import of cheap factory cloths, while in the 1930s experiments in growing cotton showed promise. Most peasants looked on livestock as their main source of wealth. Almost a third of the area of the country was pasture and animal products were major export items. The best cattle were on the alpine pastures of northern Albania, but even their quality was not high. Sheep were kept for wool and milk rather than meat, while Christian families kept pigs.

Apart from the Reich and parts of Bohemia–Moravia and western Poland, the picture was a gloomy one. Both peasants and landowners seemed too inflexible to break the vicious circle of overpopulation and undercapitalisation. While the landowner was to become the scapegoat after 1945, the peasant was far from blameless.

6.2 The development of industry before 1945 (figure 6.1)

An important consideration in the later development of industry in Eastern Europe was the social organisation that left some areas without an enterprising middle class of townspeople anxious for economic advancement. The peasants generally lacked the skill and capital, let alone the legal freedoms, to become entrepreneurs, while the landowning aristocracy saw no need to augment their wealth nor possessed the enthusaism to accept the responsibilities that industrialisation demanded. In the Russian empire, unless industrial development was for the state's purposes, there was little encouragement and the market was anyway desperately poor. In Austria–Hungary development came in the more advanced areas, such as Bohemia–Moravia, that could provide some of their own investment, and in northern Hungary after the creation of the Dual Monarchy in 1867, while the capitals of Vienna and Budapest also attracted industry. The rapidly growing Prussian state encouraged industrial development, with early developments in Silesia and in the Saxon lands, though the northern Junkers were lukewarm. The lands where the Turks held sway were most backward, for the Ottoman system stifled or stagnated economic life.

Wherever development had taken place, the initiative had come from British, French, German or Belgian capital, though Vienna had become a late source, but in an age when foreign aid to developing countries was an unknown philanthropism, investment was far from devoid of political undertones. Extractive industries or industries part-processing local produce for manufacture back in the investors' own country were most attractive, while transport—railways and ports—was a valuable investment that allowed deeper penetration of the emerging, part-developed countries. While the cheapness of labour in most of Eastern Europe, even when rates were low in Western and Central Europe, cannot be gainsaid, its skill was low and many believed it could not be trained to an adequate level. Cheap labour and peasant poverty made low purchasing power unattractive to manufacturing industry. The real economies of scale in production could not always be guaranteed and it was anyway more attractive to investors to see manufacturing done in their own country. Manufacturing industries in Eastern Europe could not be readily developed in the face of cheap imports from established industry elsewhere with lower overheads. When in the inter-war years of economic nationalism, governments came to develop local manufacturing industries behind tariff barriers, it was found that costs rose and the already poor market contracted further.

Investment brought competition between powers, but the Danubian lands and the Balkans, extending into Turkey, before 1914 had become a particular German interest. Much centred around the vague concept of the Berlin–Baghdad Railway, though realisation of German dreams was marred by fluctuating relations with the Habsburg empire. The concept of a vast German 'common market' was crystallised in Friedrich Naumann's *Mitteleuropa*. The collapse of the Central Powers gave the French an opportunity to penetrate further through such organisations as the Little Éntente, but the 1930s saw the rebuilding of a German trade area in the Danube basin and in the Balkans, forcing countries as reluctant allies but anxious trading partners into the German orbit, helping some countries to overcome their problems of economic nationalism and the legacy of

Figure 6.1. In 1914 industry was markedly developed in the German empire—notably in Saxony, Thüringen and in the Silesian lands—and in Austrian Bohemia, though it was also emerging in the Danube valley between the important industrial centres of Vienna and Budapest. In South-eastern Europe mining was more important than industry, which had developed only on a most limited scale. Various sources.

disruption left by the new boundaries created in 1918–20. It did not, however, encourage manufacturing industry, though some states tried against the great odds of the world depression to develop their own manufacturing industries on a broader front than simply light consumer goods and foodstuffs.

Within the study area the territory of the German Democratic Republic was already well industrialised by the last quarter of the nineteenth century in the Saxon lands, Berlin and Thüringen, where the great chemicals industry of the Elbe–Saale basin was beginning to emerge. Within the present Polish territory industry under Prussian encouragement had become well established in the latter nineteenth century, particularly on the coalfield of Upper Silesia. At the same time, Russian Poland was a focus of industrial development within the Tsarist empire, although the size of industrial plants was modest. In 1914 the present territory of Czechoslovakia comprised one-fifth of the area of the Habsburg empire but contained three-quarters of its industrial capacity. In Slovakia, Magyar initiative had begun some development, but the Austro-Hungarian empire's industrial core had been created by the enterprising German and Jewish population in Bohemia–Moravia. In Transylvania German and Hungarian initiative had founded modest local industries, while Croatia and Slovenia had also experienced Habsburg encouragement to industry, and there were plans afoot to resurrect the ancient iron industry in Bosnia. Only modest industries existed in Serbia, while foreign capital had begun the development of petroleum working in the Old Kingdom of Rumania and some small industrial plants had been founded in Bulgaria. In South-eastern Europe, what limited industrial development took place owed much to Greek entrepreneurs or to a few far-sighted Bulgarians and Serbs, but it required foreign capital and even foremen and managers from Western Europe.

The important contribution of German and Jewish communities cannot be gainsaid. In mediaeval times German miners, mostly from Saxony, had spread into the fringing mountains of Bohemia, into Slovakia (for example, Zips, in the thirteenth century) and into Transylvania. The mines of Joachimstal in the Erzgebirge supplied silver and tin for the *Taler*, one of the most common monetary units in Central Europe. As mining began to decline, the miners turned to smithy and foundry work out of which arose in the nineteenth century modern manufacturing industries. The guilds of German miners and artisans and the Jewish communities of artisans and traders had tended not to accept outsiders as apprentices, so inhibiting the development of skills among the other ethnic groups, but the Germans were also in a privileged position in the Prussian and Austrian empires. In the later nineteenth century, as industry expanded and the German and Jewish communities could no longer provide all the labour required, Czech, Polish, Hungarian and other peoples were attracted into industrial employment.

6.2.1 Central Germany

The foundations of the industrial infrastructure in the German Democratic Republic lie in the policy of Prussia after the Napoleonic wars in stimulating economic growth in the German states, while Saxony also provided a congenial atmosphere for industry. The Thirty Years' War had badly affected the mines of the Erzgebirge and thereafter many miners turned to making paper, glass, toys, textiles or even dyestuffs. In the 1780s the first textile mills had appeared (Ernst-tal, Mittweida), but were blighted by the shortage of raw cotton during the *Continental System*, while later they had a hard struggle against the flood of cheap English calico. The wider market provided by the Zollverein after the 1830s gave the industry its chance to get well-grounded, while use of coal after 1820 had attracted the mills from the waterside sites in upland valleys. Lack of suitable ore and adequate coal in Saxony did not encourage smelting of iron, so that engineering became important to former miners—textile machinery and railway goods after 1850 were major items. Saxony provided good technical education at an early date: Freiberg Mining Academy (1766), Chemnitz Industrial Design School (1800) and the Mittweida Technical High School (1867). In the hills domestic industry making such things as musical instruments (Klingental) turned to factories, while in Thüringen similar trends were seen, including a highly advanced optical goods industry in Jena through the genius of Karl Zeiss.

In the basins of the middle Elbe and the Saale, industry came later, though lignite began to be mined in the eighteenth century. By the mid-nineteenth century, the immense deposits of potassium salts on the Harz flanks had begun to be exploited, but it was not until the last decades of the nineteenth century that a large-scale chemicals industry grew and the real impetus came with the cutting off of supplies of Chilean nitrates in the First World War. Another focus was Berlin, where Huguenots fleeing persecution had settled to found a textile industry. Government demand in the eighteenth century stimulated smelting and foundry work for armaments, followed by engineering. In 1836 Borsig founded his railway works, while in the 1870s the city became the centre of the electrical engineering industry.

6.2.2 Silesia and Adjoining Areas

The forces that had stimulatd *Mitteldeutschland* carried the impetus into Silesia, where brass making (using calamine) and the smelting of bog iron ores had long been practised. When Prussia annexed the province in 1742, there were already twelve blast furnaces. Lead mining had been conducted from the thirteenth century, reaching a peak in the sixteenth and seventeenth centuries, thereafter declining because of inadequate pumping techniques. The coal deposits, though worked, were in little demand, because it was easier to exploit the vast forests. In the eighteenth century, Silesia had become the arsenal of Prussia, but poor char-coal hampered the expansion of iron making and in 1789 coke was first used. A decade later a large new blast furnace plant supervised by English and Scottish foremen was opened at Gleiwitz and in 1862, the *Königshütte* opened on an even grander scale. As iron making grew and the railways demanded more coal, mining also expanded, both in Upper Silesia and in the Waldenburg field, while better pumping engines made work easier. Lead mining received a new lease of life and after 1809 there was a rising production of metallic zinc.

In Russian Poland around Dąbrowa with relatively easy conditions, coal mining began in the 1790s, with the coal sent to Warsaw and other Russian markets while more suitable coal and coke were imported for iron making. The coal mines were backed by French and German capital. After 1830 iron making had been conducted at the Huta Bankowa, but later crude pig iron was imported for further processing from Prussian Silesia. A sharp increase in customs duty on imported pig after 1884 encouraged local industry and stimulated development at Czestochowa (using local and imported ore) and at Radom, financed by foreign capital. At Olkusz and Będzin there was some lead and zinc mining. Engineering was developed, though German interests predominated financially.

6.2.3 Bohemia

Coal was also mined in the Jaworzno area of Austrian Western Galicia, but the main coalfield was in Bohemian Silesia where some of the best coking coal in Silesia was found. The coal lay at considerable depth and the geology of the field was imperfectly understood. This part of the field was developed mostly after 1850. Iron making using charcoal had existed since early times, but the first modern works was established in 1826 by the Archbishop of Olomouc at Vitkovice. Local coal and ore were first used, but later ore came from Sweden. Later other works were added, with ore brought from Slovakia, Bohemia and Steiermark. Bohemian Silesia thus became the heavy metallurgical centre of the Habsburg empire and using its iron and steel, engineering plants began to develop elsewhere in Bohemia, particularly where German communities were seeking new economic opportunities. Prague, with largely German initiative, grew as an engineering centre, but one of the largest plants in the empire opened in the mid-nineteenth century at Plzeň, where the Škoda works were to become a great armaments producer. By 1841 a tenth of all factories in Bohemia–Moravia were engineering or metal-working shops. Other industries were glass-making in northern Bohemia where cheap jewellery for the British Indian market was made. Ceramics from local clays were produced at Karlovy Vary and pencils from graphite deposits at Česky Budějovice. Liberec was a major centre for textiles, while Brno in Moravia became the 'Czech Manchester'. Cheap cloths were made for Balkan and South American markets, while a fez-making industry flourished at Strakonice. Using local lignite and raw materials imported along the Elbe, Bohemia developed a chemicals industry in the Ohře and Labe (Elbe) valleys late in the nineteenth century; the earliest plants were the Kraslice dyestuffs works and several Bohemian sulphur works. Several big, modern plants were erected after 1870. There was also a considerable food-processing industry, with Olomouc, for example, refining sugar from local beet, and Plzeň using Žatec hops for its famous beer.

6.2.4 Hungary

After 1867 the Hungarians pursued an increasingly separate economic development. Slovakia and Transylvania provided numerous minerals, though fuel was a serious deficiency. Budapest began to emerge as the main industrial focus of the country, with large-scale engineering and other manufacturing industries, even if financed from Berlin and Vienna. It has been said that the Hungarians sought after 1880 to turn Slovakia into 'a new Bohemia'. There was, however, a marked shift of iron and steel making into Bohemia–Moravia after 1875 despite increased output from Slovakia. Using local ores, iron works were developed at

Krompachy, Zvolen and Podbrezova, while others were built in Hungary at Ózd, Salgótarján, Diósgyőr and other sites, though all were small even by contemporary standards. Copper refining was done at Banská Bystrica. Some Slovakian pig iron went to the Vitkovice works in Austrian Silesia. Along the Danube (notably at Budapest), Tisza and Drava there was some shipbuilding (using hard oak from the mountains to the south). Elsewhere in provincial towns, industry such as linen-making, soap-making or food preparation was on a small scale.

6.2.5 South Slav Lands

The South Slav lands were among the last in Europe to feel the impact of the industrial revolution. In the lands held by Austria–Hungary, textile factories replaced domestic industry after 1850, notably in Slovenia and the Voivodina. Other early industries were all connected with food processing, such as steam-driven flour mills in the Voivodina by 1850. In Slovenia metallurgy had flourished in Roman and in medieval times, but the modern iron works at Jesenice dates only from 1869 and the Slovenian ferro-alloy plant from 1918. Other Austrian enterprises were a ferrosilicon plant at Split, the Celje ironworks and the Šibenik ferro-manganese plant. In Serbia the first steam-driven flour mill appeared in 1863, the first steam sawmill in 1901. In 1906 a textile mill was opened and a large modern sugar works followed at Ćuprija in 1911. Mediaeval Serbia's silver mines had held the key to the economy of Europe. In 1846, in Bosnia, iron-mining was resumed at Vareš and coal-mining was stimulated by the railway construction of the 1880s. In 1891 the Vareš ironworks opened, followed in 1892 by the Zenica plant, for which major plans were projected, while a ferro-alloy plant started at Jajce. The copper and iron pyrites mines at Majdanpek, worked in ancient and mediaeval times, were worked briefly under the Austrian occupation of 1719–39, but did not come into modern production, along with the Bor copper mines, until the twentieth century.

In the old Turkish garrison towns of Bulgaria guild industries had flourished, but once an influx of cheap manufactured goods began they suffered heavily. In the 1890s the Bulgarians started a number of plants, backed by Western European capital, to process agricultural produce, but even these needed high protective tariffs to survive. Corn and oil mills, leather works and textile mills were the main branches. Railway building brought a demand for coal and consequently mining, while the reforms of 1857 encouraged factory-style industry. In Wallachia and Moldavia especially backward conditions prevailed, with primitive salt and gold mining (Gypsies in particular washed placer deposits). After 1858 petroleum began to be exploited, but the development of industry was generally retarded by a lack of banking and commercial facilities that hampered the inflow of capital and modern methods.

6.3 Industrial geography between the two world wars

The sweeping away of the Habsburg empire and the restriction within tightly drawn boundaries of the new Soviet state and the Weimar Republic, broke into established patterns of industry and trade. New states had to create new economic structures for themselves, but the whole process was complicated by the Great Depression (1929–32), the acute economic nationalism, and German economic imperialism which began to emerge in the middle 1930s.

6.3.1 Central Germany

In the territory of the German Democratic Republic, war was reflected in the varying fortunes of its several main industries, while during the Nazi period this formed the larger part of the great economic expansion of *Mitteldeutschland*. The inter-war years were a period of increasing output of electricity and gas from plants based on lignite, the mining of which was greatly expanded, notably west of the Elbe, where massive opencast machinery was used. To take advantage of the large plants established near the lignite mines, a network of gas pipelines and electricity grid lines was built and there was substantial growth in demand for electricity from electrochemical and electrometallurgical plants. The Nazi rearmament plans put a premium on the expansion in output of aluminium, based largely on Hungarian raw materials. One of the main industries in the Elbe–Saale basin was the chemicals industry, which included a number of large plants developed during the First World War, which used lignite and salts from the Harz fringe, and the energy and water supplies available. After 1919 these plants had to compete with the French control of potash deposits in Alsace. The creation of a monopolistic trust, *IG Farbenindustrie*, in 1925 brought a rationalisation of the chemicals industry to the advantage of *Mitteldeutschland*, and the chemicals industry became the mainstay of the Nazi attempt to create self-sufficiency through the introduction of a wide range of ersatz substances. Of particular importance was the manufacture of synthetic petroleum (Böhlen, Zeitz, Schwarzheide) and synthetic rubber (Schkopau), based on lignite.

Inspite of the disturbance to production of iron and steel in the major producing areas of the Ruhr and Upper Silesia, as well as the French control over the Saar's production, *Mitteldeutschland* continued to depend on these areas for its supply, and there was little change in the small local industry, though during the Depression a few old plants closed. The inter-war years marked, however, a great stimulus to the different branches of engineering and, although expansion began in the 1920s, the main push came in the Nazi rearmament policy when numbers employed rose sharply. Aircraft building (for example Junker at Dessau) and motor-vehicle construction were new directions, while precision engineering and optical goods expanded. Berlin remained a centre of electrical engineering, though shortly before the war decentralisation moved some plants to South Germany. The emphasis in Nazi regional economic development on *Mitteldeutschland* was reflected in the establishment of two major new undertakings—the Volkswagen works at Wolfsburg and the Salzgitter steel works; both these major plants fell to the territory of the West German Federal Republic through the boundary delimitation of the original occupation zones in 1945.

Saxony and Lower Silesia remained major textile producers during the inter-war years, freed in part from the competition in home markets of the Alsatian industry, but increasingly dependent on synthetic fibres.

6.3.2 Poland

The new Polish state had its industry predominantly in the west, in either former Prussian or Austrian provinces, with the main concentration in the south-west in the Polish sector of the Upper Silesian coalfield, but there was also heavy industry in the former Russian district of Dąbrowa and Częstochowa. The towns of the former Prussian lands, notably Poznań and Bydgoszcz had some engineering, also developed on a modest scale near Warsaw and Starachowice. There was a large textile industry, concentrated particularly in Łódź and in Białystok, but the capacity was too large for the Polish home market as the mills had been geared to the former Russian market. However, during the 1930s there was some development of linen mills in the backward central and eastern provinces, taking advantage of markets in Western Europe. Although Poland had inherited the oil deposits of Austrian Galicia, output could not be raised to pre-1913 standards and even fell short of home needs by the latter 1930s. Inspite of its possession of efficient food processing plants in the former Prussian territory, Poland was unable to compete effectively with Denmark, Ireland or the Baltic countries. During the 1920s some new industries appeared, such as radio assembly, electrical engineering and even a small aircraft industry.

The British General Strike of 1926 gave Poland a chance to break into the coal exporting trade (notably in the Baltic), particularly as mines in the Polish part of Upper Silesia had lost their former German customers. Although labour costs were low, Polish industry was forced to buy raw materials in overseas markets with the aid of expensive foreign investment and found it hard to hold prices to a competitive level in the deteriorating economic conditions of the late 1920s. After 1936 some recovery in European economic life brought in more cash by expanding coal sales, while a measure of central planning on a four-yearly basis was introduced. Emphasis was put on development of a central Polish industrial area for strategic reasons as well as to lap up labour in the overpopulated rural districts. The new area had Sandomierz and Stalowa Wola as main centres and contained a considerable armaments industry and a chemicals industry for military purposes.

6.3.3 Upper Silesia

Upper Silesia was peculiarly dependent on heavy industry—coal-mining, lead- and zinc-mining and iron- and steel-making—so that it felt the harsh impact of the Depression. The partition left the bulk of industrial plant and mineral resources in Poland, though before 1914 65 per cent of the iron and steel goods and 90 per cent of the zinc had been sold in Germany, but only 40 per cent of the coal had been sent to Germany. The lead and zinc mines lay in Germany but the processing plant lost to Poland was replaced in 1934 by a new electrolytic plant at Magdeburg. The intricate system of roads, railways, gas and electricity supply lines as well as water pipes that had grown up within the pre-1914 boundaries of the *Reich* were disrupted by partition. The German–Polish Geneva agreement of 1922 tried to overcome this disruption by joint supply systems and a joint railway administration, while social security and working conditions were to be unified throughout the area. Such agreements could only function so long as German–Polish relations remained amicable.

While German Upper Silesia could still retain its links with inland domestic markets, it lost business confidence, despite valiant attempts to improve efficiency and reduce costs. Conditions were worse in Poland, for in the general weakness of the economy, Polish Silesia was asked to carry an undue burden in creating wealth for the new state, while the frontier situation together with the lack of confidence in the Polish economy made it hard to attract foreign capital, though some French, Swiss and American money was sunk in the area. A critical problem was to create new markets for Polish coal, especially after shipments to Germany broke down in 1925 and were only partly offset by gains in former British markets in 1926. To improve transport links with the new port of Gdynia a costly railway was built from Silesia to the sea, but in 1938 coal production was only 9 per cent higher than in 1923. The Polish iron and steel industry was forced to export a large share of its output, since there was no adequate home market for tubes and sheets, while it lagged markedly behind the German sector in technical standards and depended on ore imports in an unfavourable foreign exchange position. After the German victory over Poland in 1939, a number of new plants were built in the attractive strategic location of Upper Silesia.

6.3.4 Czechoslovakia

The new Czechoslovak state was fortunate in having remarkably self-contained industries even though their productive capacity was considerably greater than likely home demand and they depended on finance from faltering Viennese and Budapest banks. Inspite of the overall national surplus of manuacturing capacity, the less efficient Slovak plants had to be kept in being. Until 1923 the Czechoslovak manufacturers enjoyed a period of prosperity, catering for the demand from war devastated countries. A major setback was the decline in the German market in the inflation of 1923 and thereafter, while Czechoslovakia was badly hit by the 1929 Depression, since it was not only delicately balanced financially but also depended heavily on the export trade. Devaluation helped some industries, but made it hard for the Bohemian textile industry, dependent on imported raw fibres. A serious problem was also its interior continental position that forced the movement of its goods and raw materials in the export–import trade across the national territory of others.

Bohemian industry was concentrated in the German settled areas, so that the German minority felt the impact of the Depression in 1929 more heavily than the Czech farmers. Notably hard hit were the small factory industries in the semiluxury field, such as button-making, artificial jewellery and glassware, in all of which German participation was high. Heavy industry, which employed a larger Czech element, recovered more quickly but the lignite mining industry with a large German labour force and dependent on glass making also remained behind the general recovery after 1932. The German community accused (perhaps too readily and harshly) the government in Prague of failing to act adequately to relieve their distress, while the Czechs failed to convince the Germans that the measures taken had been designed to give aid where most needed, while Bohemian–German banks were embarrassed by the German inflation of 1923 and could hardly act effectively thereafter.

New industries began to appear in the 1930s, notably the building of motor cars, which were exported to Central and Eastern European markets. Electrification brought a growth in electrical engineering, notably in Usti and Labem, Brno, Plzeň and Prague. Instrument making developed, and the chemicals industry (particularly fertiliser manufacture) showed promise. A remarkable development was the Bat'a factories, centred at Zlín in the Moravian Uplands where they could draw on large supplies of cheap labour, to make low-priced shoes for Eastern and South-eastern European markets. Czech Silesia suffered less from the troubles that beset the Polish and German sectors, because it was more self-contained, though it depended on foreign ore, and its markets lay strongly in Czech engineering plants.

Slovakia, cut from its links with the Hungarian industrial scene, found itself in a difficult position, because industry was of poorer quality than Bohemia and most strongly developed in sectors where there was already excess capacity in Bohemia, while craft industries suffered disastrous competition. Slovakian industry also suffered from the disruption in the railway system focused on Budapest with relatively poor routes into Bohemia–Moravia. Industries based on Danube cargoes (oil shipments from Rumania, oil seeds from Danubia, and so on) grew in Bratislava and Komárom and there was a small but growing Bat'a shoe plant at Poprad, though in general the mountains came to depend on tourism.

6.3.5 Hungary

Before 1914 Hungarian peasants had shown little enthusiasm to move to towns in spite of financial benefits and estate owners had not encouraged such moves. Industries came to depend on non-Magyar peoples in plants inside Hungary proper as well as in Slovakia, Transylvania and Slovenia. The country found itself stripped after 1918 of much of its heavy industry and with many of its remaining plants cut from their raw materials sources, especially the engineering and electrical goods industries of Budapest, while food-processing industries were severed ruthlessly from their traditional markets. Any prosperity the country enjoyed collapsed with the Depression of 1929 and thereafter Hungary came to depend increasingly on Germany, notably after 1935. Hungarian foodstuffs and raw materials (notably bauxite) found a ready market in exchange for cheap manufactured goods and coal, with eventually two-thirds of exports going to Germany, and raw materials went to Germany instead of to home industry. This was not helpful to all branches—the textile industry had a predominance of weaving over spinning and demanded large yarn imports yet could not buy in the cheapest market, while German investment made the engineering industry an assembler of German parts and German designs under licence.

6.3.6 South Slav Lands

Jugoslavia brought together a collection of industries that had previously served different backgrounds, with the former Austro-Hungarian territory makedly more developed than Serbia. During the inter-war years, Jugoslavia suffered similar economic ills to the other Eastern European countries—a lack of capital, shortage of skilled labour, as well as the small purchasing power of the home market. Development was mainly in industries that covered the everyday needs of the home market and was achieved behind a high tariff barrier, which in turn tended to make production expensive and further penalised the low purchasing power of the peasants.

Reconstruction of wartime devastation (chiefly in Serbia) had no sooner been achieved than the country was swept up in the Depression of 1929, suffering heavily because of its dependence on the export of raw or semi-processed materials. Serbian industry faced intense competition within the country, no longer protected by the high customs barriers under which it had been accustomed to operate. The Croatian and Slovenian lands were better organised, better equipped and could outmanoeuvre Serbian industry. In the export trade Jugoslavia was hampered by the Italian control of major ports, particularly Trieste and Fiume (Rijeka), though for a time Jugoslav industry was supported by the insatiable demand from war-torn Central Europe. After 1920 increasing efforts were made to expand markets through the Ljubljana and Zagreb trade fairs. The paralysis of the export–import trade in the Depression and the subsequent monetary troubles briefly benefited home industry, though several branches were crippled by lack of raw materials imports and opportunities to export. The sharp fall in world prices for agricultural goods reduced the low purchasing power of the peasants (still 75 per cent of the population) and made the position of the large milling and brewing industries of the Voivodina difficult, aggravated by the loss of the former large Austro-Hungarian market.

Like other Balkan countries Jugoslavia fell increasingly into the German trading sphere in the 1930s, as the Germans were prepared to pay above world price levels for raw materials, provided German manufactured goods were taken in exchange. After 1938 Germany also took over the considerable Austrian investment in Jugoslavia, although the inflow of German manufactured goods tended to inhibit local manufacturing industries. After 1938 re-equipment of the metallurgical industries began, with a modern iron and steel plant erected by Krupp at Zenica, a site to have been developed in Austro-Hungarian days and a choice influenced by state intervention in an attempt to get new plants established in inland sites for strategic reasons.

6.3.7 Rumania

Rumania was heavily dependent on foreign capital for its industrial development, with over 75 per cent of the invested capital provided by West European and American investors and a growing German element after 1935. A primary interest was in raw or semi-processed materials, with a major British concern in the oil industry. Nevertheless, between 1929 and 1938 there was 55 per cent growth in industrial production, attributable to increased customs protection, with over half the industrial output coming from the consumer goods industries, mostly food processing, leather goods and textiles. The chemicals and metallurgical industries developed only shortly before the Second World War, but engineering remained backward and in 1937 under a fifth of the domestic demand for farm machinery was covered by Rumanian producers and was less in volume than in 1927. Chemical fertilisers, vital in a largely farming country formed less than one-hundredth of the value of chemical products. Branches like motor vehicle building, electrical engineering and machine tools were virtually absent. There was also an underuse of capacity: for example, the Hunedoara ironworks worked at only 20–40 per cent of capacity and the Vlahita plant was closed for several years, while conditions in other industries were little better (the large-scale milling industry operated at a mere 18 per cent of capacity). Industry was also concentrated in six main groups that employed 60 per cent of the total labour force, 71 per cent of the installed motor power and produced 67 per cent of the output. Three of these concentrations were in former Hungarian territory and accounted for over half the total industrial production. In the late 1930s the Rumanian economy became closely integrated into the German Balkan trading sphere, with the Ploiesti oil deposits of critical strategic importance to the Nazi rearmament plans.

6.3.8 Bulgaria and Albania

In 1937 some 40 per cent of the capital in Bulgarian industry was foreign—mostly Franco-Belgian or German. The main industries in which this money had been put were cement, sugar and tobacco, besides paper-making, chemicals and electricity generation. The units were, however, small—in 1934, only 322 out of 88 000 businesses in industry and handicrafts employed more than fifty persons. Before 1944 metallurgy was represented by small plants in Sofia and Dimitrovo that smelted scrap, while the Elisejna copper plant was outdated. Engineering was limited largely to maintenance work and contributed before 1944 less than one per cent of total industrial output. The chemicals industry produced only products such as glue, paints, soap, glycerine and cosmetics, while the bulk of chemicals goods were imported from Germany. In contrast, the textile industry, using home-grown cotton, was one of the largest factory industries. Albania remained a backward pastoral and agrarian economy, with a little mining and some simple industries, but even these would have been still more primitive had it not been for Italian initiative.

The general inter-war picture was gloomy, with few countries making more than a modest recovery from the great Depression of 1929–32. Where industrial development was taking place, it was usually associated with rearmament and strategic needs. The prosperity and growth of 1914 had been swept away with the collapse of the great empires and the new succession states huddled in their own boundaries with a jealous economic nationalism and protectionist policy that damped down trade until the German economic offensive of the mid-1930s.

7 Transport

There is considerable regional variation in the intensity of development of transport in East Central and South-east Europe, ranging from the dense systems of roads and railways at a high technical level in the German Democratic Republic and western Czechoslovakia to the sparse system of a widely meshed net with many dead-ends formed by poor or indifferent roads and modestly equipped railways in Jugoslavia and Bulgaria. The railway systems evolved principally before 1914 and were designed to serve the political alignments of the period. On this pattern was imposed the new political–geographical orientation after the First World War and before adjustment to this pattern could be completed, a further new alignment was demanded by the political–geographical conditions created after 1945.

7.1 Roman and mediaeval transport systems

In Roman times within the boundaries of the empire that stretched over Europe south of the Danube and had a tenuous hold north of that river in Dacia, there was road building in comparative peace and stability, primarily for military purposes but undoubtedly giving rise to trading movements. Roman roads remained in use under the Byzantine power, but thereafter fell into disrepair as there was no central authority to supervise their maintenance, though their remains were used even in mediaeval times. These roads generally made the best use of terrain and followed as far as possible the shortest distance between places, though movement was slow—the journey from Rome to Byzantium by the Via Egnatia usually took 20 days, including the short crossing by sea from Brindisi to Durrës.

Mediaeval Europe squandered the legacy of Roman roads, and trade began to move increasingly on the rivers, while Venice and Genoa traded by sea, as did Byzantium. North of the Danube, rivers were particularly important as trading routes, but there was also pack animal transport. Trade was encouraged by the German town laws, while the *Hanse* stimulated trade in the Baltic, so that important ports such as Stralsund, Danzig, Königsberg and Riga rose to prosperity in the fourteenth and fifteenth centuries. The Baltic encouraged navigation, for it had many useful inlets for harbours, a lack of strong tidal movements and a useful anticlockwise current. It was a stipulation (not rigorously applied) that towns applying for membership of the *Hanse* should be near the sea or on navigable waters. Ultimately the 'Baltic trade' spread to the North Sea and was joined by the English and the Dutch after the mid-fourteenth century. The Hanseatic towns became the great trade foci for the 'Baltic' products of field, forest and the sea as well as for manufactures from the Rhenish and Flemish lands, and there was trading with the metal producing regions of Bohemia for tin, silver and iron. Bohemia enjoyed an important function as a route focus in Europe, which it surrendered only reluctantly and slowly.

One of the most important mediaeval trading routes ran east to west along the northern edge of the Hercynian uplands and then along the piedmont zone of the Carpathians into the Ukraine, the great salt road—known in Germany as the *Hellweg*—linking major markets such as Hannover, Leipzig, Breslau and Kraków to the Flemish trading cities in the west and to Lvov in the east. At towns along its route it intersected with north–south routes from the Baltic into Danubia or across the Alps. Along it was distributed salt, a vital commodity for preserving fish and winter provisions, from mines at Halle, Wieliczka or other important centres. Nevertheless, trade along the *Hellweg* was commonly hampered by the rapacious gathering of customs and from frequent warfare.

In mediaeval times few roads served Danubia and South-east Europe, and in-spite of the lack of control over its course, littered by sandbanks and stranded trees, the Danube remained an important routeway. At several places navigation was hazardous, notably at the treacherous gorge below Bazias, while at high-water strong currents made sailing hard for simple craft. An attempt by Charles the Great to join the Danube via the Main to the Rhine failed and it was not revived until the nineteenth century. Danube trade was often hampered by an en-forcement of frequent customs stops, as well as trans-shipment rights held by the boatmen's guilds at staple ports. There is also evidence that in the thirteenth and fourteenth centuries, winter freezing, summer floods or intense drought made the use of the river even more hazardous. In the sixteenth and seventeenth centuries it was the Turkish threat to Danube trade that stifled navigation on the middle reaches of the river, though Turkish vessels moved on the lower reaches to collect sequestered corn from Moldavia and Wallachia and to carry it to Constantinople.

7.2 Roads

7.2.1 Road-building in the Eighteenth Century and After

In the German lands and the Habsburg territories, it was not until the eighteenth century that road-building began on a significant scale, occasioned by the growth of trade, the institution of regular postal systems and by mobility becoming militarily more important. In the Habsburg lands, Vienna, Prague and Budapest were the main foci, and some of the roads—such as those radiating from Vienna—were built in the Roman style—straight and direct. A widely meshed network appeared in Bohemia, closely linked to the Austrian and western Hungarian roads, but in Slovakia only one great road developed from Bratislava through the natural routeway of the Váh valley, dividing eastwards to serve the more important valleys and basins, with a minor route focus around Košice.

Political fragmentation of the German lands tended to retard road develop-ment, but in 1705 a postal monopoly exercised by the Prince of Thurn and Taxis introduced improved coaching services on routes such as Leipzig–Nürnberg. Travel was slow—Memel to Berlin in the early eighteenth century took 104 hours (4 miles per hour), though the Prussian authorities tried to improve their postal routes, usually improving old roads by a minimum of new construction, with a concerted policy of road building after 1788. In Silesia, after 1742, the

Prussians tried to make better roads in the hope of stimulating economic development. Nevertheless, journeys were hazardous and often sixteen to twenty horses were needed in winter to handle a postal coach. In the 1790s a modern highway of quality had been built from Berlin to Potsdam, though after 1815 over half the metalled roads in Prussia lay in the Rhinelands and Westphalia. In the 1820s the Prussians began to look on road-building as a way of integrating their newly gained territories, for which purpose roads such as Berlin–Arnsberg–Rhine and Leipzig–Frankfurt were built, often crossing other states' territories, as on the Magdeburg–Bamberg road through Thüringen.

The main period of road building in the German lands came in the early and middle part of the nineteenth century and was accelerated by the creation of a customs union, the *Zollverein*. Unlike in Britain, the turnpike played no part and roads were constructed by public funds, though the Junkers in the north and east complained that they did not get their fair share compared to Silesia, the Rhinelands and central Germany. Tolls were charged for the use of some of these roads, with the last swept away in 1915 in Mecklenburg. Passenger traffic was organised by the postal authorities and increased up to 1870 when it was overtaken by the railways, but remained important in rural districts of Eastern Germany.

After the road laws of 1803 road building in the Habsburg lands proceeded steadily and by the end of the nineteenth century the major framework was complete in the Czech lands, where there was the densest road network in the empire in 1914. In Slovakia the Magyar authorities were less active and existing roads were maintained by a primitive system of compulsory labour. Neglect of the Slovak roads was not so surprising, however, since the roads throughout Hungary were inferior to Austria, except in the mining districts and near the big towns. West of the Danube, where settlement was reasonably dense, there was a network of poor, unsurfaced roads but east of the river, roads were few and simply wide tracts, extremely dusty in summer and quagmires in winter. Similar conditions were found in the Rumanian plains, while in the mountains of the Balkan peninsula there were mostly only paths used by pack animals until late into the nineteenth century. A crude but important highway ran from Constantinople along the Maritsa valley to Sofia and across into Serbia, a military artery in Turkish times. In general the Turks had let the roads fall into disrepair, though they did in fact build a few bridges at important crossing places. It was not until the reforms of 1857 that a serious interest began to be taken by the Turkish authorities in road building. All travellers in Danubia and the Balkans remarked on the poorness of the roads and the consequently high costs of carriage, usually by ox-carts, as coaches could only be used in summer when the ground was hard. Government interest in roads in Rumania began in the 1830s but only 775 km of proper roads existed by the 1860s, while interest weakened after the coming of the railway in 1869.

In the Polish lands under Russian domination roads were sadly neglected and it was only in the 1820s that the Russians began to build proper highways in their own home territory. The very poor earth tracks by which communications were maintained in central and eastern Poland were made worse by the soft glacial materials of the North European Plain, though road metal was always to remain a problem.

7.2.2 Roads in the Twentieth Century

The rapid growth in the importance of the motor vehicle during the First World War, particularly in the Western European battle grounds, gave roads a new significance, though the motor vehicle was slower to appear in Eastern Europe. Czechoslovakia was the only producer of motor vehicles, with the exception of the flourishing German industry. In the Depression of 1929–32, road construction became for some countries a solution for unemployment, though mostly such work was concentrated on improving the existing poor surfaces and removing immediate local hazards. In Germany, however, views were more far-sighted and there was a project for the Hamburg–Frankfurt–Basel toll highway (*Hafraba*), though before this could be effectively developed, the Nazi government had instituted the system of autobahns as an entirely new conception in road design. Between 1935 and 1940 a considerable length of such motorways was built and opened to traffic, though their alignment was conceived primarily in strategic terms. A plan for an autobahn through the Moravian Corridor from Silesia to Vienna was never implemented. Inspite of the strictures placed on individual consumption, the Third Reich was one of the most 'mechanised' countries of Europe by 1937.

The Polish authorities gave much more attention to railway-building even late in the 1930s than to road construction and many good roads in western Poland deteriorated through neglect. Road traffic remained largely horse-drawn with only a scattering of motor vehicles outside the big towns. A largely horse-drawn army manned by peasants had little interest in modern roads such as were demanded by the *Wehrmacht's* motorised divisions.

Road conditions in the inter-war years in Danubia and South-eastern Europe were generally also very poor. Each of the new states pursued its own policy and devoted what it felt it could afford to road maintenance. The western part of Czechoslovakia was among the most well furnished areas and there were already local motor bus services, introduced immediately after the First World War. The Czechs also developed their own motor-vehicle industry and the government pursued an active policy of adapting the road system to the needs of motor traffic. There was a costly need for better roads between the Czech lands and Slovakia as well as for road building in Slovakia. Among the major projects was a road from Olomouc to Jasiňa on the north-east side of the Carpatho-Ukraine, while among other links was a road from Prague to Užhorod via Brno and Trenčín. By 1938 a considerable part of the formidable road programme had been achieved, though conditions in the eastern tip of the country remained bad.

The road system in Hungary radiated from Budapest, and considerable effort was devoted to making surfaces able to carry motor lorries and cars in wet weather, including improving already surfaced roads. This was not an easy undertaking for there was a general scarcity of good road metal in the great plains. The relatively short internal distances in Hungary tended, even in the late 1920s, to favour road rather than railway haulage. In Rumania conditions were less satisfactory, for before the First World War roads had been outstandingly bad in the Old Kingdom though better in Hungarian-controlled Transylvania and the Banat. Serious neglect of existing roads during the war had left most only fit for rough peasant carts. In the plains of Wallachia and Moldavia, the problem was akin to Hungary—the lack of good road metal. Roads in the mountains were generally expensive if engineered for motor traffic and few were built, apart from ones that followed well-defined natural routeways. The economic problems of the country in the early 1930s resulted in a fall in the number of motor vehicles at a time when they were beginning to increase rapidly elsewhere in Europe.

In 1918 the Jugoslav road system was only developed to any extent in the former Austro-Hungarian lands of the north-west, while there were many missing links between former political territories that now came to form the main components of the new state. Wartime neglect had also left roads in deplorable condition, especially in Serbia and in the poorer mountain areas. In 1920 a major-road development programme was introduced to speed economic development and encourage political unity. With limited capital available and apathy in the local administrations, there was slight progress and in almost a decade little over 1900 km of new road had been built and another 1440 km resurfaced. Apart from the major national highways, most roads were still built for animal rather than motor traffic, with loose gravelly surface, though considerable attention had been given to bridge building across the major rivers. A new programme with enhanced specifications was introduced in 1935, but by 1940 still less than 5 per cent of the road system was adequate for heavy traffic and another 10 per cent was considered suitable for motor vehicles with high clearances. Long stretches of road remained potholed and poorly surfaced. As in the Carpathians, winter snow in the Dinaric mountains made many roads impassable for many months.

In Bulgaria though the length of main road had increased from 8600 km in 1910 to 19 500 km in 1939, the mountainous terrain made road-building costly, while in the south, Turkish neglect before 1912 was not quickly rectified and the disputed nature of the Dobrudsha left it a peripheral area in which the government was reluctant to spend money. But by far the most primitive conditions were found in Albania, where roads were barely motorable over great distances. However, Italian initiative encouraged construction of main motorable roads in the latter 1930s.

7.2.3 Roads after 1945 (figure 7.3b)

The motor-car revolution begun in Western and Central Europe in the early 1930s had not effectively reached Eastern and South-eastern Europe even by the outbreak of the Second World War. Nor did it arrive with the end of hostilities, and planning even into the 1960s followed Soviet lines of a heavy dependence on railways, on trams and on public service vehicles rather than on the private motor car. Although in the German Democratic Republic, Czechoslovakia and Poland, not to mention Hungary and Jugoslavia, there has been a substantial increase in private motor vehicles, the proportion of private cars still remains much below the levels reached in Western Europe. Road traffic has been marked much more by a growth in lorries, buses and taxi-cabs. The feverish road development in the Western European countries has not as yet penetrated to the Socialist *bloc* on anything more than a most modest scale.

7.3 Waterways since Napoleonic times (figure 7.1)

Though waterways had been important from earliest times, it was not until after the Napoleonic wars that growth in trade began to encourage concerted action among states to maintain and improve rivers. In the late nineteenth century, steam shovels and equipment began to make possible canal construction on an appreciable scale.

The major waterway is the Danube system. Czechoslovakia, Hungary, Jugoslavia, Rumania and Bulgaria all have frontages on the river, but since 1945 the Soviet Union has had a commanding position at the delta. The uppermost reaches lie in Western Germany and Austria, so providing a waterway into the non-Socialist states of Europe. The Habsburg, in whose domains the middle reaches lay, tried to improve the river, notably in Hungary in the 1780s inspite of resistance by local interests, while numerous works were undertaken in the nineteenth entury. From 1856 international interest was taken in the river below the Iron Gates, but the international regime came into full play after 1918 when the river frontages were divided among the riparian Succession states and free navigation given to all in theory. Unfortunately, the economic depression of the inter-war period, widely felt along the Danube, stagnated traffic and countries were reluctant to spend scarce resources on schemes that demanded international co-operation. With the co-ordination of the Danubian economies within the framework of Comecon, a new role has come to the river and two important projects have been proposed and begun—a link to the Rhine via the Main and a link through the Moravian Corridor to the Elbe, Oder and Vistula. Some observers suggest that the Danube will form part of the waterway 'ring' inside the Socialist *bloc*, joined to the Volga via the Baltic and the Black Sea and other canals. Such a concept seems to have replaced the idea of 'TVA on the Danube' discussed in the early post-war years.

The Danube course presents many obstacles to navigation whose eradication requires international co-operation at a level not always easily attainable. The river profile is irregular—steeply graded sections through gorges followed by wide basins with low gradients. In the gorges, fast currents and rocky obstacles in the fairway hazard ships, while in the basin sections there is the difficulty of shifting channels and shoals as well as sharp curves round meanders. One of the most difficult sections remains the gorge section, where the river has broken through between the Carpathians and Balkan mountains.

In the Berlin Congress of 1878 the Austrians had the gorge section allocated to them. Between 1895 and 1899 channels were cut through the cataracts so that single barges up to 700 tons could be towed through. Nevertheless, conditions remained hazardous and night navigation was not undertaken. Heavy tolls were levied to pay for the improvements. Work was renewed under the International Danube Commission formed in 1920 and after long negotiations, further improvements were made in the Iron Gates section after 1932.

In the Hungarian plains work begun in the eighteenth century was continued, as numerous meanders were cut through to ease flow and prevent flooding as well as to make navigation easier. Better harbours, particularly for protection against ice were provided. In the late nineteenth century improvement work began on the reaches below the Iron Gates, where the meandering and marsh-fringed river made shipping movements slow. One of the main problems was the delta with its shifting, silting arms. In Turkish times ships had pulled anchors along the bed of the channels to raise the silt and get it carried out to sea, but this was not particularly effective. In the later period, cuts were made to ease the flow in the arms and much effort was put into deepening the Sulina arm and to removing the bar from its mouth. After 1920, the special maritime section of the International Commission working from the mouth up to the Iron Gates achieved considerable improvement.

After the Second World War the old international statutes were swept away and replaced in 1948 by the Belgrade Convention which was restricted to Socialist *bloc* states with riparian frontage on the Danube and included the Soviet Union through its frontage on the Kiliya channel at Ismail. Later Austria and West Germany were reluctantly admitted. While improvements have continued, a major project has been undertaken jointly by Jugoslavia and Rumania at the Iron Gates gorge, involving a large hydroelectric barrage that will raise the level of the river 33 m above normal and will provide locks to allow vessels up to 5000 tons to reach Belgrade and reduce time of passage from 120 hours to about 35 hours. The lake so formed will extend upstream for 150 km and the locks have been designed to allow a passage of 45–50 million tons of shipping annually.

Whatever improvements are made in the channel of the river, the problems of its hydrological regime remain. Ice in winter on many reaches can be a serious problem while in summer low water often hampers navigation (the Iron Gates section was particularly badly affected). Spring and autumn high water also interrupts navigation.

The modern period in Danube navigation may be considered to have begun when the Turks in 1784 allowed vessels from the upper reaches into the Black Sea. Conditions in the eighteenth and early nineteenth centuries were, however, difficult—grain from Budapest to Vienna took a month on the journey, using eight boatmen, forty horses and thirty drivers. Draught was limited to 1.5 m or less. A major development came with the Austrian Danube Steam Navigation Company in 1837 whose steamers operated first from Vienna to Bratislava, but later to Belgrade and then to Cernavoda and eventually to the delta. In the mid-nineteenth century a recognised route was by steamer from Vienna to Cernavoda, overland to Constanţa (or from Ruse to Varna overland) and then by steamer to Istanbul. Although by the 1870s the Company owned 140 steamers, the journey was slow and uncertain and there was little passenger traffic upstream. Baedeker remarked on the uncertain schedules and on the fact that the traffic was 'inconsiderable' in relation to the size of the Company's fleet. A frequent inconvenience was the need to travel by road from Orsova to Moldova to avoid dangerous conditions in the cataract section, with delay from trans-shipping passengers and goods. It was not until the latter part of the nineteenth century that traffic really built up, so that the volume passing through the Iron Gates after improvement of the fairway doubled between 1901 and 1913, the bulk of the increase being in upstream freights. Nevertheless, even in the best years before 1914, freight traffic never rivalled the shorter but more intensely used Rhine. For example, in 1911 some seven million tons were moved on the Danube compared to over 57 million tons on the Rhine. Most of the traffic was relatively short haul and the German dreams, expressed in Naumann's *Central Europe*, of the Danube as a great waterway in the *Drang nach Osten* policy, like Austrian hopes of opening trade with the Levant and Persia via the river, did not materialise. Trade between Austria and Germany and the Black Sea, including the ports of Brăila and Galaţi on the lower Danube, moved by sea from Trieste.

Before 1914 the main freights on the Danube were agricultural products, mostly relatively short hauls. Long distance movements in cereals were restricted, since they were mostly upstream and consequently costly. Rumania found it cheaper to send grain by sea from the ports of the lower Danube to Trieste or German North Sea ports. Some coal moved downstream from German ports or from Bratislava, while small quantities of oil were beginning to flow upstream. Some timber was shipped in raft form. Most movement was by clumsy barge trains.

The inter-war years were marked by the break-up of the river frontage between the riparian succession states, each with its own customs barriers and many pursuing an economic nationalism that hardly encouraged commerce in the depressed state of world trade. After transporting 13 million tons of goods in 1913, the quantity had fallen to 2.1 million in 1923, and 7.9 million in 1930. The growing linkage between the Danube basin and Germany, including shipments of bauxite from Hungary, became marked later and in 1936, 13.9 million tons of goods were shipped and by 1942 (including Rumanian petroleum) this had reached 16 million. Other commodities included downstream movements of coal and coke and upstream movements of ores, while movements of sugar beet and cement in both directions took place over short stretches. The dissolution of the large Austrian Danube Steamship Company and the Hungarian River and Sea Navigation Company had been a serious setback to the development of traffic after 1918, since the small, unco-ordinated fleets of the riparian states were unequal to the task.

The more strongly centralised influence of the Danube Commission after 1948 and the co-ordinating role played by Comecon, inspite of the political problems of Jugoslavia, have brought an upsurge in Danube shipping. The Commission has developed a programme of basic works to aid navigation: the major plan has been to establish standard water depths of 270 cm from Regensburg to Vienna and then of 350 cm to Brăila, while between Brăila and Sulina the aim is a depth of 730 cm. Adequate signalling and information is to be established to help shippers, and fleets are to be standardised on the 1000–1350 ton *Europa* self-propelled barge, with pushboats on the lower and middle reaches. Although steam traction has given way to diesel tugs, 70 per cent of the fleet is still composed of barges. Since the late 1940s most fleets have stagnated or declined in number, although the Czechs and Bulgarians increased the size of their own fleets. There has been a tendency to develop vessels that can sail from the river into the open sea: the Hungarians have led this development with sea-going ships for the Levant and Sea of Azov trade.

At the end of the 1960s Danube traffic stood at about 48 million tons, unimpressive compared to the 158 million tons on the Rhine. The main handler of this traffic was Hungary (over 8 million tons). Large flows of industrial raw materials moved upstream from the ports at the mouth of the river. The overall disproportion between upstream and downstream flows is 4.75:1 (Rhine 3:1), though in some reaches it reaches 8.6:1. Between 1950 and 1967 the total commodity flow increased just over fourfold; the biggest increases were Czechoslovakia (over tenfold), Bulgaria (sevenfold), the Soviet Union (sixfold), Austria (over fivefold), Rumania (almost fourfold), Jugoslavia and Western Germany (threefold), and Hungary, little over twofold. The major ports since 1950 have been Reni and Ismail in the U.S.S.R., Budapest, Belgrade, Linz and Regensburg (though not always in the same order). In 1967, the largest turnover was at Reni (7.8 million tons) but this was small by Rhenish comparisons (Duisburg–Ruhrort, 32 million tons, while Ludwigshafen, Mannheim and Köln were all larger). Some ports have shown surprising growth—Lom (Bulgaria) has grown 22-fold since 1950.

The main cargoes are building materials, ores (major growth commodity), coal, coke and petroleum products. While on the upper and lower reaches, fuels and ores or metals are important, the middle reaches rest mostly on building materials. The importance of the Soviet ports of Reni and Ismail should be noted: cargoes of fuels and ores are brought by rail or water from the Soviet interior for shipment upstream. Vienna has over 80 per cent of its traffic in shipping petroleum from local oilfields, while Regensburg ships coal and coke downstream. Dunaújváros is largely dependent on ore and coal or coke imported by river transport. Both Belgrade and Budapest depend on imports of building materials (91 per cent and 72 per cent respectively), though the customs-free port at Csepel, important in collecting East European traffic for the Levant, will become the main container port for the middle reaches. Nevertheless, only 2 per cent of total Comecon foreign trade moves on the Danube.

The navigable tributaries of the Danube handle local traffic. In Jugoslavia the Sava below Sisak handles petroleum, non-metallic minerals and fertiliser, with craft up to 1000 tons; the Drava (navigable by vessels of up to 650 tons) is unimportant. The navigation possibilities of the Tisza have been improved since completion of the Tiszolök barrage, while the Eastern Main Canal between Tiszalök and the Berettyo river will be navigable in future. Szolnok and Szeged are the main Tisza ports. Other rivers—Bodrog, Körös, Maros, etc. are of no importance. In Rumania a limited traffic is carried by small vessels on the Bega Canal from Timişoara to the Tisza confluence, for the movement of agricultural produce in the Banat. The Prut is navigable for its lower 320 km while the Mureş is used for rafts and the Siret could be made navigable. The Jugoslavs have been engaged in building a cut-off canal—the Danube-Tisza–Danube Canal—to speed river traffic, while a canal from Sisak to Zagreb has also been proposed. The Czechs have been considering building a barrage at Bratislava that would improve navigation on the upper reaches, while improvement is also needed in the braided and shallow section from Bratislava to Gönyü, perhaps by a barrage at Vác.

Considerable use is made of the main rivers of the North European Plain and some of their basins have been linked by canal. The problems of operation on these rivers have arisen particularly from a lack of speedy adjustment to new political alignments after the two world wars. Most important has been the Elbe, which before 1939 was second in rank to the Rhine in volume of traffic. There has been freedom of navigation on the river since 1821 and internationalisation was confirmed after the First World War. The river is navigable from Kolin in Czechoslovakia to the sea, but in the uppermost reaches most traffic originates on the Vltava at Prague. Rigorous canalisation in the Czech section has improved navigation in the difficult summer low water period. In the German section reservoirs on the upper Saale and near Pirna help regulate the flow. Ice is present only for a few days each year, but summer low water is a serious problem. Although the carrying capacity of the river is often given as 1350-ton barges, these can be used fully laden only at optimum flow, while most of the time, particularly above Strehla near Dresden only 600 or 750-ton vessels are suitable. Cargoes are mostly lignite, ores, fertilisers and chemicals.

Since the division of Germany traffic on the reaches below Magdeburg has fallen substantially as shipments from the German Democratic Republic and Czechoslovakia have been deflected to East German or Polish Baltic ports. Nevertheless, the Czechs and East Germans still make some use of the Free Harbour at Hamburg, but it has been proposed to build a canal from the Elbe to Rostock. The Saale is unimportant and can be used only by comparatively small vessels, navigation usually extending to Halle, but plans for extension upstream have been suggested. Completion of the Elbe–Weser section of the Mittelland

Figure 7.1. The inland waterways are dominated by the Danube system, though in the northern plain, the Vistula, Oder and Elbe have been linked by canal. Projects exist to link the Danube to the Oder, and it will shortly be joined by canal to the Rhine. The main ports are notably in the Baltic.

Canal in 1938 provided a link to the Rhine. Along with the section from the Elbe to Berlin, this canal is used by West German traffic to West Berlin as well as by internal German Democratic Republic traffic. These east–west canals can be used by 1000-ton barges. Berlin has several canals accessible to 750-ton barges and these lead eastwards to the Oder. Since 1952 a new canal has made it possible to avoid West Berlin.

The Oder dominates the inland waterway scene in Poland. It is, however, limited in use by severe spring floods, summer low water and a tendency to freeze for up to 40 days each year. Before 1939 much work had been done to improve it, but the regulation work in the nineteenth century had oversteepened the gradient by making the course too straight, making the handling of barge trains in places difficult. Though some souces give 750-ton or even 1000-ton barges as suitable for the river, much of the time it can carry only 450-ton vessels. A lot of its traffic is still in old-fashioned barge trains. It has been regulated from Wrocław to the sea, but from Wrocław to the head of navigation at Koźle it has been canalised, with a canal continuing to Gliwice in the Upper Silesian industrial district. The Oder is linked by rather antiquated canals and regulated rivers of the Warta–Noteć system to the Vistula. The Vistula is difficult to navigate and lacks many essential works to make it a useful river. It suffers wide fluctuations in level and the necessary compensating reservoirs do not yet exist in sufficient capacity. Ultimate plans foresee navigation by 1000-ton vessels from Kraków to the sea, but at present the bulk of movement is from Warsaw to the port of Gdańsk. There are also plans to link the Vistula via the Bug to the Dnepr to provide a high capacity waterway from the Ukraine to Poland.

Continued interest in waterway development, with projects such as the Rhine–Main–Danube, Oder–Danube and Vistula–Bug canals being built or planned, suggests that they will play a part in Eastern European transport for a long time.

7.4 Railways

7.4.1 Railways before the First World War (figure 7.2)

The railway remains the major means of transport and in several countries extension of the network is still taking place. Railways have been developed within the transport infrastructure in a role similar to that accorded them in the Soviet Union, inspite of the very different conditions in the East European members of Comecon. Compared to Western Europe, the railway network is more widely meshed and has a greater length of single track, while most lines have a relatively low carrying capacity. The poverty of many states after the First World War led to stagnation in technical standards and in equipment. Destruction during the Second World War took many years to make good and in a few areas the railways have not been fully restored.

In the North European Plain the first railways appeared in Germany. In a far-sighted plan put forward by Friedrich List in 1833 for an all-German railway system, Berlin and Leipzig would have been major foci, but this brave concept was rejected and a Germany without a unified customs system preferred to build piecemeal. The first line in the present territory of the German Democratic Republic was opened as a section of the Leipzig–Dresden railway in 1837, two years after the first railway in the German lands. Within 10 years the present territory of the German Democratic Republic had the greatest route length in Germany—a through route from Dresden to Leipzig and then to Berlin and Stettin, while a line went to Magdeburg and on to Hanover. By 1846 a railway from Upper Silesia to Breslau had been linked to Berlin. With encouragement from the government Prussia had the main features of its network complete by 1850, while there was also a reasonable network in Saxony. Trunk lines also penetrated into Mecklenburg, Pomerania, East and West Prussia and there were lines into the Posen (Poznań) area. Nevertheless, the Junkers complained that they had not their fair share of railways in the north and east. By 1860 at Stallpönen in East Prussia, German railways reached the Russian frontier. After 1870 there was a period of branchline construction, while in Saxony a number of narrow-gauge lines were built into the Erzgebirge. In Mecklenburg and Pomerania lightly constructed lines opened up the countryside.

In Poland the first line had opened in 1845 near Warsaw and by 1848 had been extended to join the Austrian railways at Oderberg (Bohumin) and the Prussian railways at Mysłowice. One of the most important railways was the strategically important St Petersburg–Warsaw railway through Grodno (1862) and in 1863 the Warsaw–Bromberg (Bydgoszcz) line was opened. By 1914 Russian Poland had a wide-meshed network (some broad gauge) compared to Austrian Poland, while the densest network lay in the Prussian territory.

Although a horse tram had opened from Linz to Český Budějovice in 1828, the first true railway in Bohemia opened in 1839 from Vienna to Brno. Between 1841 and 1845, Prague was connected to Vienna by a line through Přerov: by 1848 Bohemian railways were joined to the Prussian and Russian systems, and in 1851 the difficult Elbe valley line from Prague to Dresden was opened. Bratislava was put on the railway by the opening of the Vienna to Budapest line in 1850. Most main lines in what is now Czechoslovakia were built between 1870 and 1880, while between 1890 and 1900 there was rapid construction of branchlines. The Bohemian railways came to be focused on Prague and linked to Vienna, while in Slovakia, the railway system was focused on Budapest. Links between the two systems were sparse.

The Hungarians were less enthusiastic about railways. The first line ran from Budapest to Vác in 1846 and thereafter a railway was built to Szolnok. Building then lagged and it was not until after the *Ausgleich* of 1867 that building on a major scale developed a system focused more clearly on the capital than almost any other European national railway system. Ease of construction in the great plains, however, brought a density of railways well above the density elsewhere in the Danube lands and the Balkans, with many very lightly constructed 'farm railways', notably after 1880. While Sopron had been linked to Vienna in 1847, the Austrians chose to avoid railway construction in ethnically Magyar lands and the main line to Trieste, the *Südbahn*, was built across the difficult Semmering Pass (1854) to Graz and Ljubljana, reaching Trieste in 1856. It was only in 1861 that this major port was linked directly to Budapest. The Austrian railways were renowned for their heavy gradients and locomotives were typically designed for powerful traction at low speeds, whereas the Hungarian locomotives running on gentle gradients had large driving wheels for speed.

In the Jugoslav lands a complex story of railway development resulted in a system of mixed quality. In the Austro-Hungarian territories, the railways became part of the imperial system, while Serbia followed its own railway policy, influenced by outside investments. An early Hungarian plan envisaged a railway from Budapest to the Adriatic coast, but it was the Austrian *Südbahn* whose plans were realised first. In 1862 the Sava valley between Zagreb and Ljubljana was used for a railway to Rijeka, but the difficult terrain between the Sava valley and the coast as well as legal problems slowed construction and the line opened only in 1875. In Serbia railway building began in the 1880s—Belgrade to Niš, 1884 and Niš to Skopje, 1886, though Skopje had been reached in 1873 by a line from Salonika to Priština. In 1887 the international—Orient Express—line from Niš to Sofia was opened. In the 1880s and 1890s much building of secondary lines in the Banat under Hungarian initiative took place. The annexation of Bosnia and Hercegovina by Austria in 1878 brought hasty railway building with military narrow gauge equipment, though many lines were laid out for later change to standard gauge. The Slavonski Brod–Sarajevo line opened in 1879 and after many delays caused by difficult terrain and the initial bad choice of ter-minal, the line reached Dubrovnik Gruž in 1891, though it remained a military railway until 1895. In 1906 a line of outstanding difficulty, often up to heights of 1000 m, was completed from Sarajevo to Novi Pazar, part of a forerunner of a railway from Bosnia to Salonika, of great military and diplomatic importance. Disagreements between the rival factions are reflected in the late completion of a through line from Zagreb to Belgrade. A main route from Budapest to Belgrade had been opened in 1884, but the completion of the Ruma–Vinkovci line in 1891 at last gave through connection from north to south along an axial trajectory that became vitally important in the new Jugoslav state after 1918.

In 1855 an abortive Turkish proposal to build a railway from Constantinople to Belgrade was followed by a second abortive plan to build a railway from Constantinople to Burgas, Varna and Ruse that proved too grandiose for its time. The Ruse to Varna line built in 1866 was a flimsy construction that did not prove a great success as a bypass to the Danube delta. In 1869 the Turkish government granted a concession for a trunk line from Constantinople to Sofia via the Maritsa valley and then through Priština and Novi Pazar to Sarajevo and the Austro-Turkish border—the Austrians were to have continued the line to Zagreb and Vienna. A change of Turkish policy in 1871 brought the collapse of the enterprise and a swing to Turkish designs to join their railways to Russia and Rumania. Uncertain and vacillating policies, however, hampered any further progress until after 1881, when a Four-Power Convention (Austria–Hungary, Serbia, Bulgaria and Turkey) chose a route from Niš to Sofia and on to Plovdiv instead of the original trajectory via Skopje. The Orient Express started in 1883 between Paris–Vienna–Bucharest and Giurgiu and then to Ruse and Varna, continuing by sea to Constantinople, was now rerouted via Belgrade and Sofia in 1889, reducing the journey from Budapest from 56 to 38 hours. Bulgarian railways were generally lightly and shoddily built, dependent on Austrian and German money through the *Bank für Orientalische Eisenbahnen* but also some Franco-Belgian funds. Though in some respects the German idea of the Berlin–Baghdad railway had been realised, if not in the way the Germans had

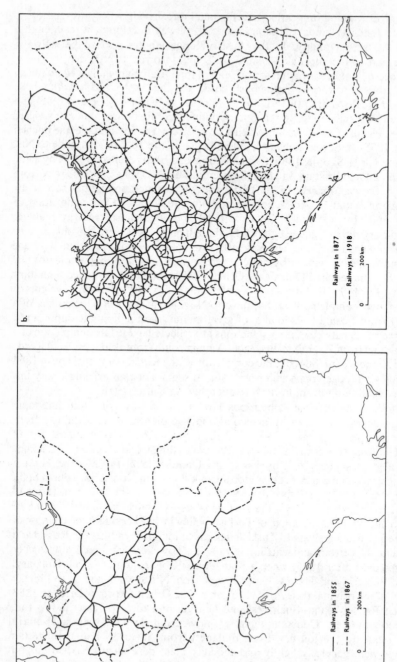

Figure 7.2. The late development of the railway network towards the east and south has marked the transport map of Eastern Europe.

Railways in 1855
Railways in 1867

0   200 km

Railways in 1877
Railways in 1918

0   200 km

a.

b.

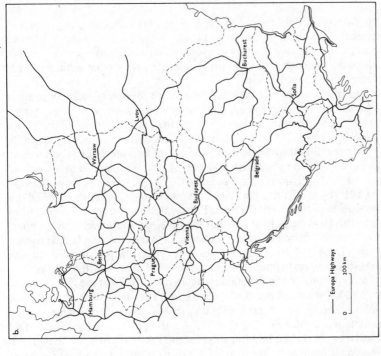

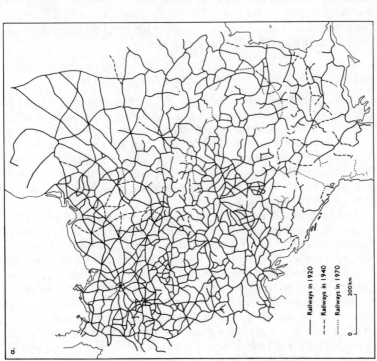

Figure 7.3. Railway building still continues in South-eastern Europe and a considerable length of new route has been added since 1945. There is also a widely meshed system of main highways.

hoped, little through freight moved to the Middle East along this route—it was mainly passengers and mail—because sea transport was much cheaper. Further building was often over long detours to avoid the cost of elaborate structures in the mountains, as for example the North Bulgarian railway from Sofia to Varna (1899) through the Danube plains.

Rumanian railway construction was the result of foreign investment in what appeared to be rewarding projects. In Transylvania, then part of Hungary, railways were built by the authorities and the main towns—Cluj, Arad, Timişoara—were linked to the rest of Hungary between 1855 and 1870, followed by more difficult routes towards the end of the century. In the north, in Bukovina, railway building was carried out by the Austrian authorities and became part of the Galician system. A classical example of the 'portage railway' was built in 1860 by the British between Cernavoda and Constanţa to avoid the difficult navigation of the lower Danube. The next line was opened in 1869 from Bucharest to the Danube port of Giurgiu. Another comparatively early important line was the route from Bucharest via Suceava to the Austrian Galician town of Lemberg (Lvov). Two early routes over the Carpathians were the Braşov-Ploieşti-Bucharest route through the Predeal Pass and the line via Orşova and Turnu Severin at the Iron Gates that managed to skirt the Carpathians' flanks. By 1900 the important route across the Turnu Roşu Pass had been opened, but it was during the First World War that considerable railway building into the mountains was done by German and Austrian railway troops. In the Old Kingdom railways had been laid out to serve the Danube ports, while in Transylvania they were focused on the heart of the Hungarian state, with consequently little attraction to build railways across the rough terrain of the Carpathians to link territories which had quite different orientations.

7.4.2 Railways in the Inter-war Period (figure 7.3)

The great territorial changes after the First World War dissected a railway network created for the political, economic and social relationships of the late nineteenth century. New flows of traffic had either to be fitted into the existing network or had to be accommodated by building new railways. Construction was, however, expensive and the new states had inadequate resources to put down railways on a lavish scale. It was, however, mostly in South-eastern Europe that building continued, largely to complete a basic network, though much work was carried out as inexpensively as possible.

Poland inherited parts of three sytems which gave a most unequal regional distribution—densest in the lands taken from Prussia, least developed in the former Russian Poland, where part of the system had to be rebuilt to standard gauge to mesh in with the remainder. The right of the Germans to operate trains across the 'Polish Corridor' between their territory in East Prussia and the main part of Germany meant extremely complex operating regulations that were made no easier by poor relations between the two states. Elaborate conditions also governed the operation of railways in the Free City of Danzig. In the south, in partitioned Upper Silesia, the railway system was also cut by the imposed boundary and disruption of the old movements of coal forced the Poles to develop new routes. A project for a coal-carrying canal to the Baltic was discarded in favour of a railway from Upper Silesia to the new port of Gdynia. Although this used some existing railways, it involved costly new building for much of its route. Another important new construction gave an all-Polish route between Poznań and Warsaw and Upper Silesia, other new lines improving links north of the Vistula between Toruń and Warsaw, while a direct line from Warsaw to Radom improved traffic to the Kielce industrial area. The general aim was to improve railway links from the capital to and between the regions, though the problem in part had been eased by military lines built in the north-east and south of the country by German and Austro-Hungarian railway troops.

The inter-war years brought limited changes in the lands of the German Democratic Republic, chiefly to adapt to the new frontier with Poland. The troublesome system of 'privilege trains' across the Polish Corridor to East Prussia, as already noted, shifted traffic between East Prussia and the rest of Germany more to the sea, so that railway shipments to Königsberg and Stettin tended to increase. There was also a decline in traffic from the reduced industrial area in German Upper Silesia, though by the middle 1930s much of this decline had been restored. Modifications in the network were designed chiefly to ease movement at junctions and provide short avoiding lines. The outer railway around Berlin begun before 1914 was again started in the late 1930s, without being completed. The emphasis was on technological improvement on the railways, with electrification of mountain lines in Silesia, routes in the Elbe–Saale basin and the main Munich–Berlin route (which was nearly complete by 1940). There was also the development of fast express diesel trains.

The Czechoslovak state was faced with the problem of drawing together into one railway system the Bohemian network focused on Prague and Vienna and the Slovak system orientated to Budapest. While the length of new route was modest, the lines were of great economic importance. There was improvement of the main east–west trunk line from Czech Silesia through Slovakia to Košice as well as the routes in southern Slovakia, mostly for defence purposes along the frontier with Hungary. In northern Bohemia and at Aš, pre-1914 working conditions remained in force, with the lines operated by the German railways. Poor relations with Poland did not encourage the improvement of lines across the Carpathians, but on the east an attempt was made to strengthen the railways ties between the Carpathian Ukraine and Rumania. Some of the work involved high capital cost and engineering skill, such as the line across the White Carpathians which required a 2410 m long tunnel.

The Treaty of Trianon had drawn the boundaries extremely tightly around Hungary, partly because of the demand for strategic railways by nations in the favour of the Allied powers. In southern Slovakia about 500 000 Magyars were left in Czech territory in order that the Czechs had command of vital railways links north of the Danube. Hungary had to surrender territory in the Pannonian Plains to Rumania in order that the latter country could have a vital strategic railway from Satu Mare to Timişoara, while new frontiers in the Banat and Bačka also gave advantage to Rumania and Jugoslavia in terms of the railway network. Only on the western frontier, where Burgenland passed to Austria, was the Hungarian interest noted in the creation of a salient of Hungarian territory at Sopron (Ödenburg) so that a vital junction remained in its control. Austria nevertheless received special rights of privilege trains through this territory.

Jugoslavia had a major problem to join together its regions, and railways received special priority from the state's limited resources in the 1920 plan to reconstruct about 1390 km of route and to build 3000 km of new route. By 1940 a large part of this plan had been achieved. Particularly important was the completion of a main axial line from Ljubljana via Zagreb to Belgrade and south of Niš and Skopje, providing an international route to carry traffic from France and the Low Countries to Greece and Turkey without using German, Austrian or Hungarian routes, resulting in the rerouting in the early 1920s of the still diplomatically significant Orient Express. The construction of a bridge over the Tisza at Senta in 1923 provided a through route from Belgrade to Bucharest, used by a branch of the Orient Express. The Italian control of Rijeka (Fiume) and the problems of operating the remaining Jugoslav port in Susak led to the building of a standard gauge line to Split across difficult mountain country (1925). Construction of 50 km of exceptionally difficult line in Bosnia, including eleven tunnels (1925), joined Bosnia to the main north–south Serbian railway system. Other building included bridges to provide better connections across the Danube and Tisza to the Banat and Bačka and construction in southern Serbia and Macedonia of an alternative route to Skopje via Kragujevac and Mitrovica, while lines were built into the far south-west (Titov Veles–Prilep–Bitola–Greece) or others improved (narrow gauge Skopje—Ohrid). Plans to build a line directly into the Scutari (Shkadar) district did not materialise, while another unfulfilled project was a north-east–south-west Trans–Balkan railway. Minor construction was also undertaken along the Hungarian border to prevent railways having to operate back and fro across the frontier.

Railway building was actively pursued in Bulgaria after the First World War but the constraint put on construction was the weak financial situation of the country. Many grandiose schemes expectedly did not materialise, but short arterial lines were built piecemeal. The major but uncompleted pre-war project was for a direct line across the centre of the country from Sofia to Burgas and Varna along the foot of the Stara Planina fault-line scarp, linking together mountain basins of considerable agricultural potential. A number of projects were for the missing north–south links: of these the Kolaróvgrad to Asparuchovo line was completed during the Second World War. A number of relatively long branch lines in very difficult country comprised part of a project to penetrate into the basins of the Rhodope, territory taken into Bulgaria only shortly before the First World War, with considerable tourist and spa potential and rich forest land. In the Struma valley a narrow-gauge line was converted to standard gauge. Other work was concerned with widening curves and improving gradients, relaying to higher standards lines built flimsily before 1914, or else to providing short avoiding links (chiefly the Sofia ring railway).

In the enlarged boundaries after the First World War, Rumania had a reasonably complete network of railways, even if the mesh of the system in the Old Kingdom was appreciably wider than in the former Hungarian territory in Transylvania. North–south and east–west links were present if not plentiful. Poorly served with railways and somewhat inaccessible was, however, the Dobrogea, while there was also a paucity of links across the Carpathians. Considerable energy was devoted to incorporating the route taken by the annexation of Bessarabia, while a number of short lines to complete links were built. A major project not completed was the double-tracking of the route from the Polish frontier via Cernăuti, Suceava to Galati, and single track, low-capacity route predominated.

Under Italian influence limited railway building began in Albania, though it remained the 'most railway-less country in Europe'.

7.4.3 Railways since 1945 (figure 7.3)

Since 1945 transport development in the Eastern European countries has reflected a considerable number of Soviet concepts and has been influenced by the strong Soviet railway lobby. Like the Soviet Union particular interest has been shown in hauls of low value bulk goods over considerable distances. Transport planning has aimed at the Soviet concept of a unified transport system in which the various media are carefully integrated, but with the railways as the prime haulier.

The emphasis on industrialisation demanded railways that could handle much greater density of traffic and were better adjusted to the new patterns of flow. On the one hand, new routes have been built to make possible the requisite flows and secondly, there has been technical improvement to increase traffic density without overload. Railways have co-ordinated much of their effort through a special Soviet bloc organisation (*Organisatsiya Sotrudineniya Zheleznikh Dorog*). The selection of the Soviet option of giving limited encouragement to road traffic and construction as well as the limited role which can be played by Eastern European waterways have helped to enhance the position of the railways, though during the 1960s a shift of favour towards road transport has appeared.

The substantial increase in freight turnover claimed by the Socialist *bloc* countries has been achieved on railway systems that were built mostly to carry low-density traffic of light agricultural produce: the main exceptions were the railways of the industrial parts of the German Democratic Republic, Polish and Czech Silesia and northern Bohemia. Before 1945 traffic was mostly a sparse service of short and light trains. Inspite of inter-war improvements, axle loadings remain light—over most of Hungary, 10–12 tons are common and 16–18 tons have been considered as heavy loadings on Jugoslav railways. Axle loads well under 15 tons are typical on the Bohemian lines built after the enactment of the Austrian light railway laws. On narrow-gauge lines axle loads of seven tons or less remain standard. A minimum of civil-engineering structures results in heavily graded and undulating track even in relatively open country while sharp curves and long detours to avoid substantial earthworks are common. Such conditions have limited use of modern high-capacity wagons, for example, in the Bohemian lignite fields. Motive power has been characteristically designed for slow but high tractive power—predominantly steam locomotives were 2-10-0 or 2-10-4 with fireboxes suitable for low grade fuels (even wood or lignite). Speeds have in the past generally been kept to 60–80 km p/h and high-speed running is even today not particuarly common, with the fastest services provided by railcar type trains. The use of diesel traction is overcoming some of the problems of steam trains though electric traction can be used only on selected routes because of its high installation cost, but proves attractive to countries like Jugoslavia with hydroelectric potential.

The large proportion of single track encourages the use of techniques proved for such route in the Soviet Union. The systems have generally lacked modern marshalling yards, apart from the German Democratic Republic, Upper Silesia and Bohemia, and most trains are marshalled in old-fashioned sorting sidings. Comecon countries have sought to arrange communal border facilities, and there are several change of gauge facilities along the border with the Soviet Union. Some 100 000 wagons have been placed in a common-user pool similar to the *Europ*-Wagon Pool in the E.E.C. in the hope of ensuring more intense utilisation and a reduction of empty running. Standard designs modelled on Soviet norms have been produced in the hope of reducing wagon maintenance.

The railway system of Eastern Europe still shows strong traits of its development and condition from before 1914, and there is also the legacy of inter-war developments and the more recently introduced ideas from Soviet experience. Like the Soviet Union the mainstay of the transport system is the railway and this is likely to remain until the end of the century, though road developments have begun, such as a proposed motorway from northern Italy to Moscow. It is unlikely that the motor vehicle will come to have the same position that it has achieved in society in Western Europe.

7.5 Ports and shipping

The countries of Eastern Europe have not been renowned as major maritime powers and it was not until the late 1950s that some turned to developing merchant marines and expanding their port facilities. For a long period, ports were underemployed and trade by sea at a low ebb. During the 1960s the growth of trade between the Soviet bloc and the outer world, however, encouraged expansion and modernisation of ports and the building of shipping fleets. None of the ports are of world rank and many have facilities that cannot be expanded to cater for the age of bulk carriers. Nevertheless, the Socialist bloc is now significant in the world shipping scene. Apart from the Soviet fleet, Poland's merchant vessels tender in the world charter market and it has shown a growing commercial ability. For example, the Polish and East German ships have been important in trade with Cuba, because of political embargoes declared by Latin America on countries whose shipping uses Cuban ports. There is a policy of trying to get at least 60 per cent of all shipments in Socialist bloc trade in Comecon bottoms. Even Czechoslovakia owns ships which operate from Polish or other ports, while Hungary owns a fleet of small vessels that sail from upstream on the Danube to Black Sea or Levant ports. The fleets have been built largely in Polish or East German yards and comprise mostly general cargo vessels.

Poland and East Germany have large modern fishing fleets operating mostly in Atlantic waters along with the Soviet fishing fleet. These are large vessels using the latest techniques, though their methods are often suspect and they have a reputation for scraping the bottom bare, contributing to serious over-fishing.

7.6 Airways

The Socialist bloc countries outside China are well served generally by the large

Soviet Aeroflot, which claims 20 per cent of world air passenger turnover. The national companies are usually primarily involved in the carriage of passengers and relatively small quantities of freight. The internal services operate principally from the capital to provincial cities and between major provincial centres. The international routes are mostly to other capitals in Europe, but the East German Interflug, for example, flies services to West Africa and the Middle East and even the small Rumanian Tarom flies to Cairo. An important element is tourist traffic in season: Málev, the Hungarian airline, flies to Slovakian and Polish Tatra resorts and even to the Crimea in summer. The machines are usually the older Soviet models, though the Czech airline ČSA and the Polish LOT have larger and more modern equipment. A co-operative agreement on traffic exists in *Sixpool*—ČSA, LOT, Tabso (Bulgaria), Tarom, Málev and Interflug—to co-ordinate their fleet of about 150 machines carrying 70 000 to 80 000 passengers annually. Probably about a third of all traffic is on the East Berlin–Prague route, followed by the Prague–Budapest flights.

The general impression is of a rapid advance in transport facilities in Eastern Europe, with the emphasis still on railways, but a growing awareness of road and air transport, besides the development of shipping fleets and ports. The system has become, however, more orientated to the east—the Soviet Union—and many links from pre-war times with Western Europe remain underused.

Part Three
Comecon and the National
Economies

8 The Genesis of Comecon and the Sovietisation of Eastern Europe

Comecon belongs to the major changes in the political geography of Eastern Europe that have taken place since 1945. It would have been hard to foresee in 1939 that one of the least expected outcomes of the Second World War would be the emergence of the Soviet Union as a politically strong and economically potentially powerful state which the fortunes of war placed in a dominant position across the eastern marchlands of Europe.

The Soviet position was, however, something of a paradox. The Soviet Union was in a strong position measured in conventional military terms—Red Army garrisons held the former German East Prussian territory around Königsberg (Kaliningrad), a strategic key to the Baltic. They also held the newly acquired Soviet territory on the great outwash fan of the Tisza around Uzhgorod and Mukachevo, a strategic key to Danubia. Soviet garrisons in central Germany could threaten the middle Rhine, especially from forward positions in Thüringen, and also the Lower Elbe from western Mecklenburg. In fact, the Baltic had become virtually a Soviet Sea and incorporation of Albania into the Soviet sphere gave a position of strength in the Adriatic. There was a weakness in the lack of Soviet strategic air power, while the detonation of the first atom bomb had posed a new threat to which there was no immediate Soviet answer, though the Soviet authorities had captured the bulk of the German rocket science installations. Military power might therefore enforce a rather tenuous political hold while a strong ruling class of Communists was developed, especially where the ideology had only weak roots among the people. The critical weakness was, however, in the economic sphere—the war had been fought by an intense scorched earth policy in the parts of the Soviet Union that fell into German hands, while resources in unoccupied areas had been stretched to the full to keep the war machine going. Now, an essentially industrially weak country was faced with maintaining a massive occupation army and rebuilding its strength, while concealing the extent of such basic weakness from its enemies. The situation was worsened by the rapid deterioration in relations with the Western Allies, who grew suspicious of Soviet intentions during the relentless winter of 1945–6, when it seemed that Communism, fed by hunger, cold and disillusionment might well spread westwards. Western European and American resources began to be devoted wholeheartedly to rebuilding as rapidly as possible the shattered society and economy of Western Europe. The emergence of grossly divergent views on the solution of political, social and economic problems in their respective spheres between the wartime allies in East and West had started the division of Europe into two, separated by the Iron Curtain, within a year of the end of hostilities.

8.1. The origins and development of Comecon

8.1.1 Marshall Aid and the European Movement

In fear of a spread of Communism, Western Europe with American help sought to organise as quickly as possible economic and social agencies to revitalise democratic life and to create a new material well-being after the years of shortage as powerful antibodies against the infection. A most potent weapon in this armoury was the immense material stimulus to reconstruction given by the brilliantly conceived Marshall Plan and this was further strengthened by the spiritual rejuvenation and solidarity provided by the Churchillian concept of the European Movement. The effect in Western Europe was a relatively rapid return to some semblance of reasonable living conditions, though many adjustments were made to the pre-war pattern. In Eastern Europe, at the same time, society and economy were undergoing a slow and painful application of Soviet theories as interpreted in the inter-war period. The highly effective results of Marshall Aid began to be reflected in the way Western European countries' economic recovery drew ahead of Eastern Europe.

8.1.2 The Birth of Comecon

Sensing the decisive victory in the impoverished continent made by the American aid and realising its longer term possibilities, the Soviet authorities set out to restrict its success by abstaining from co-operation on the grounds that the conditions of the award violated national sovereignty. As it had been offered originally to any country that wished to take advantage of it, Czechoslovakia and Poland had decided to join the programme and the former had accepted membership formally, but both were forced by Soviet pressure to withdraw. Thus no country within the Soviet bloc was to participate in the Organisation for European Economic Co-operation, the body established in 1948 to administer the American Marshall Plan aid. From 1949 to 1953 the Soviet bloc countries also withheld realistic co-operation even from the Pan-European United Nations' agency, the Economic Commission for Europe. Obviously in the situation the Soviet bloc had to offer its members and the world some tangible counter-attraction and corresponding movement.

In April 1949 in an aura of secrecy and with very little real information about it, the Council for Mutual Economic Assistance (Comecon in Western Parlance and CMEA in East bloc language) was instituted. The official handbook published to commemorate 20 years of Comecon says:

> A number of European countries embarked on the road of building Socialism after the Second World War and this dictated the need for their close economic cooperation among themselves and with the Soviet Union. Prerequisites for the development of cooperation between these countries were furnished by their state system, the same type of economic basis and their mutual interest in the early restoration and rapid development of the economy, in the building of Socialism and the necessity for mutual support and assistance.

The initial members were the Soviet Union, Poland, Czechoslovakia, Hungary,

Bulgaria and Rumania; Albania joined a month after the first communique and the nascent German Democratic Republic had become a member within a year.

8.1.3 The Soviet View of Europe

Between the World Wars the Soviet Union had existed in effective isolation, partly self-imposed and partly demanded by the attitudes of the world outside to the 'first experiment in Socialism'. In such a hermetically-sealed environment, the Stalinist interpretation of Marxism and Leninism had evolved and was consequently applied to the new Imperium in Eastern Europe. Stalin appears to have considered that the capitalist world was doomed to rapid disintegration amid post-war social upheaval and the collapse of colonial empires, so that the time was ripe for pressing ahead-with the proletarian revolution. It was, however, necessary at first to make no move that would arouse Western fears of Soviet aims nor make the Western world less ready to co-operate economically with the Soviet Union. The main aim was the speedy reconstruction of the shattered Soviet economy, with particular emphasis on trying to close the technological gap between the Soviet bloc and the Americans created by the development of atomic weapons.

The Soviet authorities had an intense fear that their economic condition would fail them and concentrated on a feverish economic rehabilitation, especially as the serious miscalculation of the resilient constitution of capitalism became apparent—it had begun to recover at an embarrassing rate for Soviet plans. To recover at a comparable rate from an initial position of weakness caused an apparent paradox in Soviet policy and action. The Soviet leaders pursued on the one hand a skilful and, within their range of experience, a well-executed political policy, but on the other hand jeopardised the success of this by a rapacious economic policy designed to maximise advantage for themselves at the expense of everybody else. Friends and former enemies alike had to find material wealth to infuse new life in the Soviet economy. So great were these demands that insufficient remained for the Eastern European countries to make an appreciable progress of their own, consequently the very social and economic conditions that had fed Communism now began to weaken its acceptance. Heavy reparations were taken from capital equipment and from current production in the Soviet Zone of Germany, inspite of an Allied agreement against the latter. Hungary was also forced to surrender reparations and wherever a 'German asset' could be claimed it went to augment Soviet economic strength. The other countries were forced to provide raw materials and manufactured goods at knock-down prices or on an exchange basis more than favourable to the Soviet Union. Only Albania, which had little to offer, and Jugoslavia, which enjoyed a measure of independence, escaped relatively lightly, and political circumstances before the 1948 *coup d'état* in Czechoslovakia helped it to escape initially. In Hungary, Rumania, Bulgaria and the Soviet Zone of Germany, numerous mixed companies, representing Soviet and local interests were formed though with the former predominant, and these commonly had strong strategic undertones, such as the Soviet interests in uranium-mining. Everywhere a multitude of Soviet 'advisers' appeared to supervise and co-ordinate operations, with a friendly if sinister guise.

In the early post-war years an important Soviet aim to be achieved as expeditiously as possible was the 'sovietisation' of the state-organisms in Eastern Europe. The continued presence of the Red Army long after the military situation demanded it impressed the view that the Eastern European countries had become a forward security zone in Soviet defence and consequently a field of major Soviet political action. In this situation Comecon added another element of Soviet influence and direction.

In the immediate post-war years there were hopes in the Soviet Union that the Eastern European people's democracies would be eventually integrated into the framework of union republics, perhaps even extending to some measure of territorial reorganisation in certain vital areas. All apparently was aimed at increasing the economic contribution to Soviet rehabilitation. As early as 1947 the Bulgarians had made it clear that, inspite of the friendship with the Soviet Union, they did not wish to become a Soviet republic but to remain a 'free and independent state with its own national and state sovereignty'. Poland rejected collectivisation because it was claimed that Polish democracy was not similar to Soviet democracy, just as Polish society was not the same as Soviet society. The trend for the Eastern European countries to follow a far too independent national line for Soviet liking came at a time when the further expansion of Soviet influence in Europe was thwarted by a reorientation of Western policies. A tentative move for a Danube union between Jugoslavia and Bulgaria—and possibly others—forced the issue. A sudden Soviet-inspired purge of Communist leadership was designed to clear away the independently minded, culminating in the expulsion of Tito and the Jugoslavs, while in the other countries (including Czechoslovakia in June 1948) new constitutions were framed, stressing the dependence on and links with the Soviet Union, followed by swift collectivisation and, where appropriate, industrialisation while Soviet views on economic regionalisation were pressed home. At this stage economic plans were formulated on the Soviet model and attempts made to co-ordinate their timing with the Soviet programme. It is claimed even output targets were geared to Soviet needs and plans for heavy industry were patently made dependent on Soviet sources of raw materials.

8.1.4 Comecon under Stalin

The first high-sounding though very general statement on the new Council was to remain the sole document of any consequence for many years. The secrecy with which the new organisation was created had been reinforced by the lack of further publicity before Stalin's death and has prompted some students to seek reasons other than those in the first communiqué as the *raison d'être* of Comecon. One theory suggests that the xenophobia of Stalin found Comecon a means of depriving the Eastern European countries of outside contacts as part of an attempt to isolate the Soviet state and its sphere of influence completely from the outside, while it has been seen as a means of countering the Western boycott imposed in retaliation for the Berlin blockade or even making the ostracisation of Jugoslavia more effective. There was also a strong centripetal element in Comecon, doubtless conceived to combat the centrifugal tendencies which had shown themselves in 1947–8.

In his *Economic Problems of Socialism in the U.S.S.R.* (1952), Stalin had explained the concept of the 'collapse of the all-embracing world market'. Each and every economic contact with the West was supposedly dangerous, just as any Western attempt to liberalise trade and expand economic contact was seen as 'a cunning attack on the principle of national sovereignty' and really reflected attempts to penetrate markets with inferior goods at dumping prices in order to strangle native industry. Stalin expounded the somewhat mistaken view that a 'unitary' world market had existed before 1939 which had now collapsed into a 'capitalist' and a 'socialist' market. In strange juxtaposition to these theories Stalin considered that ultimately the Socialist bloc countries would need to export surplus goods, though he did not say whether this was to arise from the inability of Socialist planning to prevent overproduction or from a serious economic offensive to capture capitalist markets.

8.1.5 Comecon and National Sovereignty

The reference to national sovereignty is one of the main contrasts between the Comecon and the European Economic Community. Though at the time of the creation of Comecon the Eastern European countries were more subordinate to the Soviet Union than at any other time, it was stressed in the original communiqué that the aim was 'to accelerate the restoration and development of their national economies'. Participation in the Marshall Plan, it was claimed, was impossible because it would have violated their sovereignty and the interests of their national economies. Long-standing Marxist views expressed the minor importance of national sovereignty, but no doubt the stress on sovereignty justified the dismantling of the regional coalitions which had begun to appear during 1947–8, making easier a system of *divide et impera*.

8.1.6 The Objectives of Comecon

In contrast to the copious documentation of Western organisations, Comecon was uncommunicative for the first decade of its existence. Initial information rested on the first general communiqué which remained the sole document for eight years. A proper constitution was not forthcoming for eleven years, parts of which remained unratified for even longer. The main aims, so briefly expressed, were to develop inter-member trade, accelerate the development of the several national economies and to develop and widen economic co-operation by exchange of experience and technical aid. From its inception until after Stalin's death economic co-operation and technical aid appears to have been limited to the Soviet search for know-how and skills for its own industry, while little or no widening of trade took place, but efforts were made to standardise products to Soviet types and norms. The agreement seemed to have little effect on the application of Soviet-style autarkic principles, with each member developing its own heavy industries, imitating the Soviet preference for steel, whether or not justified by the size of the domestic market. Consequently, several national development plans included projects for industries, whose products could have been obtained more cheaply and conveniently from other members, and irrespective of whether or not adequate raw material resources existed for the proposals. The difficulty of raw materials did, however, create a marked dependence of many members on Soviet supplies, even if inferior home supplies were developed. The aggregate demand of these countries for Soviet raw materials could create substantial competition for favour and thus political pressure from the Soviet Union.

8.1.7 Comecon after Stalin

After the death of Stalin important concessions were made to the Eastern European countries that changed the emphasis in economic development, though some concessions simply represented a response to events in the Soviet Union itself. There was first a reduction in the emphasis on heavy industry, especially iron and steel, while there was a small temporary swing to improving a meagre standard of living before a partial return to old policies. A major change was a relaxation in the principle of collectivisation, which apart from political reasons was coloured by the anxiety to increase the unsatisfactory output of foodstuffs. The Eastern European countries were also allowed a greater freedom in making individual economic decisions. The policy of taking reparations, which had almost destroyed the viability of the Soviet Zone of Germany, was markedly toned down, though the Soviet Union still continued to draw large quantities, at preferential prices, of manufactured and semi-manufactured goods badly needed by the Eastern European countries themselves.

8.1.8 Comecon and the Changing Soviet Economy

The broadening of the tasks facing the Soviet economy initiated in 1954 also gave new life to Comecon. The emphasis on heavy industry was put into a broader context than previously, opening a market for engineering equipment from Comecon countries, while the provision of consumer goods for the Soviet market was to be achieved by purchase from Comecon members. Finally, long neglected agriculture was to get a boost and a more significant role in the economy and in society—a development followed in Comecon countries. The move to a refined view of planning and plan economics in the Soviet Union, with studies of location of development and comparative studies of production conditions, co-ordination of planning, specialisation of production and economic integration within the Soviet bloc, brought a new importance to Comecon. The Budapest conference of 1955 examined the problems of co-ordination, especially in the field of economic plans, after lengthy studies of productive capacity and other aspects by Soviet *Gosplan* experts. There was also examination of investment agreements and conditions for industrial specialisation. To co-ordinate the work special technical commissions were formed.

The distribution of information about Comecon by the conference in East Berlin in 1956 was seen by some observers as an attempt to counteract the striking impression made in the Soviet bloc by progress towards economic integration of the several Western European agencies, in particular the European Economic Community. Though by this time the synchronisation of state plans of the Comecon countries had begun, it had hardly got properly underway before it was disrupted by the Soviet abandonment in 1957 of its 1956–60 plan.

8.1.9 The Socialist Division of Labour

At this time the first arrangements were also made for the 'rationalisation' of production between members, but unfortunately, a serious error had been made in estimating the supply of and demand for raw materials to achieve the targets set by the Gosplan experts who had examined the industrial potential and capacity of Comecon. Work also continued on improving the financial mechanism of the Soviet bloc, with an important agreement on credit. The participation of the member countries in the cost of the Comecon secretariat and related bodies, so far paid for by the Russians, was agreed. Possibly under the influence of the political upheavals in Poland and Hungary, planning was made more flexible and put on a basis of ten to fifteen year forecasts of probable requirements and targets. Consideration was given in 1958 to how the Asiatic people's democracies might be drawn into the organisation, and a year later plans were laid for development of an electricity grid to link the European members together, while discussion extended to the legal position of Comecon and the preparation of a charter of immunities.

The early 1960s brought another crisis in the failure to solve the problems of the so-called 'Socialist division of labour'. A growing resentment of the nationalistic and egotistic attitude of the Soviet Union among the members resulted in attempts to increase the authority of Comecon and to develop the technical services it offered. China and Jugoslavia, observers since 1956, and Albania, virtually a founder member, refrained from taking part in the deliberations. Discontent was not allayed, especially in Rumania, where there was concern about the subordinate role assigned it in the overall Comecon planning for which 'perspectives' had been projected until 1980. There was a growing attraction for the less developed countries with a large agricultural sector in their economy—Rumania, Bulgaria and Hungary—to trade with the West where there was a bigger demand for farm products. The situation was eased a little by economic reorganisation in the Soviet Union that allowed greater flexibility and an inclination to experiment and in which the Eastern European countries were also allowed to participate, while the growing disagreement between the Soviet Union and China made the Soviet authorities reluctant to alienate support in Eastern Europe.

8.1.10 Comecon and Asia

The growing Soviet interest in Asian affairs was reflected in an amendment to the Comecon charter in 1962 to admit Asian countries to full membership. China, North Vietnam and North Korea as well as the Mongol People's Republic were offered full membership in place of only observer status. Possibly under Chinese pressure, this was declined except by Mongolia, though in 1965 a pro-Chinese faction tried to get the country to withdraw from Comecon. Albania swung into the Chinese camp and gradually loosened its ties with Comecon, in which it has not participated since 1961. In the early 1960s, however, there was a return of Jugoslavia to an interest in Comecon, possibly conditioned by a fear of loss of markets in Western Europe with the growth of the European Economic Community, while no doubt it was useful for the Soviet Union to woo Jugoslav friendship in view of enmity with China. Jugoslavia remained, however, an observer. Cuba also began to participate in Comecon commissions, clearly keen to associate with the organisation in view of the ostracism by other American states, and became a full member in 1972. Cuba had frequently opposed Jugoslav views, which it regarded as tantamount to capitalism.

8.1.11 The Grouping of Comecon Members

Economic development during the 1960s began to group the Eastern European members into two divisions and to colour their aims and attitudes in Comecon. There appeared a group of more advanced industrialised countries—Poland, Czechoslovakia, the German Democratic Republic and, at the border, Hungary—and a group of less industrialised countries—Bulgaria and Rumania, joined by Hungary on some aspects. The Soviet Union belonged to the first group and the Mongol People's Republic fell into a sub-category of the second group. The industrialised members' main fear was for the continuance of their trading with Western Europe as new economic groupings and ideas began to appear, even though the German Democratic Republic tried to keep its relations with the West and especially with West Germany to a minimum. Rumania had set itself on a course of rapid industrialisation and some of its plans for heavy industry were unpopular or even contrary to prevailing views on Comecon planning and rationalisation that sought to restrict new heavy industry to existing producers. Rumania was unenthusiastic about a trading system that committed it to import manufactured goods against an export of raw materials—this was felt to make it a second rank member and to perpetuate the pre-war situation which it sought to escape. Bulgaria did not have such feelings, since its exports of fruits, early vegetables and non-ferrous metals met with little competition in Comecon, commanding the prices asked in both Western and Eastern markets.

8.1.12 Comecon and Planning

The 1960s brought much debate about the nature and role of central planning in Comecon as the old ideas of national autarky were abandoned and an attempt was made to find ways in which major investment projects on an international scale that would breed substantial economies of scale might be achieved. Shared investment among members and co-ordination of their plans were called for, if such aims were to be realised. Some members objected that creation of such supranational competence 'would turn sovereignty into a notion without content' and there were even threats of withdrawal if the idea were pressed, particularly by Rumania, motivated by old fears of a return—even if only partial—to its pre-war position of a 'drawer of water and a hewer of wood'. The situation was not made easier by support from the Chinese, who thought that economic assistance should always fully respect sovereignty and that any infringement on the grounds of the 'Socialist international division of labour was great power chauvinism', views which were publicly supported in Albania and in Rumania. The Soviet Union refuted these views as being outdated, abstract and dogmatist, but in the end the proposals for centralised planning were modified to a degree tantamount to discarding them.

8.1.13 Dissident Rumania

The Rumanians smarted under a proposal by a Soviet economic geographer, Valev, that Rumanian planning and industrial location was at fault and that Rumanian plans should be formulated in terms of a Danubian complex, including Bulgaria and the appropriate parts of the Soviet Union. He was violently attacked in the Rumanian press which saw such a proposal as relegating Rumania to the second rank in Comecon. The furore became so fierce that Valev was partly discredited in the Soviet Union to appease the Rumanians. Even before this Rumania had registered its dissent by signing an agreement with the Jugoslavs to build a large Iron Gates hydroelectric project, arranged through the Danube Commission without reference to Comecon.

8.1.14 'Interested Parties' and Financial Problems

The failure to establish the principle of centralised Comecon planning resulted in co-operation being put on a voluntary basis and there emerged the concept of the 'interested party', in the hope of improving central consultation to supplement bilateral negotiation. Members were left three options in collaboration—joint investments, joint enterprises and international associations. To help in the process, a bureau of integrated planning problems, instituted to advise the central executive, prepares proposals for co-ordinating economic development plans of members and gives assistance in promoting co-operation between planning bodies on specific matters.

By the middle 1960s it had become apparent that the relatively simple multilateral clearing system evolved for Comecon in 1956–7 was no longer adequate as the organisation grew and its operations became more complex. Financial problems were made more pressing by the growth of trade within the bloc and with the outside world. A special problem was to make arrangements for financial settlements between members to be brought closer to the Western European pattern, where debts might be carried over rather than settled annually, which could be a big help to poorer members. A particular need was for capital, expectedly to be drawn primarily from the Soviet Union. A most serious question was that any move towards convertability of the clearing currency would require Comecon price ratios to be closer to general prevailing world price levels. The establishment of a Bank for International Economic Co-operation in 1964 did not, however, help to eliminate simple bilateral trading, often to the disadvantage of the weaker partner, while it was only competent to deal with internal trading within the Soviet bloc.

Relaxation and decentralisation of trading in the latter 1960s further complicated the issue, especially as means of trading became more elaborate; the trends were particularly marked in Czechoslovakia, Hungary, the German Democratic Republic and Rumania. The increase in trade has been limited, however, by the import quota system and by barriers against trade with the Soviet bloc erected in the West during the Cold War. Currency has been a serious problem and the creation of the *transferable ruble* in 1965 has been acceptable only on a limited scale since such credits can only be drawn in currencies of Comecon members and the most pressing need is for greater availability of 'hard' Western currency. The Polish government has suggested that the transferable ruble should be truly convertible by each Comecon member backing it with gold or hard currency, inspite of reluctance to do this, since deficits would then be settled in such desirable hard currency for debts incurred within Comecon and thus deprive poorer members of their chance to trade in the Western market by eating into their own limited resources of Western currency.

The more sophisticated countries began to circumvent the rather crude Comecon financial system. Czechoslovak feelers in Western money markets for a large loan to restore their ailing economy was one of the events that triggered the crisis of the summer of 1968. The Czechs had begun to restore something of the quite elaborate Central European international banking system that had existed before 1945. In 1971, after all the uproar of the Czech crisis had died down, the Hungarians got a $25 million loan 'comfortably oversubscribed' in the Euro-Bond market. In the summer of 1970 an International Investment Bank was agreed upon, one of whose functions is to finance joint Comecon projects, especially if these reduce the individual countries' dependence on supplies from the West, and it has already made considerable loans. It is also thought that the bank will act as a joint Comecon venture to raise capital in the world's money markets, which its constitution allows.

These financial moves are a reflection of the growing demand for advanced plant and machinery by the Comecon countries, which has grown faster than their ability to produce industrial exports suitable for the Western market, so that the bloc's hard currency is under continual strain. The main aim is to create some suitable credit system to allow import of equipment which will greatly strengthen Comecon's productive capacity within about five years and allow it to enter world trade on appropriate terms.

8.1.15 Comecon and 'Management'—The Czech Crisis of 1967–8

One of the major conflicts of opinion between Comecon members in Eastern Europe centres around the question of 'management' in the broadest sense. In the Soviet Union decentralisation of the economy began with Khrushchev's moves in 1957 and included the brief but unhappy experiment of the *Sovnarkhoz*[1], though the process has continued, despite occasional swings back towards the old centralisation. 'Management' and 'profitability' in a quasi-capitalist sense have become a leitmotiv of recent Soviet experiments, inspite of a dilemma as to whether the economy should be managed in an overall manner by branches or on a territorial basis, but this long-standing issue has been confounded recently by new possibilities arising from computerisation. The Eastern European members of Comecon were not slow to seize the opportunity given by the Soviet experiments to develop their own interpretations, which in general have been more marked by Western European practice than the often stilted Soviet forms. Modest changes in 'management' escalated into a major ideological issue, with an overriding matter of principle in the debate on the

---

[1] *Sovnarkhoz*: Soviet term for the regional planning councils established in Khrushchev's decentralisation of planning in 1957. They proved unsuccessful and were abolished (see Mellor, R. E. H. (1968). *Geography of the U.S.S.R.*, Macmillan).

merits of centralised planning against the market economy as a method of national economic management.

Whatever reforms have been made in the Soviet Union, all-important decisions still remain in the hands of Gosplan, whereas the Jugoslavs have moved to a system where individual plants are responsible for their own survival in a competitive situation. In 1967 impatient Czechoslovak reformers, anxious to rectify the ills of their failing economy, set out on the road to the market economy, dismantling with great rapidity the superstructure of central planning and control. Unfortunately, the pace and the methods used alarmed the Soviet Union and some other Comecon members, so that pressure was put on the Czechoslovak government to change its way before abandonment of long-standing views went too far and before such new directions to the economy attracted support from other members. When this pressure failed, the Soviet authorities acted fiercely by occupying Czechoslovakia in August 1968.

Although the Czechoslovak move towards the market economy came to disaster, the Hungarians followed the course more successfully without raising Soviet suspicions, though the Hungarians have since been forced by a loss of control over the economy to consider their future course carefully. Both these countries had pressed hard to have Comecon transformed into a tariff preference area, a view also supported by Rumania, conservatively minded in planning concepts, and Bulgaria, a radical in economic reform despite loyal friendship to the Soviet Union. Rumania has pressed for easing trading relations with the Western world and has even sought closer association with the European Economic Community than many observers in Comecon would consider prudent. The German Democratic Republic, Poland and Mongolia along with the Soviet Union have in contrast been ardent supporters of planned supra-national co-ordination, though they had been thwarted by Rumanian insistence on the principle of national sovereignty in the early 1960s. The Soviet Union has on numerous occasions reiterated its view that the principle of national sovereignty has been overplayed and circumstances now warrant a more supra-national approach to problems. It is perhaps not surprising that countries such as Poland and the German Democratic Republic have supported the Soviet view and sought centralised and co-ordinated action, because any unilateral reforms might well damage their sensitive economies in tender phases of growth. Since the troubles of 1970 Poland has allowed a greater responsiveness to the market, easing central control. Since events in Czechoslovakia in 1968 the 'supra-nationalists' appear to have consolidated their position, while there has been more caution before new directions have been followed.

8.1.16 Comecon and the European Economic Community

For many years one of the greatest skeletons in the Soviet cupboard was the European Economic Community. The obvious success of the Community and the likelihood of its expansion as well as the pressure of several Comecon members for easier relations with it, forced a Soviet reappraisal of the position. Some countries, such as Poland and Hungary, would welcome easier relations with the European Economic Community because they have suffered from the problems of exporting foodstuffs to it as a result of the Common Agricultural

Policy and would like to try to ease the limitations on this trade, particularly if the Community is to expand. Overtures have been made to create some special arrangement to allow Rumanian imports a privileged position. An easing of the tensions between the two German states is likely to have substantial effects, since their trade is regarded as internal German trade and not subject to the same restrictions. It has often been said that the Hungarians 'think German' when ordering goods—a process that works for both German states. Clearly any move towards easier contacts between Comecon and E.E.C. could have considerable geographical impact along what is at present a zone of stagnation—the belt of division between the political blocs of East and West.

While Soviet bloc policy in the political and economic fields—though the division between them is not always clear—is renowned for its fluctuations and vagaries, some lines of future development seem inevitable. Consideration of the Eastern European Comecon members cannot ignore the influence of the Soviet Union, not only in the political and trading relationships established since 1945 that are unlikely to be swept away but also as a trend-setter in Eastern European affairs. Soviet planning was founded essentially on a basis of building an autarkic economy in an atmosphere of isolation, conceived in terms of developing internal resources to the maximum level to attain a high degree of regional self-sufficiency for strategic reasons, which the natural resource endowment was almost sufficiently rich to allow. The immediate post-war plans were also conceived within this framework: the countries that were to become later members of Comecon were then first seen purely as political satellites inside an enlarged 'imperium', augmenting the wealth of the Soviet Union, into which it was hoped they would ultimately merge. Later, as members of Comecon, they were tied very tightly to the Soviet economic system, but the hold has been slowly relaxed. There is little doubt that the origial aims of Soviet planning, even in the immediate post-war period, were attainable so long as the economy remained unsophisticated, with a heavy emphasis on iron and steel and simple capital goods, while agriculture could cope with the feeding of a growing industrial population at a relatively simple standard of living.

Political and military needs forced the Soviet Union to outgrow such a simple economic framework and to move towards an increasingly complex and sophisticated industrial structure in which further progress (at any rate comparable to that of the world outside) demanded reliance on buying know-how and advanced plant in the world market. With economic advance and under the pressures exerted from the Eastern European countries such as Czechoslovakia and the German Democratic Republic, the standard of living had to be allowed to improve, adding a further burden on industry and agriculture. Not only has it been imperative to import more manufactured goods of a sophisticated nature from the outside world, but the rising living standard has demanded import of foodstuffs to cover certain deficits, especially in years of bad harvests. At the same time, more complex industrial patterns have increased the need to find some raw materials outside the Socialist bloc or by increased trading within it. Such a growth of trade, though still at a low level, looks likely to continue.

The experience in the Western world has shown that as industrialisation increases and advances, growing more complex and sophisticated, marked by the emergence of a mass consumer society, the more advanced industrial countries tend to draw closer together and trade increasingly with each other. It is no longer adequate to trade on a simple system of unsophisticated manufactured goods exchanged for raw materials from the less developed countries, which in any case have generally tended to develop manufacturing industry to cover their domestic needs on a fairly broad front. It is perhaps not expecting too much that a similar situation will arise between the more advanced countries in the Eastern and Western blocs as barriers between them fall, particularly as the Eastern bloc now appears to realise that its own advance depends on buying more advanced equipment in the world markets than it can readily produce itself. When this equipment begins to increase output in the Socialist bloc, it will then seek markets for surplus production and such markets are as likely to be in the industrial countries of the Western bloc as among the Third World.

Economy of scale also tends to create trade—it was the problem of the autarkic economy of the Stalinist system that in several Comecon countries many manufactured goods could not be produced at realistic cost levels because of the limited size of the domestic market. The arguments about industrial organisation in Western Europe in seeking to support costly research and development and the maximisation and optimalisation of production advanced in Servan-Schreiber's *le Défi Americain* seem to apply equally forcefully to Eastern Europe. Another example is the dependence of Comecon on Soviet sources of raw materials that also appears to have long term limitations, if the Comecon countries are to produce at effective cost levels: raw materials carried from the deep continental interior of the Soviet Union by railway are a poor prosposition pitted against cheap oceanic bulk carriage at the lower general world price levels. The further development of Soviet mineral wealth in terms of likely demand from Comecon countries in Eastern Europe is a problem of investment—the Soviet Union has suggested that Comecon countries interested in Soviet mineral wealth should invest in it, but this is difficult for countries whose investment wealth is seriously limited and sucked up at home. Some highly attractive resources such as copper (Udokan in Siberia) have been looked at by the U.S.A., Japan and France, whose investment is as likely as investment by Eastern European countries.

As barriers between the political blocs in East and West break down, European Russia (into which over half the total national investment goes) will be drawn closer to the Eastern European members of Comecon and to the Western European countries, with which it will become closely identified in trading terms (after all, about three-quarters of Soviet population still lives west of the Volga and south of Leningrad), while for the Socialist bloc cheap oceanic bulk carriage will become more attractive than the present often unrealistic haulage distances by railway. On the other hand, the emergence of a very powerful Japanese industrial structure in the North Pacific, based notably on cheap oceanic bulk carriage, may well draw the eastern parts of Siberia (as indications already suggest) into the Pacific–East Asian trading orbit. In such circumstances, it is perhaps not too unrealistic to think of eastern Siberia importing cheap seaborne Canadian wheat rather than expensive rail-hauled Ukrainian or Caucasian grain. The political implications of such a situation are of course tremendous and probably not very palatable to the Soviet Union. On the other hand, the high level of trade expected to develop—if not already developed—between Europe and Japan makes the

Trans-Siberian route in the container revolution a most attractive proposition for high-grade manufactured goods, placing the Soviet Union and Eastern Europe in a key transport situation on a new flow diagram of world trade.

8.2 The Sovietisation of Eastern Europe

From the outset, even before the formation of Comecon, there has been a steady introduction of Soviet ideas and practices into Eastern Europe. Their success has been varied, for they were evolved in a Marxist–Leninist framework that was tested in practice if not designed in the environmental conditions of the Soviet Union. In the different dimensional situation in Eastern European countries, Soviet practices often required modification, which under Stalin was largely unacceptable, though since the early 1950s there has been a slow swing to more liberal and national interpretations. Nevertheless, political *polycentrism* has been frowned on.

8.2.1 Planning and Administration

One of the most important fields in which Soviet concepts have been applied is in regional and national planning, both within Comecon as a whole and within individual states. After initial rectification of what were considered historical errors in the territorial extent of states, strict adhesion to the 'national principle' did not allow further interference within the boundaries of states, except in a few small instances. Nevertheless, though it is hard to distinguish fact from fiction, during Stalin's time there appears to have been some attempt to plan Eastern Europe as a whole and to look forward to its ultimate absorption into the body of the Union of Soviet Socialist Republics. The plan reputedly envisaged by Stalin to create an autonomous Silesian region with a strong emphasis on iron and steel-making, carved from Czech and Polish territory seems unlikely, as a strong case could be made for a 'united Donbass' cut from the Ukraine and the Russian Republic that appeared in early Soviet plans, but was vetoed because it transgressed the 'national principle', so ardently upheld by Lenin. There is also evidence that Stalin was prepared to allow the Jugoslavs to annexe Albania and to return Szczecin (Stettin) to Germany.

Before 1945 the territorial-administrative organisation throughout Eastern Europe was largely the result of historical accident, with only slow adjustments to the boundaries of administrative units within states. The size of the units and the organisational hierarchy varied considerably from state to state, though many had been influenced by French views in Napoleonic times. A wave of reform swept through Eastern Europe in the early 1950s, recasting or at least extensively modifying the territorial-administistative pattern. Whereas before 1945 these units had been used purely for administrative convenience, the new system had a strong undertone of economic planning in the criteria used in definition. First, each unit had to be capable of development as a 'complex' economy, that is it should develop all aspects of its economic potential and fit into an overall national plan. Secondly, any specialisation which could be expressed had to be developed, though not to the exclusion of other sectors of the economy, but each of the new units had to have a distinctive functional characteristic. In designing the units not just the immediate situation had to be considered, but it was important to consider the 'perspective'—the longer term aims and ways of national development into which the units would have to fit. Particular attention was to be given to industrialisation and no unit should be ultimately solely or even predominantly agricultural. It was also stressed that each unit should aim towards a measure of self-sufficiency, especially with the aim of avoiding unnecessary transport, though this does not seem to have been taken as seriously as in the Soviet Union. The administrative centre and cultural and economic focus of each unit is a 'proletarian centre', fitting the Soviet theory of the towns as standard-bearers of Communism. Planning the units had also to consider the demographic problems, particularly of labour supply, while transport planning affected such 'rayonisation'[1] in trying to eliminate wasteful intra or inter-regional hauls and cross-flows. A final consideration was to create as far as possible a reasonable balance between the units, so that none dominated the others in economic or demographic terms. The number of units created had, however, to be sufficient to reflect major regional economic contrasts but not so numerous as to complicate the planning, fiscal or statistical processes. An important Soviet principle was to regard the boundaries of the units once created as not immutable, though boundary changes have been not so frequent nor so drastic as in the Soviet Union.

In 1945 in the Soviet Zone of Germany, Prussia had been swept away and five large states (*Länder*) created—Mecklenburg, Brandenburg, Sachsen–Anhalt, Sachsen and Thüringen. Berlin—both the eastern and western sectors—was also regarded as a *Land*. These large states were envisaged as members of an ultimate confederation, but such a degree of autonomy did not fit into the plans for the creation of a 'people's democracy'. Consequently, in 1952 the *Länder* were swept away and replaced by fourteen *Bezirke*, conceived in the terms of the Soviet-style *Oblast*[2]. As a fifteenth *Bezirk* East Berlin was included as a special situation. During the first five-year plan in Hungary, a marked simplification of the *Comitat* boundaries was undertaken, but further work on 'rayonisation' has been hampered by problems of implementing some plan decisions. The present nineteen *Comitats* plus the city of Budapest are reputedly too many in relation to the size of the country and its regional diversity, so that ten regions might seem a more appropriate number.

In Bulgaria territorial reorganisation also followed similar lines, though the more diverse nature of the country was reflected in a larger number of units than in Hungary. A drastic reshuffle of boundaries was required in Poland in order to cope with the big territorial shift westwards, but the traditional *Województwo* was retained as the major unit. It was necessary to make considerable changes in the north and west, but fewer changes were made along the new border with the

---

[1] *Rayonisation*: term taken from Soviet usage to imply regionalisation of territory for purposes of economic planning.

[2] *Oblast*: the basic territorial administrative unit in the Soviet Union. It is primarily conceived in terms of economic planning, and must have an industrial 'proletarian centre' as its focus. The principles of its design have been generally accepted into the territorial-administrative system of the East European countries.

Soviet Union. The realigned boundaries of the *Województwo* Katowice were drawn to include the Upper Silesian industrial district, while a new unit was designed to include the lower Vistula lands, with the administrative seat in Gdańsk. The five principal cities (each with over 400 000 people) were given special status, though serving as the administrative centres of the *Województwa*. In attempting to create the balance required among the seventeen *Województwa*, a particular problem has been the overwhelming industrial predominance of Upper Silesia, while in the Kielce, Koszalin and Zielona Góra *Województwa* there was a dualism of two main urban centres that weakened the regional unity. Another problem is the poor infrastructural form of the central *Województwa*—densely populated, modestly industrialised, but with poor services and communications—making their planning problems worse than the predominantly agricultural eastern *Województwa*.

The first post-war arrangements in Czechoslovakia were made primarily on administrative considerations, but in 1960 the number of units was reduced from nineteen to ten by bringing the structure into line with the economic and planning criteria on the Soviet model. Prague became a region in its own right. Nevertheless, the traditional division between Bohemia–Moravia and Slovakia was maintained. The regions are remarkably balanced in area and population, though their economic capacity is different and their long-term prospects varied. The division into a Czech and Slovak Republic within the framework of the country after the troubles in 1968 led to some decentralisation, particularly a reduction in the predominance of Prague and a growth in the role of Bratislava, though its frontier position was a disadvantage.

Rumania even before the war had had several changes in the size and number of administrative divisions, conditioned largely by political fluctuations. Immediately after the war, a return was made to administrative units based on an early inter-war division that remained in use even after the Communists took over power. It proved inadequate for the needs of economic planning, because many of the old administrative centres had no contemporary economic importance, while the boundaries often separated related economic areas. In 1950 a system of twenty-eight regions modelled on Soviet criteria was introduced, but within two years modification to bring it closer to Soviet practice followed. This included creation of a special ethnic unit for the Magyar minority (though it did not include all Magyars), apparently against considerable opposition from diehard nationalists. The number of regions was reduced to eighteen, reputedly because there were too few of the 1950 regions large and prosperous enough to achieve either self-sufficiency or specialisation to the degree required by the new plans. A further reduction to sixteen regions was made in 1956, with the abandonment of the Arad and Barlad regions because of their inadequate industrial bases, while further modifications followed in 1959 and 1960. The changes included the creation of a special status for Constanţa and its adjacent resorts and a modification in the Magyar autonomous region which reduced its Magyar element, perhaps as a concession to nationalists. New names for the regions reflected a return to the old historical traditions and a move away from the rigours of Stalinism. In 1968 a major reform was made, creating thirty-nine new divisions (*Judets*) and the muncipality of Bucharest. It was claimed that this more numerous division was necessary to take account of the great strides in economic development and the full hierarchy of central places, though in some respects the new system appears to be a departure from some of the Soviet principles.

8.2.2 Autarky

The blind acceptance of the autarky principle, much questioned by Soviet bloc economists since Stalin's death, has already left a number of white elephants; for example, the Schwarze Pumpe lignite coke plant in the German Democratic Republic. Restrictions of imports and the attempt to develop heavy industry led to unfruitful investments and overdiversification of comparatively poor and scarce resources, while the size of the domestic market was often too small to sustain manufacture on a scale large enough to get the full economies of scale. Heavy investment in industry meant that other sectors had to be starved, in which agriculture suffered most.

In following the Soviet model each national plan sought to provide 'adequate' heavy industry. The concentration on iron and steel in the early phases is seen in the large complexes such as Nowa Huta in Poland, Dunaújváros in Hungary, Pernik and Kremikovci in Bulgaria and the abortive Calbe and Eisenhüttenstadt plants in the German Democratic Republic. In the latter case the umpromising resource base and attempts to use unconventional methods to overcome this disadvantage made the products considerably more expensive than imports. In some instances these iron and steel plants served strong aims of regional development, such as at Nowa Huta (Poland) and at Košice in eastern Slovakia. The development of the chemicals industry depended on German experience, since the Soviet industry was relatively poorly developed, while an important element in development was the construction of fertiliser plants. One of the least successful branches was engineering, because autarky meant short production runs and inadequate research and development, so that projects were invariably uneconomic and valuable investment was squandered. Again, products were commonly more expensive than imports: the Polish *Warszawa M-20* car was not only produced after its design had been abandoned in the Soviet Union but it was more expensive than a superior Soviet model. There was often unrealistic development of industries, such as the German Democratic Republic's attempts to build synthetic petroleum plants and use lignite for metallurgical coke when good coke and petroleum could be readily imported from other members of the Socialist bloc.

With a wide diversity of resources among the members, though with few members apart from the Soviet Union able to approach anything like a modest degree of self-sufficiency, widening of trade rather than its restriction seemed to be the obvious choice. In the early 1950s trade between members was often a product of critical supply bottlenecks that forced countries to seek supplies beyond their own borders. After 1956 attempts were made to increase the movement of Soviet petroleum, especially as development of the Ural–Volga oilfields proceeded, as well as coal, coke and iron ore, and a similar pattern for Polish coal and coke also followed. Several of the new iron and steel complexes had been planned to be heavily dependent on Soviet supplies of ore and coke or on Polish coke. Demand for Soviet petroleum rose as the economies expanded and was an attractive alternative to expensive investment in synthetic petroleum plants. The rising shipments of petroleum from the Ural–Volga oilfields have been reflected in the development of the Comecon 'Friendship pipeline' from the Soviet Union to Poland, German Democratic Republic, Hungary and Czechoslovakia.

The turn from autarky to trade has made possible agreements within Comecon to expand iron and steel-making in countries such as Poland, Czechoslovakia and the Soviet Union, which have a reasonable resource endowment and an already well-equipped industry. Other countries will concentrate on the later stages of production, with some becoming important suppliers of certain products to the bloc—for example, Hungary supplying sheet iron, high-grade steel sections from the German Democratic Republic, hot and cold-rolled plate from Poland, wire-rod, hot-rolled plate and structural steel from Czechoslovakia; Rumania will become a supplier of pipes and the Soviet Union will supply plates in the thicker and larger sizes. Such arrangements are not always readily accepted by some members; for example, the Rumanians have been unhappy at the decision to concentrate the iron and steel-making in countries which are already large producers, since it has planned a large iron and steelworks at Galaţi on the lower Danube. To handle these patterns of supply, a joint Comecon agency, *Intermetal*, has been established to maximise iron and steel output against input by computer means for Poland, Czechoslovakia and the U.S.S.R. though Rumania has remained outside.

Hungary has been the focus of an important agreement on aluminium—Hungarian bauxite being used in Polish Silesia for aluminium production from cheap, locally generated thermal electricity, while Hungarian raw materials are also used in Czechoslovakia and in the Soviet Union. Bulgaria has been designated as a major producer of copper and lead, while Poland will concentrate on supplies of lead and sulphur, partly out of its own raw ores and partly from imported ores. Albania was to have been a major chrome supplier in co-operation with Czechoslovak mining interests. An interesting project has been *Haldex*, the joint Hungarian–Polish corporation to use Polish coal waste for briquettes. Labour shortage in Western Europe has usually been solved by migration of workers to deficit areas. In Comecon such migration is frowned on. German-made electronic components are instead assembled in Hungary, easing the central German labour shortage and providing useful assembly work for the Puszta towns.

8.2.3 The Mir Electricity Grid

Apart from the territory of the German Democratic Republic, Czechoslovakia and the former German lands now in Poland, electricity supply before 1945 was poorly developed. In the German lands a grid system had been developed and current is still traded between the two German states, though compared to pre-war the increase in West German output has been twice as great as in the German Democratic Republic. In Czechoslovakia a grid system existed in Bohemia–Moravia, but it was poorly developed in Slovakia, while elsewhere generators served only local areas and large tracts of country were without electricity supply apart from the towns. Improvements have been made since the war in Germany, while Poland has extended a grid system over the country, using the network in the annexed German Territory as a foundation. Similar developments have taken place in the other countries, even including Albania, with emphasis on national distribution systems.

Electrification was a key to Lenin's economic plans for the Soviet Union. The GOELRO[1] scheme laid down some early planning principles based on a regional structure centred around electricity generation and distribution grids, though it was in the end not implemented. There has consequently been an ideological undertone to electrification in Eastern Europe, though it has certainly been a key to successful economic expansion, particularly in the less developed countries. Technological development has now made long distance transmission of electricity a reasonable proposition, as demonstrated in many Western countries. In 1962 there came into being the Comecon international 220 kV 'Mir' Electricity Grid which links together the grid systems of the member countries and has connections to Jugoslavia, some Western European countries and to the grid systems of the western part of the Soviet Union. In 1967 the final stage was completed by a line across the Danube joining Rumania to Bulgaria. A major addition to the system will be the current fed from the large joint Rumanian–Jugoslav Iron Gates hydroelectric barrage. The main control centre for the system is Prague.

8.3 The international socialist division of labour

The new trends have been put together in a concept of the 'international socialist division of labour', which puts emphasis on trading relations as a way of achieving such classical ideas as economy of scale, economy of effort through the division of labour and specialisation. At the same time the principle of national sovereignty has been preserved and it is maintained that 'each socialist country maps out its own economic development plans based on the concrete conditions in the given country', although this must be influenced by the 'needs and potentialities of all the socialist countries'. 'The socialist countries consider it their international duty to direct their efforts to securing a high rate of development in industry and agriculture of each country commensurate with available potentialities, progressively equalising economic development levels'. Every country is guaranteed the possibility to market its specialised production and to buy the necessary raw materials, equipment and other goods. The long term aim is 'the gradual removal of historical differences in the economic development level of the socialist countries'.

It has been considered important to co-ordinate both the long and short term plans between the participants, though this has not been received with equal warmth by all members. For observers looking for sinister undertones, comparison has been made with the moves to create regional economic interdependence within the Soviet Union in order to lessen regional political independence.

---

[1] *GOELRO*: an abbreviation of the Russian for State Electricity-supply Regionalisation. Created by a commission under Kalinin in the early 1920s to plan the electrification of the Soviet State. It laid down important principles of territorial planning, which have since played a continuous role in Soviet regional planning concepts.

8.3.1 Agriculture

The concept of the international socialist division of labour recognised a fact too long ignored—'the socialist countries differ in per capita farm land and in soil and climate conditions: the exchange of farm products between them will therefore continue and increase' and 'emphasis should be on maximum increase in grain and livestock production in each socialist country'. The application without modification of Soviet forms of agricultural organisation had been introduced early into the Eastern European countryside, often with more emphasis on the ideological aspect than on the farming aspects. While collectivisation may have appeared suited to the conditions of Tsarist Russia, it was not necessarily as equally appropriate among the small or medium-sized farms of areas like Bohemia or central Germany. It was, however, reasonably well-suited to the undercapitalised countries like Bulgaria and Rumania, though this did not avoid resistance from the peasants. In trying to rectify the early mistakes of collectivisation without sufficient adaptation to local conditions, a series of widely divergent systems has evolved and change still seems the order of the day.

The growth of industry in the Eastern European countries and the process of agricultural reorganisation has produced changes similar to trends in Western Europe. There has been a marked rural exodus. Part-time farming has expanded and farming has been made more capital intensive by application of science and technology, while rural living standards have generally improved—perhaps relatively more so in Eastern Europe than in Western Europe. There has been in Eastern Europe a major change in the status of the rural farm population. The rural proletariat in countries such as Hungary were turned by the first post-war land reforms into small independent family farmers as a stage towards collectivisation (figure 8.1), which transformed them as a group into wage labourers, though in some countries like Poland and Jugoslavia, a considerable element of the independent small farmer has been preserved by the halting of collectivisation. The migration of peasants to the towns has been an important part of the process of industrialisation by providing an occupationally and educationally mobile element. Collectivisation by promoting migration from the countryside has destroyed the basis of peasant farming not only in organisational terms but also in demographic terms. Inspite of the official statistics, collectivisation in any of its forms remains markedly incomplete because of the large but largely unrecorded contribution of the private plots of farmers and industrial workers. The result of these changes cannot be missed in the countryside, in the rearrangement of field boundaries, particularly the disappearance of strip farming and its replacement by large rectangular fields. New barns and buildings can be seen in most villages, while some villages—as in parts of Czechoslovakia and the German Democratic Republic—have undergone a complete transformation. Remains of deserted hamlets often reflect the drift from the countryside or the movement into the larger villages with their better facilities.

8.3.2 Industrialisation

Feverish industrialisation has been characteristic of the Eastern European people's democracies since 1945, absorbing a major part of national investment and receiving a high priority in national plans. There has been a strong Marxist–Leninist ideological content to the locational patterns, influenced by Soviet concepts developed in the inter-war years and modified since the mid-1950s by a more polycentric interpretation of Communist dogmata. Industrial developments have been a prime factor in the spatial change in the economic geography and landscape of Eastern Europe. As the objectives of Marxist–Leninist philosophy aim at a different spatial interpretation of man's activities compared to capitalism, it is to be expected that industrial location patterns will continue to change in form and dimension. While much of the

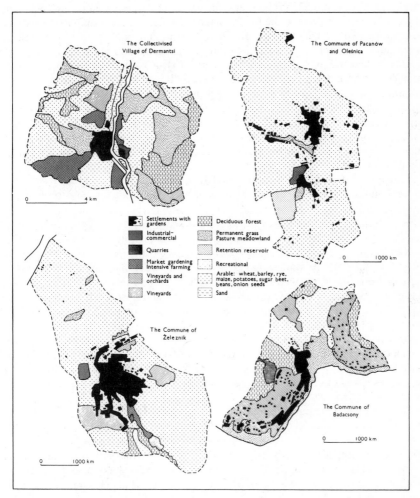

Figure 8.1 Four examples of collectivised agricultural enterprises in Eastern Europe reflect the great diversity that exists. Based on examples mapped in 'Land utilisation in Eastern Europe', *Geographica Polonica*, **5**, (1965) and 'Land utilisation in Eastern Europe', *Hungarian Studies in Geography*, **4**, (1967).

theory and practice has been from Soviet experience, it is unlikely that decisions made in Eastern Europe have been identical with similar situations in the Soviet Union and there has been a trend towards a greater diversity through adjustment to national contexts—the outcome of tolerated polycentrism—a principle recognised in the formulation of the international socialist division of labour.

Employment in industry in the area of the present Eastern European people's democracies before 1935 probably accounted for only about 15 per cent of the 55 million working people. About 85 per cent of the total industry was located in the area that is now the German Democratic Republic, Poland and Czechoslovakia. Some three-quarters of the total industry was in the triangular area encompassed by Thüringen and the Saxon and Silesian lands on the north, Bohemia in the centre and the northern part of Hungary, including Budapest, on the south, within which had lain all the locational and resource conditions necessary to establish nineteenth century industrialisation of the 'coal-iron' cycle. Elsewhere in East Central and South-eastern Europe, industry found competition with this Central European concentration difficult unless there were local advantages or intense government protection. Even in East Central and South-eastern Europe—once described as 'Agricultural Europe'—industry occurred in marked nodular concentrations. During the inter-war period, the economic nationalism that characterised the European scene helped to create industry in the under-industrialised countries of South-eastern Europe, but it was not outstandingly successful.

The inter-war industrial structure had, however, suffered very much from wartime damage or neglect, so that at the onset of Socialism the position was far from healthy. War damage had been particularly heavy in the German Democratic Republic, Poland and Czechoslovakia, while plants in the German Democratic Republic were dismantled for reparations. Population expulsion in Poland and Czechoslovakia had seriously depleted the industrial labour force, which could only be made good by the slow process of training new workers drawn from the countryside. In South-eastern Europe there was a remarkably rapid increase in industrial population as mining and unsophisticated manufacturing industries were established, whereas in the north a slower rehabilitation took place of the more complex and sophisticated industries. Nevertheless, in the long run the production performance of the northern states—the German Democratic Republic, Poland and Czechoslovakia—has been better. In South-eastern Europe, a large surplus of rural labour as a result of changes in agriculture was often a substitute for capital and allowed rapid absorption in the simpler industrial branches.

The pre-war triangular industrial concentration remains a marked feature, though its share of total industry has sunk to about a half. There has, however, been a conflicting trend in industrial development between centripetal and centrifugal location. The centripetal tendencies have been marked by concentration of new capacity in existing industrial areas, usually the result of modernising pre-war plants or by building entirely new plants. There has also been the relocation and concentration of small plants into larger units to give economies of scale. The more common trend has been for centrifugal location, reflected by industrial dispersion to follow Marxist–Leninist elimination of the differences in standards between town and country and equalisation of regional development. This probably accounts for the lack of special policies for backward or depressed regions, such as figure in the policy of the European Economic Community. Dispersion has tended to be greatest in the more underdeveloped areas where industrial development has taken place from an overall 'green field' situation rather than in the more developed countries where the attraction of existing infrastructures and the factors once termed 'industrial inertia' are operative. In backward areas mining or energy generation or industries to tap large resources of underutilised labour have been important factors in dispersion. A rather special situation—reflecting both trends—arises in the development of regional growth points in the underindustrialised regions, notably for example in parts of central or eastern Poland.

There is the initial relationship between industrial location and regional development in terms of regional specialisation and regional self-sufficiency, so that new industrial developments can usually be found to serve one or other of these superficially apparently paradoxical ideas. These concepts are also a matter of scale within Comecon at either international or intranational level. There is also the aim of an even spread of industry as part of an even spread of regional development. At an international level, however, there is often a reluctance on the part of the richer and better developed countries to encourage this trend because of losing advantages in trade with underdeveloped areas. The idea also reflects such sentiments within countries—in Jugoslavia, the reluctance of Croatia and Slovenia to sacrifice their advantages for the benefit of the less developed regions such as Montenegro or Bosnia–Hercegovina.

Although the problem of distance is not so critical in Eastern Europe as it is in the Soviet Union, the attempts to eliminate non-productive investment have produced the search to reduce transport effort. There has thus been a tendency to locate 'weight-losing' industries towards their raw material sources, either as further growth in coalfields, for example, or development in new areas of mineral exploitation—in the Lusatian lignite fields or in southern Poland for copper and sulphur. This has been a particularly marked feature of the less developed areas where basic materials-orientated industries have been the vanguard of industrial development. Likewise, industries manufacturing for the consumer have been located near to their markets, though characteristic of Soviet views, production rather than consumption has always been stressed, while centrally planned operations and the ability to manipulate prices have helped in directing and quantifying consumption without the problem of competition. This approach may have to be changed as moves are made towards the 'market economy' in which market potential becomes an important factor. In the growth point technique, the Soviet *Kombinat*[1] has been used—a full cycle of vertically integrated industry ranging from the conversion of raw materials to finished products, particularly where raw materials sources and markets overlap. As large-scale *Kombinaty* both the central German chemicals industry and the closely interrelated mining, iron and steel, chemicals and engineering industries of Upper Silesia form examples. The defence aspect has influenced dispersion of

---

[1] *Kombinat*; a Soviet industrial unit originally designed as a self-contained, full cycle of vertically integrated industries in the underdeveloped parts of Siberia and Central Asia. The concept has been applied in Eastern Europe to integrated industrial regions with marked specialisation in fields such as chemicals, iron and steel manufacture, and coal-mining.

key strategic industries, while the mining of uranium ores has produced distinct development in the German–Czech borderland around Aue and Jáchymov.

The major location problems of industry have, however, been markedly different between the Eastern European countries and the 'principles' outlined above have been applied in varying interpretations, though in most countries it is possible to see a dichotomous search for wide dispersion of industry and at the same time the further development of existing agglomerations. The main contrasts are between the more industrialised countries—the German Democratic Republic, Poland and Czechoslovakia—where in general direct Soviet applications have been limited and those countries where rapid industrialisation has been carried through, often with very considerable Soviet help. In each country, a change in practice can usually be seen as a result of the switch from the emphasis on autarky to the more liberal attitudes of the international socialist division of labour, which in itself has created a number of problems in industrial location arising from a clash between intranational and international needs.

8.3.3 Urbanisation

A noticeable impact of Soviet ideas in Eastern Europe has been in the towns where there has been a substantial growth of population, particularly in the more rapidly industrialising countries. The attraction of country people into industry in the towns has been suggested as one reason why new ideas of town design and function could be introduced reasonably easily. The growth of new towns has been the outcome of the growth of industry, often with entirely new towns on green field sites. New towns have, however, not always grown in rural areas: in Poland most new towns have been in the peripheries of the Upper Silesian industrial area, but a notable concentration lies in the emergent industrial region of central Poland. In the German Democratic Republic, new towns have grown in the new lignite mining areas of Lusatia, often in association with older communities but also in the Elbe–Saale industrial districts. The best examples of the new socialist towns are those erected on green field sites in association with major industrial developments—Nowa Huta (Poland), Dunaújváros (Hungary), Eisenhüttenstadt and Schwedt (German Democratic Republic).

Industrial location theories and practices have also influenced the development of existing towns: in the German Democratic Republic, dispersion of industry has been an important factor in the growth of small and medium-sized towns, particularly in the Baltic coast, the Oder valley and the Lusatian lignite field, though in Saxony some of the small and medium-sized towns have stagnated or fallen below their pre-war level as old industries have declined (notably in areas where lignite has been worked out). The largest towns have been slow to recover their pre-war populations, possibly because of some reluctance to invest money in their reconstruction in preference to more 'productive' branches of the economy.

In the less developed countries the small market towns have often provided the foci for new industrial developments—as, for example, in Rumania. Villages have also been turned into towns, especially where large projects have been planned, so that three small villages are now the site of the new town of Dimitrovgrad (population over 40 000) in Bulgaria. In Hungary industrialisation of the large town-like Puszta villages has been the basis of new towns, such as Törökszent-miklós, Szarvas and Orosháza, and has prevented massive migration into the Budapest area. The widespread policy of industrial dispersion has brought a steady growth in the small and medium-sized towns or the formation of new towns, while avoiding the growth of massive conurbations as found in Western Europe. In most Eastern European countries the 'primate' city dominates the urban scene (notably in Hungary, Rumania and in Czechoslovakia) in demographic and industrial terms. The trend in the countryside has, however, been to bring the village more into line with the quality of life in the towns, partly through the reorganisation of the farming system. In the 'equalisation' sought by Socialist philosophy, there is already a perceptible trend towards an urbanised society.

8.3.4 Labour Mobility

Labour in the European Economic Community has been growing more mobile, with considerable international flows, notably of 'guest workers' to the Federal German Republic. Even under the socialist international division of labour, labour migration still offends against the ideas of sovereignty and the 'national principle', so that materials and investment are more likely to migrate than labour. Labour has, however, not been a scarce commodity in most countries and large pools of under-employed or even displaced rural labour after collectivisation have been available, though shortage of labour has been a real problem in a structural sense, arising from an inadequate cadre of skilled, industrial labour and management. 'Full employment' is an important principle of the socialist economic system and in order to fulfil this command, labour is often preferable to mechanisation. Nevertheless, the labour situation in each country has been affected by the overall demographic situation, but it has usually exercised some influence over the process of industrialisation.

The German Democratic Republic had from the outset a strong pool of skilled labour and management, swollen by urban-industrial refugees from Silesia and the Sudetenland. The outflow of people, particularly in the younger, economically and demographically more productive age groups, to West Germany up to 1961 had a considerable impact on the labour force. This has been marked by a higher average age among workers than in West Germany and by a higher proportion of female labour. In 1970 nearly half the employed population was female compared to 35 per cent in West Germany. With the natural increase tending to decline, small labour classes may be expected for many years ahead. Workers from other Comecon countries have been employed only on a limited and specialised scale, inspite of reports to the contrary. Labour shortage has encouraged a search for economy, with a keen interest in automation, and attempts to carry out labour intensive operations in other Comecon countries using German components (for example in the assembly of light engineering and electronics products).

The flight and expulsion of the German industrial population from Silesia left Poland with a serious structural labour problem. It was eased a little by the creation of the concept of 'autochthonous' population in Upper Silesia to retain German workers. The resettlement of the annexed territories was achieved with people from the rurally overpopulated central and southern Poland or with Poles from territories taken by the Soviet Union. These essentially country folk required training in industrial skills as well as help with adjustment to urban life. Readjustment for many was so painful that they preferred to return to the rurally depressed areas from which they had come, leaving a continuing labour deficit in the industrial towns. A factor in the dispersion of industry was the creation of industrial occupations in rurally depressed areas in the hope of avoiding some of the readjustment difficulties that beset resettlement. Another aspect of the Polish structural labour crisis was the wartime losses of the leading professional and managerial classes (strongly Jewish), so that educational programmes were of exceptional importance.

The Polish situation had some points of similarity with problems faced in Czechoslovakia, though the loss of German population was perhaps less critical as there had been a considerable Czech industrial population before the war. The most serious loss was in the most highly skilled industries, such as glass-making and artificial jewellery production. With little surplus labour in the Czech lands, Slovaks and Gypsies were resettled in former German areas, though industrial plant from these areas was also moved into Slovakia in an attempt to improve Slovakia's industrial base. Czechoslovakia had had some experience in rapid training of rural labour for industrial occupations through the pre-war development of the vast Bat'a shoe plants at Zlín (Gottwaldov). Slovakia's position was only modestly affected by the loss of German and Magyar elements, though these had been in part a professional and managerial group, but far less important than the Sudeten Germans in Bohemia. Some 10 000 Jugoslavs are to be recruited to overcome the continuing labour shortage.

In the rapid post-war reconstruction in Jugoslavia full employment was easily attained, even though there was a large fund of labour in the rural overpopulated areas of the south, by the substitution of labour for capital since much unskilled labour was required. During the 1950s there was an increasing movement from agriculture into non-agricultural work and an absolute reduction in the number of farm workers, though a 'real' surplus of about 1.4 million agricultural workers remains. The movement into towns has been accompanied by a rise in unemployment, chiefly among unskilled workers, and it would be worse if it were not for the migration of over 300 000 workers to other countries (notably Western Germany). Unemployment has been the highest in the more backward areas—Macedonia, Kosmet, Serbia and Montenegro; more modest levels occur in the Vojvodina, Croatia and Bosnia and a low rate in Slovenia. The employment situation has deteriorated through attempts to improve the productivity of industry. Increased prices for farm products have been attempted as a means of holding more people in the countryside. There has been a failure as a result of the polycentric planning system to provide adequate employment openings in the more backward areas of highest unemployment, where there were inadequate labour-intensive projects until the mid-1960s. In the northern parts of the country, there is a deficit of skilled labour and a gross surplus of unskilled workers in the south, but there is no adequate national policy to rectify the position because of the strength of national feelings among the constituent republics.

Slow growth of the labour force in Hungary has created an overall national shortage. The main problem is to keep people in the provinces and prevent migration to the already crowded northern industrial districts, particularly Budapest, so that the establishment of new industry has been directed at the Puszta towns where underemployed population has been greatest and where reorganisation of agriculture has created a need for alternative employment. Immediately after the war, land reform had given landless peasants small holdings that absorbed agricultural manpower, but in the early 1950s collectivisation put many of these people back into the labour market to be absorbed by industrialisation. A considerable portion of the new industry established was in the labour intensive sectors of light industry to absorb semiskilled and unskilled labour in rural areas and female labour (because of a large demand for jobs from women to augment family incomes) in industrial areas. The upsurge after the liberalisation of the economy in 1968 has produced an overall labour shortage, and consequently, Hungarian planners have sought modernisation programmes, notably in the capital goods industries and in agriculture, to release more labour.

In Rumania and Bulgaria the problem of labour has been one of quality as much as quantity. Both countries began industrialisation with a substantial pool of rural labour but with virtually no skilled cadres. Their main problem has been to plan industrial growth at a rate that will not outstretch the speed with which the pool of skilled manpower—technologists and managers—can be developed. In Bulgaria though the labour force has grown at a rate great enough to allow the numbers employed in agriculture to increase, the share of agriculture in the total labour force has fallen drastically—from nearly 82 per cent in 1948 to 37 per cent in 1969. The movement from country to town was so extensive that a real shortage of agricultural labour developed at a stage before mechanisation could be effectively used in the countryside.

International labour mobility has been very low and largely restricted to specialists and workers sent to other Comecon members to erect plants or to develop new techniques. Thus German specialists have assisted industrial development in Bulgaria, while Bulgarians have worked and trained in East Germany, Czechoslovakia and the Soviet Union. Most countries have sent specialists and workers to the U.S.S.R., particularly to the Soviet atomic research and development centre at Dubna near Moscow. Countries with labour deficiencies have not sought to attract workers from neighbours with surplus labour, though clearly Marxist–Leninist views on full employment and the national principle are a hindrance to true mobility. Rumours of 'guest workers' in the German Democratic Republic from other Comecon countries in the early 1960s proved as unreliable as the reports of thousands of 'Chinese' settling in Upper Silesia in 1945–6. Personal movements between Comecon countries are more restricted than similar movements in Western Europe. Tourism is beginning to develop, with large numbers of East Germans vacationing in Carpathia, Lake Balaton and the Black Sea resorts, while some spas such as Karlovy Vary have an international clientele. Usually movement is in parties and 'delegations', while considerable flows of officials take place between the industrial and political centres. Travel to the non-Socialist world has been made difficult by financial restrictions and other formalities, though a considerable movement has begun to develop since the latter 1960s. On the other hand Western tourists and visitors are welcome on the hosts' terms in most Comecon countries as a source of hard currency. Jugoslavia is an exception in allowing a remarkably free movement of its own nationals into Western Europe and in having developed a successful tourist industry in the Adriatic littoral.

9 Sketches of National Economic Geographies: the Developed Countries

The countries of Eastern Europe vary considerably not only in population and area but also in natural endowment and in the stage of economic development. None of them has any great wealth, but they have nevertheless considerable economic potential which has yet to be really effectively utilised. From pursuing their own widely divergent national policies, they have been drawn into the application of Marxist–Leninist concepts which have tended to reduce the contrasts between them, though in recent years national interpretations have begun again to distinguish them. Collectively, they are a formidable combination and are to a considerable degree complementary to one another. With the exceptions of Jugoslavia and Albania, these nations have been tied tightly to the Soviet Union through Comecon. The orientation of their trade and political contacts to the Soviet Union has been a reversal of pre-1945 orientations and has occasioned considerable painful readjustment.

The more advanced and industrialised group comprises the German Democratic Republic, Czechoslovakia and more marginally Poland and Hungary, where agriculture still plays an important if diminishing part in the economy. The advancing and industrialising group consists of Rumania and Bulgaria and the two 'outsiders', Jugoslavia and Albania. The more advanced, industrialised countries and those with natural endowments deficient in the U.S.S.R. have been most favoured generally in Soviet dealings.

9.1. German Democratic Republic

Economically one of the most advanced parts of Eastern Europe, the German Democratic Republic, formed out of the original Soviet Occupation Zone, has been tied closely to the Soviet Union both politically and economically. Several features of its economic geography arise from the way in which its territory was carved arbitrarily from the body of defeated Germany in 1945. As the occupation zones were to have been an administrative convenience and Germany was to have been regarded as a whole, both politically and economically, by the four victorious powers, no special attention was given to territorial definition of the zones nor to the economic problems that might arise for them.

A particular problem in economic geography has arisen from the division into occupation sectors of the city of Berlin, which had had a pre-war population of over four million. Although the original intention was to administer it as a unit under four-power control, within three years of the end of the war, political disagreement between the Allied powers had brought such administration effectively to an end. In addition to West Berlin as an isolated enclave cutting across a sophisticated urban economic landscape, the western boundary of the Republic also cuts across a well-developed economic landscape, isolating central Germany from its major pre-war outlet in the port of Hamburg. The creation of a new and arbitrarily defined boundary in the east and the annexation of the port of Stettin (Szczecin) by Poland cut central Germany from its old relations with the Silesian lands and the Baltic. A further economic problem was created by the difficulties of resettlement and integration of several million refugees. Although the Soviet Zone had not suffered the same destruction from air attacks as Western Germany, the refugee problem was made more difficult by the political necessity of not appearing to treat them differently from local people.

The Soviet administration interpreted the reparations agreements liberally and in several branches of industry, poorly represented or badly damaged in the Soviet Union, three-quarters of the capacity or more in their occupation zone was dismantled. Contrary to Allied agreements, some remaining factories were used to produce for reparations; it had been agreed that reparations would only be removed from capital installations (factories, machinery, power stations and so on) and not from current production. Large sections of industry were nationalised or made into Soviet companies and production organised for Soviet requirements. Because of the breakdown of monetary and trading mechanisms and a Soviet reluctance to reconstitute them, it was difficult to rehabilitate damaged plants or to buy goods from outside the Zone.

There was also a drastic land reform in which all holdings over 100 ha were confiscated without payment, so that 2.5 million ha were available for redistribution, as well as certain other sequestered lands. Of this land 2.1 million ha were given to 119 000 landless peasants and workers, 83 000 'resettlers' and 113 000 poor peasants. A considerable amount was retained by various state agencies. Many recipients of land got only dwarf holdings and were unable to make a satisfactory existence. In 1952 these people formed the vanguard of collectivisation, while confiscated estates were commonly made into state farms. Land reform was less disruptive in the north where big estates were more common than in the south, whose small and medium farmers suffered particularly heavily under collectivisation.

The effect of land reform and the stagnation of industry as well as strong political pressures, resulted in a steady flight of people to West Germany, where living standards rose quickly after the 1948 currency reform. Migration fluctuated, with peaks when there were new and unpalatable measures. As migrants were mostly young people in the economically and demographically most productive age groups, it has left an imbalance of older people and affected the pattern of natural increase. In the twenty years from 1949 over 2.9 million people left for West Germany, but the flow was virtually stopped after 1961, when the situation had reached crisis proportions. The impact on the labour force has left the Republic with one of its most serious economic problems.

9.1.1 Industry in the GDR (figure 9.1)

In the inter-war years particularly during the Nazi economic plans, *Mitteldeutschland*, the greater part of which now formed the German Democratic Republic, had been the scene of major industrial developments in the chemicals industry, with which had been linked the growth of a large-scale

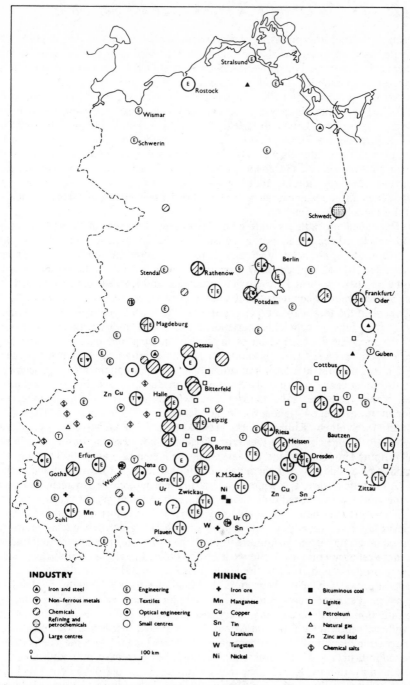

INDUSTRY

- ▲ Iron and steel
- ▼ Non-ferrous metals
- ⬘ Chemicals
- Refining and petrochemicals
- ◯ Large centres

- Ⓔ Engineering
- Ⓣ Textiles
- ◉ Optical engineering
- ○ Small centres

0   100 km

MINING

- ✛ Iron ore
- Mn Manganese
- Cu Copper
- Sn Tin
- Ur Uranium
- W Tungsten
- Ni Nickel

- ■ Bituminous coal
- ▫ Lignite
- ▲ Petroleum
- △ Natural gas
- Zn Zinc and lead
- ⬥ Chemical salts

Figure 9.1. Industry in the German Democratic Republic is concentrated in the south, notably around the important lignite deposits. More recent development has taken place on the Baltic coast and the lower Oder.

electricity generating industry. The resource bases were the rich deposits of lignite, used as a fuel for the power stations as well as a raw material in the chemicals industry, and copious deposits of mineral salts around the Harz fringes. The lignite lay in thick seams comparatively near the surface and could be worked by open-cast methods using large scale machinery. As lignite does not transport well, the big power stations were built close to the mines, such as Böhlen–Espenhain, Leuna, Bitterfeld, Zschornewitz and Trattendorf, though the big Klingenberg power station in Berlin was fired with short rail-hauled fuel. Supplies of raw materials were also brought by water up the Elbe and by canal from the Rhine basin. The chemicals plants are voracious consumers of electric current, which constitutes about 40 per cent of total costs in some instances, while they also consume large quantities of process water, drawn from the rivers of the Elbe–Saale basin.

The chemicals industry suffered comparatively little wartime damage, but it had developed the production of substances such as synthetic petrol, oils and rubber quite apart from other chemicals, considered primarily of a military character. It was consequently dismantled with a ruthless thoroughness but some plants were turned into Soviet companies and worked solely for export to the Soviet Union: when these companies were dissolved in late 1952 they held 52 per cent of the total capacity. Comparatively well-endowed with raw materials and with a fund of technical experience, the chemicals industry has become one of the most significant industries in the Soviet bloc and has been feverishly developed since the 'chemicalisation' programme introduced by Khrushchev in 1959. It is the second most important industry in the Republic after engineering, contributing nearly a fifth of total industrial production. Over half the total output comes from the Halle–Leipzig area, where five extremely large concerns dominate the scene—Leuna Works at Merseburg, Electrochemicals Combine Bitterfeld, Synthetic Rubber Works at Schkopau, the Wolfen dye works and the synthetic nitrogen works at Piesteritz. Together they account for 40 per cent of all output. The Leuna plant, the largest in the Republic, has 30 000 employees producing a wide range of chemicals. The industrial structure owes much to the *I. G. Farbenindustrie*, a vast pre-war trust that encouraged development here and some works were opened only shortly before the Second World War.

The chemicals industry is likely to develop further as more attention is given to plastics, whose expansion will depend on the rising petrochemicals industry based on crude petroleum imports through the Friendship pipeline terminating at a large refinery complex at Schwedt on the Oder. From this complex pipelines carry products and crude to the Halle–Leipzig area. Plans are also under consideration for a pipeline from an oil terminal at Rostock handling 35 000-ton tankers. Petrochemicals require less manpower and electricity per unit of production than the traditional acetylene-based chemicals. The manufacture of synthetic petroleum will be phased out. It is expected that lignite will cease to be the predominant base for the chemicals industry, which will become a petroleum-based industry. It is unfortunate that resources of petroleum and natural gas so far found within the Republic have been limited. Small petroleum deposits have been located in the north near Greifswald, near Magdeburg and near Cottbus, and there is natural gas north-west of Erfurt. Using increased imports, notably of Soviet apatite, the sulphuric acid industry, poorly represented before 1945, has been greatly expanded. Longer term Comecon plans foresee the German Democratic Republic as the main producer of synthetic fertilisers (particularly based on potash), plastics, silicones and synthetic rubber, while it has already become a major producer of pharmaceuticals.

In the southern uplands of the Republic there has been a long tradition of metal working and mining. The mining of metals succumbed to such long conflicts as the Thirty Years' War and to competition from more favoured areas, while exhaustion under technological conditions of the time forced other sources of income to be developed during the eighteenth and nineteenth centuries. Iron ore deposits are small, the iron content low and the geological conditions difficult. Even so, deposits in the Harz, the Erzgebirge and the Thüringer Wald had some local importance. Since the early 1950s iron mining has again been expanded, but even including other iron-bearing materials, such as byproducts from the chemicals industry, only about a fifth of the Republic's needs are covered. Permian sedimentary deposits are the main source of copper and the principal areas are south-east of the Harz, around Mansfeld and Sangershausen, where some ores contain up to 3 per cent copper. Lead and zinc, near Freiberg and Mansfeld, were closely related in the past to silver mining. Mining had died away in the early part of the twentieth century, but was renewed for strategic reasons in the 1930s and has continued since 1945. Of particular importance has been tin ore, often enriched by a combination of wolfram, molybdenum, lithium and other ores, and mining has been intensified, principally at Ehrenfriedersdorf and Geyer in the central Erzgebirge and at Altenberg, the most important producer, in the eastern Erzgebirge. In 1967 a special trace metals plant was opened in Freiberg to extract the rarer metals from the ores worked at Freiberg and Mansfeld. The Freiberg tin plant produces about 400 tons of pure tin and 1500 tons of lead–tin alloy annually.

With the large quantities of electric current available, the central German area had become a major producer of aluminium from Hungarian and other ores before the Second World War. Hungarian bauxite is converted to alumina at Lauta and both this town and Bitterfeld are aluminium producers. Cryolite is synthesised at the fluorspar plant at Dohna. Magnesium is imported from the Soviet Union, but it is intended by the 1980s to produce magnesium substances, based on byproducts of the potash industry.

Massive reserves of lignite (brown coal) make the country one of the world's largest producers. Though atomic energy, petroleum and natural gas will become more significant, brown coal will remain important for long into the future. The fields are grouped east and west of the Elbe, with a total extent of 563 000 ha, of which 300 000 ha are considered at present worth exploitation. Of the workable reserves 92 per cent are accessible to open-cast working. The main development of the brown coalfields came in the second half of the nineteenth century and grew substantially in the inter-war period. By the early 1950s production was twice the level of the late 1930s, but since maximum output in 1964 there has been a slight contraction with the growth of other fuels. The long-term aim is to concentrate the use of brown coal in the generation of electricity. Costs have tended to rise as the deeper layers of coal have been worked, though shaft mining has stopped. Immediately after the war, efforts were concentrated in the West Elbian fields, where output could be increased most rapidly, but since the early 1950s the rate of development has quickened most appreciably in the East Elbian fields, where the best long-term prospects now lie.

In the northern foreland of the Harz the development in the Harbke district has not been expanded, though considerable reserves remain. Briquette-making has been important, but in future most will be used in electricity generation. The shaft mining around Köthen has been stopped. In the early 1960s one of the most important areas was around Bitterfeld and its expansion to the south is expected. The coal is mostly used for generating electric current for the chemicals industry, though briquette-making remains important. A major mining area lies around Halle (Saale) especially in the Geiseltal, but its reserves are limited. The emphasis is on use in power stations, which in future will use increasing amounts of the more saline coals. Around Zeitz–Weissenfels brown coal is used mostly for distillation and carbonisation, but these branches will close by the late 1970s. The mines around Borna and Meuselwitz have been greatly expanded since 1945. Large plants in Böhlen and Espenhain distil and carbonise suitable brown coal. In the East Elbian fields mainly in the *Bezirk* Cottbus, there has been a considerable development of electricity generation and other processing plants, though the proportion used in briquette-making has declined. By the end of the 1950s mining near Frankfurt an der Oder ceased, but a new field has been opened near Zittau to supply power stations which also draw coal from the Polish Turów mines.

Only a fraction of the bituminous coal deposits are worth working, mostly around Zwickau, Lugau and Ölsnitz, though big reserves are known at great depth west of Finsterwalde. Pre-war, bituminous coal was brought from West German or Silesian fields (for which the Klingenberg power station was designed). In 1951 output was 3 million tons, but this fell as workable reserves dwindled and in the late 1960s was below 2 million tons. About 12 million tons are required annually, now drawn chiefly from Poland and the Soviet Union. Mining is expected to cease in the early 1970s, but the mining towns will continue to process imported coals.

With such an endowment of raw materials it is perhaps not surprising that no large scale iron and steel industry had grown up in central Germany. Although in pre-war times 32 per cent of total German population lived in the German Democratic Republic, it produced only 7 per cent of *Reich* iron and steel output. There was relatively little wartime damage, but dismantling for reparations was severe—85 per cent of raw steel capacity, 80 per cent of steel castings and a large part of the foundry and tempering branches. After the establishment of the new Republic, under the prevailing ideas of autarky, the development of a major iron and steel industry began, inspite of difficulties over equipment and raw materials. Pig iron is made at the eastern *Kombinat* at Eisenhüttenstadt (60 per cent), *Maxhütte* at Unterwellenborn near Saalfeld (25 per cent), and the western *Kombinat* at Calbe (15 per cent). The two *Kombinate* are products of post-war planning, but the *Maxhütte* is a modernised pre-war plant. The plant at Calbe has specially designed furnaces intended originally to use coke made from brown coal, but this was not successful. About 95 per cent of the ore is imported, while most coal and coke is from Poland and Czechoslovakia. These plants depend largely on rail-hauled raw materials, though the Eisenhüttenstadt works receives shipments along the Oder.

Steel-making, from home or imported pig and scrap of various origins, is more widespread, but most works are on pre-war sites. Scrap is the principal raw material, used cold with consequent heavy consumption of energy. The *Maxhütte* also makes steel and has rolling mills. While Eisenhüttenstadt sends its raw pig iron mostly to Brandenburg and Riesa, it has already started cold rolling (to be expanded) and steel-making. The Freital, Henningsdorf and Riesa works concentrate on special and quality steels, while Brandenburg and Gröditz are producers of standard ordinary quality steels. There are also several small rolling plants, mostly with a high degree of specialisation.

Engineering, accounting for a quarter of the total labour force and a similar proportion of total gross output, contributes just over half the exports by value. Engineering is found in most towns, particularly in the Saxon and Thüringen districts. Machine tools are a major branch, notably around Karl-Marx-Stadt, Leipzig and Berlin, but other centres are Plauen, Gera and Meuselwitz, as well as Aschersleben, Erfurt and Freital. Berlin, Ludwigsfelde, Halle, Görlitz, Gera and Meerane produce energy generating equipment (for example steam turbines), and hydroturbines are made in Meissen. Mining and heavy industrial equipment is made for the whole Comecon market in Leipzig and Magdeburg, with brown coal-mining machinery of special importance in the mining districts (Lauchhammer, Köthen and Leipzig) and Zeitz specialises in briquetting machines. One of the main Comecon suppliers of cement-making machinery is Dessau. Heavy machinery has shown the most substantial growth since the early 1950s, in part to correct the Republic's imbalance and in part to respond to Comecon needs.

There has been a substantial growth, particularly since the 1950s, in the manufactures of agricultural machinery, with the intensified mechanisation of farming. Before the war the Reich had a much more highly developed industry in this sector than other Comecon countries, but only about a fifth of the capacity was on the territory of the German Democratic Republic. The principal plants are in Saxony and Thüringen. One of the largest concerns in Europe is a group of seven interrelated plants in the Dresden area and near Bautzen, while the Weimar mowing and reaping-machinery works is also large. Along with works for tilling machinery and ploughs at Leipzig, these three groups produce almost two-thirds of the total output. Many of the works are highly specialised—the Elsterwerda milking machine works, the drill works at Bernburg, the grain cleaning and storing works near Eisenach, while near Stralsund is a works for manure spreaders. The one-time railway plant at Gotha makes parts for agricultural machinery works, including the tractor works at Nordhausen.

Eighty per cent of textile machinery is made in the textile districts of Saxony and eastern Thüringen, particularly Karl-Marx-Stadt, which exports 60–80 per cent of its production. There is a sewing machine works at Wittenberge and a plant for hatting machinery at Guben.

About 30 per cent of the pre-war German motor vehicle building capacity and 14 per cent of the components industry were in the present area of the German Democratic Republic. The reconstruction after wartime damage and reparations made the development of components important—pre-war, 98 per cent of sparking plugs had been made in West Germany, as well as 75 per cent of generators and starters and over 90 per cent of tyres and rubber parts. The largest lorry works are at Zwickau and Zittau and a smaller plant at Karl-Marx-Stadt. Motor cars are made at Eisenach and Zwickau, with motor cycles at Zschopau and Suhl. Tractors are made at Nordhausen, Brandenburg and Schönebeck. Under the Comecon specialisation agreements, the industry is to concentrate on medium and light lorries, small motor cars and two-stroke motor cycles (a pre-war speciality). A joint motor-car plant with Czechoslovakia is planned. Between 30 and 40 per cent of production is exported. Compared to the pre-war market in the Reich, demand for railway equipment is now reduced. Locomotive works have turned to diesel and electric locomotives. Important works are Halle, Erfurt and Berlin (Hennigsdorf and Babelsberg). Wagons and coaches are built for the Comecon market (notably Halle–Ammendorf). Dessau builds refrigerator trains. Shipbuilding has greatly expanded, notably at the Neptune Yards at Rostock. Many different sea-going vessels are built, but the Thesen Yard at Wismar builds river boats (mostly for the Soviet Union) and barges are built along the Elbe.

The main electrical engineering centres are Berlin, Karl-Marx-Stadt and the Dresden district. Berlin has been one of the major German centres for a long period, with a wide range of heavy and light goods. Electric motors are made in a group of towns south-east of Magdeburg, while heavy motors and generators are produced by the Dresden *Sachsenwerk*. Berlin, Dresden, Rochlitz and Stassfurt are important for radios and television sets. A semiconductor works has opened at Frankfurt (Oder) and electronic equipment is made in Teltow. A comparatively small branch of industry of unusual importance is the precision engineering and optical goods section. Several of its members are world famous, such as *Zeiss* (Jena). Rathenow is noted for its optical instruments, while Dresden produces optical glass and cameras. Typewriters and adding machines are made in *Bezirk* Erfurt and also around Karl-Marx-Stadt and Dresden. Ruhla and Glashütte make watches and clocks.

With aluminium works at Bitterfeld, Aken and Senftenberg in pre-war times, Dessau was one of the most important centres for aircraft building, while at Peenemünde on the Baltic, the large rocket propulsion research station had been established. At the end of the war nearly all these installations were dismantled and the Soviet Union took particular advantage of German skills in these fields to become the focus of the aerospace industry in Comecon.

The textile industry, the third major industry in the Republic, grew in the nineteenth century on local supplies of wool and flax and imports of cotton, but in the inter-war years there had been a substantial development of artificial fibres during the Nazi search for autarky. The main textile towns are in Saxony, Thüringen and southern Brandenburg, from which came over a third of total pre-war German textile production. Raw material supply was a critical problem in the early post-war period, though now wool and cotton came from trading partners in the Third World (notably Sudan and Egypt), but there has also been a marked expansion in the output of artificial fibres. Of five main cotton textile districts, four are in Saxony—Zittau, Grossenhain-Leipzig, Karl-Marx-Stadt and Plauen. Mühlhausen is the fifth area. As a result of the division of Germany, weaving capacity in the Republic greatly exceeded spinning, corrected by yarn imports and new spinning mills. In response to the market in Comecon and the developing countries, development has been on the coarser and cheaper cloths.

The woollen industry is chiefly in Saxony (Leipzig, Karl-Marx-Stadt, Zwickau and the Vogtland). Plauen is known for its lace, while towns such as Apolda and Karl-Marx-Stadt make stockings and related cloths. In the textile industry a surplus capacity in several branches has resulted in the introduction of 'more important' industries in several towns, though the industry could doubtless contract further if it were adequately modernised.

9.1.2 Agriculture in the GDR (figure 9.2)

Areas of good soils, particularly in the Saxon Börderland or in the Baltic littoral, inspite of a tendency to dryness, were renowned before the Second World War as some of the best farming country in Germany. Even the poorer soils developed on glacial materials in Brandenburg and Mecklenburg were farmed at standards high enough to give yields that compared favourably with other parts of the country. For a wide range of crops, better results were commonly achieved in the present area of the German Democratic Republic than in Western Germany. The land reform of 1945–6 was ruthlessly carried through to sequestrate and divide up the holdings of all owners of 100 ha or more. Resettlement brought in many people incapable of making the best of their new holdings, which in many instances were too small. The new peasant farmers often lacked experience in managing their own farms, had inadequate equipment and other resources, while the management of the Agricultural Co-operatives was inexperienced. Even where large estates had been turned into state farms, management was often politically more reliable than agriculturally efficient.

Between 1949 and 1951, farmers with 20–100 ha were similarly attacked and under strong pressure many withdrew from the land, adding to the flow of refugees to Western Germany. The process of collectivisation began with the creation of Agricultural Production Co-operatives in the early 1950s, of which three grades exist, according to the degree of involvement of the peasants. The ultimate aim is full collective agriculture, similar to the pattern in the Soviet Union. Already over 85 per cent of the agriculturally used area is in the socialised sector. Before 1939 the area of the German Democratic Republic was not self-supporting in foodstuffs, so that the fall in output resulting from organisational changes had to be made good either by imports or by rationing. To avoid the former the latter was chosen and not abandoned until 1959.

Grain cultivation occupies almost half the arable area (figure 9.2), though the proportion is less than pre-war and more of the grain required is now imported, mostly from the Soviet Union. Rye remains important though it is giving way slowly to wheat. It is usually grown not where it gives the best returns but where it is more productive than other crops on poor soils. Particular areas are the rust-coloured forest earths of Brandenburg, in the Prignitz, in the Fläming and in Lower Lusatia, particularly *Bezirk* Cottbus. Wheat, more selective, is found mostly on the dark *loessic* and chernozem-like soils, but it is also grown on brown forest soils in *Bezirk* Erfurt. The south and south-west are therefore the main areas of cultivation, where it is grown along with winter barley. Oats, cultivated less than formerly with the fall in the number of horses, is now important in the higher and cooler areas in the uplands. Winter barley is widely grown

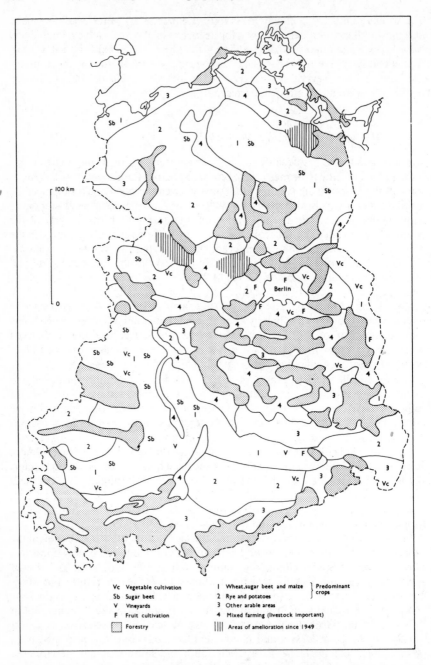

Vc	Vegetable cultivation	I	Wheat, sugar beet and maize	} Predominant
Sb	Sugar beet	2	Rye and potatoes	crops
V	Vineyards	3	Other arable areas	
F	Fruit cultivation	4	Mixed farming (livestock important)	
	Forestry	||||	Areas of amelioration since 1949	

Figure 9.2. The traditional rye and potatoes area of Mecklenburg has seen the introduction of sugar beet, while maize for fodder has become a significant crop in Saxony. By far the most productive areas lie in the south of the German Democratic Republic.

as is summer barley for brewing, which is found mostly in the rain shadow of the Thüringer Wald, and the Erfurt basin is particularly important.

The most important arable crop is potatoes, not only for human consumption but also for fodder and the food industries, while it also fills an important role in the system of rotation. The potato is cultivated widely but grows best on light soils. Potatoes have recently decreased in area—partly because of a nematode plague, partly because of a switch back to grains on some good lands (notably for wheat) and also because of larger areas of sugar beet and other roots. Nevertheless, the potato has become relatively more important on the poorer lands: this is claimed to be a result of a rationalisation of cultivation through the growth of socialised agriculture. Sugar beet is grown on a scale that exceeds home requirements and sugar is also an important export. Its area is relatively small but particularly important in the *Bezirke* Halle and Magdeburg, where almost 45 per cent of the total area lies on the good black earths. Cultivation has been encouraged on the warm brown forest soils of the north, not so well served by sugar factories, though new factories are being built (for example Güstrow). After the war the cultivation of oil seeds was expanded and there was a small expansion in fibre cultivation (hemp and flax). For a time there was also more cultivation of tobacco until supplies were obtained from South-east Europe. A new crop has been hops—grown mostly by 'resettlers' from Czechoslovakia.

Emphasis has been placed on animal production as living standards have risen. Numbers of pigs have been greatly increased, but particular emphasis has been on increasing the proportion of cattle. Nevertheless, over 60 per cent of the meat produced is pigmeat. The northern parts of the Republic, where before 1939 arable cultivation had dominated, have required a large investment programme to raise their output, so that the collectivised small and medium-sized farms of the south are still more important for animal production. Livestock consume about 60 per cent of the arable crop: over half the potato crop goes for pig feed, and the growing of green maize on the Russian model has been encouraged for silage, along with sugar beet tops and other 'waste'. The supply of adequate fodder has, however, been a major hurdle to expanding livestock production. Some encouragement has also been given to increasing numbers of sheep, primarily for wool, one of the rarer commodities of the Comecon countries. The German Democratic Republic has also built up a large deep-sea fishing fleet operating from its Baltic ports (notably Rostock and Sassnitz) to the North and South Atlantic.

The German Democratic Republic is much affected by a problem of water supply and effluent disposal. In the Elbe–Saale basin, the high demand from industry for process water and the problems of disposal of industrial effluent present the greatest difficulties, complicated by the mining of brown coal in opencast pits that adversely affects the ground water table. In 1956 a system of seven water collection regions was instituted and a thirty-year plan projected for the solution of the water supply question. The average yearly precipitation over the Republic amounts to 6×10^{10} m^3, of which $4 \cdot 5 \times 10^{10}$ m^3 are lost by evaporation. Some $1 \cdot 5 \times 10^{10}$ m^3 remain as surface and ground water, available for domestic and industrial use. In a wet year this may double in quantity, but in a dry year it may fall to 6×10^9 m^3. The present consumption amounts to 5×10^9 m^3, 60 per cent of which comes from rivers, roughly 18 per cent from ground water, just over 15 per cent from dams and almost 6 per cent from lakes, while a mere 3 per cent is from springs. Over three-quarters of the water is used by industry and the remainder divided equally between agricultural and domestic use.

While the unused balance of 10^{10} m^3 is adequate for the future, there is much regional imbalance in water supply, with serious supply problems in the major industrial districts, notably in the dry summer months. Particular attention has to be given to the supply to agriculture on the dry *loessic* soils in areas of modest precipitation in the rain shadow of the western hills. The total national water demand by 1985 is reckoned at $1\cdot5 \times 10^{10}$ m^3 (10^{10} m^3 for industry), so consuming the total natural water supply in normal years but with a deficit of up to 9×10^9 m^3 in dry years. Besides providing a much enlarged storage capacity, effective use of industrial water must be ensured, especially for its recycling, with a better distribution through an arterial pipeline system. Large ground water reserves of the Elbaue near Pretzsch and in the Annaburger Heide will be harnessed. Careful planning of future large water-consuming industries such as chemicals and atomic power stations is necessary, but a great amount of investment must be devoted to better waste water purification, including the recovery of fats, acids and albumen, to make effluent fully reusable. For example, the pollution of the Pleisse by waste water from the Böhlen and Espenhain plants is a loss of water supply for two million people.

9.1.3 Transport in the GDR

The Republic has a railway network in which main lines radiate from Berlin to distant provincial centres beyond its boundaries, for it was built for a much wider German horizon. Other than via Berlin, north–south links are poorly developed, while the division of Berlin has left two virtually separate railway systems. Considerable wartime damage was aggravated by Soviet dismantling that reduced route length from 18 500 km to 14 500 km and included complete dismantling of rural cross-country routes in Mecklenburg and Brandenburg, while double track was reduced from 37 per cent to 10 per cent of the route length. Reconstruction of the system since 1954 concentrated on building a ring railway round West Berlin, where the only remaining through line is the international Paris–Warsaw route. Improved connections are also under construction from East Berlin to Rostock. Electrification of the trunk freight routes in Saxony has been carried out, but the pre-war plan to electrify the Munich–Berlin mainline has been dropped in favour of electrification of the Elbe valley route to Prague. Of more than forty railways across the western border, only eight are now used, while disruption was caused by the new eastern border with Poland, so that trains between Görlitz and Zittau are operated across Polish territory by Polish railways and a similar situation exists at Varnsdorf in Bohemia. Conditions were so bad in the late 1940s that a railway journey from Berlin to Dresden took longer than by coach in the eighteenth century. Further new building is unlikely, apart from commuter routes in Saxony, and concentration will be on raising the capacity of the system.

The number of motor vehicles in the German Democratic Republic was decimated by war and fell from 220 000 motor cars, 3 400 buses and 79 000 lorries in 1936 to 41 700 motor cars, 908 buses and 56 200 lorries in 1947. The application of Soviet concepts in transport laid emphasis on railways and waterways rather than roads. Motor transport was seen as purely a feeder to other media or as public transport for goods and passengers in towns. Since the latter 1950s however, road transport has been the fastest growing sector, with the number of persons carried exceeding the railway share in 1962. Particularly important has been opening of bus services to replace abandoned railway branch lines and for commuter traffic.

Inspite of the growth of motor transport, investment in roads has been meagre and the network is virtually the same as in 1938. Most striking has been the lack of extension of the autobahn system, though with some justification, it is claimed that it does not fully meet the needs of the Republic in its alignment. With relatively little long distance road haulage in the German Democratic Republic, it is possibly less important than in West Germany. It is surprising that the Berlin Ring autobahn has not been completed to help traffic circulation avoid the isolated island of West Berlin. It is proposed to build a Berlin–Rostock motorway, however, to serve the country's main port, while it is also proposed to link the autobahn near Magdeburg via Halle to Leipzig and Dresden and to a proposed Czech motorway at Schmilka. Easing of tension with West Germany may also bring reinstatement of the motorway links across the frontier. These proposals were supposed to begin in 1972, though some stretches of new road have been built in the development area of Halle-Neustadt and in Rostock.

The ports of the German Democratic Republic were unimportant pre-war and their hinterlands overshadowed by Hamburg, Stettin and Lübeck. To reduce reliance on West German and Polish ports, port development began after the mid-1950s, but even in the early 1960s over half the Republic's seaborne traffic passed through foreign ports (particularly Hamburg). Wismar was the leading port until the early 1960s, handling ten times the pre-war volume of cargo, and numerous improvements were made. Rostock–Warnemünde has been selected to become the main port and a new deep harbour (including an oil terminal) has been built to handle ships up to 35 000 tons. A new high-capacity railway and motorway link to Berlin and the south is also under construction. It still handles, however, less than a fifth of Hamburg's turnover. The development of Rostock has been unpoplar in Poland, since it has drawn away Hungarian and Czechoslovak traffic from Polish ports. Wismar has also suffered, but it remains an important bulk cargo port. Stralsund is a small port in Baltic trade used mostly by Scandinavian ships. Train ferries operate from Warnemünde to Gedser (Denmark) and from Sassnitz on Rügen to Trelleborg (Sweden).

The German Democratic Republic has emerged as the major industrial country in the Eastern European group, having overtaken Czechoslovakia and drawn further ahead of Poland. It is likely to maintain its lead as the Comecon economic scene becomes more sophisticated, though it is not without problems. Much will depend on how relations with West Germany and the European Economic Community develop.

9.2 Poland

The shift westwards of Polish territory in 1945 presented an entirely new economic geography of much greater potential than pre-war, but it has created serious demographic and organisational problems. Large eastern territories, mostly poor farming country with much forest and bog, were exchanged for a broad western strip of well-developed German territory, the port of Danzig and the southern part of German East Prussia. Poland thus inherited a plethora of ports—Gdańsk, Kolobrzeg and Szczecin to add to its own Gdynia—plus two important coal basins, in Upper Silesia and in Wałbrzych (Waldenburg), as well as other mineral resources in the Silesian lands, where there were also important textile and engineering industries.

By losing large Ukrainian and Byelorussian minorities in the east and driving out the Germans in the new western territories, Poland has become a more truly national state than pre-war, but it meant resettling large numbers of people in un-familiar circumstances in the newly gained lands. The resettlers came either from the territories lost to the Soviet Union or from rurally overpopulated areas of central and southern Poland. These were largely country people, unused to living in towns and working in industry. Replacement of the town-dwelling and in-dustrially employed Germans represented a hurdle that occupied the first fifteen post-war years by a slow resettlement and the training of an adequate industrial labour force throughout the whole country. Feeling unhappy and strange, many of the people settled in the western territories preferred to return to their old homes in the rurally overpopulated parts of Poland and yet were anxious to use the new industrial skills they had learnt. By creating the status of 'autochthone', it was hoped to retrain some of the skilled workers—particularly miners—who were German or German in sympathy, so that probably 800 000 people are in this category, mostly in the industrial towns of Upper Silesia.

The boundary changes have made Poland the main storehouse of bituminous coal resources among the East European Comecon members. The greatest out-put comes from the Upper Silesian coalfield, a triangular area of 5200 km² of which about a fifth extends across the boundary into Czechoslovakia. The coalfield is a structural basin, with the whole coal series preserved in the centre but only the middle and lower coals remain around the upturned margins. Saddles in the central part bring the valuable middle and lower coals up to levels workable by contemporary mining, from which are obtained much demanded coking coals. One of these saddles near Rybnik has been developed as an impor-tant new mining district. Unfortunately the coking coal quality is mediocre, being friable in blast furnaces and causing uneven combustion.

The central parts of the basin are little known and it is unlikely these will be opened up until the more accessible margins and saddles have been worked out. The coalfield contains reserves exceeded only by the Ruhr–Westphalian coalfield. It is unfortunate that the seams vary greatly in thickness and are com-monly discontinuous, making coal extraction difficult and giving a relatively low coefficient of extraction. To prevent subsidence when thick seams are extracted, sand brought from nearby heaths is forced underground. In 1938 output was 64 million tons but in 1970 it exceeded 135 million tons. The Wałbrzych (Walden-burg) coalfield lies in the Sudeten mountains, partly in Poland and partly in Czechoslovakia. The reserves are small, and faulting and folding make the seams hard to work, but a high proportion of output is coking coal of better quality than in Upper Silesia. Three working pits produce a little over 3 million tons annually.

Poland has, of course, become a major European coal supplier, not only to other Comecon countries but also widely through the Baltic and into the Mediterranean basin, though the decline of coal in Western Europe has curtailed the Polish market and restricted sales have deprived the country of valuable hard currency since the late 1950s.

Territorial changes also increased reserves of lignite. Much of the Zielona Góra *Województwo* is underlain by lignite and there are deposits further south and east, notably at Konin near Poznań. It is mined chiefly by open-cast techniques, but of eight workings, two are deep mines. Output is about 30 million tons annually compared to a mere 20 000 tons pre-war. Most lignite is used for electricity generation at large stations near the pits. The loss of the Carpathian footslope to Russia east of Przemyśl deprived Poland of valuable petroleum deposits. The western part of the field is still worked by Poland around Krosno, Gorlice and Czarna and petroleum has been discovered to the north, where there are considerable reserves of natural gas. Petroleum is also known in association with natural gas in the Odra basin near Nowa Sól. The country relies largely on petroleum imports, now mostly from the Soviet Union through the Friendship Pipeline. In future, natural gas will be used on an increasing scale.

Most of the iron ore deposits are low grade and too small for mining in modern conditions: they are quite inadequate for the large smelting industry. The ores of Upper Silesia, an historical location factor in the iron and steel industry, are now for all practical purposes exhausted, but bedded Jurassic ores of the Częstochowa district remain significant. The ores of the Góry Świętokrzyskie are also still worked. Although a number of new deposits have been found in central and eastern Poland, the position has changed relatively little. Sixteen pits produce about 2·8–3·0 million tons per annum, but iron content has tended to drop and covers only about an eighth of requirements. Several non-ferrous metals are found, but only lead, zinc and copper are important. The lead and zinc ores are found in shelly Triassic limestone overlying the Upper Silesian coalfield along the northern margin. Once taken from open pits the ore now comes from deep mines around Bytom and Olkusz and it is smelted locally. Cadmium, copper and silver are modest by-products. Of more importance has been the discovery of copper-bearing ores of about 2 per cent. Bolesławiec in Lower Silesia is an important centre, and there are mines near Złotoryja, while other deposits lie near Legnica. The main developments came during the mid-1950s, with Głogów as the processing centre. Rich deposits of rock salt, worked since mediaeval times, occur at Wieliczka and Bochnia in the south and deeper beds in a narrow belt, including some potash salts, between Inowrocław and Łódź are worked by the brine system. Gypsum and anhydrite are worked in the Nida basin and sulphur bearing rocks near Tarnobrzeg.

9.2.1 Industry in Poland (figure 9.3)

Industry has grown strikingly, not only in pre-war locations but also in new sites. With the expansion of industry there has also been a growth in electricity generation and the development of a national distribution grid linked, like other Comecon countries, into the international arterial grid. Whereas in the German Democratic Republic most electricity is based on lignite as a fuel, bituminous coal is the most important fuel in Poland. A major group of large generating stations lies on and around the Upper Silesian coalfield. There are, however, a number of small hydroelectric stations, some dating from pre-war times, in the northern lake plateaus and in the southern mountains, notably the Sudeten mountains but also the Carpathians. Plans for regulation of the Vistula for navigation also include the building of power stations. Like the other Eastern European countries industrial investment has been predominantly in heavy industries and has tended to keep the major concentrations of industry on pre-war sites which possessed many locational advantages that have tended also to attract new industries to them, in spite of hopes of a more widespread distribution of manufacturing. There have been, however, deliberate developments of industry in new sites, particularly for socio-economic reasons. Four heavily industrialised districts dominate the scene—Upper Silesia–Kraków, Warsaw, Łódź and Lower Silesia. As a second echelon, the areas around Wrocław, Opole and the Staropolski district may be enumerated, while to these may be added Gdynia–Gdańsk and Bydgoszcz.

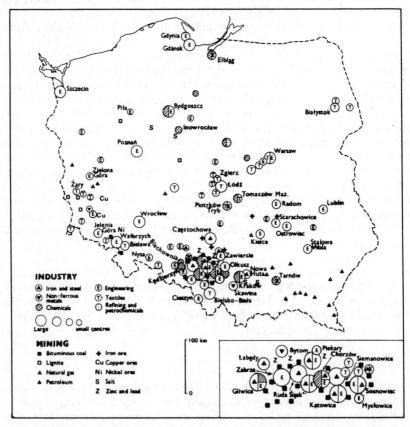

Figure 9.3. Polish heavy industry is still concentrated in the Silesian lands, though the pre-war encouragement to development in central Poland has been continued.

Poland has become one of the larger producers of iron and steel in Eastern Europe, using mostly its own coking coals but depending heavily on iron ore imported from the Soviet Union and on a limited scale from Sweden. The iron and steel industry dates back to the early nineteenth century in former Prussian Silesia, but during the inter-war years the industry was in a parlous state and output amounted in 1938 to only about 1.4 million tons of steel (a further half million tons were produced in the German part of Upper Silesia). There was, however, some increase in the pre-war capacity by the construction of a special steels plant at Stalowa Wola in association with the strategically conceived plan for a Central Industrial Region. Throughout the inter-war years, much of Polish industry suffered from the loss and disruption of traditional markets resulting from the territorial changes of 1919 and the depressed condition of trade in the period 1929–34. In 1945 Poland added the steelworks of German Upper Silesia and the small blast furnace plant at Szczecin (Stettin), though some of these German works had suffered from Soviet reparations dismantling.

The Upper Silesian coalfield, the focus of the iron and steel industry, has long established works modernised and expanded since the early 1950s. Over a dozen large plants lie in the area, but only six are integrated iron and steelworks—the largest is the *Kościuszko* works at Chorzów. Others are at Bytom, Ruda Ślaska, Świetochłowice, Dąbrowa Górnicza and Sosnowiec. Large steel and rolling mills operate at Łabędy, Siemianowice, Katowice and Gliwice. Whereas the plants of then Polish Silesia had supplied over 90 per cent of pig iron, steel and rolled goods produced in 1938, their share has now fallen to a little over 50 per cent, except for rolled steel (81 per cent). The fall in the share has been the outcome of the construction of new iron and steel plants, of which the largest is the *Lenin* plant at Nowa Huta. Completely equipped by the Soviet Union, it produces about three million tons of steel annually, with a plan to expand output to over five million tons. With other plants, it sends pig iron for further processing to Upper Silesia. The works were located to use labour from a rurally over-populated area and to receive railborne shipment of Ukranian ore.

The second important plant is the greatly expanded *Bierut* iron and steel works at Częstochowa, using local Jurassic ores, which has been operating since 1952. Another new special steels plant has been built at Młociny in Warsaw. Whereas the Młociny plant has a capacity of under half-a-million tons, the Częstochowa works are geared to a million tons per annum. Other steelworks outside Upper Silesia include the Zawiercie plant to the north-east (which is a small integrated works). As part of the Central Industrial Region are the Ostrowiec Staropolski steel works (0.3 million tons) and the Stalowa Wola special steels plant (0.3 million tons). Near Opole there are also small works (Ozimek and Zawadzkie), while the Szczecin works uses ores brought by sea in its blast furnaces. Some steel conversion (mostly from scrap) is done near Wrocław. As might be expected, manganese is obtained chiefly from the U.S.S.R., while some nickel comes from Ząbkowice in the Sudeten mountains. Annual steel production is about 12 million tons.

Since 1960 aluminium has been made from Hungarian bauxite at Skawina using electricity from the big station at Jaworzno, while in 1966 a large aluminium plant was opened at Konin.

Before the Second World War, engineering works were found chiefly in the towns which had been in Prussia before 1914, though a few were founded in Tsarist times in the Warsaw district, in Łódź and in the Dąbrowa area. A well-developed engineering industry was inherited in 1945 in the lands annexed from Germany. Machine tools are produced mainly in the towns of Upper Silesia, Warsaw, Pruszków and Wrocław, as well as Poznań, Łódź, Katowice, Bydgoszcz and Kraków, but there are also some smaller centres. Boilers and steam-raising equipment are made in Racibórz, Łódź, Kielce and Sosnowiec. Elbląg produces turbines. Warsaw and Andrychów build diesel motors, as well as Świętochłowice, Poznań and Gdańsk. Upper Silesia and Wałbrzych are the main centres for mining equipment, with 75 per cent from the Katowice area. Most output is exported to other Comecon members or to developing countries (for example, India). A similar distribution of heavy engineering for iron and steel works and also chemical engineering occurs, but it is also found in Toruń and Kielce. Świdnica builds sugar refineries, while plants in Warsaw, Wrocław, Gniezno, Olsztyn, Białystok and Kraków make machinery for food processing. Casting and die-impressing machinery is made in Kraków, Cieplice Śląskie makes paper-making machines, Bydgoszcz produces cement-making equipment and Łódź, Bielsko, Zduńska Wola and Zielona Góra produce textile machinery.

Important agricultural machinery plants are situated at Poznań, Płock, Brzeg, as well as Lublin, Kutno, Grudziądz, and several Silesian towns. Quite a lot of machinery is, however, imported from Czechoslovakia, Hungary and the German Democratic Republic. One of the branches with a large increase in the labour force and the share of total output has been electrical engineering. A quarter of production comes from Warsaw, but Kraków, Łódź and Wrocław are also important. Łódź makes transformers and telephones, while Wrocław and Elbląg are manufacturers of heavy equipment and plants lie in several other towns. Świdnica and Świebodzice make electrical equipment for cars and Poznań produces batteries, but much special equipment has to be imported.

Two long-standing railway works, *Cegielski*, in Poznań and the Chrzanów works, remained important until the end of steam locomotive building: in 1964 Chrzanów changed to building diesel locomotives, but Poznań turned to other forms of diesel engines, machine tools and railway wagons. Electric-railway equipment is built at Wrocław. *Cegielski* in Poznań and the *Pafawag* works in Wrocław turn out 85 per cent of all railway wagons, three-quarters of which are exported. Other works are Zielona Góra, Świdnica, Chorzów (tramcars), Ostrów Wielkopolski and Gdańsk.

In 1922 the *Ursus* tractor works opened in Warsaw and is now one of the main producers in Poland, associated with the Czech *Zetor* plant in Brno. The low priority accorded to motor vehicles leaves the industry comparatively small in comparison to the total population, though Poland is not a rich country and the market is limited. Pre-war only assembly of imported cars was undertaken. In 1948 the Strachowice lorry plant was opened, followed in 1951 by the Żerań works at Praga (Warsaw) for light motor cars based on Soviet vehicles, in which year a second lorry plant opened at Lublin. More recently, a *Polski Fiat* has been built at Warsaw under licence. Other small plants are at Nysa (vans and minibuses), Wrocław (lorries), Sanok (buses), while Jelcz produces a Czech-designed bus. There is also the manufacture of bicycles, motor cycles and mopeds.

The first ship built in Poland was launched in 1938, but shipbuilding is now a major industry. Sixty per cent of production is from Gdańsk; and the rest is almost equally divided between Gdynia and Szczecin. Almost all the ships are exported. There is a very small aircraft-building industry, but nearly all machines are supplied from outside Poland, notably from the U.S.S.R.

The chemicals industry, dependent to a marked degree on home produced raw materials, dates back to the first sulphuric acid works in Warsaw in 1822. Poland, now one of the largest producers of chemicals in Eastern Europe, is a major producer of sulphur-based substances from its own resources, notably in the Tarnobrzeg area, while deposits of salt are also used, as well as barytes and anhydrite. There are also worthwhile deposits of phosphate salts and potash salts to support chemicals manufacture. Home resources have been important in the development of a synthetic fertiliser industry. One of the most important chemicals plants is at Oświęcim, built by the Germans during the Second World War. This is particularly concerned with chemicals derived from coal and was originally a producer of synthetic rubber and synthetic petrol. It also produces carbide and acetylene compounds for plastics. During the First World War, an important nitrogen factory was built at Chorzów, while another lies at Tarnów, built during the 1930s, where there is a large factory for artificial fibres. The Kędzierzyn factory, reopened in 1954 on the basis of a German plant erected to make synthetic fuel, now produces nitrogen and ammonia products from coking processes.

The Upper Silesian coalfield is the focus of chemicals based on coking, but most recently natural gas has become a source of chemical substances at Tarnów and Puławy for both synthetic fibres and artificial fertilisers. Petrochemicals are being developed at the Płock refinery, drawing its crude from the Soviet Union. Three main soda plants are situated near Kraków, Inowrocław and Janikowie (opened in 1957 for calcinated soda production). Near Chrzanów is one of the main chlorine works. Phosphatic fertilisers come mainly from Poznań, Szczecin (imported materials), Katowice, Wrocław, Toruń and near Gryfów Śląski. The principal sulphur plants are Gdańsk, Kielce, Wałbrzych, using home deposits and by-products of zinc and tin refining. Dyestuffs and chemicals for the textile industry come mostly from Łódź and Zgierz, while Tarnowksie Góry produces dyes and paints. Pharmaceuticals are produced in several towns, but output is not large.

Like other countries Poland has devoted considerable attention to the development of artificial fibres. Cellulose is produced at Tomaszów Mazowiecki, Chodakowa, Wrocław and Szczecin. Łódź produces casein-based materials, while Jelenia Góra makes viscose yarn. Synthetic yarns are also made in Brzeg Dolny. The Gorzów Wielkopolski plant makes a nylon-type yarn and Łódź produces an orlon-style fibre. At Toruń a yarn of the terylene type is made. Poznań, Olsztyn, Grudziądz, Warsaw and Łódź are producers of rubber articles, but other factories for specialised production are near Jelenia Góra and in Kraków.

Poland has a substantial textiles industry, including factories in the annexed German lands (where there had been linen and later cotton textiles) as well as the centres of Łódź and Białystok. Nearly half of total production still comes from Łódź and district, while over 30 per cent comes from Silesia. The cotton industry is particularly associated with Łódź and surrounding towns. The Wrocław area is also important, but mills are found in Bielawa and other provincial towns. Investment in new plants has tended to disperse the industry, notably in the Białystok district (Zambrowa and Fasta). The woollen industry is dominated by Łódź *Województwo*, but mills also operate in Bielsko-Biała, Częstochowa, Sosnowiec, Zielona Góra, Lubsko and Żagań. Silk comes chiefly from the Łódź district, but it has been largely replaced by synthetic fibres. Lublinec and Częstochowa, Kłodzko, Kamienna Góra make sackings and industrial cloths.

The food industry has a number of large processing plants (1000–2000 employees) as well as numerous small works. It is widely dispersed and many plants date from well before 1914, especially in the western part of the country where much of the industry was concentrated before 1939, particularly distilleries and sugar refineries. The main areas are now the *Województwa* of Poznań, Katowice, Wrocław, Bydgoszcz and Olsztyn. Sugar-refining is largely on the left bank of the Oder, in Kujawy, around Bydgoszcz, and in southern parts of the *Województwa* Kielce and Lublin. Poland is usually about fifth world producer of sugar. The tendency is to build new refineries in the eastern part of the country where sugar-beet cultivation has been encouraged. There are over 5000 flour mills, with the largest plants in the big cities, notably in the central and eastern part of the country, where many small mills have been replaced by new large plants. Poznań, Gdańsk, Gdynia, Szczecin, Łódź and the large Silesian towns are main producers of fats. Oil and soap combines have been developed near Zamość (Białystok), Matwy (Inowrocław), Brzeg Dolny and near Kraków. Of over 100 breweries, some have a reputation beyond Poland, like the Okocim plant. Large new breweries have been built in Lublin, Warsaw and Białystok. Poznań, Koszalin and Szczecin are important districts for spirit distilleries. Some wine is produced in Silesia. Meat and fish processing have been greatly expanded, with much of the meat products exported.

9.2.2 Agriculture in Poland (figure 9.4)

Whereas almost half the gross national product in the inter-war years was derived from agriculture, it now accounts for less than a fifth. Before 1939 about 60 per cent of the population were employed in agriculture, whereas the share is now little more than a third. The dramatic increase in industrial output has not been matched in agriculture, but it is interesting that Poland has followed a pattern of organisation different to its neighbours. During the inter-war years there had been some dissolution of the large estates characteristic of the Polish lands before 1914. Though the process had not gone very far, numerous peasant holdings had been enlarged or created; but where land reform was most needed, in the over-crowded lands of the south in Galicia, there were few if any big estates to dis-member. In such areas, a programme of consolidating the scattered parcels of peasant land into more manageable holdings was instituted.

The problem of rural overpopulation was, however, far from solved by the outbreak of war in 1939 and immediately after the war in 1945 a drastic land reform was undertaken, based on a decree made in September 1944, that all private holdings over 50 ha of agriculturally used land would be liquidated. At the same time, all private forests over 25 ha were nationalised. The land sequestered was distributed to landless or small-holding peasants at a repayment spread over 10–20 years and based on the average annual grain harvest. Some of the land was kept by the state for various experimental and educational farms or for other purposes. In 1946 special decrees were promulgated for the annexed western territories, were the State had taken over more than 9 million ha and had distributed 3.6 million ha according to the conditions of the land reform in the rest of the country. At the end of the main phase 60 per cent of all holdings were between 2 and 10 ha and in the early 1950s a serious effort was made to collectivise the peasants by gathering the holdings into agricultural units similar to the

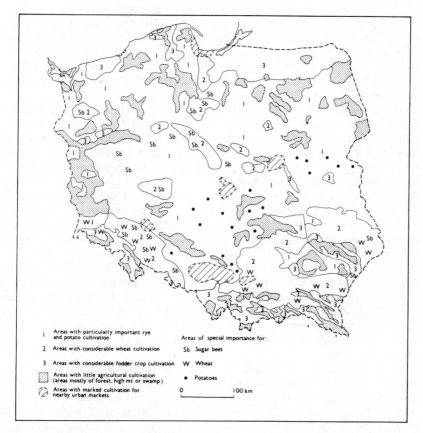

Figure 9.4. Grain cultivation is widespread in Polish farming—rye in the poorer central and northern areas and wheat on the better soils of the warmer south.

landwirtschaftliche Produktionsgenossenschaft in the German Democratic Republic. The aim was to move to full collectivisation by stages in which the commitment of the peasant to the collective principle became increasingly greater, but the process was slow and by 1954 little more than 7 per cent of the agriculturally used area was in collectives, with the majority in the western *Województwa* of Poznań, Wrocław, Szczecin and Koszalin where it was claimed that crop yield was 20–50 per cent better than on the peasant farms. Machine and tractor stations on the Soviet model were also established. State farms held about 12 per cent of the agricultural area and were more mechanised. They were the pace-makers for the other types of farms.

Though socialisation of agriculture remains the expressed aim, little has been done since the 'New Course' marked the withdrawal of many peasants from the collective-style farms in 1956. The State farms did not suffer likewise, because socialisation when carried through to a high degree is a one-way process which is virtually impossible to reverse. The strength of the State farms in the annexed western territories was another factor, because the resettled peasants had never held any rights to land, while the scarcity of labour gave full employment and consequently a rather better economic return. The individual peasant farms now hold almost 85 per cent of the farmland, while State farms have a little over 13 per cent and the collective farms have a mere 1.7 per cent. In lands that had been Polish in 1939 individual peasant farms amount to over 90 per cent of the farmland and State farms to a mere six per cent.

There are few differences between the cropping on the individual peasant farms and the socialised enterprises, though the latter tend to grow more cereals and sugar beet and to concentrate more on livestock, whereas the peasant farms give more emphasis to potatoes. Of the cropland, about half is under grains, while almost a fifth is occupied by potatoes and about a twentieth by 'industrial' crops, of which the most important are sugar beet and oil seeds. Almost a sixth of the cropland is under fodder crops. Of the grains over half the area is under rye, a traditional bread grain, but wheat has also become increasingly important. Barley occupies less than a twentieth of the cropland. The cropland occupies the highest proportion of the total area—over 50 per cent—in central Poland, between Warsaw on the east and Poznań in the west, covering the historical provinces of Wielkopolska, Kujawy and Mazowsze and is also important on the *loessic* lands of Silesia, where over 60 per cent of the surface may be cultivated, though the total area is not as large as in central Poland. It is also significant on the good soils along the foot of the Beskides and Carpathians. Cropland is least important on the poorer glacial sands of the north, in Pomorze and Masuria, as well as in the sandy lands of the *Województwo* Zielona Góra and in the mountains of the south.

In general, there remains a large element of self-supporting peasant communities, with only limited acreages of cash and industrial crops, a basic cause of the food shortages that have plagued Poland since the war, since the peasants have not been geared to increase the food supply to the growing urban-industrial population. The State farms and collectives, though much smaller, have been more orientated to the market, mostly supplying produce for export. Some regional differences in crop patterns occur. Rye is the principal crop in central Poland, often taking more than 40 per cent of the arable land. It is particularly common around Łódź and Warsaw but relatively unimportant on the *loessic* soils of Silesia and in southern Poland, where better climate and more responsive soils favour wheat. Wheat is particularly concentrated in the south—occupying over a fifth of the arable land in Silesia and in southern Poland, notably around Kraków, Rzeszów and Wrocław and Opole. Its cultivation has been spreading in the far west and in the lower Vistula. Barley is also grown in the south-east, in

Silesia, the lower Vistula and Masuria, but it nowhere exceeds 8 per cent of the arable area, whereas wheat may take up to 28 per cent. Oats is important in the Pomeranian coast, around Białystok and in the far south. Maize, though now more important, remains insignificant in the total cultivated area and much of it is cut green. The potato, one of the most common crops, covers almost a fifth of the arable land and annual production amounts to over 15 per cent of the world crop. It seldom occupies less than 10 per cent of the arable area and around Konin and Kielce as much as 30–2 per cent, and over 25 per cent of the arable area around Warsaw, Łódź and Kielce. Pre-war the potato was also very important in the German territories east of the Oder, but it is now only grown on a limited scale, except around Opole and in the *Województwo* Katowice. Sugar beet cultivation has been expanded in a broad belt from the lower Vistula through Bydgoszcz and Poznań to the Wrocław–Opole area. In the north and west rape seed and flax are grown, while in the east and south-east, hemp and tobacco are found.

Over the decade from 1960 there was little change in the share of crops in the total sown area, but production showed an upward turn as a result of higher yields, brought about by better husbandry and also by using more fertiliser, whereas in the years of collectivisation, grain yield in particular took a sharp downward turn. Yield on co-operatives has been somewhat better than on individual farms but surprisingly poor on the State farms. Mechanisation has increased, but the field pattern of the individual farms makes it hard to introduce effectively and farm labour remains plentiful enough not to make it more pressing, while the use of horses by peasants tends to increase the smaller and lighter horse-drawn machinery. There has been a large increase in the use of fertilisers: in the present area of Poland there were 29 kg per ha of cultivated ground pre-war (in the then boundaries, only 4.9 kg), whereas in 1968–9 the equivalent was 109.5 kg. Lime has been used more freely on the heavy clayey soils of central Poland and there has been extensive draining and clearing of stones. In 20 years conservation and amelioration work covered 5 million ha of arable land and 2.3 million ha of meadow and pasture. One of the most important tasks was reclamation of ground made saline by flooding in the Bay of Danzig over an area of 140 000 ha. Other reclamation works include 30 000 ha in the Noteć basin, 25 000 ha in the Obra basin, 15 000 ha in the Barycz basin and 10 000 ha in the Łeba basin, while substantial works have been undertaken in the *Województwo* Lublin. Much attention has been given to improving soil quality. There has also been electrification in the villages and the government has sought to buy out old and inefficient farmers.

Usually peasant farms have kept a horse for the cart and the plough, as well as two or three cows and as many pigs fed on farm and domestic waste, as well as hens and ducks or geese. The lack of proper grazing and the sharing of meadow with other peasants have been restrictive factors, so that the tethered goat or cow is still a common sight. In spite of poor conditions, the quality is often remarkable and Polish geese, for example, have a high reputation. The main encouragement has been given to livestock rearing, though again output has fluctuated substantially to give periodic shortages. The herds had been devastated during the war and a considerable period elapsed before numbers could be raised to the 1938 levels. The State farms have become centres of livestock farming, including such special activities as race-horse rearing (Posadowa near Poznań). Cattle are widely distributed, but the greatest density is in the centre and particularly the south, around Rzeszów, Kraków and Opole. The pig is widespread even on small farms and particularly abundant in the potato-producing areas and where there is waste from sugar-refining. The pig population is about 14 million compared to about 9.6 million in the present territory of Poland in 1938. Pig meat in various forms has become an important export item, though it has suffered from restrictions created by the European Economic Community. Sheep have also been encouraged as a source of wool and meat, notably in the hillier lands of Silesia and the Carpathian Foreland, but they are also important in the Białystok area.

Poland has developed a considerable fishing industry, mostly for home consumption, but fish is also sold to other Comecon members. Landings are over seven times greater than in 1938. The main fishing harbours are Kołobrzeg, Darłowo, Ustka, Władysławowo and Hel, but Gdynia and Szczecin are also important, while Świnoujście has been redeveloped. The main catches are made in Atlantic waters.

9.2.3 Transport in Poland

Poland's bodily shift westwards included much territory with a developed railway network and the loss of eastern territory with a broadly meshed net. In the territories annexed from Germany many country lines were dismantled in order to help rebuild the war damage. Emphasis was on improving east–west connections between the Soviet Union and its Occupation Zone in Germany: the main international route was developed from Frankfurt–Oder via Poznań and Warsaw to the Soviet frontier at Brest: but there was also the strategic route across southern Poland from Lvov to Przemyśl and west to Kraków, across Silesia and into central Germany.

The most important new lines have been south of Warsaw to keep freight traffic away from the capital and improvements made in the Radom–Kielce area where considerable economic development has taken place, but a route from Kielce south to Tarnów remains unfinished. A project for a major new trunk route from Warsaw to Katowice and other projected route east–west across southern Poland have not yet been undertaken. On existing lines, improvements have been made to the route from the Silesian industrial area to the port of Szczecin and from Warsaw to Silesia and to Szczecin via Poznań. Electrification has been undertaken on main trunk routes. Of just over 23 000 km route of normal gauge line, almost 3500 km are electrified.

Poland has become the main transit country for railway goods to the Soviet Union, with crossing points and change of gauge facilities at Kuźnica, Brest and Mostyka. Large quantities of coal are moved by Poland's railways to neighbouring countries, while there is a steady flow of iron ore to Polish steel plants from the Soviet Union. Until completion of the pipeline from the U.S.S.R. to Poland and the German Democratic Republic, there were also considerable petroleum shipments.

Road transport since 1945 has provided Poland with a means of improving internal communications at a lower capital cost than railway building. There has been a massive growth in motor bus transport, especially in 'Congress Poland' where the mesh of the railway network was much broader than elsewhere. The comparatively good quality of the road network in the former German lands has, however, also encouraged motor traffic. In the areas taken from Germany in 1945 Poland inherited three sections of 'disembodied' motorway—from the new frontier to just east of Szczecin, from Elbląg to the new frontier with Russia as part of the Elbląg–Kaliningrad motorway and from the Neisse river to just south of Wrocław. This latter section is now being extended to join a very short section of motorway near Gliwice, so providing a link throughout Silesia. The effect of boundary changes can be seen in the fact that whereas in 1938 only 19 per cent of the roads had a hard surface, the post-war figure was 38 per cent and the density of roads per 100 km^2 had risen from 16.5 to 30.7. Heavy damage to roads and bridges had to be repaired though since 1965 new building and improvement has begun. The motor-vehicle park comprises mostly buses and lorries, but there is a growing component of private cars. Although Poland has a motor-vehicle industry, most motor vehicles originate from Soviet, East German or Czech works. Horse-drawn vehicles are still common in the countryside and in the smaller towns.

Freight turnover in Polish ports rose in the 20 years after 1946 from 7.8 million tons to 36.6 million tons. Through a vigorous policy of restoration, inspite of wartime damage and reparations dismantling in Szczecin, the Poles were able to attract a considerable part of the Central European traffic, notably from Hungary and Czechoslovakia (which was accorded special rights). Before 1939 about three-quarters of total Polish trade passed through Gdańsk (in which special rights were accorded) and Gdynia, built in 1921 as a coal shipping port. In 1950 coal amounted to 70 per cent of the cargo turnover in Polish ports, but had fallen to 40 per cent a decade later. Ore imports pass chiefly through Szczecin and along the Oder, though three-quarters of the total imports arrive in Poland by rail from the Soviet Union. The main ports for grain and food produce are Gdynia-Gdańsk. Compared to West European ports, Polish ports show an absence of petroleum and petroleum products. Pre-war, transit traffic accounted for only a minor part of the trade of Polish ports, but now accounts for over a fifth of all seaborne cargo (a third of the cargo at Szczecin). About half Czechoslovak foreign shipments have been handled through Polish ports.

Inspite of many failings, Polish achievements have been considerable. It remains to be seen whether the country can adjust its economic structure to a more sophisticated economy in Eastern Europe as the demand for coal and iron and steel slacken.

9.3 Czechoslovakia

Czechoslovakia, one of the more industrialised Eastern European states, has been dogged by problems of modernisation and the loss of an important part of its skilled labour in the expulsion of the German minority (almost a fifth of the pre-1945 population). A basic problem in Czechoslovak economic geography has been the development and integration of Slovakia arising from the historical differences between the well-developed and industrialised Austrian lands of Bohemia–Moravia and the backward but potentially rich Hungarian lands of

Slovakia. The Czechs emerged in the nineteenth century as a thrusting and go-ahead society, while the Slovaks remained a mountain peasant people dominated by Magyar officialdom. Relatively little progress was made in the inter-war years, but Marxist–Leninist planning dogmas have demanded a more rigorous approach since 1948. Development of major projects in Slovakia deflecting resources and attention from basic infrastructural problems in Bohemia–Moravia has contributed to the slow growth of the Czechoslovak economy. Both the German Democratic Republic and Poland have caught up and, in some sectors, overtaken the Czechoslovak position. With limited natural wealth, Czechoslovak prosperity has depended on a well-developed manufacturing industry with a relatively good balance in the heavy and light sectors.

The country has a varied mineral wealth, but few minerals are present in quantities commensurate with modern industrial needs. Lead and zinc ores continue to be worked at the old mines of Příbram and Banská Štiavnica. Important lead deposits occur, however, in central Bohemia at Kutná Hora and in northern Bohemia at Horní Benešov and Zlaté Hory. Some copper ore with low metal content is found in the Slovakian Ore Mountains and at a few places in the Bohemian Ore Mountains and the Sudeten Mountains, while prospects of these ores also exist in northern Moravia. Central Bohemia and the Slovak Ore Mountains contain numerous deposits of antimony, but the deposits of the Low Tatra are worked out. The working of home deposits of nonferrous metals is more expensive than buying from abroad and home production can cover only a part of national needs. In mediaeval times Kremnica was an important gold and silver centre and still has a mint. After 1945 Jáchymov in Bohemia became an important uranium mining centre for Soviet nuclear development.

Of numerous occurrences of iron ore recorded, only a few are of any importance. Two main workings occur in central Bohemia (Nučice near Prague and Ejpovice near Plzeň) and in eastern Slovakia at Spišská Nová Ves, Gelnica, Rožňava and Tisovec. Exploitation began in the nineteenth century but output today covers only a small part of the national requirements and has declined from over 3 million tons in the early 1960s to little more than a million tons in 1970. The Bohemian sedimentary ores are relatively low in ore content, but they are easy to mine. In contrast, the Slovakian ores have a better iron content but are expensive to mine and their cost has been steadily rising. Larger reserves may be discovered by a more intense study of the deeper lodes in Slovakia. Iron-ore deposits in northern Moravia are still imperfectly known, while a number of otherwise reasonably sized and good quality deposits are unlikely to be worked because of difficult geological conditions. Most imported ore comes from the Soviet Union, but ore is till imported from Sweden—a onetime important supplier—and from other trading partners. Before its swing into the Chinese political camp, the Czechs had been hoping to get iron ore from Albania. Manganese ore is known in eastern Bohemia, but at present it is worked only near Poprad and Spišská Nová Ves in eastern Slovakia. Molybdenum, nickel and other alloy metals are worked on a small scale, but metal content is low and imports are made.

Salt is worked near Prešov in eastern Slovakia, where magnetite is also mined. Pyrites for sulphur are important at Chvaletice, north-east of Kutná Hora, but deposits are also known near Rožňava. Barytes occur in northern Moravia and in the Slovak Ore Mountains, also fluorspar and gypsum (Opava, Spišská Nová Ves) and there is much limestone.

The energy resources have been based on a generous endowment with coal and lignite, but recently water power has been harnessed and there has been a shift to natural gas and petroleum, of which home resources are meagre (petroleum—Hodonín and Malacky and natural gas near Ostrava). Annual production runs at about 25–8 million tons of hard coal, 58–75 million tons of brown coal and lignite, but only 140 000–200 000 tons of crude petroleum. Since 1960 electricity generation has virtually doubled, but imports of power have also risen. Petroleum as a source of energy has increased since the construction of the pipeline from the Soviet Union, while natural gas will be supplied to Western Europe from the Soviet Union across Czechoslovakia, so that its consumption by Czechoslovak industry may be expected to increase. Coal still supplies, however, about 90 per cent of the energy required.

Coal and lignite mining grew rapidly in the late nineteenth century as Bohemia–Moravia became the arsenal of Habsburg heavy industry. There was also a modest development in Slovakia, where Handlová was worked shortly before 1914. The main bituminous coal deposits of Bohemia–Moravia are in Czech Silesia, the Ostrava–Karviná basin, and their share of total output has increased. The other important though smaller field is at Kladno (north-west of Prague) and mining is also undertaken near Plzeň. Small Bohemian producers are Trutnov in the north and the Rosice–Oslavany basin near Brno. Bituminous coal is not produced in Slovakia. Coking coal amounts to three-quarters of the production in the Ostrava–Karviná field, where mining has spread recently to the area north of Frýdek–Místek. The Kladno basin produces steam coals but no coking coals and already shows signs of exhaustion. Lignite comes principally from the large Most basin in the Ohře valley of north-west Bohemia and from the Sokolov basin to the south-west. These fields produce a good quality coal in large open-cast pits. The Nováky–Handlová basin is the main supplier in Slovakia and smaller producers are near Lučenec and on the Slovak–Moravian border near Hodonín. During the 1950s demand for all types of coal grew more rapidly than production and a large modernisation and expansion programme was undertaken, notably in the Ostrava–Karviná field. Compared to the German Democratic Republic Czechoslovakia has had no serious problem of fuel and coke for heavy metallurgy, but in comparison to Poland it has had far less surplus bituminous coal for export, though it does export considerable amounts of lignite.

Electricity generation began on a muncipal scale in the 1880s and some large thermal generators had been built before 1914 but distribution networks, though extended, were not connected together on any great scale before 1939. In both generation and consumption Czechoslovakia lagged behind Germany though exceeding other Eastern European countries. Since 1945 the greatly expanded consumption has been helped by a more effective distribution system through a grid network, linked to the international Comecon grid. Large new power stations, mostly thermal plants located on or near the coalfields, have been built. Development possibilities for hydroelectricity are limited and only the Váh and the Vltava have 'cascades' of small generating plants, constructed in association with other hydrological aims. A small nuclear power station (110 kW) operates at Jaslovské Bohunice in western Slovakia. Rural electrification had been completed by the early 1960s and by the early 1970s it was aimed to install capacity to cover demand for the coming decade, of which 90 per cent will be covered by thermal generation.

9.3.1 Industry in Czechoslovakia (figure 9.5)

During the inter-war years Czechoslovakia survived the great depression in the world's iron and steel industry, but its plants received insufficient modernisation and were mercilessly exploited during the Second World War. Consequently, a major modernisation and investment programme was needed in the immediate post-war period. By the end of the 1960s output of pig iron and steel exceeded the pre-war level fourfold, while Czechoslovakia usually stands about eighth in world rating. Five modern integrated plants produce over 90 per cent of the steel output and almost all the pig iron. Over half the metallurigcal industry is concentrated in the Ostrava district. Three completely integrated plants are sited at Vítkovice, Třinec, and the very modern Nová Hut, while self-contained rolling mills work in Bohemia and Frýdek–Místek. The plants have been attracted by the nearby supply of good coke, the good transport for imported ore and supplies of limestone. A very wide range of products is made. The second important district is central Bohemia, with large plants at Kladno and Beroun, while there are ore mines and works at Příbram, but coke is brought in because the Kladno coals are not suitable. The engineering industry of central Bohemia consumes much of the produce but also returns large quantities of scrap. The newest centre opened in 1965 is the large integrated iron and steel plant outside Košice in eastern Slovakia, fed largely with Soviet raw materials, particularly Ukrainian ore, though coal and coke come from Ostrava. Tube works (one of the largest in Europe) and rolling mills are also found at Chomutov, a steel works at Most, and several plants in the Děčín–Ústí-nad-Labem area. There are non-ferrous plants scattered throughout the country, but a large aluminium works has been built at Žiar-nad-Hronom to use Hungarian bauxite and locally generated electricity. Prague is also an important centre for lead and non-ferrous alloys. Near Ústi-nad-Labem and Bílina copper and zinc are refined.

Over a third of industrial output comes from engineering, widely scattered throughout the country and Marxist–Leninist planning dogma has tended to accentuate its dispersion. The many different branches of engineering have found in common a good iron and steel base, a solid domestic market and a fund of skilled labour. After 1918 much sophistication of production took place,with the making of motor cars, electrical equipment and complex machine tools, as well as aircraft, and this skill and design know-how was harnessed after the Second World War to make Czechoslovakia the machine-shop of the Socialist bloc, though the re-emergence of the engineering industries of the German Democratic Republic caused an unwelcome intensification of competition. Nearly half of all Czech exports are engineering products. Thirty per cent of production is of vehicles, railway goods and aircraft; 19 per cent is electrical goods, while 15 per cent heavy machinery and 6 per cent comprises precision engineering goods. Weaknesses have been in the over-diversification of production and in the lack of co-ordination between plants, while it has been suggested that there is scope for rationalisation of location of interdependent component plants.

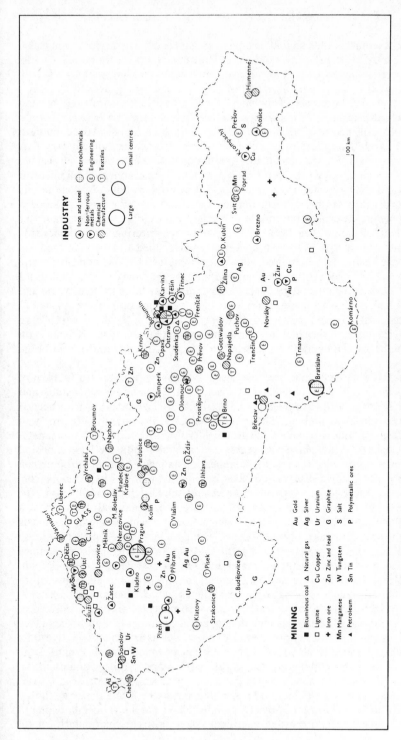

Figure 9.5. Western Czechoslovakia still remains the focus of industrial activity despite planning aid to industrial development in Slovakia, where heavy industry has been established in the east near Košice.

Almost a third of the capacity in engineering is found in central Bohemia. The largest centre is Prague and its outskirts. The main plants are for machine tools, while electrical engineering and precision engineering are important. At Mladá Boleslav is the Škoda car plant and at Klín a motor works as well as wagon building. Over 10 per cent of the engineering capacity is concentrated around Brno, where machinery of many types, tractors, small arms, boilers and bearings are made. A big centre is Plzeň, with the largest single enterprise in the country in the vast Škoda works. Railway locomotives and electrical equipment as well as heavy machine tools are among the wide production programme. The Ostrava district includes the Tatra motor works at Kopřivnice, mining equipment at Opava and railway wagons at Studénka, but a serious labour shortage in this area makes further development unlikely. In Slovakia, as a result of modern developments, the central part of the Váh valley and Bratislava are the main centres. Plentiful labour has been used in simple engineering and components assembly. The central Moravian area is more diversified and includes the farm machinery plant at Prostějov and also manufacture of food-processing machinery. In northern Bohemia engineering (for example in Děčín and Ústí) also includes textile machinery, recent lorry-building at Jablonec-nad-Nisou and wagons built in Česká Lípa. Eastern Bohemia makes food processing machinery (Hradec Králové) and conveyor systems (Chrudim). In the south České Budějovice has a motor plant and Strakonice makes motor cycles. Komárno on the Danube is a shipbuilding centre while Prague and Mělník build vessels for the Elbe.

A fast-growing sector has been the chemicals industry in spite of a problem of water supply. The first impetus was given by the demand for dyestuffs and materials for the textiles and leather industries as well as soda and acids needed for paper and glass making. The modern industry has turned increasingly to producing synthetic substances and artificial fertilisers for farming. Unfortunately, particularly in the inter-war years, the chemicals industry lagged behind domestic requirements as a result of competition and lack of adequate home raw materials. The Ostrava–Karviná coalfield became the focus of byproducts from coking, but there is also superphosphates and sulphuric acid production. The country's largest works are at Záluží near Most, supplied with water from a 40 km-long pipeline from the Elbe, which produce a wide range of chemicals from a brown coal base. Ústí-nad-Labem is the second main centre, producing dyestuffs, sulphuric acid, artificial fertilisers and other chemicals. Neštěmice makes soda products, using raw materials brought by river from the German Democratic Republic. Lovosice makes artificial fertilisers and fibres—another major fibre-producer is Neratovice near Mělník, which also makes saccharin, sulphuric acid and soda ash. Kolín uses imported materials and waste substances for a wide range of chemicals including cyanide compounds. Pardubice makes explosives and processes various forms of oil, as well as artificial fibres, dyestuffs and aniline. Hradec Králové has a photographic chemicals plant. Prague is the centre of the rubber industry, using both natural and synthetic materials. In Slovakia, Bratislava is now a major centre and produces sulphuric acid, viscose yarn, rubber goods, pesticides and phosphatic fertilisers. There is also a refinery for petroleum piped from the Soviet Union. Rožňava has a large cellulose plant.

The chemicals industry has a critical water problem, particularly in the

Ostrava–Karviná area and along the Elbe, and effluent disposal is difficult. The old-fashioned cellulose and wood chemicals works, using home timber, pollute the upper reaches of the Elbe, but new plants will replace them further downstream. The developing chemicals industry in Slovakia has an easier availability of water and the rivers are still less polluted. There is also a better labour supply.

The long-established textile industry has tended to decline in its share of total industrial output. It flourished when the whole Austro-Hungarian market was open to it, but in the inter-war years, the difficulty of trading put it under critical strain. After 1945 the large sector in northern Bohemia suffered through the loss of the German labour force. Small, scattered plants with old-fashioned machinery have been a serious hindrance since 1945 in its rehabilitation, so that works have been closed or transferred to Slovakia to provide industrial employment. The industry is dominated by cotton textiles, though there is a steady change to artificial fibres, but flax and wool are also represented. Northern and eastern Bohemia, Moravia and western Slovakia are the main foci. Liberec is noted for its cotton mills and Krnov for its woollen mills, while Trutnov is the specialised linen district and Varnsdorf, the centre of the hosiery industry. New factories to provide employment for women in otherwise heavy industrial areas have brought woollen mills to the lignite fields of western Bohemia and cotton mills to Frýdek-Místek. Brno remains an important cotton centre and there are big woollen mills in Humpolec, Jihlava and Slavonice. Large modern factories typify Slovakia (one of the oldest centres is the cotton town of Ružomberok) and woollens are made in Trenčín, Lučenec and Žilina, with a large new knitted goods industry in Svit.

One of the most remarkable industrial enterprises of inter-war Central Europe, the Bat'a concern at Gottwaldov (Zlín), aimed to use cheap labour in an area of rural overpopulation. Today it produces half the total boot and shoe output of the country. The success led to branch factories in similar sites at Partizánske, Zruč-Sazava and Třebíč. The availability of high quality glass sands and ceramic clays as well as an ancient tradition of glass-making in Bohemia have been the foundation of world-renowned glass-making in the north and ceramics in the west that produce for the domestic and artistic market as well as for special industrial uses. A large part of the output goes for export. A severe blow to the glass industry—particularly for fine glassware and artificial jewellery—was the expulsion of the Germans of northern Bohemia. New developments include glass fibres in Litomyšl and fused refractory basalt in western Bohemia, and considerable development of the sheet and plate-glass industry around Teplice and Sokolov.

9.3.2 Agriculture in Czechoslovakia (figure 9.6)

Agriculture plays an important part in the Czechoslovak economy, not only in feeding the industrial population but also in the export trade, contributing about 11 per cent of the total national income. The country enjoys a measure of self-sufficiency, though foodstuffs are imported, but in some sectors there is a surplus for export, notably hops, malted barley and beet sugar. About 7 million ha of agricultural land are available, but this has shown a slight but steady decline over

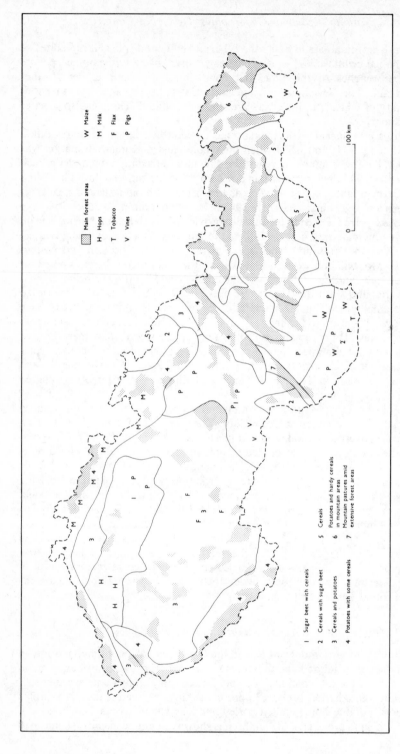

Figure 9.6. In Czechoslovakia, the better and warmer soils of the Polabí and the warm but rather dry lands of Moravia are most important for farming. On the higher lands of Bohemia and Slovakia, forestry is widespread.

the decade 1960–70. Of this area, 5 million ha are arable lands; 1.6 million ha pastures and meadows and small areas of vineyards and hop gardens. Almost 4.5 million ha are forest land. As the ratio of agricultural land to inhabitants is markedly lower than in the other Comecon countries, careful agricultural management and the maximisation of productivity is important to the Czechoslovaks. While 3.4 million people sought their livelihood in agriculture in 1936, the present agricultural employment is only 1.2 million people. Czechoslovakia carried through collectivisation, so that by the middle 1960s almost 90 per cent of agricultural land was socialised. In 1930 there were about 1.5 million farms, of which 45 per cent held less than 2 ha, whereas now there are about 6300 'united farmers' co-operatives' (collective farms), with an average of 600 ha of arable land, and some 400 state farms and related establishments (total holding of agricultural land 1 470 000 ha). 627 000 ha are divided among almost 800 000 private farmers; the great majority of these tiny farms are really part-time holdings of industrial workers. The small individual farmer remains most important in the mountain lands of Slovakia where the organisation of collectivised agriculture is difficult and where mechanisation is not easily introduced.

The collective farms are formed by farmers pooling their holdings and resources, graded according to the degree of commitment to the full collective principle. In Type 1 the farmers join together in certain work while the land remains in private holding. In Type 2, the land is pooled, but the products are distributed according to the value of land, cattle and machinery being put at the disposal of the co-operative on joining. In Type 3 there is consolidation of land holding and animal husbandry is also pooled, income being divided according to the work done by each member (though up to 15 per cent can be related to property put into the farm on joining). Type 4 (now predominant) is similar to Type 3 but income is divided solely according to work done. In the two latter forms, each member has a private plot of about 0.5 ha.

About 8 per cent of the area is fertile black earth; together brown forest soils and podzols form 70 per cent and 17 per cent comprises skeletal soils unsuited to farming, but much has to be done to improve soil quality. Improved drainage in parts of central and southern Bohemia and in central Slovakia has been carried out and irrigation systems built in southern Moravia and in lowland Slovakia, though drought remains serious, particularly in southern Moravia and southern Slovakia. Attention has been devoted to the restoration of land after open-cast mining, around Most but also in the Ostrava–Karviná basin. Investment made in new farm buildings is strikingly seen in parts of Bohemia and southern Slovakia, with new buildings particularly devoted to livestock farming. The shortage of labour in agriculture, most accute in the areas from which the Germans were expelled, has also forced the intense use of machinery.

Grain crops occupy 51.4 per cent of the sown area. The share of bread grains is 26.4 per cent, but since the early 1950s fodder grain has expanded in response to the development of livestock rearing. The greatest areas are sown to wheat (14.0 per cent), barley (13.5 per cent), rye (8.0 per cent) and oats (8.0 per cent). Grain maize occupies only 4.2 per cent. The grain harvest does not cover home requirements and efforts have been directed at a better yield to cover the deficit rather than to expand the area sown to grain. Ninety per cent of the wheat area is in winter varieties, mostly in the more fertile lowlands—the Polabí country, the

Moravian lowlands, the Danubian lowlands and the West Slovakian lowlands, though yield in Bohemia is better than in western and southern Slovakia. Wheat has steadily replaced rye since 1945, though the area sown to wheat is less than pre-war, while only half the pre-war area is now sown to rye. With low demands on natural conditions, rye is found on the poorer soils and in the higher areas—southern and western Bohemia, the Bohemian–Moravian Highlands, but it is seldom grown in Slovakia. Barley, mostly a spring crop, is important to the large Czech brewing industry, grown chiefly in areas along with sugar beet, in the Moravian lowlands, the Polabí and south-west Slovakia. Fodder barley is found mostly in the poorer lands less suited to the demanding brewing barley and its cultivation has expanded in Slovakia at the expense of wheat and rye. Oats is also mostly in the poorer upland, reaching up to 1000 m above sea level in northern Slovakia, though a decrease in area has been offset by increased yield. Following Soviet practice, maize has been cultivated more widely, concentrated in the warmest parts of the country where the grain ripens well—southern Slovakia and southern Moravia. In southern Slovakia it may occupy up to a fifth of the sown area. To a home output of 300 000–400 000 tons a year are added 300 000 tons imported mostly from the Soviet Union. Green maize for silage is grown on a larger scale in the cooler parts of the country.

The most extensive area of 'technical crops' is sown to sugar beet (the country is one of the world's largest exporters of beet sugar). The annual crop is about 8 million tons in a good year. The beet, a demanding plant, is grown in the most fertile soils—the Polabí and the lowlands of Moravia, so that it occupies between 15 and 20 per cent of the sown area in the districts of Kolín, Mělník, Nymburk, and the Olomouc basin, where the main concentrations of sugar refineries lie and there is also the use of waste for pig rearing. The textile industry imports cotton from trading partners such as the U.A.R. and the Soviet Union, but flax for the linen industry comes from home and imported supplies. The main cultivation is in the Bohemian–Moravian Uplands, northern Moravia, south and west Bohemia and in the Slovakian foothills, with a large increase in the area under flax compared to pre-war times. Hemp is grown in the Váh and upper Hron valleys and in eastern Slovakia. Two-thirds of Czechoslovakia's tobacco is imported: the rest—mostly medium quality—comes from southern Slovakia. Of particular importance to the Czechoslovak economy, hops are grown mainly in the Ohře basin—Žatec, Louny, Rakovník and Litoměřice, with a surplus for export.

About 400 000 ha of potatoes are sown annually, on loose light soils particularly common in Czechoslovakia. The main areas are the Bohemian–Moravian uplands, where potatoes occupy about a fifth of the sown area, and southern and western Bohemia, but the crop is unimportant in the Danubian lowlands. The area and yield of potatoes have fallen, primarily because of a shortage of labour but also because of pests.

During the post-war years there has been an increase in the importance of animals in the Czechoslovak farming scene. As a result of war losses the herds were very much reduced. The increase in livestock since 1948 has been of such proportions that imports of fodder have risen sharply. Cattle for meat and milk are most important, though there is a greater density in the Czech lands than in Slovakia. Milk production is characteristic of the richer agricultural areas, as in the lower parts of Bohemia and southern and central Moravia, where there is abundant green fodder. Yield per cow is lower than in Poland, Hungary, France and the two German states. Milk production and consumption are still below the pre-war level and there are distribution difficulties, consequently there has been the import of butter and cheese. In the mountainous areas beef cattle are raised, but are prepared for slaughter in the intensive farming areas of central, southern and eastern Bohemia, where they can be fattened, but only 40 per cent of home beef requirements are covered and meat is commonly short.

The pig, accounting for over half the meat consumed, has doubled in number since 1948, with western Slovakia and southern Moravia as the leading areas, using locally produced maize as fodder. Sheep numbers increased rapidly after the Second World War, only to fall again as emphasis was shifted to raising cattle. They are important in the mountainous parts of Bohemia and especially in central and eastern Slovakia. Horses have been largely replaced by lorries and tractors, but remain important in the mountains, though there are studs for high class horses. Poultry keeping is important, especially among small farmers, while bees are kept in the main fruit-growing regions. Fish are reared (notably carp for the Christmas market) in southern Bohemia, where the number of ponds has been increased.

With over a third of its area covered by forest Czechoslovakia is one of the most densely wooded countries in Europe, with three-quarters of the reserves in coniferous trees. The State and co-operative sectors hold 98 per cent of the wooded land, though forestry only accounts for one per cent of the national income. Forests supply important quantities of timber and serve vital environmental purposes. The main forest lands are in the mountains of Slovakia, but important forests also occur in the Bohemian frontier areas, notably the Šumava, Krkonoše and the Hrubý Jeseník mountains. Most wood is used for domestic articles, but just under a sixth goes for pulp. Of timber exports nearly 40 per cent moves to the United Kingdom.

9.3.3 Transport in Czechoslovakia

As an inland country in Central Europe, Czechoslovakia has played a significant role as a transit land in north–south movements from the North European Plain to Danubia, whereas the east–west movement of passengers and freight is more important in domestic traffic. The railway system is well developed, particularly in Bohemia and Moravia and during the inter-war years, much attention was given to linking Slovakia more effectively with the western part of the country.

Without appreciable territorial change Czechoslovak railways have been little extended since 1945. Emphasis has been on modernisation and the completion of short lines to relieve congestion on heavily loaded routes (for example Havlíčkův Brod-Křižanov-Brno, 1955). In Slovakia a new route has been introduced largely to open up mineral resources, but an unusual line has been the 88 km-long broad gauge railway from the Soviet frontier to the new East Slovakian steelworks to simplify coal and ore deliveries. Electrification has been undertaken on the main east–west artery (the *Friendship Railway*), which carries 35 per cent of all freight traffic, forming the core of the system from Prague via Kolín, Púchov and Košice to the Soviet border at Čierna and Tisou, where there is a large trans-shipment and change of gauge station. An improved electrified route extends from Prague to Děčín to absorb growing freight from the German Democratic Republic, a large proportion of which is in transit to Danubia and the Balkans. About 21 per cent of the route is double-track. The closure of underused lines in rural areas will leave the present route length little changed. Of about 250 million tons of freight handled, 11 million tons are in transit movements. Traffic turnover is four times greater than pre-war, but nearly 40 per cent of all freight is solid fuels; nearly a fifth, building materials; and some 15 per cent is ore, metallurgical and engineering products.

There is a dense road network but as yet no proper motorways, though there are plans for one from the German border near Děčín to Prague, Brno and Bratislava. Improvements in road links between Moravia and Slovakia are still needed. Road traffic is mostly short haul goods and passenger movements in town and country. An elaborate system of motor-coach connections has been developed (190 000 km). Road transport will take over all hauls of under 80 km. As yet Czechoslovakia does not play the role in road transport that it provides for railway transit movements.

Water transport is mainly along the Labe (Elbe) up to Kolín and up the Vltava to Prague (above Prague is only pleasure traffic). Before the war, the Labe (Elbe) was the main exit for Czechoslovak waterborne traffic to the port of Hamburg. The journey by water to Szczecin is roundabout and unimportant, while there is no adequate connection yet to Rostock. Danube traffic uses Bratislava. Plans have been made for the canalisation of the Odra (Oder) from Koźle in Poland to Ostrava, with a new canal through Moravia to the Danube near Bratislava. An Elbe–Danube link has also been proposed. Water transport is used for heavy bulk freights through Hamburg and Szczecin or from the Danube (Komárno, bulk freights; Bratislava, general cargoes). The country owns eight ocean-going vessels (80 000 gross tons) and two small vessels capable of sailing from the Danube to Levant destinations. Czechoslovak ships use Baltic or Black Sea ports for sailings to Cuba and the Far East.

The Czechoslovak problem is to weld the Czech and Slovak lands together firmly and to overcome the problems of modernising the economy. Internal political strains and the disaster of the summer of 1968 when the Soviet forces invaded have prevented progress being made. Improved relations with Austria and Western Germany are also important factors in its future prosperity.

9.4 Hungary

The dissolution of the Austro–Hungarian empire left the Hungarian State within exceptionally tightly drawn boundaries that not only put large Magyar minorities outside the national state but also many sources of raw materials upon which industry within its new boundaries had been based. The inter-war years were occupied by intense efforts to remould the economy to the new straitened circumstances, made particularly hard by the economic nationalism of the period and the faltering of the world economy in 1929–32. Though no further territorial change was made after the Second World War, the old patterns of Hungarian trade—such as the flow of bauxite to Germany—were disrupted.

Hungary, one of the smaller members of Comecon in both area (93 000 km²) and population (10.2 million), depended heavily on agriculture until the mid-1950s, but now about a third of the working population is in industry, which contributes about half the country's exports. In 1938 industry contributed 37 per cent of national income, 45 per cent in 1950 and over 68 per cent by the end of the 1960s.

The mineral resources of Hungary are varied if not great and occur in a broad belt running from north-east to south-west. One of the most valuable resources is bauxite, discovered earlier this century. The deposits lie primarily along the flanks of the block-faulted Bakony Forest: the main centres are Gánt, in the Vértes hills, Halimba, Iszkaszentgyörgy and Nyírad in the Bakony hills. Most deposits are of good quality and easy to process. Some manganese is mined at Úrkút and Eplény and exceeds domestic needs, so that exports are made. Hungary is second to the Soviet Union in manganese production in Europe. Other ores include copper-bearing gold ore in the Mátra hills, where some lead–zinc ores are also found. In the Zemplén hills veins of gold and silver are known but largely exhausted. The most important of the magmatic ores is the siderite of the Rudabánya district, where in places oxidised siderite occurs as limonite, richer in iron. The iron ore output does not, however, cover domestic requirements and imports are made.

Deposits of lignite of various quality extend north-east–south-west across the north, but in the south, in the Mecsek hills near Pécs, there are deposits of Jurassic coal with coking qualities. The coals of Ajka in the Bakony Forest are intermediate between the lignites and the bituminous types, while good lignites occur around Tatabánya in the Vértes hills and in the Dorog–Tokod field between the Gerecse and Pilis hills and in several smaller scattered basins. Together they produce about a third of Hungarian output. Around the northern hills of the Bükk and Mátra are big fields of Miocene brown coals, while poorer quality deposits occur near Várpalota, but the coals all have a very low calorific value. Hopes have been entertained that the resources of oil and natural gas will be enlarged through exploration with modern methods. The overwhelming part of the present resources lie in south-west Transdanubia in the Zala area. Promising areas are the Danube–Tisza interfluve and east of the Tisza. There has been overworking of some deposits, for example at Nagylengyel. A few strikes have been made around the foot of the Bükk hills, and resources of natural gas discovered in the Great Plains. The Zala oil and gas is piped to the Budapest area, where it is largely consumed. Hungary is also a producer of uranium, mined in the Mecsek hills, a venture with strong Soviet interest.

9.4.1 Industry in Hungary (figure 9.7)

Industrial development came effectively only after the Compromise between Austria and Hungary in 1867. There was stimulus from the growth of the railway system and also from an inflow of foreign capital, but nevertheless growth was modest. Until the end of the nineteenth century processing agricultural produce and manufacturing of farm machinery remained the main body of industry, but engineering and heavy industry were stimulated by the growing demand for armaments before 1914. After 1918 heavy industry suffered a severe setback, having been cut by the new boundaries from most of its raw materials and with a domestic market too small to support it effectively. On the other hand, with new customs frontiers, branches such as food processing and textiles began to flourish. Foreign companies invested money in Hungarian telecommunications, electrical goods and chemicals plants, so that industry began to provide the greater part of the national income. Plants in inter-war Hungary financed by Germany, were taken over by the Soviet Union as German assets in 1945 and operated for reparations, though later most of them passed to the Hungarians.

Figure 9.7. Hungarian industry remains on the northern axis from Miskolc through Budapest towards Ajka. Efforts have been made to site new industries in the large townlike villages of the Puszta.

Hungary has developed its heavy industry along new lines to fit the concepts of autarky during the Stalinist period. At the same time branches such as light engineering and textiles were reorganised and new industries such as machine tools, instrument-making and ball-bearings were started. There was a large increase in the industrial labour force at the expense of farming, while female labour began to play a significant role. The territorial distribution of industry is particularly uneven, with the major concentration in and around Budapest, which has the largest part of the country's manufacturing industry, supplied with raw materials or semi-processed goods from provincial towns. Inspite of efforts to get a more even spread of industry there remains an uncomfortable concentration around the capital, and the northern part of the country is still the focus of industrial activity. Only about a tenth of industrial capacity lies in the Great Plains east of the Danube.

The modest natural endowment has made the supply of energy a problem. Coal supplies are small and oil and natural gas is also comparatively restricted, while the cost of harnessing water power is high. Various types of coal supply together over three-quarters of the energy requirements, but substantial imports of bituminous and coking coal are made, mostly from Czechoslovakia, Poland and the Soviet Union. Three-quarters of all coal is consumed by industry. Domestic natural gas output has grown in the last two decades, but gas is imported from Rumania. The modest growth in home petroleum production has been accompanied by big increases in imports of crude and refined petroleum. Crude petroleum is brought by pipeline from the Soviet Union (and a duplicate line is planned), but larger imports are projected through the Jugoslav terminal at Bakar. The main refineries are Csepel (Budapest), Pét, Almásfüzitő and Szőny, with a new plant at Zalaegerszeg.

Three hydroelectric stations are planned on the Tisza—at Tiszalök, Tiszabo and Szeged, but power generation is secondary to irrigation and river control, while plans for three stations on the Danube have also been formulated. Electricity is, however, primarily generated in thermal stations. Since 1945 large thermal power stations have been built to serve a regional grid distribution system. These include Inota, Oroszlány, and the Százhalombatta station (using waste from the oil refinery), while a big lignite-fired station is being built at Gyöngyös. Other stations—such as Tatabánya and Lőrinci—have been enlarged. Generation does not meet domestic needs and current is imported from Czechoslovakia, the Soviet Union and Jugoslavia. Rural electrification is reputedly complete. With uranium available from Kővágószőllős in the Mecsek, a 400 000 kW power station using atomic energy has been planned.

Iron and steel-making depends both on home and imported sources for coking coal and ore, though imports form the larger part of its requirements. Iron ore comes from the Soviet Union by railway and by the Danube, while it is also shipped up the Danube by Bulgaria. Railway shipments of coking coal from Poland, Czechoslovakia and the Soviet Union are also made. Fortunately, Hungarian manganese production covers home needs and leaves a surplus for export. The iron and steel industry had been established in the northern hills before 1914—near to its coal and ore sources, while elsewhere were a few small steel-conversion plants in engineering centres. Iron and steel suffered a severe setback after 1918 through the disruption of its raw materials and did not recover until the later 1930s, but since 1945 industrial plans have emphasised its development and a large increase in output has taken place. The oldest but modernised plant is the Diósgyőr works, with iron and steel-making, rolling mills, and the largest cast-steel works. The second large plant is at Ózd, which also smelts and makes steel as well as rolling and there is a sheet mill at Borsodnádasd. A foundry operates in Salgótarján and in Györ, while Zagyvaróna has a ferro-alloy works (another is in the Zagyva valley at Apc). The Csepel plant (Budapest) uses scrap and pig imported from other plants for steel conversion and its rolling mills. The most important plant is the large post-war complex at Dunaújváros (Sztalinváros) on the Danube. It gets its coking coal from the Mecsek field and sends most of its produce to Budapest, while its ore comes from the Soviet Union and Bulgaria and some coking coal and coke from Czechoslovakia or Poland. When complete it will have large rolling mills for plate and thin sheet.

Although bauxite production reached a high level by the end of the 1920s, it was not processed in Hungary, where alumina output began only shortly before the Second World War. During the war a complete plant was opened at Ajka, but up to 1945 the bulk of bauxite was shipped raw to Germany. German finance had been important in the industry. Reconstruction and modernisation of the older plants began after 1945. Two-thirds of the alumina comes from the Almásfüzitő works and a fifth from Ajka, with the rest from Mosonmagyaróvár. The main smelters are Tatabánya, Ajka and Budapest, and there are rolling mills in Budapest and Székesfehérvár. Soviet assistance was used to build the Inota plant, a large supplier of unrefined aluminium. A major problem in expanding the industry has been its high demand for electricity. Alumina is shipped via the Danube and Black Sea to the Soviet Volgograd plant and finished aluminium returned to Hungary at an agreed rate. The Polish link is with the large processing plant at Skawina in Silesia. A similar link also exists with Czechoslovakia and Hungarian raw materials supply the aluminium industry of the German Democratic Republic. A little over half the total alumina output is exported.

Engineering has done much to establish the international reputation of Hungary as an industrial country. In the inter-war period, engineering was particularly concentrated in transport equipment—railway locomotives, rolling stock, river boats—and in electrical equipment and farm machinery, with little development of standardised production and a lack of specialisation. Since 1945 new directions have been the making of machine tools, mining equipment and motor vehicles, but production has been rationalised. The industry shows a strong concentration in and around Budapest, while another important group of plants lies west of the Danube and in the Borsod district. Transport equipment, which mostly goes for export, is concentrated in Budapest, though other plants are located at Győr (buses), Balatonfüred (ships), Gyöngyös (railway goods), Eger (vehicles), and Székesfehérvár (buses). Budapest is also the main centre for farm machinery, but other plants are Mosonmagyaróvár, Szombathely, Makó and Törökszentmiklós. Machine tools are made in Budapest, Győr, Esztergom and Békéscsaba. General mechanical engineering is found in Budapest, Miskolc, Győr and Pécs, while Budapest and Debrecen make roller bearings. High-voltage and heavy electrical equipment is manufactured in Budapest, but Debrecen and Pápa are also important. Light electrical equipment and radio and television equipment is made notably in Budapest with other major works at Székesfehérvár and Vác. Small assembly industries have been started in towns of the Alföld, where some plants assemble components made in East Germany.

The chemicals industry developed between the wars on the basis of small plants, but it has been strongly encouraged since 1945, with a special chemical university at Veszprém. Pharmaceuticals, long a major branch, are concentrated in Budapest (90 per cent of output), but there is a large penicillin and antibiotics plant at Debrecen and a morphine combine at Tiszavasvári. Hungary is a large producer of codeine and vegetable-based drugs. A big new petrochemicals plant is sited at the Százhalombatta terminal of the pipeline from the Soviet Union.

Leninváros makes plastic materials from natural gas piped from Rumania. Fertilisers are made from lignite at Várpalota and other plants are Peremarton (an old explosives works), Balatonfüzfő, Szolnok, Kazincbarcika (also plastics). Szeged imports rubber latex and synthetic rubber from the Soviet Union and the German Democratic Republic, while rubber goods are also made in Budapest. Besides home raw materials, apatite, rock salt, potassium and other substances are imported. Imports of cellulose are augmented by home-made material from rye, rice husks and rushes (at Szolnok), while it is produced from imported timber at Csepel. It is used in the rayon and paper industries.

The textile industry before 1914 had to compete with the more advanced Austrian and Bohemian industries and its main development came in the interwar period. The largest branch is cotton textiles, followed by the making-up industry and then wool, linen and hemp. There is also knitwear and hosiery. About 60 per cent of the textile industry is located in Budapest. Most of the factories outside the capital lie west of the Danube. Much rationalisation, particularly in the creation of larger units has been undertaken, with new mills equipped with Russian and even Chinese machinery. New spinning mills have been established in Budapest, Szeged, Kaposvár, Szombathely and Miskolc to overcome the shortage of home-produced yarn. Seventy per cent of the raw cotton supplies come from Socialist countries, while 45 per cent of the production is exported. Weaving mills operate at Györ, Sopron, Pápa and Mosonmagyaróvár. Using imported wool, woollen mills account for a quarter of the textile industry, with 70 per cent of the capacity concentrated in Budapest and another quarter in Györ, Sopron, Szombathely, Kőszeg and Tata. About 60 per cent of the raw wool is imported and over a third of all production is exported. Linen is mainly in Budapest and Szeged (two mills turn out four-fifths of the total output). Threequarters of the raw flax is imported—mostly from Poland and the Netherlands. The same two centres dominate jute production. A one-time substantial silk industry has declined in the face of synthetic cloths and the cultivation of silk worms has shrunk severely. Two-thirds of the making-up industry is in Budapest, but it is spreading to the countryside and small provincial towns where there is labour available. Hungary is an important leather producer and also makes shoes (notably ladies fashion shoes) sold widely throughout Comecon.

9.4.2 Agriculture in Hungary (figure 9.8)

Although the rapid pace of industrialisation has displaced agriculture's domination of the economy, it still remains a vital sector and Hungary is commonly described as an 'industrial–agricultural' country. Before the Second World War over half the population was supported by agriculture, but now only a quarter remains dependent on farming and since the war, agricultural employment has fallen by 40 per cent. The country is virtually independent for food supply and a surplus of 20–5 per cent remains for export. The harvest of several crops falls between the earlies of Mediterranean Europe and the main crops of Central and North-western Europe, giving Hungary a particular advantage in Western European markets. Many feudal survivals remained in 1945, with the Church holding 600 000 ha, the Esterházy family 140 000 ha, Prince Festetics over 65 000 ha, while a further eighty estates held over 5000 ha each and another 1070 estates

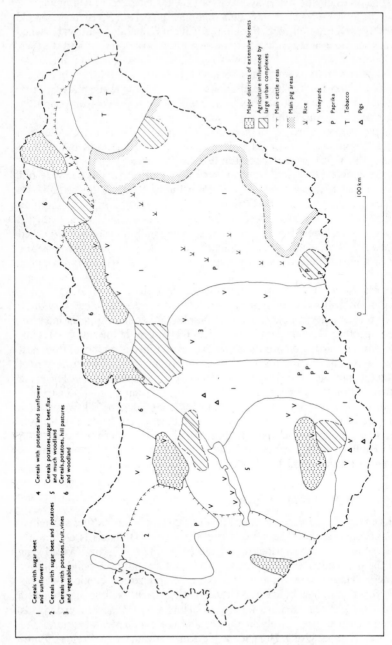

Figure 9.8. Conditions favour cereal cultivation over much of eastern Hungary, where sunflowers are also grown. West of the Danube, the pattern is more diverse, with considerable fruit production.

1 Cereals with sugar beet and sunflowers
2 Cereals with sugar beet and potatoes
3 Cereals with potatoes, fruit, vines and vegetables
4 Cereals with potatoes and sunflower
5 Cereals potatoes, sugar beet, flax and much woodland
6 Cereals, potatoes, hill pastures and woodland

Major districts of extensive forests
Agriculture influenced by large urban complexes
Main cattle areas
Main pig areas
V Rice
V Vineyards
P Paprika
T Tobacco
△ Pigs

0   100 km

each held more than 575 ha. One per cent of the agricultural population thus held 57 per cent of the total land, another 63 per cent held 43 per cent of the land and 36 per cent of the farming population were without land whatsoever. The land reform in 1945 sequestered almost 35 per cent of the area of Hungary and 642 000 landless or small peasants received land. Where land was not sufficient locally, peasants were resettled in other parts of the country where land was available. As the new holdings were in general too small to be profitable, the peasants were encouraged to join collectives. State farms held 11 per cent of the land, 10 per cent is controlled by the State Forests and 64 per cent by the Agricultural Production Co-operatives, while a mere 6 per cent remains in private farms.

The Agricultural Production Co-operatives comprise largely members' private property, who receive a ground rent, even if they do not take part in the work of the collective. If a member leaves, he receives land of equal value. Each member's family has a small plot of their own, comprising 13 per cent of the total co-operative area. The 'lower grade' co-operatives cover only bulk purchase and disposal of materials, whereas the 'higher grade' co-operatives (true collectives) cover all the operations of the farm. As a result of organisational failings, the collective movement suffered a severe setback in the mid-1950s, though it recovered during the 1960s.

Farm machinery is imported as well as made domestically, but following Soviet developments, the original machine and tractor stations were changed to repair stations and the machinery taken over by the collective co-operatives. Irrigation and watering has been a major investment programme, and about one million hectares require watering because of the liability to drought or because of adverse relief and hydrological conditions. Since 1945 the watered area has been increased from 14 000 to 400 000 ha, mostly along the Danube, Tisza and Körös. A major work has been the Eastern Main Canal, branching from the Tisza at Tiszalök and crossing the most arid parts of the Alföld—the Hortobágy and Hajdúság. There are also big irrigation schemes in the middle Tisza and along the Körös in the south-east. The growth of the chemicals industry has brought the intensified use of artificial fertilisers—in 1938 only 13 kg per ha were used, compared to 450 kg per ha in 1968. Special problems have had to be overcome in the amelioration of acid and saline soils and in sandy areas.

Over 90 per cent of the area of Hungary is used for farming or forestry. There has been a fall in the percentage of arable land, though better yield of most crops has offset this decline, whereas there has been an increase in forest land and in fruit and vineyards, but pastures have also declined. Considerable regional variations occur—the Alföld is almost treeless and devoted to arable farming; the Tisza–Danube interfluve is largely vineyards and orchards, while the northern hills are the forest lands. Inspite of its reduced percentage, the proportion of ploughland remains among the highest national levels in Europe.

Cereal crops including maize account for about two-thirds of the arable land. The proportion under these crops has, however, tended to shrink and there has been a shift from bread to fodder grains. Three-quarters of the bread grain area is under wheat, though its area is now less than maize. Winter wheat is usually sown, but spring wheat is sown after frost or flood damage. 'Hard' wheats are typical of the Tisza basin. Wheat is important in the Great Plains (apart from the sandier lands), the Danube–Tisza interfluve, the southern fringes of the northern hills and west of the Danube. Wide variations in yield occur in the Great Plains because of fluctuations in rainfall. In some years, wheat production does not cover home requirements and imports are made. In areas unsuitable for wheat rye becomes the main bread grain—it is often found on sandy and on acid soils. Yield is generally low, because it is sown on the poorest soils. Important rye lands are the sandy parts of the western border areas. The Nyírség produces the best rye. Since 1945 there has been a big increase in the cultivation of rice, now common in the central and eastern parts of the Great Plains, often on alkaline soils unsuited for other uses. Some rice is exported. Winter barley has also been cultivated on an increased scale, notably in the Mecsek, where it has shown steadily improved yield, while as an early crop, it is possible to get two harvests. Spring barley is grown mostly for brewing—principally in the Kisalföld—and its area has decreased substantially since 1945. Oats are cultivated on a small scale. Maize is now the most important crop in Hungary and both grain and green maize are used, mostly for fodder. Maize covers about 25 per cent of all arable land—the greatest concentrations are on *loess* and alluvial soils of the Danube basin and in the south-east of the country. Maize demands high rainfall and high temperatures: it is consequently open to wide fluctuations in yield in dry summers or in cool years. It has been a significant factor in the expansion of livestock production.

Potatoes are cultivated in much the same regions as rye, with the main areas on acid sandy soils in the Nyírség and Somogy districts. They are also important near Budapest and in the northern hills. Sugar beet was a typical large estate crop before 1945, consequently concentrated in the Kisalföld, where the most advanced estates were found. Other important districts were the sugar mill areas of the Mezőföld and in the Somogy and Mátra districts and some parts of the Great Plain. Since 1945, production has shifted to southern and eastern parts of the Alföld, on the soils rich in humus and of a calciferous nature. There is also a considerable cultivation of fodder roots—associated with the development of stall-fed livestock farming. Sunflower was widely cultivated during the war years and immeditely afterwards as a substitute for imported fats, but during the late 1950s as trade among Comecon countries and with the outside world developed, it lost ground to more intensive crops. Able to survive on poor quality soils and drought-resistant, it is still found in the Nyírség, in the south-western Alföld and Mezőföld. Rape and castor as well as peanuts are grown, and poppy seed is cultivated. Flax and hemp are grown for fibre and for oil, with linseed from the hotter and drier south-east, and the cooler and moister north produces flax. An attempt to grow cotton on a large scale failed because of inadequate preparation.

Though occupying only a modest area the cultivation of vegetables is important. Onions and paprika are notable products for export. Home-grown tobacco of the best quality is suitable for cigar production and a small but interesting culture is the production of medicinal herbs. Fruit is widely cultivated, but the main area is the sandy interfluvial land between the Danube and the Tisza; apricots are particularly renowned but other fruits are grown for home and export. The vine is grown notably west of the Danube in Transdanubia and over three-quarters of the vine area in the Great Plains lies between the Danube and the Tisza, where the nineteenth century phylloxera epidemic had forced the use of immune sandy flatlands, but conditions are marginal and wide fluctuations in the crop result. The most famous wines of the Tokaj vineyards are grown on *loessic* soils on a volcanic rock base in the Hegyalja where there is abundant sunshine and special treatment of the grapes. Another important wine is the red Bulls' Blood of Eger, while the volcanic Badacsony district contributes a good wine. Some export of wines has developed.

Until the middle of last century livestock breeding was remarkably independent of crop farming, with cattle kept in the open all the year and little effective use made of their manure. The once great grazing lands have shrunk and are now limited to the poorer areas unsuited to crops, while meadow remains on moister lands. The expansion of fodder crops has lagged behind the break-up of the grazing lands, so that feed has been a major bottleneck to increasing the numbers of animals. Consequently, until recently, livestock farming has been extensive rather than intensive. Numbers of cattle have increased more slowly than pigs and sheep, while mechanisation has reduced the number of horses, though Hungary still breeds riding animals. Stock-breeding contributes about 45 per cent of total agricultural production—nearly half coming from pigs and a quarter from cattle, while poultry provides a fifth.

Forest cover has been extended by plantings on poor sandy ground, but still covers only 14 per cent of the country's area. Nearly half the forest is oak and there are large acacia groves, artificially planted. Coniferous plantations are found on sands in the Great Plains, but conifers only occur naturally on the northern uplands and on lands west of the Danube. Nearly half the wood, much of it softwood, used in the country has to be imported.

9.4.3 Transport in Hungary

The transport system of Hungary was shaped originally as part of the Austro–Hungarian system. Particularly well-developed were links with the western part of the country and to Vienna. The predominance of Budapest is reflected in the radiating system of roads and railways to the corners of the state. There is a paucity of north–south or direct east–west links, which are hampered in any case by the Danube and the Tisza. Since 1945 a north–south line has been built to Dunaújváros and also an avoiding line around Budapest. Railways handle over 40 per cent of all originating goods and account for three-quarters of the total freight traffic. Their share has, however, tended to fall and there has been a shift to road traffic. Lorries handled 36 per cent of all originating goods in 1960 but almost 52 per cent in 1970, while their share of total freight traffic was just under 6 per cent in 1960 but almost 11 per cent in 1970. A small increase had also been shown in the share of total traffic moving to the rivers. Railways dominate the passenger scene, though buses have been taking a larger share. Only about 12 per cent of route is double-track and traffic is concentrated in the north—on the double-track and electrified lines Budapest–Györ–Hegyeshalom and Budapest–Miskolc–Záhony (the main route to the Soviet border) and the alternative route Budapest–Cegléd–Szolnok–Nyíregyháza–Záhony. Electric traction accounts for about a quarter of all traffic and another 40 per cent is handled by diesel locomotives. 90 per cent of all railway traffic moves on well under half the route length.

The growth in road traffic, inspite of a rigorous control on the number of vehicles, has made it imperative to improve the poor quality of the roads and a motorway has been built from Budapest to Székesfehérvár for the traffic to the Lake Balaton resorts. The road system radiates from Budapest and about 30 000 km of road exist, but only a fifth has a modern surface.

The Danube is the main navigable river, with ships sailing from Hungarian river ports to the Black Sea and Levant ports. Budapest is the main port, with some international transit traffic. Completion of the Tiszalök barrage and locks make navigational possibilities on the Tisza better, though Szolnok and Szeged are already ports. It is hoped that river boats will use the new eastern main canal to carry away farm produce.

Hungary has made desperate efforts to overcome the problems of its political geography after 1919 and since 1945 has put all its resources into industrialisation, particularly trying to spread industry into the rural backwaters of the Great Plain. It has sought co-operation with its fellow members of Comecon to achieve these objectives. Through this pattern, it belongs to the more advanced countries, now on the threshold of great economic change that makes it important for them to join in a wider horizon of world contacts and trade.

10 Sketches of National Economic Geographies: the Developing Countries

Rumania, Bulgaria, Jugoslavia and Albania form a group of countries in South-eastern Europe that have many characteristics of emerging economies, in which rapid industrialisation and a move of people from country to town have had a considerable impact on the agricultural scene. All of them before 1939 were predominantly agricultural economies. In several respects the application of Marxist–Leninist planning criteria here has had a more impressive influence on the landscape than the more subtle changes in the advanced economies of Czechoslovakia and the German Democratic Republic or, to a less subtle degree, in Poland and Hungary. Not all the countries in this group are members of Comecon. Jugoslavia has had vacillating relations with the Organisation and has been a Socialist country that has followed its own line of development since 1948. Albania, originally a member of Comecon, drifted away in the 1960s when it preferred the Chinese to Russian policies.

10.1 Rumania

Rumania, one of the larger countries of Eastern Europe, emerged after the First World War, when the Old Kingdom was enlarged by the addition of Hungarian Transylvania, Austrian Bukovina and the Russian Bessarabian lands. After the Second World War it reappeared in its old boundaries, though stripped of the Bukovina and Bessarabia. The major Rumanian territorial problem has been welding together across the formidable barrier of the Carpathians the historical provinces of Wallachia and Moldavia, essentially Lower Danubian and Black Sea orientated, and Transylvania, whose natural orientation is towards Pannonia.

The pre-war Rumanian economy had been geared to the production of raw materials and semi-processed goods from the Country's sound endowment in natural resources. After the war a feverish development policy began that emphasised manufacturing industry and a change to the Stalinist search for autarky. As the Soviet hold on the country weakened in the late 1950s, the Rumanians reverted to the creation of an 'agrarian–industrial' economy. During the 1960s Rumanian policy began to clash increasingly with Comecon plans for integration and specialisation—especially as some of the more advanced Eastern European countries conceived the Rumanian role as 'passive in-dustrialisation'. The Rumanians have not been ready to concentrate on the sup-ply of raw materials and to reduce their industrialisation through cutting back on their industries which duplicate or are still less efficient than plants elsewhere in Comecon. While Rumania has not denied the attractions of specialisation in Comecon, it has been adamant that this should follow rather than supplant establishment of a broadly based industrial structure. Rumania has been actively pursuing establishment of contacts with trading partners outside Comecon.

Before 1939 development of its valuable petroleum resources had received much foreign investment, notably by Germany, the United States and British and Dutch interests. The larger part of production had been exported and briefly at the turn of the century, Rumania had been one of the world's major producers. It now ranks twelfth in world order. Known for many centuries, petroleum was first worked in the seventeenth century. The first simple refinery opened in 1856 near Ploieşti, while after 1860 digging for petroleum in pits gave way to drilling, with much loss through explosions and inability to control the flow. After 1883 output increased rapidly. Petroleum had been encouraged by strong German interest in the 1930s and output, fostered by undesirable techniques, began to fall during the Second World War, when Rumania was the main German source of natural petroleum. Rumania has become an important supplier to neighbouring countries, though the growth of Soviet petroleum output suggests that its role will decline in future.

The most important occurrences of petroleum lie in the pre-Carpathian hills, notably along the Southern and Eastern Carpathians. The most promising deposits occur in Pliocene formations, though some good reservoirs are found in the older Tertiary beds of the outer Flysch zone of the Eastern Carpathians (the Bacău region of Moldavia). Modern methods of exploration have brought not only new finds in existing areas, but also in the Getic plateau, the southern Moldavian plateau, in the Danube plain and in the western part of the country. Before 1939 90 per cent of production came from the Ploieşti area: this has fallen to a third. The Argeş district and the Oltenian district each contribute a quarter, while the remainder comes from Bacău. Although new refineries have been built in the Bacău region, the Ploieşti district remains the focus of refining. Pipelines join the oilfields together and to the port terminals in Giurgiu and Constanţa. About half the production is today consumed internally.

Another important source of energy is natural gas, either occurring in association with petroleum deposits or separately, usually in young Tertiary formations. Its presence has long been known as 'eternal fires' and mud volcanoes. The gases in association with petroleum comprise 64–90 per cent methane and have a heating value of about 40 MJ per m^3, with commonly 250–300 m^3 of gas for each ton of crude petroleum. Pre-war, as much as two-thirds of this gas was flared off or otherwise wasted, but much is now bottled. Since the 1950s it has been used increasingly for industrial purposes or for the generation of electrical power. The gases, which occur separately and are of unusual purity (98–9 per cent methane), lie in subterranean structural domes in Transylvania, which is a focus of a rapidly expanding pipeline system, with gas piped into northern Hungary. The natural gases form an important raw material in the petrochemicals industry.

About a third of the coal reserves occur in the Petroşeni field in the Southern Carpathians which produces over half the total output. Although dating from Cretaceous times, the coal is well carbonised with a heating value of 26–30 MJ per kg and it will coke satisfactorily. In the Banat in the upper Carboniferous and lower Lias, in small, strongly folded basins, there are reserves of excellent coking coal, with a heating value of 27–33 MJ per kg (8 per cent of total output). These deposits are well placed in relation to iron and manganese deposits for the iron industry of the Reşiţa district. There has been a substantial growth in the mining of lignite of various qualities, rising from a fifth of total fuel output in 1938 to well over 40 per cent in 1970. The largest deposits (from Pliocene and Oligocene times) are near Comăneşti (Bacău) and Almaş(Cluj). The heating value ranges from 21–6 MJ per kg. The poorer qualities occur in the Muntenian pre-Carpathians (15 per cent of total output) and in the Danube plains, usually near the surface and easy to work by open pits or adits. These Pliocene lignites have a heating value of 15–17 MJ per kg. There are several small scattered occurrences elsewhere in the country. They are used mostly by industry for steam-raising but small amounts also go for domestic use in towns.

10.1.1 Industry in Rumania (figure 10.1)

A main task since 1945 has been creation of a large scale electricity generation and distribution system. The pre-war system was unevenly distributed over the country—Bucharest and district, the Prahova valley and the area of Braşov had almost half the installed capacity, while the bulk of the remainder was in the towns of Transylvania. The Dobrogea, Oltenia and Moldavia had little generating capacity, so that only 29 per cent of the population had an electricity supply. To overcome the bottlenecks in the supply of electric current and to cover the needs of a rapidly expanding industry, a Ten Year Electrification Plan was run, ending in 1960. Under this, over twenty major power stations were built, besides a large number of small stations for local supply, while a basic national grid was also developed. Thermal generators account for the overwhelming part of the current produced and only a small fraction of the water power potential has yet been used. The largest hydroelectric project is the 210 000 kW Lenin station at the Bicaz dam, though two other large projects are under construction: the Iron Gates dam, in association with Jugoslavia, and the Turnu Măgurele project on the Danube with Bulgaria. Over two-thirds of the thermally generated power is delivered from gas-fired stations, 17 per cent from lignite-fired stations and 7 per cent from oil-fired stations.

Early attention after 1945 was given to the development of an iron and steel industry. Before the Second World War, small plants were working at Reşiţa and Hunedoara, producing Bessemer and open-hearth steel. Reşiţa had a coking plant that covered 60 per cent of its needs, while the rest of the country's coke was imported from Germany, Poland and Czechoslovakia. Seven of the eleven plants processing iron and steel were in the Banat and Transylvania—the others were Bucharest, Galaţi, Brăila and Roman.

Two-thirds of the iron ore mined comes from the Poiana–Ruscă Massif. The other important centre is the Banat Hills, while an untapped source lies in the Dobrogea, and there are some ores in the Harghita Mountains. Manganese is mined in the upper basin of the Bistriţa and in the Dornei depression, while deposits also occur in the Banat Hills, and Tirnăveni has a ferro-manganese plant. In serpentine rocks of the Orşova district, chrome and nickel occur, and the Banat also has some molybdenum.

Of total iron and steel output, almost a third comes from the Hunedoara plant; 25 per cent from Reşiţa; just over 6 per cent from Oţelul Roşu; 2 per cent from

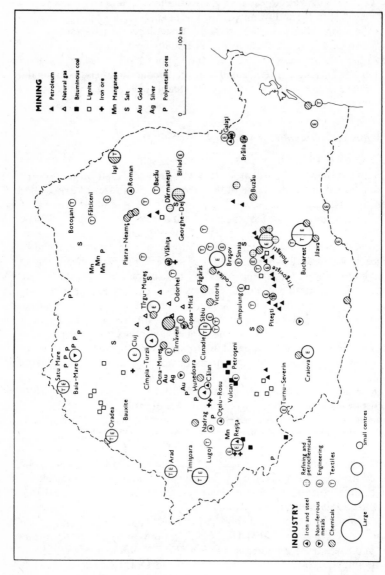

Figure 10.1. Rumania has a significant variety of mineral wealth and was once an important world petroleum producer. The Transylvanian lands received an impetus to industrialise under the Austro-Hungarian regime. Development in the south and east is still limited, apart from a new heavy-industry complex at the mouth of the Danube.

Călan and a little over 1 per cent from Nădrag. Hunedoara has been reconstructed since 1945 as a full cycle plant, with new blast furnaces, open-hearth furnaces, electric steel mills, rolling mills, a cokery and a power station. It is supplied by a cableway with ore from Teliuc and also from other mines. The Reşiţa plant, completely modernised after over-use during the war, is supplied with ore from Ocna de Fier and Drognecea, while coke is made at the plant, but pig iron and coke are also brought from Hunedoara. It is most important for heavy and medium-rolled goods. The works at Călan was modernised with new blast furnaces, but produces grey cast iron (also at Vlăhiţa), while reconstruction of the Oţelul Roşu works has doubled its output of steel and light-rolled goods compared to 1948. The Cîmpia Turzii plant (with electric furnaces) has been rebuilt to produce more light-rolled sections, also produced at Brăila and Nădrag. Bucharest has a tube works and there are new pipeworks at Roman and Iaşi. The strip mill at Galaţi will be near the large new iron and steel plant, viciously criticised in Comecon, using river-borne Petroşeni coal and coke and Brazilian and Indian ore. Inspite of a large increase in domestic production Rumania must still import finished rolled goods and special steels from the Soviet Union, while increased steel production demands imports of Silesian coke and Ukrainian coke and iron ore.

Non-ferrous metals occur in two main groups: in the volcanic mountains of Maramureş and in the Apuseni mountains. In the north polymetallic sulphides yield copper, zinc and lead, and there are also some precious metals. In the western Carpathians gold and silver occur and between the rivers Crişul, Alb, Arieş and Mureş is the so-called *Gold Polygon*, one of the richest auriferous areas in Europe. Lead deposits occur in the Banat; at Balan in Transylvania and in the Dobrogea, copper ores occur. Recent exploration has located new rich lead, zinc and copper occurrences in the Bistriţa mountains, the Maramueş mountains, in the Banat and the Dobrogea. Near Oradea are valuable bauxite deposits. A mercury-bearing ore is found in the *Gold Polygon*. Output is now several times greater than pre-war and new installations have been built to refine and process the metals, including a wide range of chemical by-products. The main pre-war plant was at Baia Mare, where lead, zinc and copper were refined and sheet and pipe lead made. Silver, gold, lead and copper were also processed at Ferneziu, while gold-bearing concentrates came from the Zlatna works. Using non-ferrous metallic waste, the Solex plant at Bucharest, opened in 1932, produced mainly lead and copper. During the Second World War, the Copsa Mică zinc works was opened. After the war flotation plants were opened at six new sites, while existing works were enlarged and modernised. Particular emphasis has been given to copper refining and production, a metal short within Comecon and vital in the electrification programme. A new alumina plant built in Oradea to use local bauxite ships its produce to the aluminium combine at Slatina.

Engineering contributed only 10 per cent of the total industrial output in 1938, but it is now almost 30 per cent. The output of engineering is now more than twenty times greater than in 1939, but there has been overdiversification within the limited domestic market. The main centres are the principal towns: Bucharest produces a wide range of products, Braşov, Cluj, Arad and Reşiţa have a diversity of general engineering besides special products such as machine tools. Ploiești, Tirgoviște, Brașov, Bacău and Bucharest are producers of oilfield and mining equipment, exported to Comecon and overseas. Electrical equipment is now made in Rumania, whereas pre-war all requirements were imported: the main centres are Bucharest, Brașov, Timișoara and Ploiești. Along the Danube, shipyards lie at Turnu Severin, Oltenia, Brăila and Galați, while on the Black Sea coast, Constanța is important. Lorries have been built since 1953 at Brașov and buses made in Bucharest, but since 1969, Renault cars have been assembled at Pitești. In 1947 after retooling a wartime aircraft factory, tractor production began at Brașov. Farm machinery is now made in many centres, but important plants are at Bucharest, Craiova, Timișoara, Ploiești and Sibiu.

The pre-war chemicals industry was very small, though raw materials were amply present. The drive in the Soviet Union for 'chemicalisation' in the late 1950s gave a stimulus to the industry in Rumania, with heavy investment in large production units. From 2.7 per cent of total industrial output contributed by chemicals before the war, the share is now over 10 per cent. Inorganic chemicals are particularly important. As well as the pre-war sulphuric acid plants of Valea Călugărească, Cîmpina, Mărășești, Baia Mare and Zlatna, new plants have been opened in Copșa Mică, Victoria and Năvodari. Sulphur is obtained from roasting pyrites or as a by-product of non-ferrous metal refining. The large resources of gypsum may also be used for sulphur recovery, notably on the Someș plateau and in the Muntenian pre-Carpathians. Large and remarkably pure salt deposits at Slănic, Tîrgu Ocna, Ocna Mureșului and Ocna Dejului supply the soda plants of Turda, Tirnăveni, Ocna Mureșului and the new works of Govora. The output of caustic soda, chlorine and hydrochloric acid has greatly increased, while ammonia is made in combines at Făgăraș, Victoria and Tirnăveni.

Particular attention has been devoted to the artificial fertiliser industry—at Valea Călugărească, Făgăraș, Tirnăveni and the Victoria chemical works. A large phosphate fertiliser plant has opened at Năvodari and a nitrogenous fertiliser plant at Piatra Neamț, while works have been constructed well into the 1960s. Natural gas and petroleum have provided significant bases for chemicals production—acetylene at Borzești, Craiova and Rîsnov; hydrogen cyanide for artificial fibres at Săvinești; at Copșa Mică methane is oxydised for formaldehyde. Petroleum provides a base for synthetic rubber at Bucharest (Jilava) and Onești, while benzene, ethylene and propylene for detergents and plasticisers are made mostly around Ploiești. The sophistication of this branch has been possible with the increase in post-war refinery capacity. Rumanian 'Relon' has established itself as an artificial fibre in Eastern Europe, using a petrochemicals base, but more conventional cellulose-based fibres are also made at Lupeni and Popești-Leordeni. Coal has been used for the production of such items as xylol and benzol at Hunedoara, while carbon substances come from Cluj. The development of the chemicals industry has been achieved through co-operation of neighbouring countries—particular help has been given by the German Democratic Republic and Czechoslovakia in the building of a large paper and cellulose combine at Brăila using reed from the Danube delta.

Inspite of a long period of ruthless exploitation, 27 per cent of the area of Rumania remains in forest and a vigorous reafforestation policy has been making good the losses of the past. The forests are mostly in the Carpathians and in Transylvania, while the plains of Wallachia and Moldavia and the Dobrogea have relatively little forest. Three-quarters of the forest is deciduous, with beech as the most common tree, useful for plywood production. The high quality spruce of the northern forests has long been used as a resonant wood for musical instruments. By the outbreak of the Second World War, the wood-working industry was one of the most important branches in the country, with two-thirds of the plants and over 80 per cent of the workers in the sawn timber section. Since 1945 a drastic rationalisation closed two-thirds of the old-fashioned and small plants, replacing them by large-scale *kombinaty*. Reed has tended to replace wood in the paper and cellulose industry.

The small and rather antiquated pre-war textile plants have been enlarged and modernised and new textile mills built. Cotton textiles are made in Timisoara, Arad, Lugoj, Sf. Georghe, Pitesti, Brănesti and Iasi. Woollen cloths come from Cisnădie, Sibiu, Brasov, Prejmer, Ghimbav; silk from mills in Bucharest, Timişoara, Sighişoara, Lupeni; while flax and hemp fibres are worked at Iaşi, Ploieşti, Fălticeni. Folk-weave textiles also remain significant. Bucharest is the biggest single centre of the industry.

The pre-war food-processing industry was one of the largest industries in Rumania, but it was essentially composed of small units. Large factories were found primarily in the milling trades and in sugar and edible oils, branches which accounted for 80 per cent of the total output. Since 1948 new plants have been built and old ones modernised, while new branches have been developed, such as canning and preserving of fruit and fish, with considerable exports. The milling industry is found in many large towns of the plains, but particularly in the ports. Sugar plants are mostly in the districts where sugar beet is grown; the Siret valley, the Danube plains, the Bîrsa plains, in the western plains and the plains of Transylvania. Inspite of a substantial increase in domestic sugar consumption, a surplus remains for export. Over 90 per cent of the vegetable oil is derived from sunflowers and a considerable expansion in production, already seven times greater than pre-war, is envisaged. Expansion of the dairy industry—with well-established local cheeses—has been on a considerable scale, while Rumania has exported butter to Western Europe.

10.1.2 Agriculture in Rumania (figure 10.2)

Before the war agriculture was the predominant source of employment in Rumania: even in 1950 it still included almost three-quarters of the employed population, whereas by the early 1970s this share was a little above 50 per cent. In 1938 agriculture and forestry contributed over 38 per cent of the national income: by 1969 this had fallen to 24.1 per cent. Agriculture claims 63 per cent of the area of the country; arable land alone covers 41 per cent and pastures and meadows, 18.6 per cent. The share of arable land is tending to increase, particularly in the south-east where it encroaches on pasture and forest. In other parts of the country, however, there has been some decline as greater emphasis has been laid on animal farming. Cereals occupy a little under 70 per cent of the arable area compared to 87 per cent in 1938, though this decline has been more at the expense of maize, barley and rye rather than of wheat, which has maintained its share. Big improvements in maize yield have allowed a smaller area to

Figure 10.2. Rumania is still an important producer of forest products, notably from Carpathia and the Bihor. Elsewhere, grain growing is important, with large areas well suited by their steppelike regime. Transylvania is agriculturally more diverse.

1 Cereal cultivation with subsidiary animal husbandry
2 Animal husbandry with subsidiary cereal cultivation
3 Areas of predominant vegetable cultivation
4 Areas of predominant viticulture
5 Predominantly pastoral areas
   Forests with some livestock
   Areas with farming influenced by large urban populations
   Sunflower
   Sugar beet

0   100 km

be devoted to it, while better living standards have also reduced demand for maize, rye and even barley. The socialised structure of agriculture has made possible the cultivation on a larger scale of industrial crops, while the importance of potatoes and vegetables has risen. The greater interest in livestock farming has also increased the need for fodder crops.

A marked feature of land-use and farming patterns in Rumania is the contrast between the extensive plains with their wooded steppe and steppe-like conditions and the rough forested mountain country of the Carpathian structures. The plains of Wallachia and Moldavia and the eastern fringe of Pannonia, with extensive red-brown forest soils and chernozem-like soils, high summer temperatures, low precipitation and a long annual frost-free period, are ideal for cereals such as wheat, which develops here a high gluten content. Maize and other cereals also do well in the slightly moister Pannonian fringe. On the degraded chernozem soils, red-brown forest soils and more fertile podzols of Transylvania, grain crops are also widely grown, as are sugar beet, potatoes and flax, though sunflowers, important in the southern and eastern plains, are missing. The lower slopes of the Carpathians in the south and south-east, with good drainage and absence of frosts, are important for fruit and vines, though vines are also grown within Transylvania. The mountains remain a land of forests, though grains suited to the cooler conditions—barley and oats—and potatoes are raised in the valleys and depressions, where there are also some orchards.

The lifting of the Turkish trade monopoly in 1829 brought an upsurge in the area sown to grain, which became the most important item in Rumanian foreign trade and many of the social and economic problems of the peasantry arose from the rapacious policy of landowners to extend their grainlands, with wheat as the main crop. Inspite of increasing competition from outside Europe after the 1870s, grain remained a key to the Rumanian economy even after 1918. Maize and wheat now occupy 90 per cent of the land sown to grains, with almost a third of the total arable area sown to wheat, predominantly winter varieties. Rumanian wheat has played an important part in feeding the Socialist bloc countries. Maize occupies a third of the total arable land and Rumania is usually about sixth world producer. In the past over-dependence of the peasants on maize caused serious dietary deficiencies. Green maize is sown for silage. Rice is grown in wet lands along the Danube and Tisza.

The area sown to cotton is little larger than pre-war in contrast to large increases in other industrial crops. Flax and hemp are also cultivated. Of particular importance are oil plants, dominated by the sunflower, cultivated in Moldavia, the Bărăgan steppe, the Tisza plains, the Dobrogea and the plain of Oltenia, as well as in Transylvania. The crop completely covers home demand, but linseed, rape and soya are the other sources of oil. Sugar beet growing, introduced late in Rumania, has been greatly extended compared to pre-war, while further large increases in the sown area are anticipated. It is most common in the Transylvanian hills, the western plains and also in Moldavia and the Danube plains. Tobacco cultivation has also been increased since 1938—in the Bîrlad plateau of Moldavia, the Dobrogea, Muntenia and Oltenia, in the Mureş valley and in the Tisza plain. Potatoes, cultivated since the eighteenth century, are most important in the uplands of Transylvania, and Carpathian depressions. In the nineteenth century the high quality of Rumanian wines found a wide market in

Russia, Poland and Black Sea, but overcoming the phylloxera plague was slow. The best wines come from the Cotnari district of Moldavia, though the largest vineyards are on the lower reaches of the Siret. Good white and red wines originate in the Oradea district. Rumania has become an important supplier of wine and table grapes through the Comecon bloc. A traditional peasant culture has been developed in medicinal plants (similar to Hungary) and Rumania now claims to be the world's largest commercial producer of such plants.

Livestock raising was the most important part of the economy until the rapid expansion of grain cultivation in the nineteenth century, when grazing land was taken for wheat and the area available for fodder growing limited, posing critical problems for the livestock farmers. Even between the wars, livestock was raised extensively on natural pastures and meadows. The number of animals, much reduced during the Second World War, has slowly increased since 1945 and, with the exception of horses, now exceeds pre-war stocks. There is still dependence on the use of the vast alpine pastures of the Carpathians, the abundant grass of the Danube floodplains and the delta, but at the same time there has been the development of fodder production.

Attention has also been given to the improvement of breeds, though cattle belong to many strains, not only of Rumanian origin but also imported types such as Pinzgau and Simmenthaler, while in the Bărăgan steppe red steppe cattle from the Soviet Union are now bred. Cattle are found throughout the country, though their density is greatest on the Carpathian foreland, particularly between the Prahova and Motru rivers. Dairy cattle are kept mostly near to the larger towns. Horses are also reared throughout the country, but they are becoming less significant with mechanisation. Both native and imported breeds are kept and a number of state stud farms exist. One of the biggest increases has been in the number of pigs, with particularly high concentrations in the Banat, Brasov and Suceava regions. The lard-bearing curly-haired Mangalitsa pig is common, but both native and foreign breeds—including the Landrace pig—are reared. Much effort has been devoted to improving breeds of the numerous sheep and to providing an effective fodder base for them. Special attention has been given to raising sheep with fine fleece, notably in the Dobrogea, the Bărăgan steppe and the Tisza plains, which now account for over half the total flock compared to a quarter in 1950. Sheep are particularly numerous in the mountains and the Dobrogea and poorer steppe areas. Poultry is also widely kept in both special poultry farms and on peasant holdings. Bees are also important, with good forest and meadow conditions. Even the breeding of silkworms has been expanded in the south and south-west where it has long been practised by peasant women.

The land reform of 1921 was carried out within a politically restricted framework in fear of the radical measures pursued in the Soviet Union against which the Rumanians wanted to insulate themselves. Under Soviet influence a far more radical land reform was carried out after 1945 and the change completed by 1962, after which there was no further collectivisation. This has limited private farms to parts of the upland and mountain lands where application of collectivisation would be difficult. To win peasant support through elimination of the last vestiges of landlordism, estates were cut back to 50 ha, so that 1.5 million ha were available for redistribution. At the same time close central control channelled investment and planned production. State Agricultural Enterprises account for just over 17 per cent of the total arable land, but their number has been reduced by organisation into larger units. Almost three-quarters of the arable land is held by the Agricultural Producer Co-operatives—organised in a similar way to collectives—while the land for the personal use of members of co-operatives accounts for a little over 8 per cent of the total arable. Only 4.6 per cent of the arable is held by individual farms, though they still hold 43.6 per cent of the meadows. Vineyards are markedly in the hands of members of Agricultural Producer Co-operatives, who hold just over 30 per cent as well as 11.6 per cent of the orchards and nurseries.

10.1.3 Transport in Rumania

In 1938 the railway route length was 9900 km and by 1970 it was 11 012, slightly below the maximum of 11 023 km of 1967. The route length of narrow-gauge railways had been reduced from 752 km in 1948 to 625 km in 1970. Important links completed since 1945 include the Craiova–Roşiorii de Vede–Bucharest line across southern Wallachia and the Tirgu Jiu–Iscroni line across the Carpathians, while the Bucharest–Făurei–Tecuci line reduced loading on the busy Bucharest–Ploieşti–Focşani route. In the north the Salva–Vişău railway joined to the main system a number of lines isolated by frontier changes with the Soviet Union. A plan for a northern Trans-Carpathian line from Vatra Dornei to Bicaz exists. Double tracking of the more heavily laden lines will increase capacity and a modest electrification programme has begun. Diesel and electric traction handled 79 per cent of all traffic in 1970.

Of the 76 000 km of road, only 10 600 km can be considered of modern standard and only 70 per cent of the arterial national highway system is described as 'modern'. Nevertheless, the length of 'modern' roads has risen from 3600 km in 1956 compared to little change in the total length of roads. A major highway—described as an 'autostrada'—is under development from Sibiu via Bucharest to Constanţa. The roads are used largely by lorries and buses, with relatively few private cars, though consideration has been given to road improvement in areas of tourist interest. Since 1960 road transport has overtaken the railways in movement of originating tonnage, though the railway still maintain a traffic volume (in ton/km) ten times greater than road transport. In passenger traffic intercity buses slightly overtook the railway in number of originating passengers in 1969, though in terms of passenger traffic (passenger/km), railways still handle two-and-a-half times the volume of buses.

The main waterway is the Danube, on which Rumania has a frontage of 1075 km: far less important are the Bega canal and the lower Prut. Rafting takes place on the Bistriţa, Siret, Mureş and some other rivers. A plan to join the Danube to the Black Sea by a canal from Cernavodă to Constanţa was abandoned in the early 1950s and development shifted to the delta, where Ismail and Reni had become important Soviet ports. Most recently port development for the new iron and steel complex at Galaţi has begun, though between 1958 and 1964 the port of Constanţa had been modernised. Rumania has also developed pipeline transport. Whereas crude oil and oil products ranked as first railway freight in 1938, they now lie fourth. Since 1960 pipelines have been third among the transport media for originating tonnage handled, though only fourth or fifth in terms of ton/kilometres.

Development in Rumania appears to have progressed relatively smoothly, partly by a skilful policy that has related growth of industrial development to availability of suitable labour. Nevertheless, Rumania has been a dissident in Comecon against a policy that has sought to relegate it to a second-rank position: such a challenge seems to have encouraged the Rumanians to further advance in the level of their economy with the greatest possible smoothness. The country has also sought to cultivate the best possible relations with Western European countries.

10.2 Bulgaria

Bulgaria, one of the last countries to be released from the dead grip of the Turkish empire in the late nineteenth century, has had unhappy relations with its neighbours, largely arising from long-standing territorial claims for a Greater Bulgaria. As a dissident 'revisionist' power under the Treaty of Neuilly (1919), the country fell readily into the German sphere of influence in the mid-1930s.

Since 1945 Bulgarian economic development has rested heavily on Soviet, Czech and East German aid. A major hindrance to economic development has been a shortage of skilled labour and a town-dwelling population, though in the late 1950s the vigorous flow of labour from the countryside produced a shortage of agricultural workers. Major national investment had to be made to complete the transport system. Railway route was increased from 3454 km in 1945 to 4196 km in 1969, and there has also been feverish road construction, a need made more pressing by growing transit traffic from Western Europe to Turkey and the Middle East.

The natural resource endowment of Bulgaria for industrial development is good. Good quality brown coal has been used increasingly for thermal generating stations as well as for chemical by-products. The main workings are in the eastern half of the Upper Thracian Plain around Dimitrovgrad, but there are also subsidiary workings, and a second important area is around Sofia. Unfortunately, bituminous coal is less generously endowed, with some Jurassic coals in the west near the Jugoslav border and there are also small deposits in the Balkan Mountains near Teteven, Sofia and Trojan, though the Upper Cretaceous coals worked at Trjavna and Sliven are of coking quality. Coal for metallurgical purposes has, however, to be imported. Anthracite occurs near the Isker gorge north of Sofia. A search for petroleum and natural gas, started after 1945 with Soviet help, brought finds in the north and in the Black Sea coast. The heavy oil was exported for refining, but a large refinery has recently been built at Burgas for local and imported petroleum, with a substantial increase in imports. Natural gas is used locally to fire industrial plants.

About one-third of the electric current comes from hydroelectric plants, which have to contend with the long winter freeze and the summer drought. Nearly two-thirds of all current is consumed by manufacturing industry. The most important group of stations producing about 40 per cent of national output, lies around Sofia and Pernik (mostly thermal generators, but there are also some hydroelectric plants). In the Rhodope there are a number of hydroelectric stations, which produce about a fifth of the total current generated. Important plants are also found around Dimitrovgrad, including the large Maritsa stations, using coal mined locally, and at Varna, where both brown coal and diesel oil are used, while a large new thermal power station fired by Donbass coal is being built 12 km west of Varna. The current is distributed through a grid system of 110 kV and 220 kV lines, linked to the Comecon international grid.

Before 1944 there had been a few small plants smelting scrap in Sofia and Dimitrovo (Pernik), as well as an old-fashioned plant smelting copper at Elisejna and a small lead–zinc flotation plant near Kirdzhali. During the 1930s mining nearly came to a standstill, but was stimulated by the demand for metal for the German rearmaments drive. Mining has been greatly expanded since 1944 and new plants built, including a copper refinery near Zlatica and two flotation plants in the Burgas region. The main focus of non-ferrous metallurgy is the eastern Rhodope in the new towns of Madan and Rudozem. Kirdzhali and Plovdiv are important lead and zinc-processing centres. Tin is an important metal, short in the Socialist *bloc*, found in association with zinc.

10.2.1 Industry in Bulgaria (figure 10.3)

Considerable attention has been devoted to iron and steel manufacture. Bulgaria has good supplies of iron ore—haematite, siderite, magnetite and limonite —with four-fifths of the reserves around Kremikovci near Sofia, where about 60 per cent of the ore is mined. The remaining 40 per cent comes mostly from the mines in the Jambol district. The Kremikovci mines are to produce a much larger share of the total in the future. Bulgarian ores seldom exceed 30 per cent iron. Manganese is worked near Varna as well as at Kremikovci. Chrome occurs in the Rhodope and molybdenum is found in the upper Maritsa. The first modern iron and steel plant, the Lenin plant at Pernik, opened in 1953, is a full-cycle plant with iron and steel-making, ferro-alloy production, foundry works and rolling mills. A much larger full-cycle plant has been under construction at Kremikovci, immediately in the neighbourhood of its ore supply and with its own cokery.

Engineering, established since 1944 on a much wider scale, now contributes almost a fifth of total industrial output, though, as in Hungary and Rumania, its range and diversity might be criticised in such a small home market. About 40 per cent of the labour force is in plants with more than 1000 employees. About one-third of total production comprises transport goods, notably railway wagons and river and sea-going ships. Motor cycles and mopeds are produced, while fork trucks and earth-moving equipment as well as tramway cars are made. Soviet and Czech cars are assembled at Plovdiv. Farm machinery and food-processing machinery are made and electrical equipment manufactured. Of the labour force of over 140 000, 30 per cent is in Sofia, 11 per cent in the Plovdiv area and about 9 per cent in the district of Stara Zagora, while 7 per cent work in Ruse and Varna. Heavy machine tools and much specialised equipment have, however, to be imported.

The pre-war chemicals industry was largely concerned with light chemicals for the domestic market, and other chemicals were imported from Germany. The new development has been in the heavy chemicals sector, with help from the

Soviet Union and from the German Democratic Republic, particularly in the production of artificial fertilisers and in plastics. Chemicals contribute a little under 7 per cent of all industrial production. Sofia has rubber works, dyestuffs, paints and soap; rubber is also processed in Pazardzhik; artificial fertilisers in Dimitrovgrad—one of the largest plants—as well as a range of acids; Asenovgrad produces calcium carbide; plastics are made in Ruse and Gabrovo, while calcium carbide, plastics and many sodium-based substances and chlorine are produced by the large Reka Devnja plant near Varna, where there is production of artificial fertilisers, also made at Stara Zagora. A polyethylene plant has

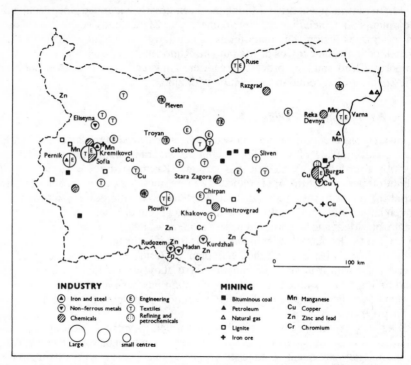

Figure 10.3. In Bulgaria heavy industrial development has been encouraged since 1945, though many older industries like textiles are still important. The eastern part of the country has a number of new chemicals plants.

been under construction at Burgas. Cellulose is made in a German-designed plant at Oryakhovo as well as at Plovdiv. The pharmaceuticals industry is found in Sofia, Stanka Dimitrov and Razgrad (penicillin). Petrochemicals have been established at a refinery to process Soviet crude oil at Burgas, while a large nitrogen fertiliser plant is planned at Vraca. Cement-making has been developed on a considerable scale and substantial exports made, while glass goods are made for export to the Near East. With the growth of food processing, a large glass container factory has been built in Razgrad and another in Plovdiv. From Bulgaria's forests, wood is used for a chemical extraction industry and for cellulose and paper-making. The paper mills are, however, of limited capacity and paper is imported. To increase the output of cellulose, a factory to process straw has been built near Oryakhovo.

The woollen industry dates back to the Sliven mill opened in 1834, and the main mills are now Gabrovo, Sofia, Trojan and Kazanlik, dependent on substantial imports of raw wool. The cotton industry has been a product of the twentieth century, with mills in Varna, Sofia, Ruse, Gabrovo and Jambol. Most cotton is grown in Bulgaria, apart from cotton for the finer cloths, though the mills are not in the cotton-growing districts. Home production of silk cocoons now only just meets needs for fine silk cloths still manufactured in a number of small mills. An ancient home industry is carpet-making: Ciprovici, Panagyurishte, and Zlatica are centres in the west and Kotel in the east.

10.2.2 Agriculture in Bulgaria (figure 10.4)

In 1948 82 per cent of the labour force in Bulgaria was engaged in agriculture; by 1960 55 per cent was still in this sector, but by the opening of the 1970s it was less than 37 per cent. Nevertheless, the total number of agricultural workers had increased from 148 196 in 1960 to 266 106 in 1970, but whereas in 1957 19.7 per cent of the labour force was female, by 1970 this had risen to 49.7 per cent. There has, however, been an appreciable fall in the share of the national income derived from agriculture. Unlike other pre-war Eastern European countries, Bulgaria has shown a remarkable prevalence of small peasant holdings, though methods of cultivation were simple, with variable and relatively low crop yields and a backward form of livestock farming. Subsistence farming predominated, with no more than a third of total output destined for the market. At the same time population pressure was increasing on the land as industry and other sectors of the economy grew slowly, while inheritance was resulting in ever smaller holdings. In 1900 the average holding had been 7 ha but by 1940 this had been nearly halved. Cattle and animal manure was insufficient for most farms and artificial fertilisers little known and too expensive.

The Bulgarians have pursued collectivisation with great vigour, so that 1.1 million peasant holdings divided into between 12 and 13 million parcels of ground were reduced to 3290 large Production Co-operatives. In 1959 a further drastic reduction in the number of units was made, with the co-operatives reduced to 792, each averaging between 4000–4500 ha. State farm enterprises have been set up, often with specific objectives such as seed raising. About 18 per cent of the cultivated land is held by the state farms and the co-operatives (including the private plots of their members) control about 81 per cent; whereas private holdings account for only 0.6 per cent of the cultivated land. The co-operatives and State farms may comprise such small, intensive horticultural units that there are two or three in a village or they may be extensive grain-growing units in the steppelands of the southern Dobrudsha. The relatively small number of co-operatives makes quick implementation of policy changes easy: in 1953 a plan for self-sufficiency in cotton was rapidly scrapped and five years later, a wholesale slaughtering of goats was undertaken. The Agricultural Co-operatives are remarkable in some instances for their specialisation, concentrating on such things as table grapes or wines. The State farms have been significant in moder-

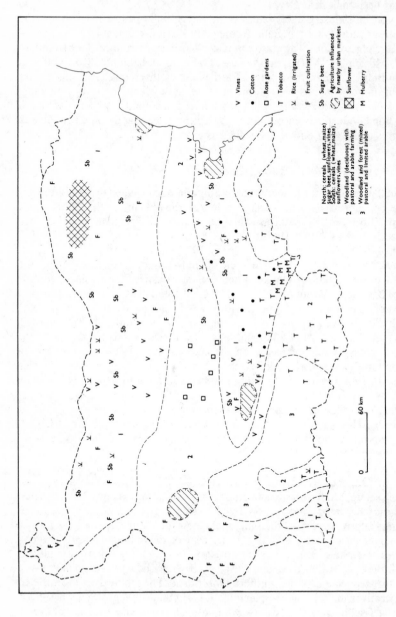

Figure 10.4. On the plains south of the Danube, grain cultivation is important, but Bulgarian farmers have a long reputation for their skill as market gardeners and such farming is found extensively in the main valleys and basins of the centre and the south.

nisation, though they have been less effective in improving livestock quality than might have been expected.

The chemicals industry has provided artificial fertiliser that before the war had to be imported, while better fodder supplies and stall feeding have given more natural fertiliser. Substantial improvement, through the efforts of state farms, has been made in the strains of crops. Irrigation, practised for a long time, has been extended since 1945, allowing more varied crops to be grown and removing the uncertainties of natural precipitation. Before the war only about 40 000 ha were irrigated—half of the area lay round Plovdiv and Pazardzhik—while another 45 per cent was in the Struma, Mesta and Tundzha valleys. In 1960, 290 000 ha were irrigated, and in 1969, 973 000 ha. It is planned to irrigate eventually about 3 million ha. Development of irrigation has been associated with water storage projects for hydroelectric and other amelioration systems, but in general the stored water capacity has outstripped the use of water for irrigation, so that a larger area could be watered if investment was made available. The use of sprinkling machines on slopes has been a potential cause of soil wash and special methods of hoed cropping introduced. Increase in irrigated land in the north (less than 5 per cent of the total) has been mostly in the drained marshy lands along the Danube.

One of the most fertile areas is the Maritsa valley and some of its tributaries, where alluvium and chernozem are readily cultivated and there is a long growing season in spite of low January temperatures. Irrigation is essential if more than one crop is to be grown, since precipitation in summer is low and evaporation very high. This part of the country has a reasonably developed transport system and there are numerous processing factories. Most farms have only a modest proportion of their area under grain and devote the remainder to a very wide range of fruit and vegetable crops. The Bulgarian ability for horticulture has also been fully developed. Besides such things as paprika, aubergines and tomatoes, there is considerable vine cultivation (though Bulgarian wines have not yet established a strong image) and also fruit, while tobacco has long been an important commodity and many smokers in Comecon prefer Balkan to Virginian tobaccos. Half the tomato crop and almost as much of the potato crop are exported as well as large proportions of other crops. It is planned to extend irrigation and to move vineyards to the lower foothills to release land for more profitable crops.

To the east, around Stara Zagora, where irrigation is only conducted in the Tundzha valley, a much larger proportion of the ground is devoted to cereals—notably wheat. This is also the area of the bulk of the cotton crop, a much more widespread crop until the early 1950s. Fruit farming is expanding here. North of the Stara Planina the northern tableland plains are less easily adaptable to irrigation, though the irrigated area is being extended. This *loess*-covered plateau underlain by largely calcareous rocks still remains a predominantly grain-growing land, notably for wheat and also maize, though the proportion sown to cereals has tended to decline. Maize, hemp and lucerne are the main crops of the drained but irrigated land along the Danube. In the east sunflowers and other crops which do well without irrigation are common. Fruit cultivation—such as apricots—is being encouraged. In the north-west, where strawberry cultivation for preserves and jam has developed since 1960, there has been the establishment of large agrarian-industrial complexes, linking state farms and processing industries with co-operatives. These have tended to encourage local specialisation and to concentrate crops in the most favourable areas, with areas of 4000 ha or more sown to a single crop. There is also a tendency to separate livestock farming from arable farming. Some livestock units aim at annual fattening capacities of 100 000 pigs or the holding of 3000 dairy cattle. Such large units demand a high level of management, but it is expected that this form of organisation will spread throughout the country.

The mountains remain largely pasture land or forest (33 per cent of total area), but on the lower and middle slopes are considerable areas of fruit cultivation, such as the plum orchards of the northern slopes of the central Stara Planina. The elevation, poor soils and summer drought are factors influencing the low grain yield and long fallows are practised, but in some areas, wheat is important (around Kyustendil and Kurdzhali), though the usual grain is rye. The southern parts of the mountains are significant for an expanding tobacco cultivation. Potatoes are also being grown on a large scale as the upland soils are more suitable than the compact lowland soils, with the Smoljan and Sofia districts particularly important As they are ready before the Central European crop, they find a good export market as well as good home demand. Development of hybrid maize to ripen in cool conditions has also become important. The Sofia basin is important for fodder crops and dairying based primarily on the large local urban market.

Expansion of livestock farming has been limited by fodder supplies and by the need to improve the quality of animals. Numerically, sheep predominate, though numbers fell as more pasture land was taken into cultivation, but recently some increase has taken place as a result of better provision of fodder. The sheep belong mostly to local breeds and provide wool and meat but also milk for cheese-making. Wool is, however, the most important product, which has been improved in quality by crossing local animals with merinos. The plateau south of the Danube and the areas of Burgas and Jambol in the south-east are the main sheep-breeding lands. Cattle are fairly evenly distributed, but most important in the north on the plateau along the Danube, with a concentration in the north-east. South of the Balkan range the main concentrations of cattle are in the industrialised areas of Sofia and Dimitrovo. Cattle are less important in the plains of Upper Thrace, though cattle breeding around Kurdzhali goes back to Turkish times when the local Moslem population would not breed pigs. In the southern mountains cattle are on the whole small and of moderate quality. Cattle are no longer used for field work and conditions have been improved, notably on state farms, so that better milk and meat yields are being attained. Buffalo are declining as tractors and lorries become more widespread though Bulgaria still has more than any other European country. Horses are likewise declining in numbers, though mules and donkeys are still kept, particularly in the vineyards and tobacco fields.

The development in agriculture has been accompanied by a growth in the food-processing industry, which has changed from semi-processed goods of pre-war to high quality fully processed goods such as jams, tinned fruit, puree and alcoholic drinks and cigarettes. The milling industry, however, has had considerable excess capacity resulting from the decline in grain exports. The oil-extracting industry also had a surplus capacity which arose after 1918, when import of olive oil and other edible oils was reduced and an emphasis laid on home production of sunflower oil. The oil mills are mostly in the eastern plains, where sunflower and cotton seed are available. 90 per cent of production is for edible oils. Sugar mills working home-grown beet are found at six locations, but the major centre is Gornja Oryakhovitsa. A large new plant has been built at Reka Devnya and others will be needed if an annual target of 500 000 tons is to be sustained. The pre-war tobacco industry scattered in small units is being replaced by large modern combines, with many of the workers released to canning factories in the summer. The food-processing industry, one of the largest branches of industry in the country, has benefited from the record of productivity in farming which has been better in Bulgaria than in other Eastern European countries.

10.2.3 Transport in Bulgaria

Before 1939 the transport system of Bulgaria was still underdeveloped. An important factor was the high cost of construction in the mountainous terrain, so that many vital links between the regions of the country were still incomplete. Railway-building had begun late and had moved slowly because of political conditions. Bulgaria had been reluctant to allow too much foreign investment in railways and yet had not had the resources itself to build much needed lines. The road system was particularly backward and the rivers of no significance. Roads in particular were unsuited to motor vehicles and the inter-regional movements depended primarily on railways. Since 1944 investment has been made to complete and modernise the transport system. Railway building has completed an axial through route from Sofia via Kazanlik and Nova Zagora to the Black Sea ports; the railway from Sofia along the Struma valley has been joined to the Greek railways; and since 1953 a 2200 m-long bridge across the Danube at Ruse has provided a rail link to Rumania. In 1972 a railway to Silistra opened up the far north-east, while a direct link to Turkey was opened, avoiding territorial complications in the lower Maritsa. A further extension of the route length by about 25 per cent is foreseen, though half investment in railways will be for technical modernistion and electrification.

Road building continues at about 5–10 km daily, so that by 1980 over 70 per cent of the road length should have hard asphalted surfaces. There is growing road transit traffic across Bulgaria between Asia Minor and Western Europe, using Europa Highway 5N, while Bulgarian long-distance road haulage for perishables to Western Europe has grown substantially. Ox carts and horse carts are still used, with mules on mountain paths. Bulgaria has developed its own Danube fleet and its sea-going vessels operate from the modest ports of Varna and Burgas.

Bulgaria has been distinguished by its better agricultural record than the other Eastern European countries. It has also made formidable strides in industrial development, based on a relatively good raw-materials endowment. These achievements have been made with the help of long-standing good relations with the Soviet Union and with the Germans. It nevertheless remains a country with a great potential for development and with a long road to complete modernisation.

10.3 Jugoslavia

Jugoslavia, one of the most complex states of Eastern Europe, comprises an uncomfortable union of the South Slav peoples. Though a Socialist state, it defected from the main body after rejection of subordination to the Soviet Union. The state is a federal republic comprising the six people's republics of Serbia, Croatia, Slovenia, Bosnia-Hercegovina, Macedonia and Montenegro. The Jugoslavs have been associated with Comecon through Article X of the Constitution that allows for observer status, while they have pursued a juggler-on-the-fence attitude, maintaining overt contact with both capitalist and socialist camps. The contrast between the Adriatic littoral, with its Mediterranean characteristics, the bare Dinaric mountains backbone, and the plains of the Sava and Drava of a Pannonian nature, give the country a great potential economic diversity. The northern part of the country is truly 'Central European', while the south is quite impressively 'Balkan'. Nevertheless, the regions tend to look away from each other, so that welding them together becomes a trying test.

The basic endowment of Jugoslavia with minerals provides a sound foundation on which to develop industry. Nevertheless, it is only since 1945 that the true extent of this mineral wealth has been appreciated, while it is likely that further substantial additions to the inventory will be made in areas where detailed geological survey has still to be completed. Reserves of coal were greatly increased by intensive prospecting in the 1950s, though 99 per cent are of low calorific value. Bituminous coal, in short supply, has high sulphur content and ash that make it unsuitable for coking, but it is, however, valuable for electricity generation. Imports of high quality coals remain considerable. The coal basins are widely scattered about the country, though many are quite small, while some are already exhausted or unworkable for various reasons. There are three main bituminous coalfields: Raša in the Istrian Peninsula, Rtanj-Timok and Ibar in the east. Nearly three-quarters of the better lignites are found in Bosnia in the basins of Zenica–Sarajevo and Banovići, and small but important deposits occur in eastern Serbia—Despotovac-Senjski Rudnik and Aleksinac—while another basin lies at Zagorje in Slovenia. The largest resources are, however, in the five big lignite fields—Valenje in the north, Kreka in Bosnia, Kolubara and Kostolac in northern Serbia, and Kosovo (claimed to be the largest lignitė basin in Europe). Since 1945 the industry has been modernised and rationalised, with a tendency for production to become more important in Bosnia and Serbia and to be less important in Croatia, while Slovenia has also lost its earlier rank.

Since the 1950s considerable reserves of petroleum have been found, greatly augmenting the first workings before 1939 in the Lendava area on the Hungarian frontier. Three-quarters of the oil and half the gas output now comes from fields along the Sava valley near Zagreb. In the latter 1950s a new field in the Banat came into operation. There are also good prospects for oil and gas discoveries elsewhere in the Sava–Drava basin and along the Adriatic littoral. In Dalmatia there are also oil shale deposits, but the main workings have been at Zletovo in Macedonia and Aleksinac in Serbia. While crude and refined production of domestic petroleum has grown substantially, a large oil terminal is being built at Bakar near Rijeka to handle imports from North Africa and the Middle East for the Danubian countries. Refineries are situated at Rijeka, Sisak and Bosanski

Brod, through petro-chemicals have not as yet been developed.

One of the greatest potential sources of energy is hydroelectricity and Jugoslavia could become an important exporter of current to neighbouring countries. Hydroelectricity is already the primary source of energy in the country. After modest developments in the inter-war period, based largely on surveys before 1914 by the Austrian authorities, a major programme of detailed investiation began after 1945. It was found that only Norway had a greater total potential. Almost three-quarters of the potential is in the Alpine–Dinaric lands, where there is good precipitation, adequate run-off and river profiles that provide a high possible power output from each catchment. The Karst is particularly rich, with use of underground water. The lower precipitation, the smaller run-off and the gentler river gradients restrict the potential in Pannonia and parts of Serbia and Macedonia. The large potential of the Iron Gates on the Danube is at present being harnessed by a joint Jugoslav–Rumanian scheme, which on completion will account for 10 per cent of total Jugoslav resources. Inspite of massive post-war investment in harnessing water power, only about a fifth of the total is at present utilised. The grid system allows exchanges of current between regions, so that current generated in the karst lands when Mediteranean rainfall is at its peak can be transmitted to northern Jugoslavia during the high demand period of winter. Conversely, when water levels are low in the Karst during the summer, the stations in the northern alps are generating at full power as water becomes available from snow melt. Like other Eastern European countries Jugoslavia has plans to develop some nuclear power; uranium ores are available from Kalna in eastern Serbia.

10.3.1 Industry in Jugoslavia (figure 10.5)

The iron ore deposits are among the most considerable in Eastern Europe. Almost three-quarters of the reserves lie in Bosnia, near Vareš and Ljubija, but are modest in quality though they can be worked by open-cast. There are big un-worked deposits of low grade ores with high phosphorus content in western Macedonia. The main deficiency is in coking coal, which has had to be imported mostly from the U.S.S.R., West Germany and the U.S.A. The political implications of this supply have led to attempts to blend good Bosnian lignite with imported bituminous coal to produce a utilisable coke. An attempt to produce coke from lignite at Tuzla in the early 1950s was a failure and the plant, located away from the consumers, now uses imported coals. The main coke ovens are Zenica and Tuzla-Lukavac. The fuel problem has tended to encourage the use of electric processes in the iron and steel industry. Scrap is imported for steel-making.

Before the Second World War, the main development had been in the north, where iron-making had received encouragement from the Habsburg authorities, which led to establishment of the Jesenice ironworks and the ferro-alloy works at Ruše in Slovenia, Austrian initiative had also developed the Dalmatian ferro-silicon plant at Split, the *Elektrobosna* ferro-alloy plant at Jajce, the Štore ironworks at Celje, the Šibenik ferro-manganese plant and the steel plant at Ravne, Slovenia. Austrian initiative was also planning a large iron complex in Bosnia in 1914, from which the forerunners of the Vareš works and the Zenica

plant developed. Between the wars, the Jugoslav policy of industrial dispersal for
strategic reasons resulted in modernisation of the small and outdated plant at
Vareš and Zenica, while a ferro-tungsten plant opened in Serbia near Kučevo
and an important new iron and steel plant was created at Sisak. A plant away
from raw material supplies was opened at Smederovo near Belgrade, though work
on this site began in 1913. After 1945 further expansion and dispersal was continued, with a policy of establishing works near to domestic raw materials
supplies and as near as possible to depressed and overpopulated areas.

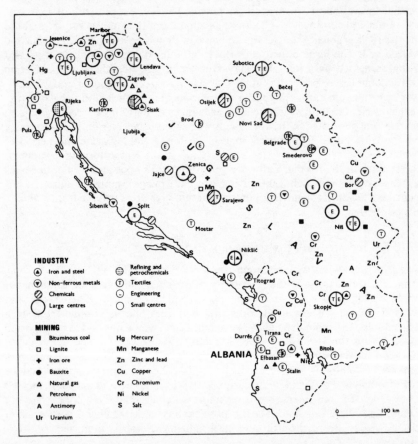

Figure 10.5. Jugoslavia and Albania have both undergone considerable industrial
development since 1945. The Jugoslavs have sought to decentralise industry from its
earlier concentration in the north. In Albania small plants using local resources and
supplying local markets have been established.

Consequently, development in Slovenia has been small, with the Štore and
Ravne plants turned to electric processes for special steels, while the modernised
and integrated Sisak plant uses natural gas from the Slavonian field and the
Smederevo plant, natural gas from the Banat. Expansion has given the

Zenica–Vareš region about two-thirds of the total capacity, including the Ilijaš ironworks opened in 1956. These plants use local ores, coke from Tuzla-Lukavac and Doboj limestone. The steelworks at Nikšić in Montenegro (opened in 1951), the result of social and political more than economic considerations, uses pig iron shipped from Zenica and poor quality fuel from the Mostar basin. A similar concession to political demands was made in the Skopje plant, with its electric pig iron furnaces and the latest LD converters, where production first began in 1967 and large further extensions are planned. A high-cost producer, it uses low grade Macedonian ore and coke made from Kosovo lignite. In 1957 a ferro-tungsten plant was opened near Skopje. In spite of rapid growth and establishment of new plants, the iron and steel industry has seldom achieved the ambitious targets set for it and recent interest has shifted to more favourable locations. There are plans for a large steel plant at Split and a big foundry at Prijedor.

Non-ferrous metals have been an important item in Jugoslav trade since the Second World War and there has been a substantial development of smelting and refining facilities, while geological exploration has sought additional deposits. The country is a major European producer of antimony, chrome, copper, lead, molybdenum, mercury, zinc and bauxite. A considerable proportion of the deposits are in Serbia and Macedonia, though important mines lie near the Dalmatian coast and in Istria. The most important commercial deposits are the copper mined at Bor and Majdanpek, though other deposits are known in western Serbia and in Montenegro, Originally only blister copper was exported, though some was rolled in Slovenia. It is now handled completely by the refinery at Bor, the alloy and rolling mills at Sevojno and the wire works at Svetozarevo. Lead and zinc are mined at several localities, the largest centre being Trepča in the Kopaonik mountains. In Slovenia, Mežica is a centre, with Zletovo in Macedonia, Rudnik in northern Serbia, Srebrenica-Majdan in the Drina basin and Pljevlja-Mojkovac in Montenegro. A large zinc-electrolysis plant at Sabac provides waste gases for sulphuric acid production. The Šar Planina chrome deposits are processed in an electro-metallurgical and chemical combine at Tetovo in Macedonia. Other resources include manganese (worked near the Vareš iron ore deposits) and pyrites from Majdanpek and from lead–zinc flotation plants. Idrija (Slovenia) has important mercury deposits and antimony is found in the Drina basin. Wolfram is found near Majdanpek and molybdenum near Surdulice. Deposits of nickel, cobalt and cadmium are also known. Bauxite occurs in Istria, the Dalmatian coast (Obrovac), in western Bosnia and near Mostar (Hercegovina) and also in Montenegro (Nikšić, Kotor). There is also ample caustic soda, coal and electricity for production, which was retarded by lack of capital and poor planning. The first large plant was Kidričevo in Slovenia, 250 km from the bauxite mines. The integrated plant at Šibenik has been expanded: near to its raw materials, it has been made partly dependent on alumina and aluminium from Kidričevo. Other integrated plants include Titograd and Mostar.

The large pre-war cement industry was orientated to the Italian market from Istrian and Dalmatian centres, but since the war new plants have been opened to serve inland markets on a regional basis.

Engineering has developed sectors poorly represented or even non-existent before 1939. The pre-war engineering plants were markedly in the north—in Slovenia, northern Croatia and in the Vojvodina, while the Sava–Morava axis still remains the most important belt. The heavy industrial development of Zenica–Vareš in Bosnia has also attracted engineering, just as similar development at Skopje has been accompanied by engineering plants. The main towns such as Ljubljana, Zagreb, Maribor, Rijeka and Sarajevo have machine tool as well as general engineering, while there is also heavy constructional engineering. Rijeka, Pula, Karlovac and Ljubljana build turbines and diesel motors. Agricultural machinery is built at several towns in the farming lands of the north. There is a small electronics industry, with a radio factory at Niš, and electrical engineering found in many of the main towns. Belgrade is the principal centre for engineering, with a wide range of plants. Railway equipment comes from Slavonski Brod, Smederevska Palanka, Kruševac, Kraljevo and Niš. A Fiat assembly plant operates at Kraguljevac, with Citroen cars built at Koper (Istria), and there are also Volkswagen and Daimler–Benz assembly plants. Shipbuilding on the Adriatic coast has been expanded from annexed Italian capacity, with main yards at Rijeka, Split and Pula. Smederovo builds river craft. Attempts have been made to establish simple engineering assembly plants in areas with acute unemployment and overpopulation.

Foreign investors had developed chemicals plants in Jugoslavia before 1914 to process local resources. The inter-war development was mainly in soaps, dyes, and domestic chemicals, from works in the main towns where reasonable markets existed. After 1945 development encouraged both heavy and light chemicals in order to reduce imports in a growing home market, with extended and modernised pre-war plants and new integrated plants using complex chemical processes to produce a wide range of by-products. An example is the integration of nitrogen fertiliser and sulphuric acid plants with the Lukavac cokery or the use of waste gas for by-products at the Bor and Trepča smelters. Important centres for acids, soda and nitrogen compounds and oxides are Zemun (Belgrade), Šabac (also artificial fertilisers), Subotica (also a fertiliser producer). For chlorine, sodium and sulphur-based chemicals, plants at Lukavac, Jajce, and Kruševac are major producers. The Goražde plant also produces these substances as well as nitrogen compounds, while oxygen and other gases are made in Belgrade, Novi Sad, Kraljevo and Niš. Plastics production is mostly at Kastel Sucurac (Split), Zagreb, Osijek, Novi Sad and Loznica. There is a carbide plant at Dugi Rat, which along with Prahovo also produces artificial fertiliser. The soap and detergents industry is mostly in large towns—Osijek, Maribor, Zagreb, Subotica, Pančevo, Belgrade and Niš. Ljubljana makes glycerine and dyes, while in several large towns pharmaceuticals are prepared. The rubber industry is mostly at Borovo, Pirot and Niš.

High pre-war tariffs on imported goods protected the growth of light industries and foreign investors found the large supply of cheap labour attractive, so that firms such as the Czech shoemaker, Bat'a, opened plants. After the war, light (consumer) goods industries received low priorities, but nevertheless have been a source of many new jobs. There has been some structural adjustment—cotton spinning to replace imported yarn for home weaving mills, substitution of cotton cloth for woollens, and clothing and rubber industries to reduce dependence on imports, while export of hides and skins has been replaced by manufactured leather goods. Although these industries have tended to remain chiefly in the north (Zagreb, Kranj, Varaždin, Maribor, Osijek, Subotica, Belgrade) often using existing skill (as in the onetime Bat'a works at Borovo-Vukovar), there have been new plants located to provide labour demand in underdeveloped areas.

10.3.2 Agriculture in Jugoslavia (figure 10.6)

Jugoslavia remains a strong agricultural economy and a markedly peasant society. In 1938 about 80 per cent of the population depended on agriculture: in 1971 it was still 49 per cent. Agriculture uses 58 per cent of the country's area, while forests cover 35 per cent and another 7 per cent is unproductive. Cropland covers almost 30 per cent and meadows and pastures extend over 25 per cent, while almost 3 per cent is in orchards and vineyards. Just over half the gross national product is contributed by agriculture.

Over much of the country, winter is severe and, in the mountains, protracted, while along the Adriatic littoral there is summer drought. Cold air drainage from the mountains into the coast lands, plains and mountain basins is a serious hazard. Soils in the mountains are poor and often only skeletal. The large areas of karstic limestone result in quick percolation of rainwater, so that they are arid lands for the farmer. Better soils are found in the Morava–Vardar Corridor, in the Voivodina and the Banat–Bačka, where open plains are admirably suited to grain. Good arable and orchard country covers the northern flanks of the Dinaric uplands and the northern Slovenia. It is unfortunate that many of the best riverine lands of the Pannonian Plains are subject to serious floods, while some of the *loess*-covered interfluves suffer acute dryness.

Present-day problems of agriculture usually have roots deep in history, especially in the Turkish period. The great migration of people from the Turkish controlled plains into the mountains produced an anomalous pattern of population distribution, with extensive destruction of forest and overgrazing, while the rich plains were neglected or irrationally tilled. The rapid upsurge of population after the coming of independence, first in Serbia and later over the whole country, brought decreased farm sizes and more fragmented holdings, with extensive subsistence farming. The rich north and north-east exported food direly needed in the impoverished and overpopulated mountains of the west and south. For long, all the land cultivable within the limits of peasant technology has been cultivated, though wet lands in the Pannonian valleys could be further reclaimed and sandy lands of the Bačka and Banat could also be made useful. Yet, on the other hand, many marginal lands in the mountains and the mountain basins might be better abandoned.

Land reform after 1918 was only partially completed and had mainly affected non-Slav landowners, but it swept away remaining feudal obligations. The more radical land reform of 1945 expropriated any holdings exceeding 25–35 ha of cultivated land (depending on soil conditions and the ratio of arable to pasture) while even more drastic measures were taken on estates and farms belonging to absentee landlords. All land of German, Hungarian and Italian owners expelled in 1945 was taken. Of the 1.57 Mha taken, over 770 000 ha were used to establish large-scale socialised agriculture, while amost 800 000 ha were sold to 316 400 families of landless labourers and smallholders. Because of an im-

320   *Eastern Europe: A Geography of the Comecon Countries*

balance between land confiscated and the demand for land, some 60 000 families were resettled from the mountains to the plains of Pannonia. The division of the commercially run estates and the resettlement on them of people with backward farming skills had a catastrophic effect on productivity long into the 1950s, and large grainlands in the Banat and Bačka were reduced to extensive stock rearing of mediocre animals. A law of 1953 restricting the maximum private holding to 10 ha resulted in a process of agglomeration of holdings in the 4–8 ha category and accelerated a shift from the land of young people, aggravating the problem of agricultural labour shortage. The farms in the 4–8 ha category are the mainstay of food production, providing 60 per cent of the food marketed.

The socialist sector has been enlarged by creating 'socialist farms' and by extending government influence to peasant farms through co-operatives. Four million ha of land are state-owned, about half comprising poor karstland

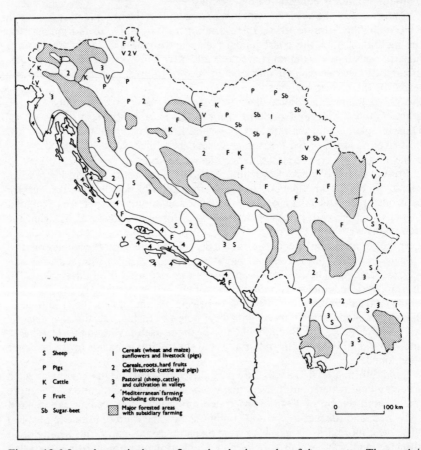

Figure 10.6 Jugoslav agriculture reflects the physiography of the country. The north is characteristically 'Danubian' with sugar beet and cereals, while the Adriatic littoral has tree crops and fruits, whereas poor pasture on the extensive limestone tracts and forests on the moister country are typical of the Dinaric lands.

pastures. About 15 per cent of all farmland is in government hands, organised in over 2300 state and co-operative farms. In 1945 state farms on the Soviet model were introduced and collectives designed for both upland and lowland environments were encouraged. Peasant response was lukewarm, but in 1948 forced collectivisation was initiated, with four types of collective depending on the extent of pooling of resources by the peasants. These showed many weaknesses, while government planners set them impossible tasks and starved them of the necessary funds and materials, and peasant opposition and alienation did little to improve the situation. In the northern lowlands, in better natural conditions, and with an immigrant peasant community less emotionally attached to the soil, they performed best, with yield 20–30 per cent above that of peasant holdings. It was perhaps surprising their success was not greater, for the Jugoslav peasant might have been expected to favour communal cultivation, for which there was a long communal tradition in the *zadruga*. In 1951 freer conditions were introduced and shortly after emphasis moved from land nationalisation to intensification of agricultural productivity. Many peasants left the socialist sector, which fell to one-third of its maximum extent, though it later recovered and has since substantially expanded, largely through purchase or lease of unwanted peasant land from dwarf holdings. In general, more land is now offered to the socialist sector than it needs. Peasants have discovered the advantages of membership of co-operatives, both for the credits given and for their marketing organisation, while they provide employment for peasants with holdings inadequate for subsistence or even with no land. Reorganisation of the state farms in the mid-1950s put them into a position to stimulate agricultural methods and standards, with access to better machinery, seeds and animals.

Almost three-quarters of the farmland is used for crops: gardens and meadows take in another fifth, and a fourteenth is accounted for by orchards and vineyards. The plains of the Voivodina, Banat and Bačka, predominantly under the plough, cover only about one-tenth of the country's area but produce half the bread grains, over three-quarters of the sugar beet, vegetable oils, vegetable fibres, and almost half the maize. In the hilly country of Croatia, northern Bosnia and much of Serbia (wetter than the northern plains) cropland is less extensive and animal husbandry becomes important, though here are important orchards and vineyards. The poor soils, high rainfall and long, severe winters of the mountains do not encourage farmers, except in the better lands of the valleys and *polja*. This is a land of grazing and animal husbandry with less than a fifth of the cropland found amid the mountains. It is the proportions between the various crops and species of animals in these different regions rather than differences in crops and animal species that make the distribution pattern. Two regions of dry summers and low rainfall stand out. In Macedonia, cropland covers only a small part of the country and about one-third is irrigated, and the crops demand great warmth and much sunshine, for example tobacco, rice and even cotton. Sheep and goats (much discouraged by the state) graze on dry hills, while a narrow strip along the Adriatic coast has typically Mediterranean conditions, giving a land of vineyards and fruit gardens, with some sheep on the hills.

Of the arable land 77 per cent is taken up by grain crops, industrial crops occupy 4.5 per cent, while root crops and potatoes cover 7.4 per cent and fodder crops account for 11 per cent. Grains, most important in the north, are dominated by maize (34.5 per cent of the sown area), of which Jugoslavia is one of the largest European producers. Maize is most important in the Pannonian Plains and the lower valley of the Morava. Considerable quantities are exported. Wheat occupies 30.3 per cent of the sown area, mainly in the Pannonian Plains and in some of the central Serbian valleys. It is almost all winter sown and is becoming more important. About 5 per cent of the area is sown to barley and a mere 2 per cent to rye, which like oats are crops of the hilly areas. Rice is cultivated on irrigated ground in Macedonia.

Cabbage is a significant crop in Croatia around Varaždin and in the Bačka and Voivodina, while beans are commonly rotated with maize. Potatoes (for food and industrial products) are found mostly in the north-west, in Slovenia and Croatia, but the area is small and yield is low. Vegetable cultivation is everywhere widespread. Fodder crops are grown wherever cattle breeding is important—clover is found mostly in Slovenia and northern Croatia, while lucerne is important in the Voivodina. Industrial crops include hemp in the Voivodina and in Slavonia, with flax in the Drava–Sava interfluve and in the Voivodina. Cotton has been grown in Macedonia. Croatia and the Voivodina are the main areas of sugar beet cultivation, but sunflower, an important source of oil, is cultivated in the Pannonian Plains, while olive groves are found on the Dalmatian coast and islands and in parts of Montenegro. Hops are found only in Slovenia and the Voivodina. Tobacco is grown in Dalmatia, Montenegro, the Voivodina and in Serbia, while Macedonia and Hercegovina produce export quality. In the north and north-west plums, pears and apples are grown, with citrus fruits and figs on the Adriatic coast, forming an important export. Vineyards are scattered over northern Croatia, the Dalmatian coast and on south facing slopes of hills in the Danubian Plains and in northern Serbia. Wherever the Moslem tradition was strong, vineyards are poorly developed. Jugoslav wines have established a modest reputation in European markets.

Pig-rearing in the oak and beech forests of Serbia was once a mainstay of the rural economy and vast herds on the hoof were exported to Austria–Hungary. Although pastures and meadows cover such a large proportion of the country, animal farming is less important than might be expected, because peasant farming is not conducive to good livestock. In the lowlands it has been encroached on by more intensive cropping, while livestock suffered heavily during the war years and rebuilding of the herds has been slow. Numerically most important are sheep and pigs—the former are found on mountain pastures and in areas with dry summers, but the latter are no longer forest animals and are most numerous in the arable lands of the north and north-east, fed from the surplus and waste of the best farming country. Pigs have never been important where Moslem traditions were strong. Goats, once important on the poorer grazings and the Adriatic scrub, have been reduced substantially in numbers by government action. Cattle are widely and relatively evenly scattered, except in the poor karstlands, on the Adriatic littoral and in southern Macedonia, areas with an acute lack of summer fodder and conditions not suitable for cattle. Dairy farming is best in the hills of Slavonia, northern Croatia and parts of Bosnia and Serbia. Horses remain important though declining in numbers, while mules and asses still play a part in peasant transport, notably in the mountains.

A most antique feature in Jugoslavia has been seasonal movement of flocks and herds between mountain and valley, but this becomes increasingly difficult as competition with cropland increases. Though not on such a scale as formerly, cattle in Slovenia are still sent into the Alpine pastures in summer, while in the Adriatic littoral sheep are taken up to the mountains to escape the great heat and drought. In Macedonia, though the permanent villages are in the uplands, animals are sent down to the valleys in winter.

The forests cover a third of the area of Jugoslavia, making it one of the most forested countries in Europe. There are, however, large areas of poor woodland of no commercial importance. Of the economically valuable reserves, almost three-quarters are deciduous trees such as beech and oak. Softwood conifers are most important in Slovenia. The main commercial forest areas are in east-central Bosnia, parts of western Serbia and in the northern alpine lands and parts of Slovenia. Important forests occur in south-west Croatia and neighbouring areas of Bosnia, central Slavonia and the Jugoslav–Bulgar frontier area. Nearly three-quarters of the forest is state-held. Quick-growing conifers have been planted where soil erosion has been a problem, while controlled grazing has also helped to protect forests.

10.3.3 Transport in Jugoslavia

The transport system inherited by the new state in 1919 was uneven in quality and incomplete, compounded of elements contributed by Austrian, Turkish, Serbian and Hungarian interests. The main deficiency was a lack of modern routes across the mountains between Pannonia and the Adriatic, while there were numerous missing interregional ties arising from the earlier political–geographical pattern. Though improvements were made between the wars, conditions did not encourage massive development, and much was destroyed in the Second World War.

The mainstay remains the railways, which handle three-quarters of the freight traffic that has quadrupled since 1945. Over 2000 km of new route have been built and technical improvement—including electrification—undertaken. A fifth of the route remains narrow gauge, inspite of closures and change to standard gauge. Much standard-gauge route has a low carrying capacity, while less than a tenth is double track. After 1948 much international traffic from Western Europe to Turkey and Greece moved to Jugoslav tracks to avoid passing through Soviet-controlled countries, so that the Zagreb–Belgrade–Skopje route was double tracked and later electrified to handle the increase. Much work has been done to improve links across the Dinaric mountains, partly by gauge conversion, but also by building new lines or electrifying existing route. A major uncompleted project across Montenegro from Belgrade via Titovo Užice to the potentially important port of Bar would avoid long detours from Serbia to Split or Rijeka and might attract traffic now going to Greek Salonika. It has been criticised by some observers as satisfying only Serbian nationalism. The high cost of construction in mountain country has retarded realisation of the east–west axial route from Rijeka to Belgrade via Ogulin, Bosanski Brod and Tuzla.

Roads before the Second World War were exceptionally poor and motor vehicles few. After 1945 reconstruction began but investment was limited and, like other Eastern European socialist countries, efforts concentrated on the railways. With growing contacts with Western Europe, road development became a more realistic proposition. A major improvement was the building of the axial Belgrade–Ljubljana 'motorway'. Since the mid-1950s road transport has become increasingly competitive and during the 1960s the number of motor vehicles increased with explosive speed, demanding new road construction. Much road transport from Turkey and the Middle East, and food shipments by road from Bulgaria, now cross Jugoslav territory, while there is a growing tourist traffic, catered for along the Adriatic coast by a major new highway of well-engineered proportions.

The Austro-Hungarian empire developed Trieste as a major Adriatic port and provided it with contemporaneously good rail links. It remained important for Danubian and Central European traffic in the inter-war years. Inspite of Jugoslav claims it was retained by Italy after 1945, though territorially virtually an enclave and ill-placed in the prevailing political conditions to recapture its lost importance. The disadvantage of Trieste has been Rijeka's gain (a port held by the Italians in the inter-war period), along with its satellite port of Sušak to which the Jugoslavs have sought to attract much Danubian and Central European trade. It was originally developed by Hungary to compete with Austrian Trieste. Facilities have been extended by building a dry cargo port at Koper south of Trieste, replacing Istrian Pula, while plans have been put forward for an oil terminal at Bakar near Rijeka to serve Danubia. In the inter-war years, when Rijeka and Pula were in Italian hands, the Jugoslavs developed Split as their main port, but like Gruž near Dubrovnik, poor rail communications restricted its growth. The coasting trade once so marked along the Adriatic littoral has been eroded by motor lorries using newly built roads along the coast. Other new ports developed in Jugoslavia include Ploče (replacing pre-war Metković), but it can only handle about a quarter of its 600 000-ton capacity because of poor railway links inland. Development is also planned at Bar on completion of a good railway connection to the Serbian interior. Inter-republic rivalry has led to excessive port development and a diffusion of effort so that in some respects Jugoslavia suffers from a plethora of ports.

Inland waterways are concentrated in the north, predominantly the Danube, which carries both Jugoslav and international traffic. The Sava below Sisak also carries domestic traffic in boats up to 1500 tons, while such vessels can also use the lower Tisza. The Drava and Begej rivers handle smaller craft. Completion of the Danube–Tisza–Danube canal will help to speed Danube traffic. Belgrade is a close competitor with Split for the place as second port of Jugoslavia, while Osijek, Sisak, Bosanski Brod, Novi Sad, Smederovo and Prahovo are also important river ports. Great increase in river traffic is expected after completion of the Iron Gates hydroelectric scheme. There are also plans to link Zagreb with the Sava by canal. Cargoes are nearly all bulky, low value freights—coal, coke, ore, ballast and aggregate.

Jugoslav problems have arisen from the conflicting interests and loyalties of its component peoples as well as from the considerable difficulties of its physical geography that have to be overcome to knit the country together. It is a potentially rich country that history has deprived of a chance to develop its wealth. It has been in a strange position between the two main power blocs since 1948, though it has over the 1960s developed reasonable relations with both camps. In many respects Jugoslavia holds the key to the future trends and developments in South-eastern Europe.

10.4 Albania

The Albanian Republic, one of the smallest countries in area and population in Europe, has shown rapid demographic and economic growth, but it remains relatively little known. Since 1961 it has swung into the Chinese political orbit, which brought considerable setback to the economy that had come to rely on help from the Soviet Union and other Eastern European countries and it has taken no effective part in Comecon. Modern economic development did not begin until the inter-war years under Italian pressure.

The country has appreciable mineral wealth (figure 10.5). In the east along the Jugoslav frontier, there are deposits of chrome, nickel and iron ore, worked in- initially after 1945 with Czech help. In the north there is also some copper ore, while between Tiranë and Elbasan and in the Korçë basin, are resources of brown coal. North-east of Vlorë deposits of petroleum and bitumen have been found. Petroleum as well as chrome were first worked in the 1930s by Italian interests. The crude oil was first piped to Vlorë for export, but later small quantities were refined at Kucovë (Qytet Stalin). Output has been concentrated mostly in the Fier area since 1945, with over half the output refined in the country, principally at Cërrik. Most recently, deposits have been found near Lushnje, where natural gas occurs. The brown coal is only of secondary importance, though mining has been stepped up since the late 1940s. Albanian plans for industrialisation rest primarily on developing the favourable conditions for hydroelectric power. In 1938 there was one small hydroelectric generator near Korçë and most current in towns came from diesel generators. In 1951 a 5MW hydroelectric station was opened near Tiranë and later development on the river Mat included a 25MW station at Burelli (1957), followed by further stations near main towns and electrification extended to the countryside, with effort to create a national grid system. Output now exceeds the 1938 level more than eightfold, with two-thirds from hydroelectric stations, though there is a large new oil-fired station near Fier.

Metal ores comprise an important part of Albanian exports, with iron ore and chrome going to Czechoslovakia and to Jugoslavia. A small smelter for blister copper was built at Rubik during the Second World War, while Kurbnesh and Kukës mines have concentration plants. At Laç a smelter produces sulphuric acid as a by-product from ferro-chrome and in Shkoder there is a small wire- works. The deposits of good haematite with a high level of nickel are presently mined for export and for the Elbasan steelworks, a project started with Russian help but later dependent on Chinese aid. It uses home ore but depends on imported coal and coke. By 1975 its output will have been expanded to 250 000 tons of steel.

Most Albanian industrial plants date from the mid-1950s and later. Some of the first industries were brick-making, cement (Tiranë, Vlorë) and glass-making (Korçë, Tiranë), while leather and rubber shoes are made at Tiranë. One of the largest branches is textiles—cotton and woollen mills operate in Tiranë and there is a knitwear factory in Korçë. The Chinese have contributed a cotton mill for

Berat. Improvements in agriculture have resulted in factories for food-processing—there is tobacco-curing and cotton-ginning and a considerable woodworking industry using home timber. Engineering is still on a modest scale, mostly making spare parts, doing maintenance work or producing simple farm machinery, concentrated in Tiranë. The oil refinery at Cërrik has been the core of the chemicals industry, but a superphosphates plant has been built at Laç and one for nitrogen fertilisers at Fier.

Cultivated ground accounts for only 17 per cent of the area of the country; forests cover almost 44 per cent and pastures extend over a quarter of the area, while over 13 per cent is agriculturally unusable. 'Forest' is often poor forest-scrub and real reafforestation is now being undertaken. Much of the old forest is deciduous, with a large element of oak. The lowland plains were ridden with malaria until the 1930s, when there was much bog and marsh, though in the summer irrigation was needed. During the inter-war period, American organisations did much to help in malaria control, while the state and Italian interests carried out land amelioration. The work has continued since 1945, so that the area under cultivation has been extended by more than two-thirds and irrigated land increased from 10 per cent to over 40 per cent of the cultivated area. The irrigated coastal lowlands allow two crops a year to be cultivated.

In 1945–6, land reform eliminated private ownership of ground and instituted agricultural collectives and state farms, with land redistributed among small farmers and landless peasants. There were, however, many difficulties to overcome, with 85 per cent of the population in villages and only 10 per cent of the country's area cultivated, while soils were often too dry, too wet or had other undesirable properties, and crop rotations were simple and methods primitive. The peasants who received land under the reform were among the first to agree to collectivisation and by 1948 there were 56 collectives with 10 000 ha of land and 2300 peasant families. At the same time, there were 16 state farms responsible for providing good seed and better breeds of animals. The state controlled all the pastures and natural meadows—over 800 000 ha or 62 per cent of the country's area. In 1949 under a new statute for co-operatives, peasants were allotted 0.3 ha of private plot and a number of animals in accordance with the size of the family, and an agricultural association for cultivation introduced, which became widely distributed, notably in the lowlands, though in the mountains, individual farms remained. In 1955 the process and collectionisation was accelerated and by 1958, per cent of the total village land was organised collectively, but a process of turning the small units into larger farms was introduced. In 1961 collectives and state farms accounted for 88 per cent of the cultivated ground, while mechanisation was actively pursued through state machine stations.

Although most kinds of grains are cultivated maize is particularly important, but on the lowlands, where there is irrigation, rice is grown. Other crops include tobacco and cotton, while in the Korçë basin there is sugar beet cultivation on the drained floor of Lake Maliq. Vegetable cultivation is widely spread and there are many areas with edible chestnuts, plums, figs and citrus fruits as well as olives. Animal farming (mostly sheep and goats) has an ancient tradition in Albania, especially in the hill and mountain areas where there are good pastures, but standards in general have been low. In an attempt to improve animal farming, more leguminous fodder crops have been grown. Horses, mules and donkeys are used for transport. Dairy cattle and pigs have become more important (though pigs remain few in Moslem districts). A small fishing industry has some of its catch processed in a cannery at Vlorë.

The railway system—170 km—dates almost entirely from the post-war period, with the 37 km mainline joining Tiranë to the port of Durrës. Road transport has depended on the building of proper roads and new bridges, while coastal boats carry an important traffic between the ports. Tiranë has an airfield.

Albania is the best example of a 'developing country' in south-eastern Europe, particularly in its demographic pattern. Having chosen to support China instead of the Soviet Union, it has recreated some of the isolation that was beginning to break down, though it has tended to remain aloof. It is potentially rich and could trade to great advantage with the rest of Europe, but it is still a poor and small domestic market, so that it is questionable whether more than a limited industrial development can be expected. It needs a larger neighbour to lean on, but the most likely—Jugoslavia and Italy—are for past misdeeds unacceptable.

Together these countries are in a phase of rapid growth. Whatever changes come in the economies of the more developed countries, the biggest changes in the geography of Europe can be expected to take place in south-eastern Europe. Over the next quarter century, the centres of gravity of many phenomena in the Continent will most likely shift towards this south-eastern corner. Consequently, these countries that have for long been passive members of the community of nations in Europe can be expected to play a larger part, particularly in relations with the Soviet Union.

Alternative Names for the Principal Places

This list contains only the more common forms likely to be met. It is by no means exhaustive.

German Democratic Republic

Bautzen	Budyšin (Sorb)
Cottbus	Chośebuz (Sorb)
Eisenhüttenstadt	Stalinstadt
Forst	Baršć (Sorb)
Hoyerswerda	Wojerecy (Sorb)
Kamenz	Kamjenc (Sorb)
Karl-Marx-Stadt	Chemnitz
Niesky	Niska (Sorb)
Spremberg	Gródk (Sorb)
Weisswasser	Běla Woda (Sorb)

Poland

Bielkso-Biała	Bielitz (Ger)
Bolesławiec	Bunzlau (Ger)
Bydgoszcz	Bromberg (Ger)
Bytom	Beuthen (Ger)
Brzeg	Brieg (Ger)
Chorzów, Królewska Huta	Königshütte (Ger)
Cieszyn	Teschen (Ger), Těšín (Cz)
Częstochowa	Tschenstochau (Ger)
Elbląg	Elbing (Ger)
Gdańsk	Danzig (Ger)
Gdynia	Gdingen, Gotenhafen (Ger)
Gliwice	Gleiwitz (Ger)
Glogów	Glogau (Ger)
Gniezno	Gnesen (Ger)
Gorzów Wielkopolski	Landsberg (Ger)
Grudziądz	Graudenz (Ger)
Gubin	Guben (Ger)
Jelenia Góra	Hirschberg (Ger)
Kalisz	Kalisch (Ger)
Katowice (Stalinogród)	Kattowitz (Ger)
Kłodzko	Glatz (Ger)
Kołobrzeg	Kolberg (Ger)

Kostrzyn	Küstrin (Ger)
Koźle	Cosel (Ger)
Kraków	Krakau (Ger)
Legnica	Liegnitz (Ger)
Łódź	Litzmannstadt (Ger)
Malbork	Marienburg (Ger)
Mysłowice	Myslowitz (Ger)
Olsztyn	Allenstein (Ger)
Opole	Oppeln (Ger)
Oświęcim	Auschwitz (Ger)
Poznań	Posen (Ger)
Pszczyna	Pless (Ger)
Raciborz	Ratibor (Ger)
Rzeszów	Reischshof (Ger)
Sandomierz	Sandomir (Ger)
Słupsk	Stolp (Ger)
Sosnowiec	Sosnowitz (Ger)
Świdnica	Schweidnitz (Ger)
Świętochłowice	Schwientochlowitz (Ger)
Świnoujście	Schwinemünde (Ger)
Szczecin	Stettin (Ger)
Tarnowskie Góry	Tarnowitz (Ger)
Toruń	Thorn (Ger)
Wałbrzych	Waldenburg (Ger)
Warszawa	Warsaw (Eng), War Schau (Ger)
Wrocław	Breslau (Ger)
Zabrze	Hindenburg (Ger)
Zgorzelec	Görlitz (Ger)
Zielona Góra	Grünberg (Ger)

Czechoslovakia

Aš	Asch (Ger)
Banská Bystrica	Neusohl (Ger), Besztercebánya (H)
Banská Stiavnica	Schemnitz (Ger), Selmecbánya (H)
Bohumin	Oderberg (Ger)
Bratislava	Pressburg (Ger), Poszony (H)
Břeclav	Lundenburg (Ger)
Brno	Brünn (Ger)
České Budějovice	Budweis (Ger)
Česká Lípa	Böhmisch Leipa (Ger)
Cheb	Eger (Ger)
Chomutov	Komotau (Ger)
Čierna nad Tisou	Csernö (H)
Domažlice	Taus (Ger)
Gottwaldov	Zlín
Hlučín	Hultschin (Ger)
Hradec Králové	Königgrätz (Ger)

Jablonec	Gablonz (Ger)
Jáchymov	Joachimsthal (Ger)
Jihlava	Iglau (Ger)
Karlovy Vary·	Karlsbad (Ger)
Karviná	Karwin (Ger), Fryštát
Kežmarok	Käsmark (Ger) Késmárk (H)
Košice	Kaschau (Ger), Kassa (H)
Kremnica	Kremnitz (Ger), Körmöcbánya (H)
Kutná Hora	Kuttenberg (Ger)
Levoča	Leutschau (Ger), Löcse (H)
Liberec	Reichenberg (Ger)
Litoměřice	Leitmeritz (Ger)
Litomyšl	Leitomischl (Ger)
Mariánské Lázně	Marienbad (Ger)
Martin, Turčiansky Svätý Martin	Turóc-Szt. Márton (H)
Mladá Boleslav	Jungbunzlau (Ger)
Most	Brüx (Ger)
Nitra	Neutra (Ger), Nyitra (H)
Olomouc	Olmütz (Ger)
Opava	Troppau (Ger)
Ostrava	Ostrau (Ger)
Pardubice	Pardubitz (Ger)
Plzeň	Pilsen (Ger)
Praha	Prague (Eng), Prag (Ger)
Prešov	Eperies (Ger), Eperjes (H)
Rožňava	Rosenau (Ger), Rozsnyó (H)
Ružomberok	Rosenberg (Ger), Rózsahegy (H)
Slavkov (u Brna)	Austerlitz (Ger)
Sokolov (Falkov)	Falkenau (Ger)
Spišská Nová Ves	Neudorf (Ger), Iglo (H)
Svitavy	Zwittau (Ger)
Teplice	Teplitz (Ger)
Těšín	Teschen (Ger), Cieszyn (P)
Trenčin	Trentschen (Ger), Trencsén (H)
Trnava	Tyrnau (Ger), Nagyszombat (H)
Ústí-nad-Labem	Aussig (Ger)
Žatec	Saaz (Ger)
Žilina	Sillein (Ger), Zsolna (H)
Znojmo	Znaim (Ger)

Hungary

Budapest	Ofenpest (Ger)
Debrecen	Debreczin (Ger)
Dunaújváros (Sztalinváros)	
Eger	Erlau (Ger)
Esztergom	Gran (Ger)
Györ	Raab (Ger)
Komarom	Komorn (Ger), Komarno (Cz)

Köszeg	Güns (Ger)
Mosonmagyarovár	Wieselburg (Ger)
Nagykanizsa	Grosskanizsa (Ger)
Pécs	Fünfkirchen (Ger), Pecuj (SC)
Sopron	Ödenburg (Ger)
Szeged	Szegedin (old form)
Székesfehérvár	Stuhlweissenburg (Ger)
Szombathely	Steinamanger (Ger)
Vác	Waitzen (Ger)

Rumania

Alba Julia	Gyulafehérvár (H), Karlsburg (Ger)
Baia Mare	Nagybánya (H)
Băile-Herculane	Herkulesbad (Ger)
Bistriţa	Beszterce (H), Bistritz (Ger)
Braşov (Oraşul Stalin)	Brassó (H), Kronstadt (Ger)
Bucureşti	Bucharest (Eng), Bukarest (Ger)
Cluj	Kolozsvár (H), Klausenburg (H)
Constanţa	Konstanza (Ger), Kjustendza (B)
Galaţi	Galatz (Ger)
Giurgiu	Giurgevo (B)
Haţeg	Hátszeg (H)
Hunedoara	Hunyadvár (H), Eisenmarkt (Ger)
Oradea	Nagyvárad (H), Grosswardein (Ger)
Ploieşti (Ploeşti)	
Reghin	Regen (H), Sächsisch Regen (Ger)
Satu-Mare	Szatmár (H), Sathmar (Ger)
Sibiu	Nagyszeben (H), Hermannstadt (Ger)
Sighişoara	Segesvár (H), Schässburg (Ger)
Suceava	Suczawa (P)
Timişoara	Temesvár (H), Temeschburg (Ger)
Tirgu Mureş	Marosvásárhely (H), Neumarkt (Ger)
Turda	Torda (H), Torenburg (Ger)

Bulgaria

Most apparent alternative names in Bulgaria are the result of different systems of transliteration from the Cyrillic alphabet.

Blagoevgrad		Gorna Dzhumaya
Botevgrad		Orchanie
Pernik		Dimitrovo
Plevna		Pleven
Plovdiv	Philippolis	Filibe (T)
Ruse	Ruschuk	Ruscuk (T)
Shumen		Kolarovgrad
Sliven		Slivno
Stanke Dmitrov		Dupnitsa

Tolbukhin	Dobrich
Trnovo	Tirnovo
Varna	Stalin
Vraca	Vratsa

Jugoslavia

Bar	Antivari (I)
Beograd	Belgrade (Eng)
Bitola, Bitolj	Monastir
Celje	Cilli (Ger)
Dubrovnik	Ragusa (I)
Karlovac	Karlstadt (Ger)
Karlovci	Karlowitz (Ger)
Kočevje	Gottschee (Ger)
Koper	Capodistria (I)
Kotor	Cattaro (I)
Ljubljana	Laibach (Ger)
Maribor	Marburg (Ger)
Novi Sad	Neusatz (Ger), Újvidék (H)
Niš	Nisch (Ger)
Ohrid, Ochrid	Ochrida (Ger)
Osijek	Esseg (Ger), Eszék (H)
Pančevo	Panscova (H)
Peć	Ipek (T), Pejë (Alb)
Petrovaradin	Peterwardein (Ger), Pétervárad (H)
Požarevac	Passarowitz (Ger)
Prilep	Perlepe (T)
Priština	Prishtinë (Alb)
Prizren	Prizreni (Alb)
Ptuj	Pettau (Ger)
Rijeka	Fiume (I)
Šibenik	Sibenico (I)
Skopje, Skoplje	Üsküb, Uskub (T)
Smederovo	Szendra (H), Semendria (Ger)
Split	Spalato (I)
Subotica	Szabadka (H), Maria-Theresiopel (Ger)
Tetovo	Tetovë (Alb), Kalkandelen (T)
Titograd	Podgorica
Ulcinj	Dulcigno (I)
Varaždin	Varasd (H)
Vrsac	Versec (H), Werschatz (Ger)
Zadar	Zara (I)
Zagreb	Agram (Ger), Zágráb (H)
Zemun	Semlin (Ger), Zimony (H)
Zrenjanin (Vel. Bečerek)	Nagybecskerek (H)

Albania

Some differences exist between Tosk and Gheg spellings of names.

Dürres	Durazzo (I)
Gjirokastër	Gjinokastër Argyrokastro (Gk)
Korçë	Korytsa (Gk), Corizza (I)
Krujë	Croia (I)
Lesh, Lezhë	Alessio (I)
Sarandë	Santi Quaranta (I), Porto Edda (I)
Sazan	Saseno (I)
Shëngijn	San Giovanni di Medua (I)
Shkodër	Skadar (SC), Scutari (I)
Tiranë	Tirana (I)
Vlorë, Vlonë	Valona (I)

Names in SOVIET TERRITORY formerly within the territory of Eastern European states.

Baltiysk	Pillau (Ger)
Belgorod Dneptrovskiy	Cetatea Alba (Rum), Akkerman
Brest, Brest Litovsk	Breść nad Bugiem (P)
Chernovtsy	Cernăuţi (Rum), Czernowitz (Ger)
Chernyakhovsk	Insterburg (Ger)
Chop	Čop (Cz), Csop (H)
Kaliningrad	Königsberg (Ger)
Kiliya	Chilia Noua
Kishinev	Chişinău (Rum)
Lvov	Lwów (P), Lemberg (Ger)
Mukachevo	Mukačevo (Cz), Munkács (H)
Sovyetsk	Tilsit (Ger)
Uzhgorod	Užhorod (Cz), Ungvár (H)
Vilnius	Wilno (P)

Other towns with alternative names found in literature on Eastern Europe

Alexandroupolis	Dedeagatch (B), Dedeagaç (T)
Edirne	Odrin (B), Adrianople
Gorizia	Gorica (SC), Görz (Ger)
Istanbul	Tsargrad (B), Constantinople
Klagenfurt	Celovec (SC)
Trieste	Trst (SC)
Thessaloniki	Solun (SC), Salonika

Bibliography

Note. Explanations of the abbreviations for some of the publishers are on page 347.

General Works

Aschenbrenner, V. *et al.* (1967). *Die Deutschen und ihre Östlichen Nachbarn*, Diesterweg, Frankfurt.

Authors' Collective (1966). *Geographical Outline of the Socialist Republic of Romania*, Meridiane, Bucharest.

Author's Collective (1964). *Republica Populară Romîna—noua Geografie a Patriei*, Meridiane, Bucharest.

Barbag, J. and Berezowski, S. (1956). *Ökonomische Geographie der Volksrepublik Polen*, Verlag der Wissenschaften, Berlin.

Berezowski, S., Ed. (1969). *Geografia Ekonomiczna Polski*, PWN, Warsaw.

Beškov, A. (1960). *Volksrepublik Bulgarien—Natur und Wirtschaft*, Die Wirtschaft, Berlin.

Beškov, A. and Valev, E. B. (1961). *Geografiya na Bulgariya*, 2 vols, Akademiya na Naukite, Sofia.

Bernát, T. (1969). *Magyarország gazdasági földrajza.*, Mezögazd asági kiadó, Budapest.

Blanc, A. (1965), *Géographie des Balkans*, PUF, Paris.

Blanc, A., George, P. and Smotkine, H. (1967). *Les Républiques Socialistes d'Europe Centrale*, PUF, Paris.

Blašković, V. (1962). *Ekonomska Geografija Jugoslavije*, Birozavod, Zagreb.

Blažek, M. (1959). *Ökonomische Geographie der Tschechoslowakischen Volksrepublik*, Die Wirtschaft, Berlin.

Blažek, M. (1964). *Ekonomická Geografia ČSSR*, Bratislava.

Breu, J. (1967). *Zur Wirtschaftsgeographie der Tschechoslowakischen Republik. Geographie und Wirtschaftskunde*, Vienna.

Busek, V. and Spulber, N. (1957). *Czechoslovakia*, Free Europe Committee, New York.

Cucu, V. and Roşu, A. (1966). *The Physical and Economic Maps of the Socialist Republic of Rumania*, Meridiane, Bucharest.

Cvijić, J. (1918). *La Péninsule Balkanique*, Colin, Paris.

Demek, J. *et al.* (1971). *Geography of Czechoslovakia*, Academia, Prague.

Droz, J. (1960). *L'Europe Centrale*, PUF, Paris.

Elkins, T. H. (1969). *Germany*. 2nd edn, Chatto & Windus, London.

Fleure, H. J., Ed. (1936). *Eastern Carpathian Studies*, Le Play Society, London.

Fleure, H. J., Ed. (1939). *Eastern Carpathian Studies*, Le Play Society, London.

Fischer-Galati, S. A. (1964). *Eastern Europe in the Sixties*, Praeger, New York.

George, P. and Tricart, J. (1954). *L'Europe Centrale*, 2 vols, PUF, Paris.

George, P. (1964). *Géographie de l'Europe Centrale*, PUF, Paris.

Geco, P. (1964), *Gjeografia Ekonomike e Shqipërisë*, Universiteti, Shtetëror, Tirana.

Hamilton, F. E. I. (1968). *Yugoslavia—Patterns of Economic Activity*, Bell, London.

Haseganu, M., Ed. (1962). *Wirtschaftsgeographie der Rumänischen Volksrepublik*, Die Wirtschaft, Berlin.

Harrington, R. (1967). Albania—Europe's least-known country. *Canadian Geog. J.*, **74**, 132–43.

Hartshorne, R. (1934). Geographie and political boundaries in Upper Silesia. *Ann. Ass. Am. Geog.*, **23**, 195–228.

Häufler, V., Korčák, J. and Král, V. (1961). *Zeměpis Československa*, NČAV, Prague.

Herbst-Rădoi, A. (1969). *Geografia Economică a R.S. România*, Editura Stiintifică, Bucharest.

Hoffman, G. W. (1963). *The Balkans in Transition*, Van Nostrand, Princeton, N.J.

Hoffman, G. W., Ed. (1971). *Eastern Europe—Essays in Geographical Problems*, Methuen, London.

Hoffman, G. W. (1973). *Regional Development Strategy in Southeast Europe*, Praeger, New York.

Ilinicha, Yu. V. (1965). *Polsha—Ekonomiko-geograficheskaya Monografiya*, Izdatelstvo Mezhdunarodnyye Otnosheniya, Moscow.

Jelavich, C. and B., Eds. (1953). *The Balkans in Transition*, University of California Press, Berkeley.

Kohl, H., Ed. (1969). *Ökonomische Geographie der Deutschen Demokratischen Republik*, Haack, Gotha.

Kremky-Saloni, J. (1961). *Rumania*, PWE, Warsaw.

Leszczycki, S. and Kosiński, L. (1967). *Zarys Geografii Ekonomicznej Polski*, PWN, Warsaw.

Leszczycki, S. (1969). Spatial structure of Poland's economy. *Geog. polon*, **11**, 77–96.

Macartney, C. A. and Palmer, A. W. (1962). *Independent Eastern Europe*, Macmillan, London.

Markert, W. (1954). *Jugoslawien-Osteuropa Handbuch*, Böhlau, Cologne.

Markert, W. (1959). *Polen-Osteuropa Handbuch*, Böhlau, Cologne.

Maruszczak, H. (1971). *Bulgaria*, PWE, Warsaw.

Markos, György (1971). *Ungarn—Land, Volk, Wirtschaft in Stichworten*, Hirt, Kiel.

Milojevic, B. Ž. (1958). *Yugoslavia—Geographical Survey*, Commission for Cultural Relations, Belgrade.

Milojevic, B. Ž. (1960). *Monografia Geografica a Republicii Populare Romine*, 2 vols, Editura Stiintifică, Bucharest.

Moraru, T. *et al.* (1966). *The Geography of Rumania*, Meridiane, Bucharest.

Naumann, F. (1915). *Central Europe*, King, London.

Naval Intelligence Division (1944–5). *Jugoslavia, 3 vols, London.*

Naval Intelligence Division (1945). *Albania*, London.

Nernheim, K. (1966). Albanien—eine Landes–und Wirtschaftskunde. *Zeitschrift f. Wirtschaftskunde*, **10**, 10–117.

Newbigin, M. L. (1915). *Geographical Aspects of Balkan Problems*, Constable, London.

Osborne, R. H. (1967). *East Central Europe*, Chatto & Windus, London.

Partsch, J. (1903). *Central Europe*, Frowde–Heinemann, London.

Pécsi, M. and Sárfalvi, B. (1964). *A Geography of Hungary*, Collets, London.
Penkov, I. and Christov, T. (1965). *Ikonomicheska Geografiya na Bulgariya*, Akademiya na Naukite, Sofia.
Pounds, N. J. G. (1964). *Poland between East and West*, Van Nostrand, Princeton, N.J.
Pounds, N. J. G. (1969). *Eastern Europe*, Longmans, London.
Poznáváme Svět 1 (1965). *Československo*, USGK, Prague.
Poznáváme Svět 8 (1965). *Balkánské Státy*, USGK, Prague.
Poznáváme Svět 12 (1965). *Střední Evropa*, USGK, Prague.
Radó, S., Ed. (1962). *Ökonomische Geographie der Ungarischen Volksrepublik*, Die Wirtschaft, Berlin.
Raus, O. and Freytag, S. (1961). *Deutsche Demokratische Republik—politisch-ökonomisch-geographische Übersicht*, Die Wirtschaft, Berlin.
Rychłowski, B. (1967). *Województwo Katowickie*, PWN, Warsaw.
Sárfalvi, B., Ed. (1964). Applied geography in Hungary. *Studies in Geography*, 2, Akadémiai Kiadó, Budapest.
Schacher, G. (1936). *Central Europe and the Western World*, Allen & Unwin, London.
Schmidt, G. (1961). Albanien: ein landeskundlicher Abriss. *Geog. Rundschau*, 13, 396–409.
Schmidt-Renner, G. (1962). *Wirtschaftsterritorium DDR*, Die Wirtschaft, Berlin.
Singleton, F. B. (1965). *Background to Eastern Europe*, Pergamon, London.
Skendi, S., Ed. (1957). *Albania*, Free Europe Committee, New York.
Staar, R. F. (1971). *The Communist Regimes in Eastern Europe*. 2nd edn, Hoover Institute, Stanford.
Straszewicz, L, Ed. (1970). *Geografia Gospodarcza Europejskich Krajów Demokracji Ludowej*, 2 vols, TWE, Warsaw.
Střída, M. *et al.* (1963). *Oblasti Československa*, NČAV, Praha.
Todorov, N. *et al.* (1965). *Bulgarie—Aperçu historique et géographique*, Akademia na Naukite, Sofia.
Tyagunenko, A. (1960). *Razvitiya Ekonomiki Narodnoye Respubliki Albanii*, Izdatelstvo Mezhdunarodnyye Otnosheniya, Moscow.
Valev, E. B. (1955). *Ekonomicheskaya Geografiya Bolgarii i Albanii*, Izdatelstvo Mezhdunarodnyye Otnosheniya, Moscow.
Van Cleef, E. (1933). Danzig and Gdynia. *Geogrl. Rev.*, 23, 101–7.
Wanklyn, H. G. (1941). *The Eastern Marchlands of Europe*, Philip, London.
Wanklyn, H. G. (1954). *Czechoslovakia—A Geographical and Historical Study*, Philip, London.
Wrzosek, A. (1960). *Czechosłowacja*, PWN, Warsaw.

Physical Environment

De Martonne, E. (1917). The Carpathians: Physiogeographic features controlling human geography. *Geogrl. Rev.*, 3, 417–37.
Dorn, P. and Lotze, F. (1971). *Die Geologie Mitteleuropas*, 4th edn, Koeltz, Frankfurt.

Gellert, J. von (1969). Karte der Grossformentypen und Morphostruktur Bulgariens im Masstab, 1:2.5M. *Geog. Berichte*, **51**, 118–22.

Kendrew, W. (1964). *Climates of the Continents*, Oxford University Press, London.

Kunský, J. (1968). *Fyzický zeměpis Československa*, SPN, Praha.

Lencewicz, S. and Kondracki, J. (1964). *Geografia Fizyczna Polski*, PWN, Warsaw.

Marković, J. (1963). *Fizika Geografija Jugoslavije*, Nauchna Kniga, Belgrade.

Mavrocordat, G. (1971). *Die Böden Rumänians*, Dünker u. Humblot, Giessen.

Pécsi, M. (1970). Geomorphological regions of Hungary. *Studies in Geography*, **6**, Akadémiai Kiadó, Budapest.

Soó, R. de (1929). Die Vegetation und die Entstehung der Ungarischen Puszta. *J. Ecol.* **17,** 329–50.

Historical Development

Barker, E. (1950). *Macedonia—its Place in Balkan Power Politics*. RIIA, London.

Betts, R. R., Ed. (1950). *Central and Southeast Europe, 1945–1948*, London.

Bowman, I. (1929). *The New World*, 4th edn, World Book Co., London.

Breu, J. (1971). Grossmachtbildung im Donauraum. *Geoforum*, **6**, 17–19.

Cahnmann, W. (1949). Frontiers between East and West in Europe. *Geogrl. Rev.*, **39**, 605–24.

Dvornik, F. (1949). *The Making of Central and Eastern Europe*, Polish Research Centre, London.

Dvornik, F. (1962). *The Slavs in European History and Civilisation*, Rutgers University Press, New Brunswick, N.J.

Erickson, J. (1964). *Panslavism*, Historical Association, London.

Fejtö, F. (1971). *A History of the People's Democracies*, London.

Gewehr, W. M. (1967). *Rise of Nationalism in the Balkans, 1800–1930*, Arcon, Reissue, London.

Gimbutas, M. (1956). *The Pre-History of Eastern Europe*, Harvard University Press, Cambridge, Mass.

Halecki, O. (1961). *A History of Poland*, Dent, London.

Ionescu, G. (1965). *The Break-up of the Soviet Empire in Eastern Europe*, Penguin, London.

Kohn, H., Ed. (1960). Die West- und Südslawen. *Die Welt der Slawen*, **1,** Fischer, Frankfurt.

Kohn, H., Ed. (1962). Russen-Weissrussen-Ukrainer. *Die Welt der Slawen*, **2,** Fischer, Frankfurt.

Macartney, C. A. (1942). *Problems of the Danube Basin*, University Press, Cambridge.

Macartney, C. A. (1962). *Hungary—A Short History*, University Press, Edinburgh.

Macdermott, M. (1962). *A History of Bulgaria, 1393–1885*, Allen & Unwin, London.

Marriott, J. A. R. (1924). *The Eastern Question*, Oxford University Press, London.

Moodie, A. E. (1945). *The Italo-Yugoslav Boundary—A Study in Political Geography*, Philip, London.

Roglić, J. (1970). Die Gebirge als die Wiege des geschichtlichen Geschehens in Südosteuropa. *Colloq. Geograph. Argumenta Geographica.* **12,** Bonn.

Schreiber, H. (1965). *Teuton and Slav,* Constable, London.

Seton-Watson, R. W. (1934). *A History of the Roumanians,* University Press, Cambridge.

Seton-Watson, R. W. (1946). *Eastern Europe between the Wars, 1918–1941,* Cambridge University Press, London.

Seton-Watson, R. W. (1963). *A History of the Czechs and Slovaks,* Hutchinson, London.

Shute, J. (1948). Czechoslovakia's territorial and population changes. *Econ. Geogr.,* **24,** 35–44.

Szaz, Z. M. (1962). *Die Deutsche Ostgrenze,* Bechtle, Munich.

Thomson, S. H. (1944). *Czechoslovakia in European History*, Oxford University Press, London.

Wagner, W. (1964). *The Genesis of the Oder-Neisse Line,* Brentano, Stuttgart.

Warriner, D., Ed. (1965). *Contrasts in Emerging Societies,* University Press, London.

Wilkinson, H. R. (1951). *Maps and Politics: A Review of the Ethnographic Cartography of Macedonia,* University Press, Liverpool.

Wilkinson, H. R. (1967). *Perspective on some Fundamental Regional Divisions in Yugoslav Illyria, Liverpool Essays in Geography,* Liverpool University Press, London.

Wiskemann, E. (1956). *Germany's Eastern Neighbours,* RIIA, Oxford.

Wiskemann, E. (1967). *Czechs and Germans,* 2nd edn, Macmillan, London.

Wolff, R. L. (1956). *The Balkans in our Time,* Harvard University Press, Cambridge, Mass.

Population and Ethnography

Ancel, J. (1930). *Peuples et Nations des Balkans,* Colin, Paris.

Berent, J. (1970). Causes of fertility decline in Eastern Europe and the Soviet Union. *Popul. Stud.,* **24,** 53–8.

Breu, J. (1966). Das Völkerbild Ostmittel- und Südosteuropas in Zahlen. *Mitt. öst. geogr. Ges.,* **108,** 325–39.

Buchhofer, E. (1967). *Die Bevölkerungsentwicklung in den polnisch verwalteten deutschen Ostgebieten, 1956–1965,* Schriften d. Kieler Universität, Kiel.

Carter, F. W. (1972). *Dubrovnik—a Classic City State,* Seminar Press, London.

Ciborowski, A. and Jankowski, S. (1966). *Warszawa Odbudowana,* Polonia, Warsaw.

Compton, P. A. (1965). The new Socialist town of Dunaujvaros, *Geography,* **50,** 288–91.

Compton, P. A. (1972). Internal migration in Hungary between 1960 and 1968, *TESG,* **63,** 25–38.

Coon, C. S. (1939). *The Races of Europe,* Macmillan, London.

Dawson, A. (1971). Warsaw—An example of city structure in free-market and planned socialist environments, *TESG,* **62,** 104–13.

Dinew, L. (1966). Geography of population and settlements in Bulgaria, *Przegl. geogr.,* **38,** 199–204.

Dziewoński, K. (1962). Procesy urbanizacyjne we współczesnej Polsce, *Przegl. geogr.,* **34,** 457–508.

Eissner, A. (1965). *Bevölkerungsprobleme im Europäischen Osten,* Atlantic Forum, Bonn.

Francastel, P., Ed. (1960). *L'Origine des villes polonaises,* Mouton, Paris.

Francis, A. J. (1971). Urbanisation processes in Poland. *Geography,* **56,** 133–5.

Frumkin, G. (1952). *Population Changes in Europe since 1939,* Allen & Unwin, Geneva.

Georgescu, F., Ed. (1965). *Istoria Orașului București,* Editura Sciintifică Bucharest.

Gimbutas, M. (1971). *The Slavs,* Thames & Hudson, London.

Häufler, Vl. (1968). Ein Beitrag zur Bevölkerungsgeographie der Böhmischen Länder, *Acta Univ. Carol.,* Prague.

Häufler, Vl. (1968). *Changes in the Geographical Distribution of Population in Czechoslovakia,* NČAV, Prague.

Hoffman, G. W. (1964). Transformation of rural settlement in Bulgaria, *Geogr. Rev.,* **54,** 45–64.

Horvat, B. (1971). Nationalismus und Nation, *Wiss. Dienst Südosteuropa,* **8/9.**

Huxley, J. S. and Haddon, A. C. (1935). *We Europeans—A Survey of Racial Problems,* Cape, London.

Jasiński, J. (1972). *Kraków—Rozwój Miasta w Polsce Ludowej,* PWN, Warsaw.

Kielczewska-Zaleska, M. (1965). The Definitions of urban and non-urban Settlements in East-Central Europe, *Geogr. polon.,* **7,** 5–17.

Kielczewska-Zaleska, M. (1965). O typach osiedli wiejskich w Polsce i planie ich przebudowy, *Przegl. Geogr.,* **37,** 457–80.

Kielczewska-Zaleska; M. (1965). Distribution of rural dispersed settlements in Poland, *Przegl. Geogr.,* **42,** 225–34.

Kosiński, L. (1961). Demographic Problems of the Polish Western and Northern Territories. In *Geographical Essays on Eastern Europe* (ed. N. J. G. Pounds), Indiana University Press, Bloomington.

Kosiński, L. (1966). Migrations of population in East-Central Europe from 1939–1965, *Geogr. Polon,* **2,** 259–69.

Kosiński, L. (1965). Warschau. *Geogr. Rdsch.,* **17.**

Kosiński, L. (1969). Changes in the ethnic structure in East-Central Europe, 1930–1960, *Geogr. Rev.,* **59,** 388–402.

Kulischer, E. (1943). *The Displacement of Population in Europe,* International Labour Office, Montreal.

Lewis, W. S. (1938). Some aspects of *Tanya* settlement in Hungary, *Scot. geogr. Mag.,* **54,** 358–66.

Malisz, B. (1962). *Poland Builds New Towns,* Polonia, Warsaw.

Markos, Gy. (1963). Wandlungen der Siedlungsstruktur in der Volksrepublik Ungarn, *Geog. Berichte,* **8,** 30–46.

Martonne, E. de (1920). Essai de Carte Ethnographique des Pays Roumains, *Annales de Geog.,* **29,** 81–98.

Mellor, R. E. H. (1963). A minority problem in Germany, *Scott. Geog. Mag.*, **79**, 49–53.

Milojević, B. Z. (1953). Types of villages and village houses in Yugoslavia, *Prof. Geographer*, **5**, 13–17.

Niederle, L. (1925). *Slovanské Starožitnosti*, Prague.

Pacuraru, I. (1961). Populația R.P. Romine, *Natura*, **13**, 15–22.

Pallis, A. A. (1925) Racial migrations in the Balkans during the years 1912–1924, *Geogrl J.*, **66**, 315–31.

Penkoff, I. (1960). Die Siedlungen Bulgariens—ihre Entstehung, *Geogr. Ber.*, **5**, 211–27.

Popov, P. (1969). Statistika Migrace a Migračnich Procesu v Bulharsku, *Demografie*, **11**, 137–47.

Portal, R. (1969). *The Slavs*, Weidenfeld & Nicholson, London.

Pounds, N. J. G. (1971). The Urbanisation of East-Central and Southeast Europe. In *Eastern Europe: Essays in Geographical Problems* (ed. G. W. Hoffman), Methuen, London.

Prinz, Gy. (1924). Die Siedlungsformen Ungarns, *Ungarische Jahrbücher*, **4**, 125–32.

Radó, S. (1964). Städtentwicklung in der Ungarischen Volksrepublik, *Wiss. Veröff. dt. Inst. Länderk.* 191–6.

Rosenstein-Rodan, P. N. (1943). Agricultural surplus population in eastern and southeastern Europe, *RIIA*, London.

Șandru, I. and Cucu, V. (1964). Classification of towns in Romania, *Rev rom. Géol. Géophys. Géogr.*, **8**, 210–15.

Sárfalvi, B., Ed. (1969). Recent population movements in the East European countries, *Stud. Geogr.* (Budapest), **7**.

Schechtmann, J. B. (1962). *Postwar Population Transfers in Europe, 1945–1955*, Oxford University Press, London.

Schröder, K-H. and Schwarz, G. (1971). *Die ländlichen Siedlungsformen in Mitteleuropa*, Institut für Raumordnung, Bad Godesberg.

Srb, Vl. (1968). Obyvatelstvo Československa v Letech 1918–1968, *Demografie*, **10**, 289–306.

Straszewicz, L. (1966). Aglomeracja Berlina, *Przegl. Geogr.*, **38**, 77–105.

Straszewicz, L. (1969). Capitals of the socialist countries in Europe, *Geogr. polon.* **16**, 27–40.

Střída, M. (1965). Probleme der Siedlungsstruktur der Tschechoslowakei. in *Festschrift für Leo Scheidl*, Vienna.

Turnock, D. (1970). Bucharest: The selection and development of the Romanian capital, *Scot. geogr. Mag.*, **86**, 53–68.

Vrišer, I. (1971). The pattern of central places in Yugoslavia, *TESG*, **62**, 290–9.

Wanklyn, H. G. (1941). The role of peasant Hungary in Europe, *Geogrl. J.*, **97**, 18–35.

Wöhlke, W. (1964). *Zum Problem der ländlichen Übervölkerung und der Verstädterung in Polen*, Schriften d. Universität Kieler, Kiel.

Economic Development
Basch, A. (1944). *The Danubian Basin and the German Economic Sphere*,

Kegan Paul, London.
Bicanić, R. (1967). *Problems of Planning—East and West*, Nijhoff, Den Haag.
Breyer, R. and Hinkel, H. (1959). Verwaltungsgliederung und Raumplanung in Polen und Ostdeutschland, *Z. Ostforschung*, **8.**
Caesar, A. A. L. (1962). Yugoslavia; geography and postwar planning. *Trans. Inst. Br. Geogr.*, **30**, 33–43.
Čižovský, M. (1970). *Mezinarodní Plánování Zkušenost a možností RVHP*, NČAV, Prague.
Degn, C. (1959). *Die Sowjetisierung Ost-Mitteleuropas*, Umschau Verlag, Frankfurt.
Dobb, M. H. (1970). *Socialist Planning—Some Problems*, Lawrence & Wishart, London.
Faddejew, N. A. (1965). *Der Rat für Gegenseitige Wirtschaftshilfe*, Die Wirtschaft, Berlin.
Feigin, J. G. (1956). *Standortverteilung der Produktion im Kapitalismus und im Sozialismus*, Die Wirtschaft, Berlin.
Fikus, D. (1966). *RWPG—Fakty*, PZWS, Warsaw.
Fisher, J. C. (1962). Planning the city of socialist man, *J. Am. Inst. Planners*, **28.**
Hacker, J. and Uschakow, A. (1966). *Die Integration Osteuropas, 1961–1965*, Verlag Wissenschaft und Politik, Cologne.
Helin, R. A. (1967). The volatile administrative map of Rumania. *Ann. Ass. Am. Geogr.*, **57**, 481–502.
Hoffman, G. W. (1967). The problem of underdeveloped regions in southeast Europe, *Ann. Ass. Am. Geogr.*, **57**, 637–66.
Hutira, E. (1963). *Le Developpement de l'Economie nationale de la Republique Populaire Roumaine*, Meridiane, Bucharest.
Kaser, M. (1967). *Comecon—Integration Problems of Planned Economies*, 2nd edn, RIIA, London.
Kiss, T. (1971). *International Division of Labour in Open Economies (CMEA)*, Akadémiai Kiadó, Budapest.
Klinkmüller, E. and Ruban, M. (1960). *Der wirtschaftliche Zusammenarbeit zwischen den Ostblockstaaten*, Duncker u. Humblot, Berlin.
Leptin, G. (1970). *Die Deutsche Wirtschaft nach 1945—ein Ost–West Vergleich*, Leske, Opladen.
Logan, M. I. (1968). Regional economic development in Yugoslavia, 1953–1964. *TESG*, **59**, 42–52.
Maergoiz, I. M. (1967). Fragen der Typologie in der ökonomischen Geographie—auf der Grundlage von Materialen über die Industriegeographie der sozialistischen Länder Europas, *Petermanns geogr. Mitt.* **111**, 161–78.
Markos, Gy. (1969). Grundsätze der territorialen Planung in Ungarn. *Wiss. Abh. geogr. Ges. DDR.*
Mellor, R. E. H. (1971). *Comecon—Challenge to the West*, Van Nostrand, New York.
Moore, W. E. (1945). *Economic Demography of Eastern and Southern Europe*, League of Nations, Geneva.
Morosov, V. I. (1964). *SEV—soyuz ravynch*, Izdatelstvo Mezhdunarodnyye Otnosheniya, Moscow.

Popov, I. V. (1969). *Osnovnyye Napravleniya Tekhnicheskogo Progressa v Stranakh SEV*, Izdatelstvo Mezhdunarodnyye Otnosheniya, Moscow.
Pounds, N. J. G. and Spulber, N. (1957). *Resources and Planning in Eastern Europe*, Indiana University Press, Bloomington.
Pounds, N. J. G. (1959). Planning in the Upper Silesian industrial region, *J. Cent. Eur. Affairs*, **18**, 409–22.
Pritzel, K. (1966). *Die wirtschaftliche Integration der Sowjetischen Besatzungszone Deutschlands in den Ostblock*, 2nd edn, Bonner Berichte, Bonn.
Pryor, F. (1963). *The Communist Foreign Trade System*, Allen & Unwin, London.
Roglić, J. (1949). O geografskom položaju i ekonomskom razvoju Jugoslavije, *Geogr. Glasn.*, **11**, 5–26.
Secretariat CMEA (1969). *The Council for Mutual Economic Assistance—Twenty Years*, Secretariat C.M.E.A., Moscow.
Sergeyev, S. D. (1964). *Ekonomicheskoye Sotrudnichestvo i vsaipomoshch sotsialisticheskych Stran*, Izdatelstvo Mezhdunarodnyye Otnosheniya, Moscow.
Spulber, N. (1957). *The Economics of Communist Eastern Europe*, Wiley, New York.
Stephan, H. (1959). Rebuilding Berlin, *Tn Plann. Rev.*, **29**, 207–26.
Stolper, G. (1966). *Deutsche Wirtschaft seit 1870*, Mohr, Tübingen.
Uschakow, A. (1962). *Der Rat für gegenseitige Wirtschaftshilfe*, Verlag Wissenschaft und Politik, Cologne.
Valev, E. B. (1964). Problemy Ekonomicheskogo Razvitiya Pridunayskych Rayonov Rumynii, Bolgarii i SSSR, *Vestnik Mosk. Universiteta*.
Vikentyev, A. I. and Miroshnichenko, B. P. (1969). *Proizvodstvo i Potrebleniye v Stranakh SEV*, Izdatelstvo Mezhdunarodnyye Otnosheniya, Moscow.
Werner, F. (1972). *Zur Raumordnung in der DDR*, Kiepert, Berlin.

Transport

Arnautovitch, D. (1937). *Histoire des Chemins de Fer yougoslaves*, Colin, Paris.
Beaver, S. H. (1941). Railways in the Balkan Peninsula, *Geogrl J.*, **97**, 273–94.
Dost, P. (1965). *Zur Geschichte der Warschau-Wiener Eisenbahn*, Boettcher, Dortmund.
Grimm, F. (1970). Die Donau und ihre Nutzung, *Geogr. Ber.*, **15**, 1–14.
Gumpel, W. (1967). *Das Verkehrswesen Osteuropas*, Wissenschaft und Politik, Cologne.
Herbst, A. and Herbst, C. (1971). Transformations du paysage consécutives à la construction du système hydroénergétique et de navigation "Les Portes de Fer", *Geoforum*, **6**, 57–62.
Herbst-Rădoi, A. (1972). Aspecte Actuale ale Geografiei Transporturilor din Ţara Noastră, *Terra*, **2**, 30–40.
Hoffman, G. W. (1968). Thessaloniki: The impact of a changing hinterland, *E. Eur. Q.*, **2**, 1–29.
Hundert Jahre Deutsche Eisenbahnen (1935). Verkehrswissenschaftliche Lehrmittelgesellschaft, Berlin.
Korompai, G. (1971). Changes in the structure and direction of expanding commodity transport on the Danube, *Geoforum*, **6**, 63–74.

Lijewski, T. (1959) *Rozwój Sieci kolejowej Polski*, PWN, Warsaw.
Lijewski, T. (1961). Powojenne Przemiany Transportu Bułgarii, *Przegl. Geogr.*, **33**, 679–89.
Markós, Gy. (1965). *Összehasonlitó gazdasági földrajz idegenfogalmi szakemeberek számára*, Budapest.
May, A. J. (1952). Trans-Balkan railway schemes, *J. Modern History*, **24**, 352–67.
Myers, T. C. (1965). The Danube. In *International Rivers: Some Case Studies* (Ed. N. J. G. Pounds), Indiana University Press, Bloomington.
Sander, E. (1971). Verkehrswirtschaft Südosteuropas, *Z. Wirt. Geogr.*, **15**, 84–92.
Spulber, N. (1954). The Danube–Black Sea canal and the Russian control over the Danube, *Econ. Geogr.*, **30**, 236–45.
Štěpán, M. (1958). *Přehledné dějiny československých železnic*, Dopravní Nakladatelství, Prague.

Industry
Antal, Z. (1966). *The Economical Geographical Questions of the United Electric Power System of the European Socialist Countries*, Eötvös Loránd University, Budapest.
Antal, Z. (1966). *Some Hungarian References to the Socialist International Division of Labour*, Budapest.
Blažek, M. (1965). Die Konzentration der Industrie in der Tschechoslovakei, in *Festschrift für Leo Scheidl*, Vienna.
Borgstrom, G. and Annegers, F. (1971). An appraisal of food and agriculture, *TESG*, **62**, 114–25.
Carter, F. W. (1970). Natural gas in Romania, *Geography*, **55**, 214–20.
Childs, D. (1966). Recent East German economic progress, *Geography*, **51**, 367–9.
Elkins, T. H. (1957). The central German chemical industry, *Geography*, **42**, 183–6.
Hamilton, F. E. I. (1970). Changes in the industrial geography of Eastern Europe since 1940, *TESG*, **61**, 300–5.
Jordan, C. N. (1955). *The Romanian Oil Industry*, University Press, New York.
Khristov, T. (1962). *Geografiya na Promishlenostta v Bulgariya*, Akademia na Naukite, Sofia.
Kohl, H. (1964). Standortprobleme der Kaliindustrie der Deutschen Demokratischen Republik, *Petermanns geogr. Mitt.*, **108**, 85–90.
Kohl, H. (1966). *Ökonomische Geographie der Montanindustrie in der Deutschen Demokratischen Republik*, Haack, Gotha.
Kondracki, J. (1960). Types of natural landscape in Poland, *Przegl. Geogr.*, **32**, 23–33.
Kortus, B. (1964). Donbas and Upper Silesia—A comparative analysis of the industrial regions, *Geogr. polon.*, **2**, 183–92.
Kramm, H. J. (1966). Ökonomisch-geographische Probleme der VR Ungarn dargestellt am Beispiel der Aluminiumindustrie. *Wissensch. Veröffentlich. des Deutsch. Inst. für Länderkunde*, **23–4**, Dresden.

Lesczycki, S. (1968). Wandlungen in der räumlichen Struktur der Industrie in Volkspolen in den Jahren 1949–1965, *Acta geogr. Debrecin.*, **7**, 161–7.

Maergoiz, I. M. (1970). Ökonomisch-geographische Entwicklungsaspekte der Arbeitsteilung zwischen den Staaten der RGW, *Petermanns geogr. Mitt*, **114**, 29–33.

Pounds, N. J. G. (1958). Nowa Huta—A new Polish iron and steel works, *Geography*, **43**, 54–6.

Pounds, N. J. G. (1958). The spread of mining in the coal basin of Upper Silesia and Northern Moravia, *Ann. Ass. Am. Geogr.*, **48**, 149–63.

Pounds, N. J. G. (1958). *The Upper Silesian Industrial Region*, Indiana University Press, Bloomington.

Seraphim, P. H. (1953). *Industriekombinat Oberschlesien*, Müller, Cologne.

Sinnhuber, K. (1965) Eisenhüttenstadt and other new industrial locations in East Germany, in *Festschrift für Leo Scheidl*, Vienna.

Smotkine, H. (1967). Un type de complexe industriel: le district de Karl-Marx-Stadt en RDA, *Annls Géogr.*, **76**, 152–67.

Sperling, W. (1966). Das Gebiet der ostslawischen Eisenwerke. *Erdkunde*, **20**, 60–2.

Strużek, B. (1963). *Rolnictwo europejskich krajów socialistycznych*, PWN, Warsaw.

Turnock, D. (1970). The pattern of industrialisation in Rumania, *Ann. Ass. Am. Geogr.*, **60**, 540–59.

Zaubermann, A. (1964). *Industrial progress in Poland, Czechoslovakia and East Germany, 1937–1962*, RIIA, London.

Agriculture

Beuermann, A. (1967). *Fernweidewirtschaft in Südosteuropa.*, Westermann, Brunswick.

Biegajło, S. (1972). Spósoby Využivania Ornej Pôdy porovnávacia štúdia na priklade Pol'ska, ČSSR a Maďarska, *Geogr. Čas.*, **24**, 9–17.

Cousens, S. H. (1967). Changes in Bulgarian agriculture, *Geography*, **52**, 12–22.

Davies, E. (1940). The patterns of transhumance in Europe, *Geography*, **25**, 156–68.

Entwistle, E. W. (1972). Agrarian-industrial complexes in Bulgaria. *Geography*, **57**, 246–8.

Enyedi, Gy. (1969). Geographical types of Hungarian agriculture, *Stud. Geog.*, **3**, Akadémiai Kiadó.

Enyedi, Gy. (1964). Le village hongrois et la grande exploitation agricole, *Annls Geogr.*, **73**, 687–700.

Enyedi, Gy. (1967). The changing face of agriculture in Eastern Europe, *Geogr. Rev.*, **57**.

Halpern, J. M. (1963). Jugoslav peasant society in transition, *Anthrop. Q.*, **36**.

Häufler, V. (1954). Veränderungen im Hirtenleben in der Tatra . . . während der letzten 25 Jahren, *Przegl. Geogr.*, **26**, 89–96.

Hoffman, G. W. (1961). The Changes in the Agricultural Geography of Yugoslavia. In *Geographical Essays on Eastern Europe* (ed. N. J. G. Pounds), Indiana University Press, Bloomington.

Jaehne, G. (1968). *Landwirtschaft und landwirtschaftliche Zusammenarbeit im Rat für Gegenseitige Wirtschaftshilfe,* Dünker u. Humblot, Giessen.

Kostrowicki, J., Ed. (1965). Land Utilization in East-Central Europe—Case Studies, *Geogr. polon.,* **5.**

Lefevre, M. A. (1930). La Zadruga: forme de propriété collective de type patriarcal, *Annls Géogr.,* **39,** 316–20.

Matley, I. M. (1970). Traditional pastoral life in Rumania, *Prof. Geogr.,* **22,** 311–16.

Piekarczyk, K. (1962). Rozprzestrzenianie się stonki ziemniaczanej, *Przegl. Geogr.,* **34,** 75–97.

Roubitschek, W. (1960). Zur Bevölkerungs- und Agrarstruktur Rumäniens, *Petermanns geogr. Mitt.,* **104,** 23–32.

Roubitschek, W. (1964). Die regionale Struktur der pflanzlichen Bruttoproduktion in der DDR 1955 und ihre Veränderung gegenüber 1935, *Petermanns geogr. Mitt.,* **108,** 69–78.

Sárfalvi, B. (Ed.). (1966). Geographical types of Hungarian agriculture, *Stud. Geogr.* (Budapest), **3.**

Sárfalvi, B. (1967). Land utilization in Eastern Europe, *Stud. Geogr.* (Budapest), **4.**

Sárfalvi, B. (1971). The changing face of the Great Hungarian Plain, *Stud. Geogr.* (Budapest), **9.**

Turnock, D. (1970). Geographical aspects of Romanian agriculture, *Geography,* **55,** 169–86.

Warriner, D. (1954). Some controversial issues in the history of agrarian Europe, *Slav. East Eur. Rev.,* **32,** 168–86.

Warriner, D. (1964). *Economics of Peasant Farming,* 2nd edn, Oxford University Press, London.

Atlases

Atlas zur Bodenkunde (1965) Bibliographisches Institut, Mannheim.

Atlas zur Geologie (1968) Bibliographisches Institut, Mannheim.

Atlas zur Geschichte der Deutschen Ostsiedlung (1958) Velhagen u. Klasing, Bielefeld.

Atlas Östliches Mitteleuropa (1959) Velhagen u. Klasing, Bielefeld.

Atlas der Deutschen Demokratischen Republik (1972) Landkartenverlag, Berlin.

Atlas po Bulgarska Istoriya (1963) Akademiya na Naukite, Sofia.

Atlas Československe Socialisticke Republiky (1966) Ústřední správa Geodesie a Kartografie, Prague.

Atlas Československých Dějin (1965) USGK, Prague.

Atlas za osnivu Skolu (1962) U.Č.I.L.A., Zagreb.

Atlas der Donauländer (1970) Deuticke, Vienna.

Atlas për Schkollet Fillore (1966) N.I.S.H. Hamid Shijaku, Tirana.

Atlas Geograficzny Polski (1969) PPWK, Warsaw.

Atlas Historyczny Polski (1967) PPWK, Warsaw.

Atlas Ziem Odzyskanych (1947) PPWK, Warsaw,

Atlas Statystyczny Polski (1970) PPWK, Warsaw.

Atlas Polski (1954–6) Zeszyt I–IV. PPWK, Warsaw.
Atlas Narodov Mira (1964) Glavnoye Upravleniye Geodesii i Kartografii, Moscow.
Atlas Geografic Republica Socialistă România (1966) Editura Didactică, Bucharest.
Atlas Istoric Romania (1971) Editura Didactică, Bucharest.
Atlasul Republicii Socialiste Romania (1972) Editura Didactică, Bucharest.
Csati, E. (1965 et seq.). *Cartactual,* Cartographia, Budapest.
Jazdziewski, K. (1949). *Atlas do Pradziejow Slowian,* PPWK, Lodz.
Kovalevsky, P. (1961). *Atlas historique et culturel de la Russie et du monde slave,* Elsevier, Paris.
National Atlas of Hungary (1967) Cartographia, Budapest.
Shkolski Istorijski Atlas (1965) Geokarta, Belgrade.
Školní Atlas Československých Dějin (1959) USGK, Prague.
Sudetendeutscher Atlas (1954) Sudetendeutsche Arbeitsgemeinschaft, Munich.
Történelmi Atlasz (1967) Cartographia, Budapest.
Westermann Atlas zur Weltgeschichte (1963) Westermann, Brunswick.

Journals and Periodicals
Harris, C. D. and Fellman, J. D. (1971). *International List of Geographical Serials,* 2nd edn, Chicago.

Abbreviations

NČAV	Nakladatelstvi Československé Akademie Věd
PPWK	Państwowe Przedsięborstwo Wydawnictw Kartograficznych
Przeg geogr.	Przegląd geograficzny
PUF	Presses Universitaires de France
PWE	Państwowe Wydawnictwo Ekonomiczne
PWN	Państwowe Wydawnictwo Naukowe
PZWS	Państwowe Zakłady Wydawnictw Szkolnych
RIIA	Royal Institute of International Affairs
SPN	Státni Pedagogické Nakladatelstvi
TESG	Tijdschrift voor Economische en Sociale Geografie
USGK	Ustredni Správa Geodesie a Kartografie
VSAV	Vydavatel'stovo Slovenskej Akadémie Vied

Index

towns (*contd*)
  'socialist' 142, 244, 245
town planning 161, 162
town status 141
trace metals 253
trade 89, 179, 193, 194, 195, 197, 198, 203, 204, 205, 225, 227, 229, 232, 294, 303, 318, 327
trams 201
Trans-Danubia 21, 176
transhumance 100, 104, 177, 322
transit traffic 272, 273, 284, 306, 313, 323, 324
transport 141, 148, 159, 235, 243, 260–1, 272–3, 283–4, 293–4, 305–6, 307, 313, 323–5
transport planning 215
Transylvania 4, 5, 8, 16, 17, 79, 86, 100, 101, 108, 133, 177, 183, 187, 194, 212, 295, 301
Trianon, Treaty of 75, 108, 133, 171, 213
Trieste 87
Triple Monarchy 74
Tsar Simeon 47
Turkish influence on agriculture 175, 176
Turks 49–52, 58–60, 102, 139, 185
  depredations of 33, 108
  Ottoman 33, 49, 60, 74, 179
  Seljuk 49

Ugrians 133
Ukrainians 117, 120, 126, 131–2
unemployment 246
unified transport system 215
United Nations Organisation 83, 222
uranium 223, 244, 274, 285, 287, 315
urban land use 141
urbanisation 97, 118, 170, 244–5
Urbarium 177
Urstromtäler (pradoliny) 9, 10, 97

Vandals 42
Variscan; *see* Hercynian
Via Egnatia 136
Vienna Agreement 121
village types 101, 136, 162–9
vines, vineyards 172, 175, 183, 291, 292, 293, 303, 304, 305, 311, 321
Vistula 207
Vlachs 78, 79, 133, 134
Voivodina 182, 183, 190, 246
volcanic landscapes 6, 12, 15, 16
vulcanism 8, 15, 16, 17, 296, 299

Wallachia 30, 79, 134, 166–7, 178, 190, 295, 301, 303
Wallachian Plains 5, 8, 22–3, 30, 173, 177, 183
war damage to industry 242, 255, 273
Warsaw (Warszawa) 151–4
water supply 252, 259, 260, 275, 278, 287
Weimar Republic 66, 190
Western Europe 201, 221, 222, 223, 224, 225, 226, 227, 229, 245, 248, 306
wheat 172, 183, 184, 303, 311, 321
Wilno (Vilnius) 69, 85
wines 175, 183, 293, 304, 309
Województwo 235, 236, 263
wolfram 317
women's rights 135
world price levels 233

yields 180, 181, 309

Zadruga 321
zinc 11, 188, 192, 253, 263, 274, 276, 285, 299, 307, 317
Zollverein 188, 199
Zurück ins Reich 120